# BY THEIR BLOOD

Christian Martyrs from the Twentieth Century and Beyond

THIRD EDITION

## James and Marti Hefley

**BakerBooks**

Grand Rapids, Michigan

Copyright © 1979, 1996, 2004 by James C. and Marti Hefley

Published by Baker Books
a division of Baker Book House Company
P.O. Box 6287, Grand Rapids, MI 49516-6287
www.bakerbooks.com

Updated and abridged version published 2004 by Baker Book House
and used with permission of copyright owner.

Printed in the United States of America

Library of Congress Cataloging-in-Publication Data is on file at the Library of Congress, Washington, D.C.

ISBN 0-8010-6515-1

# BY THEIR
# BLOOD

"I saw under the altar the souls of them that were slain for the word of God, and for the testimony which they held."

(Revelation 6:9)

"These all died in faith, not having received the promises, but having seen them afar off, and were persuaded of them, and embraced them, and confessed that they were strangers and pilgrims on the earth. . . . Others were tortured, not accepting deliverance; that they might obtain a better resurrection: and others had trial of cruel mockings and scourgings, yea, moreover of bonds and imprisonment: they were stoned, they were sawn asunder, were tempted, were slain with the sword: they wandered about in sheepskins and goatskins; being destitute, afflicted, tormented; (of whom the world was not worthy): they wandered in deserts, and in mountains, and in dens and caves of the earth."

(Hebrews 11:13, 35–38)

# Contents

# Part Five: Martyrs of the Asian Pacific Islands

# Part Six: Martyrs of Nazi Germany and Occupied Europe

# Part Seven: Martyrs of the Soviet Union and Eastern Europe

# Part Eight: Martyrs of the Middle East

# Part Nine: Martyrs of Sub-Saharan Africa

## Part Ten: Martyrs of the Caribbean and Latin America

# Preface

C hristian martyrs! The words stir the imagination. A saint singing above flames that crackle around his stake. A believer kneeling serenely before a blood stained block; the gimlet-eyed executioner preparing to swing his sword. A missionary bound with vines beside a bubbling pot, his eyes lifted confidently to heaven, while loin-clothed cannibal aborigines dance wildly around to the beat of booming drums.

But burning at the stake passed out of style after Reformation times. Death by the sword rarely occurs today. And only a few missionaries have ever been cooked by cannibals. Such macabre martyrdoms more often occur in the imagination of novelists.

Martyrs of the twentieth century have met their earthly end in more conventional, up-to-date methods such as gunshots, bombs, banditry, debilitating prison diseases, and starvation.

A second oversimplification is that Christian martyrs always die strictly for their testimony of Christ. This idea persists because accounts of martyrdom often do not include sufficient backgrounding of the events. When all the details are known, it is apparent that most Christian martyrs die in circumstances *related* to their witness for Christ. For example, five young American missionaries were speared to death in 1956 by Auca Indians in Ecuador because of the Indians' fear that they were cannibals. And nurse Mavis Pate was killed by gunfire from a Palestinian refugee camp because Arab commandos mistook the Volkswagen Microbus in which she was riding for an Israeli army vehicle. However, some Christians are killed primarily for their allegiance to Christ. Most martyrs to communism in China and the former Soviet Union fit into this category.

So the first dictionary definition of martyr—"One who submits to death rather than renounce his religion"—cannot always be strictly applied to the violent death of Christians. The second definition—"One who dies, suffers, or sacrifices everything for a principle, cause, etc."—is more inclusive. By this delineation, Lottie Moon, the heroine of Southern Baptists, who died from self-imposed starvation in China was as much a martyr as John and Betty Stam, who were brutally murdered by cold, calculating Chinese Communists.

Recognizing this, we have included many martyrs who might be excluded in some books because they did not die a violent death. At the same time we have not classified as martyrs those who died in accidents which might have happened to them in their homeland. Admittedly, the line is hard to draw here.

We have sought to provide stories of the deaths of Christian nationals where reliable information is available. This is often not the case. Young churches, developing amidst persecution, are less likely to keep records than established congregations with more time and freedom. National believers, also, because of educational and communicational disadvantages, do not document and preserve the stories of their own who have died for Christ. These stories are usually transmitted orally and later written down by educated leaders and/or missionaries. In contrast, the stories of most missionary martyrs and nationals who die with them are well attested. Books by eyewitnesses or close relatives have even been written about some of them.

We have generally restricted our time limit to the twentieth century, although in giving background and introducing the martyrs of a country or area, we have usually summarized hostilities to Christianity before the year 1900. In instances of both martyred nationals and missionaries, we have also sought to understand the political, national, and social forces behind great outbreaks, such as the Boxer Rebellion of China and the later Congo massacre.

We have organized the narrative by geographical units, with the chronological being subordinate to the geographic. Large nations such as China and the Soviet Union are treated as units within themselves, as is Nazi Germany. Smaller nations where little bloodshed of Christians has occurred in the twentieth century are encompassed in larger units and given less attention.

We have excluded the United States, Canada, Australia, and New Zealand, although some Christians have died in these countries in connection with their Christian service. We have noted some instances of martyrdom in Western European countries during the Nazi occupation. Independent western governments have been neutral, if not encouraging, to the advance of Christianity in modern times, with Spain, Italy, Portugal, and Greece to some degree excepted. There has been no particular policy of physical persecution of evangelicals in the democratic western countries, although in recent times Bible-believing evangelicals have suffered discrimination from the media, the courts, government, and business.

We must plead imperfection and the subjectivities of our rearing and national loyalties in failures to adequately define Christian martyrdom in many instances. We are humbled at the devotion and commitment of these thousands of Christians who were willing to lay down their lives for the Cause in which they believed.

We found it impossible to include a biography on every Christian martyr of the twentieth century. The *World Mission Digest*, published by the Foreign Mission Board of the Southern Baptist Convention, cites the World Evangelization Database as accounting for the martyrdom of 119 million Christians during this century. Many, if not most, of these martyred believers died as the result of genocidal attacks by brutal dictators and political and religious zealots. Though little known on earth, their names will be heralded in heaven.

We do believe that every martyr, whether included in this classification or not, has died for a purpose within the sovereign will of God. God was there when every human life was taken, not setting up the deaths, but permitting evil men to exercise free will and to do their dastardly deeds under the temporary dominion of Satan. Yes, our God was there in grace abounding over sin, beauty growing out of ashes, victory triumphing over death, and the Church advancing beyond defeat.

James C. Hefley, Th.M., Ph.D., Litt.D.
Marti Hefley, Dip. Theology, B.A.

# PART ONE

# Martyrs of China

# 1

# China, 1900

## *The Fury of the Boxers*

BY IMPERIAL COMMAND EXTERMINATE THE
CHRISTIAN RELIGION! DEATH TO THE FOREIGN DEVILS!

In June 1900, crazed mobs bannered this terrible proclamation as they rampaged through cities of north China, looting and burning churches and the homes of missionaries and Chinese Christians. They were led by bare-chested fanatics called Boxers who brandished long, curving swords and cried for the heads and hearts of Christians and missionaries.

*Item.* In Manchuria, where all missionaries managed to escape, a Chinese pastor was caught. When he refused to deny Christ, his eyebrows, ears, and lips were cut off. Still he would not recant. His heart was then cut out and put on display in a theater. His fourteen-year-old daughter, following the example of her father, suffered a like fate.

*Item.* In Shansi Province Mary Huston and Hattie Rice, two young single women affiliated with the China Inland Mission, strove to flee an angry mob. Miss Rice was beaten to death by the roadside. Miss Huston, seriously injured by a cart run over her to break her spine, died a month later.

*Item.* At remote Tsun-hua the Chinese Methodist pastor was forced into a pagan temple, mocked before idols, then left tied to a pillar. He spent the night preaching while friends pleaded with him to recant. In the morning a thousandstrong mob descended on him and literally tore out his heart. Two Chinese women teachers who were captured also refused to renounce Christianity. The feet of one were chopped off and she was then killed with a sword. The other—shouting to her pupils, "Keep

15

the faith!"—was wrapped in cotton, soaked with kerosene, and burned alive. One hundred sixty-three Chinese Methodists in Tsun-hua were martyrs for Christ in June 1900. Only four or five escaped.

As the blood flowed, newspaper headlines abroad screamed:

CHINESE MASSACRE MISSIONARIES

and a shocked world asked why.

## Intrigue Leads to Tragedy

The world's most populous nation had appeared to be moving from idolatrous darkness toward the light of Christianity. Converts had been doubling and redoubling in recent years, with circulation of Scripture running in the millions. The China Inland Mission (CIM; now Overseas Missionary Fellowship), largest of the evangelical agencies in China, had welcomed over a thousand new workers in the past decade. Other missions were also expanding, but on a lesser scale.

Western churches spoke of China as "our largest and most promising mission field." Yet ironically, Christianity had reached China centuries before Columbus sighted America. In fact, an eighth-century Chinese Nestorian church leader claimed the Magi, returning from Bethlehem, had brought the first news of the Savior.

Christianity had waxed and waned until around 1300 when Franciscans arrived and tried to dominate the Chinese church. Their actions provoked intervention by Asian Muslims who had been abiding by a truce. The aroused Muslims killed hundreds of thousands of Christians, piling seventy thousand heads on the ruins of one city. Organized Christianity was swept from Asia.

The Jesuit order came in the sixteenth century and in 1705 convinced the Chinese emperor to make China a Catholic state. A sharp rebuff came from the pope who said the emperor could not be a Christian and continue to worship his ancestors. In 1724 Christianity was banned, and hundreds of Catholic missionaries and converts were put to death.

The first Protestant missionary, Robert Morrison, went out as an employee of the East India Company in 1807. He translated almost the entire Bible into the main Chinese language, but when he died in 1834 there were only three known Chinese Christians in the whole Empire.

Western military and political pressure opened the door for the entrance of foreign missionaries in the latter half of the nineteenth century. Hundreds poured in and took up stations across the vast mysterious land.

Disease, travel accidents, and violence took a heavy toll. The average life expectancy dropped to forty. The countryside rumbled with frequent rebellions against the central

Manchu government in Peking. Missionaries were often caught between opposing forces, and some gave their lives. For example, an early Southern Baptist worker, J. Landrum Holmes, and an Episcopal missionary were killed while trying to intercede with rebels for the safety of their town.

The Righteous Ones, as the Boxers were called, bitterly opposed Christianity, which they termed "the religion of the foreign devils." In a desperate effort to preserve the old pagan religions, they had established a network of secret cells across China. Initiates repeated a sacred formula until they fell foaming at the mouth, then joined in a black magic ritual that sometimes included human sacrifices to temple idols. The Boxers claimed they were commanded by "heavenly deities," and were thus invulnerable. A potion smeared on them by their priests was supposed to make them bulletproof.

Throughout the spring of 1900 the fanatical Boxers agitated the populace by stirring up historic Chinese racial pride in their nation as the celestial center of the world. They fired hatred against foreign powers for forcing exploitative treaties on the country and sustaining the hated opium trade which kept millions of Chinese addicted. They fueled resentment over jobs lost through foreign building of railroads. In northern China, which had suffered crop failures for three years, the Boxers blamed missionaries and their foreign religion for the long drought. "The foreigners have insulted our gods," they declared. "Foreign blood must be spilled before our gods will send rain." The Boxers also capitalized on enmity which had developed against Catholic missionaries when the French government had actually forced the Chinese government to give Catholic prelates power equal to judges and magistrates.

Still the foreigners did not become alarmed until it was too late for many to flee. After all, many reasoned, China had always seethed with rebellions and banditry, and even so the CIM had lost only one missionary to mob violence, although other martyrdoms had occurred. Danger went with the work, the missionaries assumed, as they went on about their business of preaching, teaching, and healing.

## The Terror Begins

In March the empress appointed the notorious, known Boxer supporter Yu-hsien governor of Shansi, the northern province where much missionary work was concentrated. In June the German and Japanese ambassadors were murdered in Peking. The alarmed foreign community grouped in the British embassy compound and began building fortifications as Boxers paraded through the Imperial capital.

The royal edict to kill all foreigners and exterminate Christianity was given to couriers for delivery to provincial governors. Messengers to the south, however, changed one Chinese character on the decree, so that it read "protect" instead of "kill" foreigners. For this disobedience they were cut in half. But the missionaries and Christians in this area were saved, and the bloodletting was confined to the northern provinces.

One hundred eighty-eight foreign missionaries and missionary children were murdered during the Boxer wrath in the summer of 1900, all in four provinces. Most of these casualties occurred in Shansi Province under the diabolical governor Yu-hsien. Of the 159 foreigners who died in Shansi Province, 91 were associated with the China Inland Mission.

Rugged Shansi Province is the cradle of ancient Chinese civilization. The famous Emperor Yao lived and ruled from here over the "black-haired race" eight hundred years before Abraham was born. Shansi is an inhospitable land, bitterly cold in winter and fiercely hot in summer. Topographically, it is mostly high undulating tablelands, punctuated by steep hills and sandwiched between the Yellow River on the west and a rugged mountain range on the east. Shansi was not an easy place from which foreigners could escape.

## The Governor's Treachery

The bloodiest massacre took place in the ancient Shansi provincial capital Taiyuan where the gates of the walled city were closed to prevent the foreigners from escaping. Trapped in their residences were twenty-four adults and nine children, associated with the Baptist Missionary Society of England, the CIM, and the small Sheo Yang Mission which operated the Schofield Memorial Hospital in a satellite town.

The doctor for whom the hospital was named had died of typhus fever in 1883, contracted from a patient admitted by the gatekeeper without the doctor's knowledge. Shortly before his death, he had begged for reinforcements. Two medics had answered his call, Dr. William M. Wilson and Dr. E. H. Edwards. Dr. Edwards took charge of the Schofield Hospital. Dr. Wilson, who was with the CIM, operated a hospital for opium addicts in an outlying city at his own expense. To these doctors thousands of persons owed their lives.

Dr. Edwards was safely away when the crisis came. Dr. Wilson and his wife and young son were due for furlough, but had stayed on to help during the famine. Early in the summer Mrs. Wilson and son went ahead to Taiyuan for rest from the baking heat. The doctor remained to care for his patients until he fell prey to peritonitis. One of his last acts of mercy was to travel twenty dangerous miles to save the life of Pastor Si who lay severely wounded from a Boxer sword slash in his side. Before the doctor left for treatment in Taiyuan, Chinese Christians presented him with a large red satin sash, bearing the gilt inscription "God's Faithful Servant." His last letter was written on the road to Taiyuan. "It's all fog," he wrote a colleague, "but I think, old chap, that we are on the edge of a volcano, and I fear Taiyuan is the inner edge."

Besides Mrs. Wilson, two CIM single women missionaries were in Taiyuan. Jane Stevens, a nurse, was in frail health. During her last trip back to England for rest, a friend had suggested that a position in the homeland might be easier. Nurse Stevens had replied, "I don't feel I have yet finished the work God has for me in China. I must go back. Perhaps—who knows?—I may be among those allowed to give their lives for the people."

Miss Stevens had come to China in 1885. Her Taiyuan partner, Mildred Clarke, came in 1893. Upon reaching Taiyuan, Miss Clarke wrote home, "I long to live a poured-out life unto Him among these Chinese, and to enter into the fellowship of His sufferings for souls, who poured out His life unto death for us."

Of the other missionaries at Taiyuan nine were former CIM members: six had joined the small Sheo Yang Mission which operated the Schofield Memorial Hospital; W. T. and Emily Beynon were now representatives of the British and Foreign Bible Society; Alexander Hoddle was independent, operating a small Christian bookstore and teaching English to Chinese students for his support.

At the Sheo Yang Mission were T. W. and Jessie Pigott and their young son Wellesley. A friend had written of Mr. Pigott, "If ever a man lived in earnest, it was Thomas Wellesley Pigott." A man of many talents, he could fix anything. Emily Pigott, though not a doctor, was skilled at removing eye cataracts. Old China hands, the Pigotts had lost friends in an earlier massacre—four Church Missionary Society workers killed by the radical vegetarian sect in Fukien Province in 1895. Since then the Pigotts had felt their time would be short in China and had worked almost nonstop. Another prophetic note had been sounded by W. T. Beynon in the ending of his 1899 report to the Bible Society: "We trust that this coming year the God of all grace will give all of us grace to be faithful."

Violence exploded in late June 1900. Mobs roamed the streets, setting fire to the compounds of the British Baptists and the Sheo Yang group. The missionaries and a group of Chinese believers linked hands and sought refuge in the Baptist boys' school about a half mile away. After reaching the school, Edith Coombs of the Sheo Yang Mission suddenly realized she had left two Chinese schoolgirls behind, one of whom was very sick. Miss Coombs broke away and ran back to the blazing buildings to rescue them. As they were rushing out, the sick girl stumbled and fell. Miss Coombs bent to lift her and shield her from the brickbats being hurled by the mob. The mob moved in closer, forced them to separate, and drove the missionary back into the house. The mob and the Chinese girls she had tried to rescue last saw her kneeling in the flames.

The remaining thirty-two missionaries and children, along with their loyal Chinese friends, barricaded themselves in the boys' school. Day and night stones pelted the walls and doors while the group inside waited and prayed behind barricades, hoping for rescue by the provincial governor, Yu-hsien, whose palace was a short distance away.

On July 9 soldiers arrived and escorted the missionaries to the courtyard of the governor's palace where they joined twelve Catholic clergy. The missionaries, thinking they would now be saved, saw they were doomed when Yu-hsien stormed out waving his sword and shouting, "Kill! Kill!"

The governor announced that the men would die first. George Farthing, one of the English Baptists and the father of three children, stepped forward. His wife clung to him, but he gently put her aside and knelt before the chopping block without a murmur. His head fell with one stroke of the executioner's sword.

The other men were killed one by one, then the women and children. The Farthing children hung on to their mother and had to be pulled away when she was ordered to kneel. Mrs. Lovitt was permitted to hold the hand of her little boy. "We all came to China to bring you the good news of salvation by Jesus Christ," she said in a firm voice. "We have done you no harm, only good. Why do you treat us so?" In a strange act of gentleness, a soldier stepped up and removed her spectacles before she and her son were beheaded.

The priests and nuns died with equal courage. Their bishop, an old man with a white beard, asked the governor, "Why are you doing this wicked deed?" Yu-hsien answered by drawing his sword and slashing the bishop across the face.

Finally the Chinese Christians were brought forth to complete the carnage. Few escaped to report the tale of horror.

The bodies were left for the night where they had fallen and were stripped of clothing, rings, and watches under cover of darkness. The next day the heads were placed in cages for a grotesque display on the city wall. Yu-hsien was without remorse and later crowed to the empress, "Your Majesty's slave caught them as in a net and allowed neither chicken nor dog to escape." The old woman replied, "You have done splendidly."

## No Hiding Place

Eight British Baptist missionaries at Hsinchow, forty-five miles north of Taiyuan, heard the tragic news and decided to flee to the hills. They took refuge in caves where they were lovingly cared for by local Christians. Boxers roamed the area, seeking their hiding place. A Chinese evangelist was beaten to death for refusing to cooperate with the Boxers.

After their food supply was cut off, the missionaries received a message from the magistrate at Hsinchow offering them protection if they would return to the city. Upon arrival they were jailed about two weeks, then promised a protective armed escort to the coast. Rev. Herbert Dixon, one of the eight, told a Chinese preacher, "We are ready to glorify our Lord, by life or by death. If we die, there will certainly be others to take our place."

The Hsinchow eight set out in carts on August 8. As they were passing between the inner and outer gates of the city, their "escort" suddenly closed around them and other armed men sprang from hiding and brutally beat them all to death.

## Massacre at Soping

At Soping ten missionaries of the small Swedish Holiness Union were holding their annual church conference in cooperation with Mr. and Mrs. Oscar Forsberg of the International Missionary Alliance Mission. Soping was already seething with unrest. Boxer agitators were saying that the missionaries had swept away approaching rain clouds with a yellow paper broom and that the foreigners were praying to their God that it might not rain.

According to Chinese evangelist Wang Lan-pu, who managed to escape, a mob converged on the house where the missionaries and Chinese Christians had barricaded themselves and began battering the door. Just as the mob burst into the house, the missionaries and their friends slipped out the back and ran to the city hall where they asked the magistrate for refuge. The Boxer leaders learned where they had gone and led the mob there. The magistrate refused to surrender his charges, but to pacify the howling crowd he said he had been ordered to send the foreigners to Peking where they would be executed. As the mob looked on, he had his blacksmith make manacles for five of the men. Apparently satisfied, the crowd dispersed.

Later that night the mob came back with soldiers sympathetic to the Boxers. Sparing no one, they stoned to death all the missionaries and their children along with Chinese Christians who had sought refuge. They hung the heads of the missionaries on the city wall as a ghastly testimonial to the populace. Among the Chinese who died were the mother and little daughter of the evangelist who escaped.

The June 29 massacre almost wiped out the tiny Swedish mission. Only two members in another province and one home on furlough were left. The senior Swedish martyr was Nathanael Carleson. Chinese believers had often used the scriptural allusion to introduce him: "Nathanael, an Israelite indeed, in whom is no guile." The youngest martyr was Ernst Peterson. He had been in China only five months. Four of the other eight were single women, all about thirty years of age. Aware of the danger of serving in bandit-ridden north China, Mina Hedlund, one of the four, had written in her last letter, "I don't fear if God wants me to suffer the death of a martyr."

## Ambushed in the Desert

The International Missionary Alliance (now known as the Christian and Missionary Alliance—C&MA) had been founded by A. B. Simpson, a far-seeing Presbyterian minister with a vision for world evangelization. At the time of the Boxer uprising, this mission had about forty Swedish missionaries on the China field. At least nineteen adults and fifteen children met violent death.

The Olaf Bingmarks and their two young sons sensed trouble when children stopped coming to their school. Friends told them stories were spreading that Mr. Bingmark was extracting the eyes of Chinese boys for use as medicine. Duly warned, they kept inside their house. A peddler named Chao, whom they had kindly received many times, betrayed them for a price. Boxers dragged them outside and attacked them with swords and stones while an artist stood by sketching the violence. The picture, as later revealed, showed the two little boys kneeling and imploring mercy.

The Chinese evangelist who worked with them was bound for ten days without food and drink. Near death, his sufferings were mercifully ended by the sword.

Miss Gustafson, a beloved missionary teacher, lived alone at another station. When warned that Boxers were coming, she fled with another Chinese evangelist. A few miles down the road she was overtaken and stoned to death. Her body was thrown into a river and never seen again.

In far northwest China seven Alliance (C&MA) missionaries and seven children tried to flee on camels into Mongolia. Robbers intercepted them and took everything, even their clothes. In the trauma two of the missionary wives gave birth. French missionary priests found the fourteen and the two infants naked in the desert and subsisting on roots. The priests gave them covering and took them back to the Catholic mission station.

News came that a Boxer army was approaching. "Our way . . . is cut off," the Alliance's Carl Lundberg wrote. "If we are not able to escape, tell our friends we live and die for the Lord. I do not regret coming to China. The Lord has called me and His grace is sufficient. The way He chooses is best for me. His will be done. Excuse my writing, my hand is shivering."

Six days later he added, "The soldiers have arrived and will attack our place. The Catholics are prepared to defend themselves but it is in vain. We do not like to die with weapons in our hands. If it be the Lord's will let them take our lives."

When the Boxers attacked, the priests and two of the Alliance men, Emil Olson and Albert Anderson, tried to escape. They were captured, ordered to undress, then made to kneel for beheading. The others fared no better. The Boxers killed them with guns and swords, then set fire to the church.

Another seven Alliance missionaries with three children and four workers from other missions huddled in a chapel at Patzupupulong. Warned by the local magistrate that Boxers were on their way to kill them, the group set out for the coast. They ran into an ambush planned by the magistrate and all were killed except one of the wives. Left for dead, she was rescued and taken into the tent of a Mongol widow. However, the treacherous magistrate's wife learned where she was and sent soldiers to the tent. They murdered her in bed.

## The Fatal Appointment

Most local Chinese officials were protective of missionaries. The magistrate at Fenchow in north Shansi was notably kind. Because of his friendliness, Mr. and Mrs. C. W. Price and other workers of the American Board of Commissioners of Foreign Missions invited three CIM colleagues, Mr. and Mrs. A. P. Lundren and Miss Annie Eldred, to come and stay with them during July when mob violence was at its peak. However, shortly after they arrived, the vindictive provincial governor appointed another magistrate to Fenchow.

The new magistrate ordered the missionaries out of the city and assigned them an armed guard under the pretense of protection.

Apparently the missionaries expected the worst. Lizzie Atwater wrote her family on August 3:

> Dear ones, I long for a sight of your dear faces, but I fear we shall not meet on earth. . . . I am preparing for the end very quietly and calmly. The Lord is wonderfully near, and He will not fail me. I was very restless and excited while there seemed a chance of life, but God has taken away that feeling, and now I just pray for grace to meet the terrible end bravely. The pain will soon be over, and oh the sweetness of the welcome above!
>
> My little baby will go with me. I think God will give it to me in Heaven, and my dear mother will be so glad to see us. I cannot imagine the Savior's welcome. Oh, that will compensate for all these days of suspense. Dear ones, live near to God and cling less closely to earth. There is no other way by which we can receive that peace from God which passeth understanding. . . . I must keep calm and still these hours. I do not regret coming to China, but am sorry I have done so little. My married life, two precious years, has been so very full of happiness. We will die together, my dear husband and I.
>
> I used to dread separation. If we escape now it will be a miracle. I send my love to you all, and the dear friends who remember me.

Twelve days later, when they were out of the area, the guards assigned by the new magistrate murdered the seven missionaries.

## Detour to Death

Other trusting missionaries were betrayed by Boxer-inspired Chinese claiming to be their protectors. Such was the case of six CIM workers, two married couples and two single women, returning to their Shansi stations from vacations.

George McConnell, an Irish evangelist, and his Scottish wife Belle had buried their daughter in Scotland only two years before. They had just opened three new chapels and received fifty-one new inquirers. But the preacher sensed danger in the air. He quoted from Psalm 31 in a letter titled "'My times are in Thy hand.'"

John and Sarah Young had been married only fifteen months. He was Scottish, she an Indiana Hoosier. Both had made exceptional progress in the difficult Chinese language, but they lived one uncertain day at a time. In her application to CIM, Sarah had written, "I want to be found in the battle when He comes, and I want to be an instrument in the hands of God in saving souls from death." Eleven days before her martyrdom she wrote, "The winds may blow, and the waves may roll high; if we keep our eyes off them and on the Lord, we shall be all right. . . ."

Annie King and Elizabeth Burton, Britishers, were still single and strikingly attractive. They had been in China less than two years. Previous to her departure for China, Annie had been a home missionary, helping in the "Ragged Schools" for friendless child waifs in England. "Praise the Lord, I am really in China," she wrote home. "I don't know what the future holds for me, but, whatever comes, I know I have obeyed the will of our God." And later, "Often I wish I could have come before. . . . It is so nice to be in this village, where the people trust us, and love to hear of Jesus, for whose sake and the Gospel's we have come. There are numbers of villages where the name of Jesus is unknown, all in heathen darkness, without a ray of light."

Elizabeth, also a teacher, had written, "Oh, I feel so inadequate, so weak, and yet I hear Him say, 'Go in this thy might, have not I sent thee?' Yes, He has sent me; if ever I felt God has called me in my life, I feel it tonight." Then shortly before taking a fateful vacation: "Jesus is very real to me out in this land, and I would not change my present lot in spite of loneliness and occasional hardships."

Along the road to Yu-men-k'ou the group was met by soldiers who advised them to detour off the main road for safety. "We will accompany you," they said. Nearing the Yellow River, their escorts suddenly dismounted and unsheathed their swords. "You thought we came to protect you," the captain said. "Our orders are to kill you unless you promise to stop preaching your foreign religion." When the missionaries refused to so pledge, Mr. McConnell was pulled from his mule and decapitated with a quick swing of a sword. As Mrs. McConnell and their young son Kenneth hit the ground, the boy was heard to say, "Papa does not allow you to kill little Kennie." Swords flashed and two more heads rolled on the ground. The young women embraced each other as did the Youngs. Arms swung and death came quickly. The last to die was a faithful Chinese Christian servant, Kehtienhuen, who refused to deny his faith.

A Chinese Christian friend was able to escape. He smuggled a letter out describing the killings. "Men's hearts are shaking with fear," he reported. "We cannot rest day or night."

## No Mercy Shown

At Ta-t'ung on June 24 CIM missionaries, two couples and their four children and two single women, took refuge with a friendly magistrate. The official defied the Boxer mob that circled the house clamoring for the blood of the foreigners. Then orders came on the twenty-seventh from a superior, ordering them to their home. The magistrate sent them under cover of darkness with an armed guard that remained at their door. A few days later Mrs. Stewart McKee gave birth. Now there were five children sheltered in the small house, while the mob outside grew noisier.

By July 12 only two guards remained. At seven o'clock that evening an official knocked and demanded the names of those inside. They were given.

An hour later three hundred soldiers arrived on horseback in support of the Boxers. Stewart McKee went out and tried to reason with them. Instead of listening, they hacked him to pieces, then set fire to the house. In the flames and confusion, only little Alice

McKee managed to escape. In the morning the mob discovered her in a cowshed and slashed the defenseless child to death.

## Buried in a Baptistry

The CIM's Emily Whitchurch and Edith Searell were one of many teams of young single women serving in isolated towns. Their only protection was the goodwill of the people.

They worked in Hsiao-i, a town in south central Shansi Province, with slaves of the terrible opium trade from which western nations were profiting. "Mornings and evenings," a visiting colleague wrote of Miss Whitchurch, "she would gather the opium patients around and teach them Scripture. . . . The Scriptures were as the voice of God to Miss Whitchurch; they shaped her life, and she had confidence in their power to purify and to convert."

Miss Searell was one of the first New Zealanders to come to China. In May she had been seriously ill with pleurisy, but refused to leave her British partner and Chinese friends. On June 28 she wrote a close friend, "From the human standpoint [all missionaries in Shansi Province] are equally unsafe. From the point of view of those whose lives are hid with Christ in God all are equally safe! His children shall have a place of refuge, and that place is the secret place of the Most High."

Two days later a Boxer mob attacked their house and showed them no mercy. After the mob left, loving Chinese Christians risked their lives in order to place the martyrs' bodies in a baptistry bordered with flowers which Miss Searell had planted a few weeks before.

## No Earthly Sanctuary

No missionary was safe in Shansi Province. Scores were hidden by Chinese Christians at grave peril to their own lives.

"We will stand by you til death," Chinese friends vowed to the CIM's Duncan Kay, a colorful Scottish evangelist. "And we will stay until driven out," declared Kay.

When mobs threatened, Chinese believers spirited Kay, his wife and daughter Jenny, and three single women missionaries into the mountains and hid them in caves. With their help, Mrs. Kay was able to get a letter out to her three children at the CIM school in Chefoo, which was in a safe area in another province near the coast. She described their plight:

[We are] being molested every day by bands of bad men who want money from us. Now our money is all gone. We feel there is nothing for us but to try and get back to the city; this is no easy matter. The roads are full of these bad people who seek our lives.

I am writing this as it may be my last to you. Who knows but we may be with Jesus very soon. This is only a wee note to send our dear love to you all, and to ask you not to feel too sad when you know we have been killed. We have committed you all into God's hands. He will make a way for you all. Try and be good children. Love God. Give your hearts to Jesus. This is your dear parents' last request.

Your loving papa, mama, and wee Jenny

Shortly after the letter was sent, the three Kays were killed. The three young women, hiding in another cave, survived.

Another group of CIM missionaries were hidden in caves for three weeks before being captured by Boxers. "We are in God's hands," Willie Peat, who was accompanied by his wife Helen and two daughters and two single women, wrote. "I can say, 'I will fear no evil, for Thou art with me.'" One of the single women, nurse Edith Dobson, said in her last letter, "We know naught can come to us without His permission. So we have no need to be troubled: it is not in my nature to fear physical harm, but I trust, if it come, His grace will be all-sufficient."

They received a reprieve when a magistrate intervened and ordered a guard to deliver them to the town of K'u-wu. At K'u-wu a mob threatened, and they fled into nearby mountains. From their hideout in an earthen cave, Willie Peat wrote a last letter to his mother and uncle:

> The soldiers are just on us, and I have only time to say "Good-bye" to you all. We shall soon be with Christ, which is very far better for us. We can only now be sorry for you who are left behind and our dear native Christians.
>
> Good-bye! At longest it is only "til He come." We rejoice that we are made partakers of the sufferings of Christ, that when His glory shall be revealed we may "rejoice also with exceeding joy."

Helen Peat added, "Our Father is with us and we go to Him, and trust to see you all before His face, to be forever together with Him."

They were put to death on August 30.

Australian David Barratt, a veteran of only three years, was traveling when he heard of the Taiyuan massacre. "The news nearly made me faint," he wrote a colleague, adding,

> The Empire is evidently upside down. No "*Mene, mene, tekel, upharsin*" is written on the old Middle Kingdom. Our blood may be as a true center (for the foundation) and God's kingdom will increase over this land. Extermination is but exaltation. God guide and bless us! "Fear not them which kill," He says, "are ye not of much more value than many sparrows." "Peace, perfect peace," to you, brother, and all at Lucheng. We may meet in the glory in a few hours or days. . . . Not a sleep, no dinner, a quiet time with God, then sunset and evening bells, then the dark. . . . Let us be true till death.

In such trusting faith the young Aussie was killed while seeking refuge on a desolate mountain.

Barratt's partner, Alfred Woodroofe, was at their station in Yo-yang when the persecution hit. The year before he had barely escaped a mob. Then he had written, "Are we called to die? The poor, feeble heart says, 'Oh, no; never.' But, to bring blessing into the world, what has it always meant? What to the Savior? What to the Apostles? 'This is the way the Master went; should not the servant tread it still?'"

This time Woodroofe and three Chinese Christians were forced to flee into the mountains. For a week or more they slept in caves at night, retreating into remote canyons during the day. Woodroofe sent a message back to other believers in Yo-yang, stating his wish to return "so we can die together." The reply told him to remain hidden. He wrote again, describing how his feet were cut and bleeding from wandering among the rocks, but ended by quoting James 5:11: "We count them happy that endure." This was his last message. He died at age twenty-eight.

Details of how he and about a dozen other CIM workers died were not known for many months. The few who managed to slip letters out expressed similar courage and faith and wished only that the Chinese church would be strengthened through their martyrdom. Wrote Edith Nathan, who served with her sister May and with Mary Heaysman at Ta-ning: "I hope I shan't be ordered off anywhere; if my Christians are in trouble, I trust I may be allowed to stay and help. One does long for the native Church to be on the right foundation—Christ Jesus." Mary Heaysman headed her last letter, "There shall be showers of blessing." The three young women and ten Chinese believers were captured after a long and harrowing flight and put to death in a pagan temple.

## Journeys of Death

In the most terrible of the flights, two parties of missionaries fled from Shansi Province to the city of Hankow in Hupeh Province a thousand miles south.

One group of fourteen included two families with six young children and four single women fleeing from the town of Lucheng. Mobs followed them from one village boundary to the next, hurling sticks and stones, shouting, "Death to the foreign devils!" Robbers stripped them of everything but a few rags. Emaciated from hunger and thirst, shoeless, barebacked in the scorching heat, desperately trying to hold up filthy, torn Chinese trousers, they staggered from village to village half alive.

The young children displayed remarkable insight and faith. "If they loved Jesus they would not do this," seven-year-old Jessie Saunders reminded her parents. Once when they took shelter in a barn, the now fever-stricken child looked up at her mother who was fanning her and said, "Jesus was born in a place like this."

A few days later Jessie's baby sister, Isabel, died from beatings and exposure to the hot sun. As Jessie grew weaker, she cried for a place of rest. Her wish was granted a week after Isabel's death. The two children were buried beside the road.

In one village attackers dragged one of the men, E. J. Cooper, into the open country and left him for dead. He somehow revived and crawled back to his family and friends. Margaret (Mrs. E. J.) Cooper began lapsing into unconsciousness. Once she whispered to her husband, an architect whom she had married after joining the CIM, "If the Lord spares us, I should like to go back to Lucheng if possible." But her beatings were too severe, and she slipped into merciful death.

On July 12 Hattie Rice collapsed in the heat. A mob began stoning her and a man ran a cart over her naked body to break her spine. Her companion, Mary Huston, shielded her body until shamefaced men came with clothing. When she was again clothed, they took her from Miss Huston to a temple and consulted their gods about her faith. When a priest announced that the gods would let her live, the men carried her back to the other missionaries on a stretcher. She died a short time later.

The survivors somehow kept moving. They crossed and recrossed the Yellow River. They were imprisoned and released. Miss Huston suffered the worst. Part of her brain was exposed from beatings received at the time Miss Rice had been fatally wounded. Her friends could do no more for her than protect her from the sun. She died on August 11. Both young women were from the United States, Miss Rice from Massachusetts and Miss Huston from Pennsylvania. Assigned to a refuge for opium addicts, they had taken nothing from China and given everything.

Shortly before Miss Huston's death, the Lucheng group had met and joined a second group. Led by the CIM's Archibald Glover, they told a harrowing story of beatings, imprisonments, and miraculous deliverance. Mrs. Glover was in her last month of pregnancy. The last leg of their journey was made together by boat, allowing them to take the bodies of Mrs. Cooper and Miss Huston to Hankow for burial.

Three days after their arrival, Mr. Cooper laid his tiny son Brainerd beside his wife. He then wrote his own mother:

> The Lord has honored us by giving us fellowship in His sufferings. Three times stoned, robbed of everything, even clothes, we know what hunger, thirst, nakedness, weariness are as never before, but also the sustaining grace and strength of God and His peace, in a new and deeper sense than before. . . .
>
> Billow after billow has gone over me. Home gone, not one memento of dear Maggie even, penniless, wife and child gone to glory, Edith [his other child] lying very sick with diarrhea and your son weak and exhausted to a degree, though otherwise well. . . .
>
> And now that you know the worst, Mother, I want to tell you that the cross of Christ, that exceeding glory of the Father's love, has brought continual comfort to my heart, so that not one murmur has broken the peace of God within.

## The Peril at Paoting

Outside of Shansi Province the worst Boxer massacre of missionaries occurred at Paoting, then capital of the adjoining province Chihli (now Hopeh Province), where American (Northern) Presbyterians, the CIM, and the American Board of Commissioners for Foreign Missions had stations.

On June 1 CIM workers H. V. Robinson and C. Norman were seized and killed by Boxers outside the old walled city. The gates were heavily guarded, sealing off any possible escape by the eight remaining missionaries, four children, and the Chinese believers inside Paoting.

A story was circulated that the missionaries had poisoned the dwindling water supply in the wells. Another rumor charged that the Presbyterians' Dr. G. B. Taylor was extracting the eyes of children for medicine. Still another lie said the missionaries had helped build the hated railway that had taken jobs from cargo haulers.

The last letter out stated, "Our position is dangerous—very. We are having awfully hot, dry dusty days and *yao yen* [rumors] are increasing. . . . Oh that God would send rain. That would make things quiet for a time. . . . We can't go out and fight—we must sit still, do our work, and if God calls us to Him, that's all. Unless definite orders come from Peking that we are to be protected at any cost or a guard of foreign soldiers sent at once, the blood must flow. We are trying to encourage the [Chinese] brethren, but it is difficult work. A crisis must come soon—the Lord's will be done."

In this situation two friends managed to enter the city. One was Pastor Meng, the first Chinese to be ordained by the American Board's North China Mission. The missionaries begged him to leave. As a Chinese he could melt into the constant flow of human traffic and go to a safer town. "No," he vowed, "I will keep the church open as long as God allows. And after I am with the Lord, my son will keep it open."

The second arrival, Rev. William Cooper, deputy director of the CIM, had been visiting mission stations in adjoining Shansi Province and was returning to the metropolis of Tientsin on the coast. Like a Paul Revere, he had been warning missionaries at stations along the way, enabling some to escape just in time. Now he was caught.

Cooper was an old China hand, having been on the field nineteen years. A long bout with typhoid had impaired his hearing, but his spiritual senses remained strong. "One of the very few blameless lives I have ever come into contact with," declared a missionary friend. "He lived in an atmosphere of prayer," said another. "He literally drew breath in the fear of the Lord." In Paoting he joined CIM colleagues Benjamin and Emily Bagnall and their five-year-old daughter Gladys.

At the American Board station were H. T. Pitkin, Miss A. A. Gould, and Miss M. S. Morrill. Pitkin was one of the great missionary spirits of China. A classmate of Henry Luce (who later founded *Time* magazine) and Sherwood Eddy, Pitkin had served as secretary of the vigorous Student Missionary Movement before manning the American Board's mission station at Paoting.

On Saturday, June 30, the American Presbyterian Mission in the northern part of the city was attacked. Dr. Taylor went outside to plead that the missionaries had come to China only to do good. He was killed almost immediately and his head displayed in a pagan temple. After disposing of Dr. Taylor, the Boxer-led soldiers set the Presbyterian mission house on fire. One of the men, Frank Simcox, was seen walking to and fro on the veranda, holding the hands of his two sons as the flames enveloped them.

News of the martyrdom of the Presbyterians traveled rapidly to the other mission houses on the south side. The three members of the American Board, Pastor Meng, and other Chinese Christians kept a vigil through the night, writing last letters to loved ones, letters which would later be dug up by Boxers and destroyed. When morning dawned the Chinese, at the urging of the missionaries, slipped out the back door. About nine o'clock the Boxers arrived.

Miss Morrill went out to plead with the soldiers. "Kill me and let the others go," she begged. "I am ready to die for them." Her entreaty, according to the later report of one of the soldiers, touched off an argument in the crowd. Some of the older Boxers and the soldiers wanted to spare the four. The others wanted to proceed with the killing. During the controversy the missionaries were allowed to remain in their house.

The hard-liners won the dispute. Pitkin was killed defending the women. Miss Gould died of shock before the attackers could reach her. Miss Morrill was captured alive and taken to a pagan temple where William Cooper and the Bagnall family had already been taken.

Throughout Sunday they were taunted and abused as objects of sport and mockery. That evening they were taken out for execution. Mrs. Bagnall begged in vain for the life of her daughter while the cherubic-faced child with long golden curls stood by in frightened perplexity. The plea was refused, and at the captain's command they were all beheaded.

## Murders in Mongolia

The dark hand of Boxer hate reached even into bleak Mongolia. Once the fountainhead of the great Mongol Empire, the high, thinly populated desert nation was in 1900 a vassal state of China. Christian work was so difficult that mission boards hesitated to send their missionaries there, and it came to be called "the neglected field."

In 1895 the Scandinavian Alliance Mission of Chicago (now The Evangelical Alliance Mission—TEAM) sent its first worker, a red-bearded Swede. Taking a cue from pioneer James Gilmour, "the apostle to Mongolia," David Stenberg clad himself in woolen Mongolian skirts, rode a camel, traveled with the nomadic shepherd people, ate their food, and learned their language. Within three years he received support from five other hardy Scandinavian missionaries—N. J. Friedstrom, Carl Suber, Hanna Lund, and Hilda and Clara Anderson. Upon finding Stenberg, they mistook him for a Mongolian.

In the spring of 1900 they heard the rumors of danger to foreigners in China. Such rumors were common and they were from far off. They gave them little consideration.

In September they embarked on a long journey. A half day out they met a Mongol who advised them to turn back. Stenberg and the women went on under the protection of a Mongol chief. Friedstrom and Suber waited a while, then fearing danger decided

Friedstrom should search for their friends while Suber remained with the caravan. When Friedstrom did not return, Suber became alarmed and sent a friendly Mongol to investigate. He came back in two weeks with horrifying news. The chief had betrayed them. Following orders from Peking, he had sent them to a lonely spot in the desert where soldiers killed them, then preserved their heads in salt for shipment to Peking where an award was expected. Weeks later, another Mongol led Suber to the spot where the only visible remains were a blonde curl and a shoe among ashes.

## The Merciless Vegetarians

The extent of the Boxer persecutions in north China and Mongolia obscured blood-shed elsewhere by other rebellious groups. The worst violence occurred at Ku-chau in south central Chekiang Province where the Kiang-san, a secret vegetarian society similar to the Boxers, had launched an anti-foreign, anti-Christian vendetta. It was in this province that CIM founder Hudson Taylor had commenced work in 1857.

Three hundred federal soldiers had been sent to calm the agitated populace and to protect CIM missionaries D. Baird and Agnes Thompson and their two young sons, Edith Sherwood, Etta Manchester, and Josephine Desmond. The protectors were a joke. They had come without arms.

"We hear all kinds of evil reports which make us fear," Thompson wrote, "but by His grace we are able to rise above all, and take hold of our God and Savior. . . . We will just 'stand still and see the salvation of God.' . . . His will be done."

The five workers were among the best the CIM had in China. The Thompsons had not taken a furlough in fifteen years. In the Ku-chau area they had established a bustling church with a strong evangelistic outreach. Almost every night, Scotsman Thompson and national evangelists held services. Mrs. Thompson was instructing eighty Chinese women twice weekly.

Nurse Josephine Desmond, an Irish American from Massachusetts, had trained at Moody's Bible Training School in Chicago under R. A. Torrey. Miss Desmond had been caring for her co-worker Etta Manchester, a New Yorker who had been in China only three years. Friends had implored her to return home. She replied: "I am willing to come home if that is what God wants. If He wants me to remain here, I will stay. I am prepared to do the will of God, whatever the cost."

At forty-six Edith Sherwood was the eldest of the single women. She had been influenced by the Thompsons to leave missionary work in Europe and come to China. A friend had called her "a center of hope and love to old and young."

Reports from Chinese Christians described the missionaries' martyrdom. A mob attacked the mission house on July 21, wounding Thompson. Edith Sherwood and Etta Manchester ran to seek help from the magistrate and arrived as their colleague was being led to execution. Chinese friends pulled them aside just in time and directed them to a secret hiding place.

The mob succeeded in breaking down the missionaries' door that afternoon. Helpless to resist, the Thompsons, their two children, and Miss Desmond were put to death immediately. Three days later Miss Sherwood and Miss Manchester were discovered and killed.

Around the same time three other CIM missionaries were about twenty miles away, trying to reach a hoped-for haven in Ku-chau. Britisher George Ward and his wife Etta, an Iowan, had met and married on the field. The number of Chinese believers at their station in Ch'ang-shan had doubled in three years. Their companion, Emma Thirgood, was still weak from a long illness that had kept her in England for three years. She had amazed everyone by returning to China the year before.

Upon learning that the Kiang-san were in close pursuit, they decided to split into parties. Mrs. Ward and Miss Thirgood boarded a boat with the hope that they would be safer as unprotected women. They were killed at a river jetty. Mr. Ward was caught and murdered about five miles from Ku-chau.

## The Fellowship of Blood

More evangelical Protestant missionaries were killed in the Boxer bloodbath than Catholic representatives from abroad. The Catholics were often able to barricade themselves in fortress-like cathedrals. Chinese casualties, however, were just the reverse. Thirty thousand Catholics perished, while only two thousand Protestants gave their lives. Many thousands more lost all their property to burning, looting mobs who systematically sought out residences of persons listed on church registers.

Stories of bravery abound.

At P'ing-tu, Shantung Province, some twenty native Christians were seized and offered escape if they would deny their God and worship the idols. When they refused, their queues were tied to the tails of horses, and they were dragged twenty-five miles to Lai-chou where most were killed.

At Ta-t'ung, in Shansi Province, where six missionaries and five children died, eighteen Chinese believers offered themselves for baptism while the Boxer storm was mounting. Five died with the missionaries a few days afterward.

At another town in Shansi, one man who at first had denied Christ later repented and told the Boxer magistrate, "I cannot but believe in Christ: even if you put me to death, I will still believe and follow Him." For this he was beaten to death, his body cut open, and his heart extracted and exhibited in the magistrate's office.

At the town of Honchau, also in bloody Shansi, "Faithful" Yen and his wife were tied to a pillar in the pagan temple. After beating them with rods, the Boxers lit a fire behind them and burned their legs raw. Although they still would not deny Christ,

Mrs. Yen was set free. But Mr. Yen was thrown to the ground and firewood stacked around him. The fire was lit. After a few minutes of roasting in agony, he tried to roll out of the fire. A Boxer began to heap his body with hot ashes and coals. A soldier standing by could stand it no longer and cursed the Boxer. The Boxers leaped on the soldier and cut him to pieces. At that, the other soldiers rushed on the Boxers and chased them out of the temple. They then took the pitifully burned Chinese Christian from the fire and carried him still alive to the magistrate's house, only to see the official throw the man in a dark prison cell where it is presumed he died.

At Taiyuan, after the foreigners were beheaded, many of the Chinese Christians were forced to kneel down and drink their blood. Some also had crosses burned into their foreheads.

Here, a mother and her two children were kneeling before the executioner when a watcher suddenly ran and pulled the children back into the anonymity of the observing crowd. Taken by surprise, the Boxers were unable to find either the man or the children. They then turned back to the mother and asked if she had any last word. Dazed, she begged to see the face of the kind man who had taken her children. The man came forward in tears at risk of his life. Satisfied that the children would be cared for, the mother went to her death because she would not deny her Lord.

In the Hsinchow district, where eight English Baptist missionaries were killed, a Christian family—Chao Hsi Mao, his wife, sister, and mother—were driven to their place of execution in a large open cart. As they were pushed along they sang the hymn, "He Leadeth Me." When everything was ready, each in turn was asked to recant. One by one they bravely refused and were beheaded.

At Fang-su, another British Baptist station, the small church building was burned by the Boxers and the young minister Chou Yung-yao beaten nearly to death for refusing to divulge the names and whereabouts of his flock. As the mob began dragging him toward the flames, he shouted, "You need not drag me. I will go myself." He crawled into the blazing ruins. A moment later the roof collapsed over him to crown his final act of devotion to Christ.

About one hundred Chinese Christians were rounded up in the Shou-yang district, among them fourteen members of one family, and given a test of faith. A large circle was drawn on the ground and a cross inscribed in the center. To indicate their denial of Christ, all they had to do was step outside the circle. Only a few accepted this invitation. Those that stood their ground included a sizable number of teenagers. All were killed.

In a village in Shansi, another mother, Mrs. Meng, was weaving cloth on her household loom when a crowd of fierce faces appeared in her doorway. She knew who they were and what they wanted even before the inevitable question, "Will you deny your belief in Jesus?" "Wait a moment, please," she calmly replied. She stepped down from her loom and went to the closet where her family's best clothing was kept for holidays and funerals and donned her best gown. Then she walked to the door and knelt. "Now you may do as you wish, for I will not deny Jesus." A command, a flash of steel in the air, and the deed was done.

In the mountains nine Black Miao tribal Christian men, the first believers of their tribe, were called before the headman of their village on a ruse. One of the nine, sensing a trap, slipped away. Seven of the eight who appeared were seized and beheaded without trial or defense. In the days following, twenty-seven other Miao Christians were martyred and hundreds fined and forbidden to speak to one another.

In a church in Honan Province the Boxers took the roll book and went around to one hundred homes, offering each family immunity from persecution if they would renounce their faith and worship idols. Ninety-nine stood fast. Their homes were looted, their cornfields trampled down, their farm implements stolen, their cattle driven off, and they were left destitute.

A young teacher near the Great Wall was left in charge of seventeen schoolgirls in a boarding school when the missionary had to leave. Influential people offered to hide her, but she refused to leave the girls who could not get to their homes. Hiding in fields and caves, they were hunted like wild animals. Finally they were captured and led to a Boxer temple for execution.

A Christian cook was seized and beaten, his ears were cut off, his mouth and cheeks slashed with a sword, and other shameful mutilations afflicted. He remained true.

A Chinese preacher who refused to apostatize was given a hundred blows on his bare back and then asked again to deny Christ. "No, never," the half-dead man of God declared. "I value Jesus Christ more than life and I will never deny Him!" Before the second hundred blows were completed, he collapsed and his tormentors left thinking he was dead. A friend stealthily carried him away, bathed his wounds, and secretly nursed him to recovery.

No Chinese Christian was safe from the Boxer wrath, not even the most highly educated. Dr. Wang was one of the first graduates from the Peking University Medical School. When he and his little son were arrested, Boxers told him, "Dr. Wang, you are an educated man. We do not want to kill you, but we have no choice unless you burn incense to the gods."

"No, I cannot do that," he replied.

"We'll make it easy for you," the Boxers offered. "Get someone to burn incense in your place."

When he again refused, they offered to find him a substitute. "You will only have to go to the temple with us," they said.

"No, I will not," he persisted. "You may kill me, but I will not worship your gods in any way. There are four generations of Christians in my family. Do you think I would let my child see his father deny his Savior? Kill me if you must, but I will not betray my Lord."

They ran him through with a sword, lamenting, "What a pity to kill such a man."

The bravery of such Christians astounded the Boxers. Sometimes they ripped out the hearts of victims in search of the secret of their courage. Finding nothing but flesh, they would then remark, "It was the medicine of the foreign devils [the missionaries]."

## The Bravery of Blind Chang

Of all the Chinese martyrs none died with more courage than Blind Chang, the most famous evangelist in Manchuria, homeland of the Manchu rulers of China.

Chang Shen had been converted after being stricken blind in mid-life. Before his conversion he had been known as *Wu so pu wei te*, meaning, "one without a particle of good in him." A gambler, woman-chaser, and thief, he had driven his wife and only daughter from home. When he was stricken blind, neighbors said it was the judgment of the gods for his evil doing.

Chang heard of a missionary hospital where people were receiving sight. In 1886 he traveled overland for hundreds of miles to reach the hospital, only to be told every bed was full. The hospital evangelist took pity and gave up his own bed. Chang's eyesight was partially restored, and he heard about Christ for the first time. "Never had we a patient who received the gospel with such joy," reported the doctor.

When Chang asked for baptism, missionary James Webster replied, "Go home and tell your neighbors that you have changed. I will visit you later and if you are still following Jesus, then I will baptize you."

Five months later Webster arrived in Chang's area and found hundreds of inquirers. He baptized the new evangelist with great joy.

A clumsy native doctor robbed Chang of the little eyesight the missionaries had restored. No matter—Chang continued his travels from village to village, winning hundreds more, praising God when cursed and spit upon, even when ferocious dogs were turned loose to drive him away. He learned practically the whole New Testament by memory and could quote entire chapters from the Old Testament. Missionaries followed after him, baptizing converts and organizing churches.

When the Boxer fury arose, Chang was preaching at Tsengkow, Manchuria. Christians felt sure he would be one of the first targets and led him to a cave in the mountains.

The Boxers reached the nearby city called Ch'ao-yangshan first and rounded up about fifty Christians for execution. "You're fools to kill all these," a resident told them. "For every one you kill, ten will spring up while that man Chang Shen lives. Kill him and you will crush the foreign religion." The Boxers promised to spare the fifty if someone would take them to Chang. No one volunteered. Finally when it appeared the Boxers would kill the fifty, one man slipped away and found Chang to tell him what was happening. "I'll gladly die for them," Chang offered. "Take me there."

35

When Chang arrived, the Boxer leaders were at another town. Nevertheless, he was bound by local authorities and taken to the temple of the god of war, and commanded to worship.

"I can only worship the One Living and True God," he declared.

"Then repent," they cried.

"I repented many years ago."

"Then believe in Buddha."

"I already believe in the one true Buddha, even Jesus Christ."

"You must at least bow to the gods."

"No. Turn my face toward the sun." Chang knew that at this time of day the sun was shining toward the temple and his back would be to the idols. When they turned him around, he knelt and worshiped the God of the Bible.

Three days later the Boxer leaders arrived. The blind evangelist was put in an open cart and driven to the cemetery outside the city wall. As he passed through the crowds, he sang the first Christian song he had learned at the hospital.

> Jesus loves me, He who died
> Heaven's gate to open wide;
> He will wash away my sin,
> Let His little child come in.
>
> Jesus loves me, He will stay,
> Close beside me all the way;
> If I love Him when I die,
> He will take me home on high.

When they reached the cemetery, he was shoved into a kneeling position. Three times he cried, "Heavenly Father, receive my spirit." Then the sword flashed, and his head tumbled to the ground.

The Boxers refused to let the Christians bury his body. Instead, fearful of a report that Blind Chang would rise from the dead, they forced the believers to buy oil and burn the mangled remains. Even so, the Boxers became afraid and fled from the revenge which they believed Chang's spirit would wreak upon them. The local Christians were thus spared persecution.

## The Tribulation in Peking

The largest number of Chinese Christians died in the populous cities of Peking and Tientsin. Fewer died in Tientsin where a young Quaker engineer named Herbert Hoover, the future president of the United States, and other foreigners gave them refuge and the opportunity to help defend the foreign garrison against attacks by Chinese government soldiers.

But not a single missionary died in Tientsin. And only one was martyred in Peking, an Englishman known as Professor James who had been in the country since 1883. As the crisis was developing, he went out to check on Chinese Christian friends. Soldiers captured him and took him to the house of two of the leaders in the coup that had overthrown Emperor Kuang-hsu. They ordered him to kneel. The missionary refused, declaring, "I cannot kneel to anyone but my God and King." Then he was forced to kneel upon a chain for several hours. He was executed three days later and his head exhibited in a cage hanging from the beam of the Tung An Gate.

The foreigners in Peking were fast gathering in the British ambassador's compound for protection against sniper attacks. Unexpectedly, the empress's troop commander in the capital announced a short truce to permit all the foreigners to take shelter. American Methodist missionaries begged their ambassador to wait for seven hundred Chinese Christian girls who were unprotected in their mission school a mile away. "We appeal to you in the name of humanity and Christianity not to abandon them," the missionary said. The ambassador felt the risk was too great. Missionary Frank Gamewell then warned that "our Christian nation will never live down your decision." Gamewell and his colleagues could only go back and distribute money to students and faculty and instruct them to hide wherever they could.

After the foreigners were safely behind the walls of the British compound, the Boxers and their fanatical supporters struck. The tragedy they inflicted was described by Dr. George Ernest Morrison of the London *Times* who was caught in Peking:

As darkness came on the most awful cries were heard in the city, most demoniacal and unforgettable, the cries of the Boxers—*Sha kuei-tzu* [kill the devils]—mingled with the shrieks of the victims and the groans of the dying. For Boxers were sweeping through the city, massacring the native Christians and burning them alive in their homes. The first building to be burned was the chapel of the Methodist Mission in the Hatamen Street. Then flames sprang up in many quarters of the city. Amid the most deafening uproar, the Tung-tang or East Cathedral shot flames into the sky. The old Greek Church in the northeast of the city, the London Mission buildings, the handsome pile of the American Board Mission, and the entire foreign buildings belonging to the Imperial Marine Customs in the east city burned throughout the night. It was an appalling sight.

. . . On June 15th rescue parties were sent out by the American and Russian Legations in the morning, and by the British and German Legations in the afternoon, to save if possible native Christians from the burning ruins. . . . Awful sights were witnessed. Women and children hacked to pieces, men trussed like fowls, with noses and ears cut off and eyes gouged out. Chinese Christians accompanied the reliefs and ran about in the labyrinth of network of streets that formed the quarter, calling upon the Christians to come out from their hiding places. All through the night the massacre had continued, and Boxers were even now caught red-handed at their bloody work. As the patrol was passing a Taoist Temple on the way, a noted Boxer meeting place, cries were heard within. The temple was forcibly entered. Native Christians were found there, their hands tied behind their backs, awaiting execution and torture, some had already been put to death, and their bodies were still warm and bleeding. All were shockingly mutilated. Their fiendish murderers were at their incantations burning incense before their gods, offering Christians in sacrifice to their angered deities.

Several hundred Chinese Christians did reach the besieged foreigners and worked heroically digging ditches and fortifying the walls against Boxer attacks. As the first shells burst over the walls, Chinese children could be heard singing, "There'll be no dark valley when Jesus comes." Finally in August an international rescue force, marching from Tientsin, reached Peking and broke the siege. By this time the Chinese Christians were reduced to eating leaves. Arm and leg bones protruded through their skin, and they were too weak to cheer their rescuers.

The empress was overthrown and fled Peking in terror. Many of her advisers committed suicide. The victorious foreign expeditionary force allowed a caretaker government to take over. Now the Boxers became the hunted, and thousands were killed by foreign and Chinese troops. The mad governor of Shansi Province was beheaded.

## The Last Boxer Martyr

Meanwhile, the CIM missionaries who had been beaten on long marches were being cared for in hospitals. Mrs. Glover gave birth to the child she had carried on her thousand mile trek. But tiny Faith Edith lived only ten days.

Mrs. Glover helped plan the burial service choosing one of the CIM's favorite hymns which begins, "Hark, hark the song the ransomed sing." After the burial, Mrs. Glover's health improved and she was moved to Shanghai. There she took a sharp turn for the worse and began sinking fast. Late on the afternoon of October 24, she picked up the lines of "Jesus, Lover of My Soul" which her husband had been singing by her bedside. In a remarkably clear voice she sang,

> Leave, ah! leave me not alone,
> Still support and comfort me.

At four the next morning she was with Christ.

She was the last of the Shansi missionary martyrs to die. As her coffin was lowered, her husband, two sons who had been away at school, and missionary and Chinese friends sang the hymn she had sung so many times to her children at bedtime:

> Sun of my soul, Thou Savior dear,
> It is not night if Thou be near.

Afterwards her husband had inscribed on her headstone two praise notes appropriate to all the martyrs of the Boxer uprising:

THE NOBLE ARMY OF MARTYRS PRAISE THEE.
IN THY PRESENCE IS FULNESS OF JOY.

## The Power and the Glory

The Boxers had inflicted the most severe blow ever dealt to the modern Protestant missionary movement launched by William Carey. A total of 135 missionaries and 53 children had been killed—100 from Britain and Commonwealth nations, 56 from Sweden, and 32 from the United States. Of this number, 79 were associated with the CIM and 36 with the C&MA, the societies which suffered the greatest losses. Many China watchers thought Protestants were finished in China. Chinese believers, they said, are rice Christians and the native church will fade away. They further predicted that missionaries would never again be welcome in China.

The doomsayers were wrong on all counts.

When the rebellion was over, an assessment showed that the Chinese church had been battered but had never bent. For example, the Methodists in Foochow met after the missionaries had departed and agreed they would continue their educational and evangelistic work, even if they never received another missionary or dollar of mission money. When peace and order came and the missionaries returned, a delegation of twelve men came from a village to ask for a Christian preacher. "We want to know more about your religion. We will support the minister and provide him a place to live and a building in which to preach."

At Taiyuan the remains of the slain missionaries and Chinese Christians were carefully gathered up and buried in the Martyr Memorial Cemetery. Later a Martyr Memorial Church was opened at the spot where Miss Coombs had been burned to death while trying to rescue two of her Chinese students. A memorial stone, on which was inscribed the names of the Taiyuan martyrs, was placed on the porch of the new church.

At Paoting, where two hospitals were built as memorials to the slain missionary doctors, the commander of the Chinese Second Army Division, General Wang, came to the Presbyterian mission and requested Christian teachers to come to instruct his men in the gospel and biblical morality.

Powerful, soul-cleansing revivals surged across north China. Missionaries confessed sins of arrogance, pride, and ill feeling toward their co-workers and asked forgiveness. Chinese pastors and church leaders confessed failures to their flocks. Kinsmen who had been long estranged made tearful reconciliations. Prodigals came and knelt at their parents' feet and begged forgiveness. Many parents asked their children for forgiveness. The Methodists' Bishop Cassels recorded:

Scoffers might call the work by an evil name; unbelievers might laugh at the unusual scenes; hard hearts might for a time resist the influence; but those whose eyes were opened and whose hearts were touched, felt indeed that now, if never before, they had been brought into touch with the powers of the other world, and with the mighty working of the Spirit of God.

Protestants more than doubled during the six years following the massacres. In 1901 one missionary in Kiangsi Province reported twenty thousand converts.

Throughout China there was mass interest in Christianity. It was well known that most Christians, Chinese and foreign, had not demanded indemnities for loss of life and destruction of property as other foreigners had. Hudson Taylor, director of the missionary society which had suffered most, asked CIM workers to show to the Chinese "the meekness and gentleness of Christ, not only not to enter any claim against the Chinese Government but to refrain from accepting compensation even if offered." In Shansi Province, where the greatest damage had been wreaked, newly appointed officials appointed Baptist missionary Timothy Richard to help make post-Boxer adjustments. Richard suggested that a large sum be set aside as an indemnity, not to be paid to foreigners but to found in Taiyuan a Chinese university. He believed this would help dispel the ignorance and superstition which had enabled the Boxers to gain support from the populace. The proposal was accepted and another English Baptist missionary was appointed the first principal.

Chinese church leaders more than matched the spirit of the missionaries. Even those who had lost loved ones exhibited remarkable restraint and forgiveness. Chen Wei-ping, pastor of the Asbury Methodist Church in Peking, had lost his minister father and mother and sister to crazed Boxers in Yen-ching-chou. His father had been beheaded, his mother and thirteen-year-old sister hacked to pieces as they clung in each other's arms. When invited by the government to submit a claim, Pastor Chen replied, "We are not in need. We do not want payment." Instead he requested his bishop to "Appoint me to Yen-ching-chou that I may preach the message of love to the men who killed my loved ones." The bishop consented.

The families of the missionary martyrs were equally forgiving. Sherwood Eddy, the missionary statesman, told a student missionary convention in Kansas City about visiting the parents of Mrs. E. R. Atwater in Oberlin, Ohio. She, her husband, and their four children had been killed by soldiers who had pretended to be their protectors. Recalled Eddy, "They said, in tears, 'We do not begrudge them—we gave them to that needy land; China will yet believe the truth.'"

Sending churches were challenged by missionary and Chinese speakers fresh from China to embark on a crash program for evangelizing China. Yale student Fei Chi-hao told another student missionary convention, "My parents are now wearing the martyr's crown in the 'Home above.' It is my ambition to follow in the footsteps of your missionaries and carry back the blessed message to my people." Then he challenged the students about China's immediate needs. "We need colleges and universities, railroads and factories," he said. "But the thing that we need most, just now, is Christianity. The Christian religion is the only hope and salvation of China."

Such appeals brought wave after wave of new missionaries to China and millions of dollars for evangelization and education.

The Boxer martyrdoms in China bore fruit for decades following. Thousands upon thousands came to Christ as a direct result of the slaughter of Christians in 1900. Some had been direct observers of persecutions and could not, as Saul of Tarsus in witnessing the stoning of Stephen, forget the bravery and dedication of those who had died.

One of the most notable was Feng Yu-hsiang, the soldier who watched the murders at Paoting. In 1913, as a major, he professed faith in Christ at an evangelistic meeting led by John R. Mott in Peking. Afterwards he testified, "I saw Miss Morrill offer her life for her friends. And a missionary walking with his sons on a veranda in calmness and peace while flames rose to envelop them. I could never forget that."

Feng Yu-hsiang became China's most famous "Christian General." He won hundreds of his officers to Christ, forbade gambling and prostitution in his camps, and had his men taught useful trades.

The results were much less spectacular in Mongolia where the Scandinavian missionaries had given their all. But their successors were confident. Said Mrs. A. B. Magnuson:

> Looking back on our work in Mongolia it seems dark, having borne little fruit, but I lift my eyes upward to Him who can look deeper and farther than we can look and does not judge simply by the outward appearance as we do. He can change and transform all things and no work for Him is in vain. We believe there will be some saved souls from Mongolia in the great blood-washed multitude before the throne of the Redeemer. "They that sow in tears shall reap in joy."

The defeat of the Boxers and their Imperial backer marked a turning point in China's history. The feudal Manchu dynasty was soon overthrown and the Chinese Republic founded under the leadership of Sun Yat-sen, a Christian whose life had once been saved by a British missionary.

The new generation of Chinese looked to the "Christian" West for education and technical aid. Protestant missionaries were invited to start universities in every major city. By 1911 most Chinese political leaders were Protestants, including Sun Yat-sen. One official even suggested that Christianity be made the state religion.

# 2

# China in the Following Decades

## *No Ark of Safety*

The Boxer defeat opened China to greater evangelization, but it did not mark the end of violence. Scores of missionaries and thousands of Chinese Christians were martyred in the line of duty during the next half century. Most were killed by mobs, dread diseases, Japanese bombs and bullets, and Communist assassination squads—all before the Red scourge enveloped the Celestial Kingdom and cut off communication with Christianity abroad.

Superstition and ignorance continued to spur the dark horse of death. In the summer of 1902 a cholera epidemic swept parts of north China. Thirteen children died at the CIM's Chefoo school where missionaries sent their school-age youngsters. One was the son of Boxer martyrs, Mr. and Mrs. Duncan Kay. Missionaries at their stations were working to save thousands of Chinese when a rumor was circulated that they were spreading the epidemic with their poison (medicine). In Chen-chou, Honan Province, two CIM members, J. R. Bruce of Australia and R. H. Lowis of England, were attacked by a fear-ridden mob and murdered as a result of the rumor.

### The Doctor's Devotion

Anti-foreign mobs continued to lengthen the trail of blood of the Christian missionaries, who were not ordinary foreigners but humanitarians of the highest order. Dr. Eleanor Chestnut is an example. An orphan raised by a poor aunt in the backwoods of Missouri, she skimped and starved to get through Park College, dressing in castoffs from the mis-

43

sionary barrel. Determined to be a medical missionary, she lived in an attic and ate mostly oatmeal while attending medical school in Chicago. To earn money she nursed the aged. She was nurse to Dr. Oliver Wendell Holmes in his final illness.

After studies at Moody Bible Institute, Dr. Chestnut was appointed by the then American Presbyterian Board to China in 1893. She started a hospital in Lien-chou, Kwangsi, the province adjoining Hong Kong. She lived on $1.50 a month so that the rest of her salary could be used to buy bricks. Her Board learned what she was spending on bricks and insisted on repaying her. She refused the sum offered, saying, "It will spoil all my fun."

While the building was under construction, she performed surgery in her bathroom. One operation involved the amputation of a coolie's leg. The surgery was successful, except that the flaps of skin did not grow together. Eventually this problem was solved and the man was able to walk with crutches. Someone noticed that Dr. Chestnut was limping. When asked why, she responded, "Oh, it's nothing." One of the nurses revealed the truth. The doctor had taken skin from her own leg for immediate transplant to the one whom nurses called "a good-for-nothing coolie," using only a local anesthetic.

When the Boxer uprising began Dr. Chestnut was one of the last missionaries to leave. She returned the following spring. On October 28, 1905, she and other missionaries were busy at the hospital when an anti-foreign mob attacked. She slipped out to ask for protection from Chinese authorities, and might have escaped had she not returned to help her fellow workers. Her last act was to tear strips from her dress to bandage a wound in the forehead of a boy in the crowd. She was killed along with Rev. and Mrs. John Peale and two other missionaries.

## Martyrs to Bandits and Kidnappers

Disorders and rebellions continued. In June 1920, William A. Reimert, a missionary educator, was murdered by bandit soldiers. In December 1921, the C&MA's W. H. Oldfields was kidnapped by brigands in Kwangsi Province. In 1922 Dr. Howard Taylor and four other CIM missionaries were seized by bandit soldiers, but were subsequently released. In August 1923, F. J. Watts and E. A. Whiteside of the English Church Missionary Society were murdered by robbers in Szechwan Province. A few months later four American Lutheran missionaries were captured in Hupeh Province, and one, B. A. Hoff, died of injuries after his release. In 1924 George D. Byers, an American Presbyterian, was killed by bandits in Hainan Province. A few months later the anti-foreign Red Lantern Society murdered Mrs. Sible, a Canadian Methodist, at Ch'eng-tu. More kidnappings and murders followed, including the killing of several national Bible Society colporteurs.

A vast spiritual harvest paralleled the violence. For example, in Kweilin, capital of Kwangsi Province, thousands of new converts were baptized by Christian and Missionary Alliance missionaries. Three times the church sanctuary had to be enlarged. The foundation of the third building was laid during a period of near anarchy while bullets from battling military factions zinged over the construction site. C&MA missionary Cunningham was supervising the work when hit by a fatal shot. His life and the lives of other missionaries and national church leaders were part of the price of the spiritual reaping.

The violence continued to escalate. Kidnappers no longer sent sliced ears as warnings, but killed their victims immediately if demands for ransom were not met. The anti-foreign spirit, kept high by Communist agitation, was so strong that local military and civil authorities often looked the other way when attacks were made on missionaries and even on Chinese Christians.

## The Blood Keeps Flowing

President Sun Yat-sen died in 1925. His party split apart, factions fighting among themselves. China became even less safe. Six more missionaries died, among them the beloved Bishop Cassels. Before his death he had written, "We came in the steps of Him who was despised and rejected of men. Perhaps this is one of the lessons we have to learn at a time when extraordinary and bitter hatred is being stirred up against us."

The year 1927 was the worst since the Boxer violence in 1900. Mission hospitals and schools had to be closed in the interior of China. Missionaries were ordered to evacuate to the coast or return home. In that year the Protestant force dropped from sixty-five hundred to four thousand.

Crossing deserts and high mountains, missionaries were again easy prey for bandits and undisciplined troops. In one incident bandits attacked three CIM American missionaries, Mr. and Mrs. Morris Slichter, their two children, and Miss May Craig. They were traveling under military guard to a railway station in Yunnan Province. When the bandits opened fire, the guards fled leaving the missionaries unprotected in a rice field. Heedless of cries for mercy, one bandit fired at Mrs. Slichter who was holding her three-year-old daughter Ruth in her arms. The bullet passed through the child's head and ripped a gash across the mother's left wrist. Another robber stabbed Mr. Slichter in the back. He fell dead without a sound.

## Chinese Christians Were Not Spared

For every missionary who died directly or indirectly because of the violence, at least ten Chinese Christians lost their lives. One was Y. C. Liu, a promising, scholarly young preacher in Szechwan Province. He was on his way to his ordination ceremony in a CIM-related church when kidnapped by bandits. His body was later found in the woods. Another Chinese Christian from the same area was the former incense-maker, Ho. After hearing the gospel, Ho had invited missionary C. M. Tan and his Christian brother-in-law to the destruction of his idols. A man of few words, he became known for his warm smile and willingness to tackle any task in the church. While on a trip to sell cloth, he was stopped by brigands, robbed, and killed. Left to mourn were his wife and three young children.

Besides the bandit peril, Chinese Christians continued to be targets of anti-foreign and anti-Christian societies. Traveling Bible and book salesmen were especially in danger. One was seized in Kiangsi Province, his books were confiscated, and his hands tied. He was ordered to run through the streets, calling out, "I am also an imperialist, a slavish dog of the foreigners." Instead, he proclaimed at the top of his lungs, "I am a slave of Jesus Christ!" They did not kill him on the spot, but threatened to do so if he ever dared sell another Christian book. How long he lived after this is not known. Another Chinese Christian in Yonanchow, Hunan Province, was grabbed by Communists and charged with being a "running dog of imperialists" for disseminating the teachings of Jesus. When told he was worthy of death, he begged the opportunity to pray. A Communist instantly struck off his hand. "Lord Jesus, receive my spirit," the Christian shouted in a loud voice. A second blow with the sword and he was dead.

The Nationalist armies now pushed north and conquered the upper Yangtze Valley. With the fall of Nanking on March 27 many foreigners, including missionaries, were murdered. Many others escaped. Pearl S. Buck, daughter of missionaries and later to become a world-renowned novelist, hid in a peasant hut. A Southern Presbyterian doctor was pushed into a hospital coal bin by his loyal staff. After the danger had passed, he crawled out, sooty but safe.

## The Red Peril

Chiang Kai-shek purged the Communists from his armies and reversed Sun's policy of friendship with Russia. In 1928 the long civil war began between Chiang's Nationalist armies and the Communists under Mao Tse-tung. Vastly outnumbered by Nationalist troops, the Communist armies retreated to the far northwest. But infiltrators and guerrillas remained hidden in the dense population.

Undaunted, the CIM called for two hundred new workers in 1929 to serve in dangerous areas. "It will involve the most tremendous conflict [with Satan] which we have ever undertaken," said the CIM director. Within the next few months eight more missionaries were killed, thirty captured and held for ransom, and twenty of thirty-two CIM stations looted.

The price of serving in China remained high. In 1930 three missionaries of the Finnish Free Mission Society, Misses Cajander, Ingman, and Hedengren were killed by Communist outlaws. Altogether, during 1930, the Communists killed an estimated 150,000 Chinese in Kiangsi Province and burned one hundred thousand homes. One and a half million Chinese fled the province in fear.

When Chiang Kai-shek declared himself a Christian the next year, missionaries and Chinese church leaders became direct targets for Communist hostility. Propagandists nailed up posters announcing such charges as, "The church is the headquarters of murderers and incendiaries," "The missionaries have love in their mouths and hate in their hearts," and "Christians are traitors to China." Other posters urged Chinese, "Drive out these missionaries who are making slaves of us." To the testimony of one CIM missionary in Kiangsi Province that he was not afraid to die because "I know I will go to Heaven," a Communist answered, "Let him go to Heaven. We will have one less missionary in China to cheat the people."

## Muslim Marauders

The decade of the thirties began with terrible famines and plagues added to Communist guerrilla activities and other rebellions in many cities. In Minchow, Kansu, the Assemblies of God lost 150 school children out of five hundred students in a plague. Next, bandits attacked the town, seizing citizens by force and torturing them until they gave up their valuables. Hundreds were burned and beaten. Many Christians among them died. The bandits had hardly left when thirty thousand rebellious Muslims marched in and took control. Their leader made his headquarters in the front yard of the Assemblies mission house. The Muslims looted, burned, raped, and killed at will for eighteen days.

The brutalities were even worse in Tsinchow, Kansu Province. A Muslim army captured the town in May, killed twenty-seven hundred natives in three days, took over a thousand young women captive, and turned the CIM girls' school into horse stalls.

## Afraid of What?

In October 1931, widower Jack Vinson, a beloved Southern Presbyterian missionary, was captured by bandits while visiting rural churches in Kiangsu Province. A government force, loyal to Chiang, pursued the kidnappers and surrounded them in a small town. The bandits offered the missionary freedom if he would persuade the force to withdraw. Vinson agreed only if they would release other captives. The bandits refused and tried to shoot their way out. In the melee many bandits were killed, and the survivors fled with Vinson. However, the missionary could not run because of recent surgery. One bandit shot him, then another ran up and cut off his head.

Jack Vinson was the first Southern Presbyterian martyr in China. A colleague, E. H. Hamilton, was inspired by his courage to write a poem that was widely printed and became an encouragement to other missionaries and Chinese believers in constant danger.

Afraid? Of What?
To feel the spirit's glad release?
To pass from pain to perfect peace,
The strife and strain of life to cease?
    Afraid—of that?
    Afraid? Of What?
Afraid to see the Savior's face
To hear His welcome, and to trace
The glory gleam from wounds of grace?
    Afraid—of that?
    Afraid? Of What?
A flash, a crash, a pierced heart;
Darkness, light, O Heaven's art!
A wound of His a counterpart!
    Afraid—of that?
    Afraid? Of What?
To do by death what life could not—
Baptize with blood a stony plot,
Till souls shall blossom from the spot?
    Afraid—of that?

## Victory Day for the Stams

John and Betty Stam, new CIM missionaries in hazardous Anhwei Province were among those strengthened by "Afraid? Of What?" They had met at a CIM student prayer meeting at Moody. Betty, a gifted poet, had been raised in China of Presbyterian missionary parents and felt God's call to return there. John, of Dutch immigrant ancestry from New Jersey, was also drawn to the land where, as he said, "a million a month pass into Christless graves."

At that time the CIM was calling for a vanguard of single men to serve in dangerous Communist-infested areas. Even though this could mean not marrying for several years, if at all, John was willing to go. Chosen to give the Class Address for the Moody Class of '32, he challenged,

> Shall we beat a retreat, and turn back from our high calling in Christ Jesus; or dare we advance at God's command in face of the impossible? . . . Let us remind ourselves that the Great Commission was never qualified by clauses calling for advance only if funds were plentiful and no hardship or self-denial involved. On the contrary, we are told to expect tribulation and even persecution, but with it victory in Christ.

Since Betty was a year ahead of John in school, she went to China first. Assigned to Anhwei Province, she was delayed in Shanghai when the veteran CIM missionary in Anhwei, H. S. Ferguson, was captured by bandits and all the women missionaries had to leave. Ferguson was never seen alive again.

So she was in Shanghai when John arrived and after a year they were given permission by the CIM director to be married. "Truly, God seems to go out of His way to make His children happy," John wrote his parents after the wedding. They were even happier when Helen Priscilla was born in September 1934, in a Methodist hospital far up the Yangtze River.

Communist activity was said to have subsided in Anhwei Province, and they were assigned to do evangelistic work in the town of Ching-te. The district magistrate assured, "There is no danger of Communists here. I will guarantee your safety."

A few weeks later Communists did attack and the magistrate was one of the first to flee. The Reds were quick to go to the Stams. Betty served them tea and cakes while John tried to explain their peaceful intentions. When they finished their tea, the visitors politely said, "You will go with us."

At the direction of his captors, John wrote CIM that the kidnappers wanted $20,000 ransom. "The Lord bless and guide you, and as for us, may God be glorified whether by life or by death." He told the Communists, "I do not expect the ransom to be paid."

The Reds abandoned Ching-te, taking their captives with them. On the trail they discussed killing the baby to save trouble. An old farmer protested, "The little one has done nothing worthy of death." "Then you will die for her," the leader retorted. "I am willing," said the farmer. He was killed on the spot.

They stopped in the town of Miao-shou and ordered John to send another letter demanding the ransom. The postmaster recognized him and asked, "Where are you going?" "We don't know where they're going," John replied, "but we are going to heaven."

A short time later they were painfully bound, stripped of their outer garments, and quartered in a house. The next morning, still bound, they were marched through the town. As they moved along, the Communists shouted ridicule and hate slogans and called the people to the execution.

The procession stopped in a pine grove at the top of a hill. Suddenly the town physician, Dr. Wang, a Christian, ran to the prisoners and pleaded for their lives. He was dragged away to be killed.

John was asking mercy for the doctor when ordered to kneel. The executioner swung his sword and the young missionary was gone. Betty quivered momentarily, then fell beside him. Another swing and they were together with God.

## The "Miracle Baby"

The next day a Chinese evangelist named Lo arrived. The Communist soldiers had left, but the townspeople were too terrified of Communist spies to talk. Finally an old woman pointed to a vacant house and whispered, "The foreign baby is still alive." Lo found the baby lying warm and snug on a bed and took her to his wife. Then they recovered the bodies of the parents and lovingly wrapped them in white cotton for burial.

The bravery of the evangelist and his wife shamed the townspeople and they gathered to hear his funeral sermon.

> You have seen these wounded bodies, and you pity our friends for their suffering and death. But you should know that they are children of God. Their spirits are unharmed, and are at this moment in the presence of their Heavenly Father. They came to China and to Miao-shou, not for themselves but for you, to tell you about the great love of God, that you might believe in the Lord Jesus and be eternally saved. You have heard their message. Remember, it is true. Their death proves it so. Do not forget what they told you—repent, and believe the Gospel.

After the burial Evangelist and Mrs. Lo tenderly carried little Priscilla in a rice basket a hundred miles through dangerous mountains to the home of another CIM missionary, George Birch. Along the road they had asked Chinese mothers to nurse the child. Birch promised to care for her until his wife returned. Tucked away in the baby's clothing was ten dollars hidden by the mother for food.

When Mrs. Birch arrived, the couple arranged for the tiny orphan to be taken to its mother's parents, Dr. and Mrs. Charles Scott, at their Presbyterian station in Chi-nan, Shantung Province. Dr. Scott said of his daughter and son-in-law: "They have not died in vain. The blood of the martyrs is still the seed of the church. If we could hear our beloved children speak, we know from their convictions that they would praise God because He counted them worthy to suffer for the sake of Christ."

The report of the Stams' martyrdom and the survival of the "miracle baby," as Priscilla was called, was widely publicized in the United States and Britain. Hundreds of letters came to the parents of the young couple and their mission. Many contained large gifts. Some writers volunteered to go as replacements. At Moody and at Wilson College, where Betty had also attended, there were student prayer meetings. A biography was published and quickly ran through nine printings. Noting the impact, a CIM missionary in China wrote Betty's parents, "A life which had the longest span of years might not have been able to do one-hundredth of the work for Christ which they have done in a day."

## Martyrs to Disease

More missionaries died in China from dread diseases than from violence. The C&MA, for example, lost ten missionaries to smallpox, typhus, dysentery, and malaria from 1900 to 1924, while losing only two workers to afflictions common in the homeland. The larger CIM mission lost many more to dread diseases. Missionary doctors were most vulnerable to diseases such as smallpox, cholera, and typhus because they were often involved in fighting epidemics.

The multitalented J. O. Fraser—preacher, linguist, musician, and engineer—came to Yunnan Province in 1910 and mastered the difficult Lisu language. Developing his own "Fraser Script," he devoted himself to translating Scripture into the tribal dialect. In 1916 the Lisu began turning from their demon worship to Christ in large numbers. Sixty thousand were baptized in a two year period. The Lisu church continued to grow and became one of the largest tribal Christian bodies in the world. Then in 1937, in the peak of life, the "apostle to the Lisus" came down with malignant malaria while on a trip in the mountains and died.

## Shine On, Lottie Moon

Famine, the result of floods and drought, was the greatest destroyer of all. The loss of life in China in the first third of the twentieth century would have been infinitely greater without emergency relief programs funded by Christians in the United States and Britain and administered by missionaries. In 1906 one Christian periodical, *Christian Herald*, raised and forwarded $450,000 in gold. Upwards of two million lives were saved. Many impressed Chinese came to the missionaries, asking, "Tell us about your religion."

Too often the money was not available from home, and missionaries were helpless to prevent mass starvation. They had only their own small salaries for purchasing food. Some hastened their own deaths by going without.

The most celebrated martyr to hunger was Charlotte (Lottie) Moon, a household name among Southern Baptists today. Each Christmas Southern Baptist women in almost forty thousand American churches gather an offering in Miss Moon's name for foreign missions.

Born and reared in Virginia Baptist aristocracy, Lottie Moon was self-willed and rebellious through most of college. Surrender to Christ was not easy. Of her conversion she said, "I went to the service to scoff, and returned to my room to pray all night."

Her younger sister Edmonia went to China first. Charlotte went to Cartersville, Georgia, to teach. There she sought out destitute families for whom she bought clothing from her own purse. One morning the pastor spoke on the text, "Lift up your eyes, and look on the fields, for they are white already to harvest." At the close of the sermon the young teacher walked down the aisle and declared, "I have long known God wanted me in China. I am now ready to go."

She joined Edmonia in 1873 at Tengchow in northern Shantung Province. Edmonia was later compelled to leave China permanently because of poor health. Charlotte gave herself without reserve to her teaching and evangelistic work and to pleading for new workers from the homeland. She sometimes struck sparks in letters to her Baptist board. "It is odd that a million Baptists of the South can furnish only three men for all China," she wrote once. "Odd that with five hundred preachers in the state of Virginia we must rely on a Presbyterian minister to fill a Baptist pulpit [here]. I wonder how these things look in heaven. They certainly look very queer in China—but the Baptists are a great people, as we never tire of saying in our associations and conventions, and possibly our way of doing things is best!"

When more men finally were appointed, the decision was made that women should not share policy making with them. Miss Moon promptly submitted her resignation over the issue and officials backed down.

In 1887 she was preparing to leave for furlough when two Chinese men arrived. They had walked 115 miles to seek a teacher. There was no one else to send, so she went. This was the year when she suggested that Southern Baptist women designate a week of prayer and offerings for missions the week before Christmas. "I wonder how many of us really believe that it is more blessed to give than to receive," she challenged.

She was now facing persecution and hatred for being a foreigner. Frequently she was called "Devil Old Woman." After receiving a death threat, she underlined this sentence in her copy of *Imitation of Christ*: "Thou oughtest so to order thyself in all thy thoughts and actions, as if today thou wert to die."

She survived through most of the Boxer Rebellion before agreeing to evacuate to Japan for a few months. In 1911 came the Revolution, followed by famine. The Chinese churches did all they could. Miss Moon regularly gave a large part of her salary. She wrote to the Southern Baptist Foreign Mission Board again and again. Each time the reply was negative. The Board was heavily in debt and could hardly pay missionary salaries. Not one cent had been budgeted for famine relief.

She wrote a nephew, begging him to speak with his pastor about a local church offering. She told of mothers eager to give their children away and warned that "unless help comes from one to three million must perish from hunger. One penny a day up to the next harvest will save a life. How can we bear to sit down to our bountiful tables and know of such things and not bestir."

The famine worsened. Her appeals to the homeland continued to receive no response. She drew out the last of her savings from a bank in Shanghai to send to relief workers. "I pray that no missionary will ever be as lonely as I have been," she wrote in her bank book.

Fellow missionaries began noticing that she was behaving strangely and appeared befuddled. They sent for a doctor. One look told him she was starving to death. Indeed she had vowed to eat no more so long as her Chinese friends were starving.

Gentle hands gave her nourishment and put her on a ship for home with a missionary nurse escort. Enroute, the ship stopped at Kobe, Japan. There, on Christmas Eve night, 1912, she lapsed into unconsciousness. The nurse saw her lips move and bent to catch the name of a Chinese friend. Her frail, thin, almost transparent hands were moving, clasping and unclasping in the Chinese fashion of greeting. She was saying goodbye to old friends. Or was she saying hello? Finally her hands grew still, her breathing stopped, and she was in the heavenly company.

After cremation (required by Japanese law) her ashes were delivered to Virginia and buried under whispering pines. At the head of her grave her family placed a marble stone with the inscription:

LOTTIE MOON 1840–1912
FORTY YEARS A MISSIONARY OF THE SOUTHERN
BAPTIST CONVENTION IN CHINA
"FAITHFUL UNTO DEATH"

Her home church hired an artisan to design the figure of a beautiful woman in graceful, flowing garments, walking through a field of lilies, one hand clasping the Word of God to her heart, the other holding high a blazing torch. On this he inscribed in gold lettering:

GO YE, THEREFORE, AND TEACH ALL NATIONS

Back in China her Christian friends erected their own memorial stone:

A MONUMENT TO BEQUEATH THE LOVE OF
MISS LOTTIE MOON
AN AMERICAN MISSIONARY
THE CHINESE CHURCH REMEMBERS FOREVER

But her greatest memorials have been the numbers of young Christians who have been challenged by her life and the annual week-of-prayer offerings taken in thousands of Southern Baptist churches every year for foreign missions. In 1994 the collection amounted to almost 85 million dollars.

## The Real John Birch

John Birch is one of the most remarkable martyrs of this period. Unfortunately, his service to China has been all but forgotten in the controversy over the organization named after him.

Born in India of missionary parents, Birch graduated at the head of his high school, college, and seminary classes. He went to Hangchow in 1940 under the World Fundamentalist Baptist Missionary Fellowship and immediately demonstrated an unusual proficiency in learning the language and adapting to the culture. Within a year he was slipping through Japanese occupation lines and preaching in villages where missionaries had not dared go since the war began.

After Pearl Harbor the Japanese ordered his arrest. But he had fled to Shang-jao in Kiangsi Province from which he and four Chinese preachers sustained national churches for several months. Because Shang-jao was still in "free" territory, he became a conduit for American funds sent to missionaries stranded in Shanghai.

As the war progressed, he became a one-man rescue unit, helping missionaries and Chinese preachers evacuate before advancing Japanese. In one operation called "Harvey's Restaurant" he arranged for sixty missionaries and children to be flown out to safety. In another he rescued Colonel James Doolittle, the most celebrated American flier shot down during the war.

He asked to join the American Military Mission as a chaplain. Instead he was commissioned a captain in intelligence and told he could preach all he wanted. He became a legend. He was the only American who had the complete trust of the Chinese Army and could go anywhere. His commander, Colonel Wilfred Smith, said later, "John influenced more as a military officer than he did as a missionary."

But he never saw himself as anything but a missionary. "I'm just making tents," he wrote his father. "When the war is over, I'll be ready to welcome the others back."

His announced intention to remain in China after the war may have led to his death. He was sent to convince hold-out pockets of Japanese in North China that the war was over. Communists, under the guise of "agrarian reformers," were then entrenched in North China, awaiting the opportunity to resume their war of conquest. Birch and his team were intercepted by a column of Chinese who were not supposed to be there. "Let us take you to our commander," they offered. Warned by his lieutenant that he might be walking into a trap, Birch decided to go. "It doesn't make any difference what happens to me," he said, "but it is of utmost importance that my country learn now whether these people are friend or foe." His body was found the next day, punctured and slashed by bayonets.

Chinese friends tenderly wrapped his body in white silk. He was buried in a Chinese coffin with full military honors, with several missionaries and Chinese pastors looking on. On his stone they placed the inscription:

HE DIED FOR RIGHTEOUSNESS.

Only the barest details of his death were released to his family by the State Department. In the amoral game of diplomacy Communists were never blamed. There were at the time Red sympathizers ensconced in high places in the U. S. government. It was also later disclosed that the decisive U. S. atomic bombing mission had been carried out with the aid of essential weather bulletins from Mao Tse-tung's Communists in North China.

Why was John Birch killed? The best speculation is that the Chinese Reds did not want him around as a missionary after the war.

## Martyrs of Red China

The West was blind to the Red tide washing across China. But the old China hands who returned to their mission posts soon saw the handwriting on the wall. The Soviets had declared war on Japan in the closing days of the war—to grab Manchuria, some thought. The Chinese Marxists had helped the Americans defeat the Japanese in China and gained valuable experience in guerrilla warfare. All during the war they had been subverting and plotting to take over the government.

Meanwhile, the opportunities for evangelism seemed never greater. Most churches had either held their own or actually grown during the years of war and Japanese occupation. Missionaries and national church leaders began reopening hospitals and schools and launching evangelistic crusades.

The euphoria was short-lived as Communist propagandists began stirring up old hatreds against Americans. Communist armies launched new attacks. Banditry intensified, making travel as dangerous as ever.

In December 1947, Evangelical Covenant Church missionaries at Hankow became concerned about their colleagues in Kingchow, which was in imminent danger of being taken by the Communists. On January 7 Dr. Alexis Berg, Esther Nordlund, and Martha Anderson left by transport truck to consult with their friends. Some of the passengers, worried about a bandit attack, had hired an armed guard.

About two in the afternoon as they were traveling through deserted hilly country, a shot rang out. The driver stopped immediately and one of the guards fired a shot to scare off any small group. More shouts and more firing—then about sixty armed men appeared. The guard fled.

The bandits advanced on the passengers and ordered them to get off the truck and to give up their valuables. The missionaries were also forced to give up their coats and shoes. Dr. Berg asked if he might keep his passport. At that, one bandit cursed and slapped his face. The doctor handed the passport over. A passing bicyclist was stopped. When he hesitated to give anything up, the bandits shot him dead.

They then left by scrambling up a nearby hill. Part way up, four turned around and returned.

"Shall we kill these foreigners?" the leader asked. Then looking at Dr. Berg, he demanded, "Are you Americans?" When Dr. Berg did not reply, the bandit snarled, "Americans are the worst of all. They have done China much harm." Then he shot Dr. Berg through the head.

When the shot was fired, Miss Anderson burst into sobs. The bandit leader responded, "She must be a relative of his," and immediately shot her also. By this time some of the passengers were kneeling, pleading with the bandits to stop killing. The four consulted briefly among themselves, then turned toward Miss Nordlund. "Yes, you may kill me, too," she said. Then she was shot. None of the other passengers were killed.

The killers left. But the frightened passengers insisted that the driver take them on and leave the dead Americans by the roadside. The bodies were later recovered and taken to Kingchow. The missionaries there sorrowfully dressed the bodies and placed them in coffins. They were taken back to Hankow for a final service and buried in the

International Cemetery among the graves of scores of other departed missionaries who had given their all for Christ in China.

The Communist armies kept advancing. By 1949 the conquest was all but complete. There was much hand wringing and finger pointing in the West. It was said "fuzzy" liberals and hidden Communists in the U. S. government had blinded the Americans until it was too late to rescue Chiang. There was less quibbling over other factors, such as corruption in the Nationalist government, runaway inflation, and student unrest. Later even the liberals had to concede they had been duped while the Communists had followed their game plan to victory.

The Communists sought to destroy the old Confucian order of family loyalty and morality and level the social system. Millions were killed for nothing more than owning property and paying respect to parents. How many Christians died in the secret genocidal purges will never be known.

Not wanting to inflame world opinion, the new "People's Republic" pursued a more wily strategy against Christianity. First they got rid of most of the missionaries, not by execution but by cutting ties between East and West. They charged that Christianity as it existed was too closely tied to western imperialism and colonialism. Missionaries were suddenly without jobs, property, and financial support. For example, the CIM, still the largest mission, had served in China eighty-five years. By 1953 it did not have a single worker in China nor a piece of furniture to call its own. The schools, hospitals, and all properties of the CIM and other foreign missions were confiscated.

Taking a lesson from history, the CIM changed its name to Overseas Missionary Fellowship, began accepting Asian workers on a par with Westerners, established headquarters in Singapore, and began work in East Asian countries.

By 1950 only a scattering of missionaries remained in China. Some had welcomed communism as a partner to Christianity and were outright propagandists for the regime. The others were holdouts, determined to stay until they were forcibly removed, imprisoned, or killed. Along with the Protestants were not a few Catholic diehards who died in prison.

The Communists had a step-by-step plan for dealing with the immovables: false accusations, planting of evidence, arrest, showcase trial, imprisonment, interrogations, and torture until the victim signed a confession, then if life remained, release of the shattered mind and body to authorities in Hong Kong.

Many faithful evangelists and pastors were arrested, never to be heard from again. One was Pastor Wang Shih-kuang, who was conducting a morning service at Ch'in-hsien in northwest China when Communists entered. The venerable preacher had apparently been expecting arrest. Raising his hand, he said simply, "This is God's service. Kindly remain at the back until we have finished." The Communists complied.

When the service was over and the soldiers came forward, Pastor Wang had only one last request. "Permit me to change clothes first." They understood. When a Chinese believes death is upon him, he wants to be dressed in his best garments. A few minutes later Pastor Wang reappeared, properly dressed, for his trip to jail. His fate was never known. The bodies of those who died in prison were usually released with the cause of death cited as disease, accident, or suicide.

## Indomitable Bill Wallace

The diabolical brutality of twisted Marxist minds is no better illustrated than in the treatment given a Baptist bachelor surgeon from Knoxville, Tennessee.

The quiet and devout Wallace joined the staff of Stout Memorial Hospital in Wuchow in 1935. A veteran missionary on board ship had told him that during the first half century of Protestant work in China, only one missionary had reached age forty. Wallace surpassed that by only three years. He steadfastly refused all marriage prospects. One hopeful said after a short acquaintance, "Marriage to Bill would be bigamy. He's married to his work."

The first incident occurred when he returned from language school to find the other missionaries had departed in fear of an advancing bandit army. He simply pulled the Chinese staff together and went to work. An American ship anchored in the nearby river. The captain sent an officer to remind the young surgeon that he could not be responsible for his safety even if he stayed overnight. "Tell your captain," Wallace said, "that he was not responsible for my coming here in the first place and he does not need to be responsible for my staying here."

The Japanese could not bomb him out during their war with China. He stubbornly remained during World War II until Wuchow officials decided the city must be evacuated. Then he put the hospital on water by transferring staff and equipment to a barge. When enemy planes roared overhead, he had the tugboat captain pull the floating hospital into one of the many large caves along the riverbank.

After VJ Day he set up shop again in the old building at Wuchow and for four years operated in peace. Then the Communists took over. One by one his missionary colleagues had to leave. Finally only he and nurse Everly Hayes remained. Local Communists tried to impose a crippling tax. Wallace said he could not believe the new People's Republic would so handicap an institution of mercy. Local citizens rose up and demanded exemption. It was granted.

The Korean War was now on and Communists in Wuchow mounted a "hate America" campaign. But the only "American dogs" and "imperialist wolves" remaining in the city were Dr. Wallace and Nurse Hayes, and Wallace was renowned as the finest surgeon in south China. The propaganda campaign fizzled.

One pre-dawn morning more than twenty Communist soldiers came to the hospital gate claiming to have a sick man. When the gate was opened, they rushed to the doctor's house. "We hide nothing," Wallace protested. "Our only work is healing the suffering and sick in the name of Jesus Christ."

A planted pistol was excuse enough to arrest and jail the doctor for espionage. From his cell Wallace preached to peasants brave enough to come within hearing.

At a mock trial his prosecutors waved a paper they said was his signed confession. What they had gotten from Wallace was only a brief, factual biographical summary. After he had signed it, they had typed in the confession. Citizen accusers were asked to come forward. To the prosecutor's embarrassment, no one moved. No matter. At a prearranged signal, hired stooges stood to deliver false testimony.

The missionary doctor was convicted, sentenced to prison, then marched through the streets to the main prison. His hands were tied and he wore a placard bearing obscene charges. Along the way he was shoved by a guard, and he fell, badly hurting his hand.

The next days were a nightmare of almost hourly interrogations accompanied by charges of medical incompetence, murdering and maiming Chinese, performing obscene operations, and immoral conduct with nurses. Once he was forced to pose holding a radio aerial for a picture to prove the spy conviction.

Near the end of one brutal day in February 1951, one of the Catholic missionaries asked from a nearby cell how he was holding out. "Trusting in the Lord," came the weak reply. His prison mates often heard him crying out in agony. It was also learned later that he wrote short Scripture verses, affirmations of faith, and denials of guilt on pieces of paper which he stuck on his cell walls and repeated to prepare for the next grilling.

The questioning continued, the pressure unrelenting. He became delirious and lapsed into crying spells.

Perhaps in fear of punishment for not succeeding, his guards used long poles to jab him into unconsciousness. The next morning they ran along the cellblock yelling, "The doctor has hung himself." They showed the Catholic priests where he was hanging from a beam and asked them to sign a statement attesting to his suicide. They would only state that they found him hanging.

Nurse Hayes and the Chinese hospital staff, who had been held under house arrest, were asked to claim his body. Miss Hayes noticed that his eyes were not bulging nor his tongue swollen, the usual features which would indicate hanging. But his upper body was a mass of bruises.

These devoted friends took his body to a cemetery. The Communists permitted no service and required the mourners to leave immediately after his body was lowered into the grave. But the Chinese Christians could not be cowed. Defying the Communists, they returned and erected a shaft over his grave pointing heavenward. On the shaft they inscribed the Scripture which they felt described the motivation of his life:

FOR TO ME TO LIVE IS CHRIST

When Everly Hayes was released and returned home to tell the story, the head of the Southern Baptist Foreign Mission Board commented: "The Communists thought they were rid of him; instead they immortalized him." So true. *Bill Wallace of China,* by Jesse

Fletcher (Broadman Press), had multiple printings. A film was made. Scores of young men and women committed their lives to missionary service. Said a Christian and Missionary Alliance missionary friend, "There have been and there will be many martyrs, but few can so glorify Him in death as Bill did."

## The Fiery Trials of Chinese Believers

Chinese Christians and church leaders having close connections to President Chiang's Nationalist government were among the first targets of a Communist purge. Many were killed. Others managed to flee with Chiang's staunchest supporters to Taiwan.

One who escaped was Dr. Chen Wei-ping, who had been a Methodist pastor for over fifty years. In 1900 he was pastor of the First Methodist Church of Peking when the Boxers spilled their rivers of blood across North China. His church and home were burned, but he and his wife and young child escaped. His parents and brother and sister did not. Later Dr. Chen had been told the gruesome story of his family's murder. He had borne the memory for almost fifty years. Now, with the Communist takeover, he too was willing to die for Christ. But leaders of the defeated government begged, "Come with us. We need you more." He went to Taiwan and became Chief of Chaplains in the Nationalist Army. Later he became pastor of the Shih Ling Church which President and Madame Chiang regularly attended.

Many thousands of Christians stayed behind, telling departing missionaries and fleeing Chinese friends, "We ask only that you pray for us as we remain to face the storm."

The Communist rage hit Catholics harder than Protestants. The Reds tried to induce the Catholic clergy to set up an independent Chinese Patriotic Church but met stiff resistance. A crackdown resulted, and hundreds of priests were imprisoned. Before 1952 about one hundred Chinese clergy died in jail. In 1952 over two hundred perished. By 1954 an additional four to five hundred priests had joined these martyrs. Not until 1958 was the puppet Catholic church established, and then it was denounced by the pope. Most of the remaining opponents of the new church were put in prison.

The Marxist regime had more success with Chinese Protestants. In 1950 Chou En-lai persuaded a few leaders to draft a "Christian Manifesto," affirming loyalty to the government and opposition to "imperialism, feudalism, and bureaucratic capitalism." Chinese "volunteers" were then fighting the West in Korea. The anti-foreign spirit for past western aggressions remained strong. With support from liberal churchmen, some trained in liberal American seminaries, three hundred thousand Chinese Protestants signed the Manifesto.

The next tactic was the "Resist-America, Aid-Korea, Three-Self-Reform Movement" program, followed by the organization of a unified Chinese Christian Church with officers from Three-Self Committees. All denominational structures were dismantled. Services were allowed only in authorized church buildings at announced hours with a government monitor present. By 1958 only a dozen of two hundred churches in Shanghai were open; in Peking only four of sixty-five still held services.

From the beginning of the Red takeover there had been Christian resistance. In Manchuria a Christian leader protested indiscriminate killing. He was dragged into a People's Court and accused of numerous crimes against "the people." The judges ordered spectators to march by him, each to hit him with a club until he was beaten to death. But the people refused, declaring, "He's a good man."

Changing tactics, the judges promised that if he renounced Jesus he would be set free. "Which do you choose—Jesus Christ or Communism?" they demanded.

"Jesus! Jesus! Jesus!" he shouted back.

Then they took him to the riverbank for execution. Along the way he sang, "Jesus Loves Me" and the Twenty-third Psalm set to Chinese music. He asked to pray, and they granted him permission to kneel briefly. When he stood up, he was shot in the back. But instead of falling on his face to grovel in the dust as victims usually do, he fell backwards, as if he were falling into the arms of Jesus. The entire community was reportedly stirred by his testimony.

In Shansi Province, scene of bloody Boxer massacres, many evangelists and pastors were martyred. In one instance, a preacher was tortured, then told he could go but dare not preach again.

"No, I cannot do that," he replied. "I cannot obey you."

Furious, the official shouted, "Then you must die, you miserable lout."

"I am not the one who is poor and miserable," the preacher replied calmly, and he began preaching to the man. He was shot without further delay.

There was widespread resistance to joining the puppet National Christian Church. This resistance was concentrated in the communal Jesus Family and the Little Flock house churches. Neither had direct connections with missionaries. Thousands of Chinese participants in the house churches of these groups were killed or imprisoned. Best known in the West for his books was Watchman Nee, leader of the Little Flock. He was imprisoned in 1952 and lived until June 1972.

A deceitful calm came in 1957 when many political prisoners were released and Mao Tse-tung proclaimed as state policy, "Let all flowers bloom and all schools of thought contend." This was taken as an invitation to speak up. Some church leaders charged the Three-Self Movement with taking away their political rights. One churchman called the lack of personal freedom under the government "intolerable." The veteran evangelist Chia Yu-ming told theological students that the "mark of the beast" as revealed in Revelation was membership in the Communist Party. Another faculty member at this seminary displayed a poem that challenged atheism:

> I say, God is; you say No;
> Let's see who will suffer woe.
> You say, No God; I say you're wrong;
> We'll see who sings salvation's Song.

The bloom faded. Most of those who had been released from prison when the deceitful invitation was announced were rounded up and put back in jail. One of these was Henry H. Lin, who had previously been arrested in 1957. Before that time he had been president of the Baptist University of Shanghai, succeeding Herman Liu, a martyr to the Japanese. President Lin languished less than two years in prison. According to a report, he was given a higher release when he died in a jail near Nanking early in 1960.

Too late the freedom critics learned they had been tricked. The Communists now knew who the resisters were and began hauling them into court for crimes against the state.

In one city fifty-two pastors, evangelists, and leading laymen were put on trial and pressured to make confessions. During the procedure, Communist supporters were invited to display their loyalty by slapping, pulling the hair, and spitting on the accused. The inquisition continued for seven days and two nights. On September 7, 1958, one pastor collapsed and died. He was rolled up in a reed mat and dumped in a grave before his widow knew he was dead. When she asked permission to move the body to their home burial ground, the Communists jeered, "You Christians are going to heaven. Why do you worry about burial?" As a result of this pastor's death, seventeen of his codefendants denounced Communist injustice and were immediately sentenced to long terms of hard labor under inhuman conditions.

## The Chinese Church Refuses to Die

What of Christianity today behind the bamboo curtain?

In recent years hard news of the state of Christianity in China has been scarce. There were a million baptized Protestants and around three million Catholics at the time of the Communist takeover. Journalists and other visitors report seeing only a few showcase churches still open and these are sparsely attended. Unauthorized meetings of three or more persons are illegal. The "president" of the Nanking Theological Seminary admitted in 1977 that he had had no students in five years.

Relatives outside the bamboo curtain occasionally get news of their loved ones. Franklin Liu, for example, a Baptist educator in Hong Kong and the son of martyred Herman Liu, heard that his mother remained under house arrest in Peking, his brother was in a labor camp in Manchuria, and his sister was allowed to teach mathematics in Shanghai. That news was several years ago and their fate is now unknown.

But letters to the Far Eastern Broadcasting Company in Manila, stories from refugees trickling into Hong Kong, and reports from Chinese allowed to visit relatives inside China suggest that cell churches are thriving in some areas. Among a population of thirty thousand in an area near the coast, three thousand believers are said to be meeting in small house churches. But sources for this report also say that plundering Red Guards during the height of the Cultural Revolution destroyed almost all Bibles in the district.

David Adeney, dean of OMF's Discipleship Training Centre in Singapore and a veteran China watcher, tells in the November 18, 1977 issue of *Christianity Today* of a Hong Kong resident who visited his relatives and found almost all of them still professing Christians. Relatives told him many had been baptized in 1976 and numbers of young people were seeking Christ. These were being warned that the cost of commitment could be great. The times and places of house church meetings were constantly being changed to avoid a crackdown. Nevertheless, leaders continued to be arrested and sent to labor camps. At one meeting worshipers "strongly sensed the presence of the Spirit of God and the love of Christ." At the conclusion of the meeting, five visitors stood and announced they had been sent to make arrests. Now they too wanted to believe. They were then instructed to kneel and confess their sins and receive salvation in Christ.

Adeney tells of another Chinese Christian who came to Hong Kong with his five-year-old daughter to visit his father. He had left his wife behind in an area where Christians feared to confess their faith. He recalled that he and his wife sometimes prayed together in bed, but had been afraid to tell their child for fear she would tell in kindergarten and bring trouble upon them.

Adeney further reports news of a powerful revival in one section of China. In this area five hundred Christian leaders associated with Watchman Nee were arrested. The news bearer said that five of eleven who came from his village were sent to a remote spot from which only one returned. Three died from extreme cold and hard labor. One was shot because of his continued witness. But in 1976 revival swept the area and four to five thousand were baptized in secluded places.

## Has a New Era Begun?

The most astounding news came in late 1978 when President Jimmy Carter and Chinese Vice Premier Teng Hsiao-p'ing announced establishment of diplomatic relations between their two countries. Immediately afterwards, wall posters appeared in major Chinese cities calling for more democracy and friendship to the West. The Chinese government began signing contracts with American corporations for tourist hotels, airline service, and technological assistance. Train car loads of Coca Cola were shipped from Hong Kong to major Chinese cities for Chinese New Year celebrations.

The first wave of American tourists visiting large Chinese cities in 1979 reported almost no sign of Christianity. One small group did locate a Protestant worship service in downtown Peiping and boosted the crowd of worshipers to seventeen. Chinese scholars and journalists touring the United States told readers back home that religion was very important to Westerners.

With the reestablishment of diplomatic relations between the United States and China, the world's most populous nation became more open and concerned about international relations than it had been since the years immediately following World War II. During the 1970s fewer than one thousand Chinese Christians were known to be worshiping publicly. By the end of 1982 an estimated two hundred Protestant and ninety Catholic churches had been reopened. That year the government approved the printing of one million Bibles.

During the 1980s thousands of Westerners visited China for extended periods. Some came simply as curious tourists. Others pursued business opportunities. Still others came to teach in Chinese schools. Among the latter were many Christians intent on bearing a low key witness to their faith.

It soon became apparent that millions of Christians had survived the Red purges. The only question was how many. The government-approved Protestant Three-Self Patriotic Movement claimed over four thousand open churches were enjoying full freedom of worship. *Christianity Today* estimated in 1988 a membership of five million among over a billion people. Other estimates put the figure above fifty million Christians in Communist China.

The Marxist Chinese government has come to realize that tight indoctrination and harsh repression cannot stamp out Christianity. The government is also striving to put its best foot forward in trying to convince the world of a vast improvement in human rights. Life is certainly better than during the dark years under Mao Tse-Tung when millions were murdered to advance the Revolution. It took the 1989 Tiananmen Square massacre of protesting students, which included Christians, to dispel belief that the China of the 1990s was on the way to becoming a democracy.

Christian ministers and lay leaders are still kept on a short leash. The largest official seminary has less than two hundred students. One prospective student who sought to bypass government procedures for admission was arrested and put in jail. Catholic Bishop Joseph Fan Zhongliang was arrested on June 10, 1991, apparently in retaliation for the Vatican's elevation of another Chinese bishop to cardinal. The Chinese government does not recognize any linkage between Chinese Catholics and Rome. Zhang Yonglian, a Protestant house-church leader from southern Henan Province, was seized in September 1990 and detained for almost a year, during which he was reportedly beaten in an effort to obtain information about other Chinese Protestants operating outside of Marxist regulations. Zhang was sentenced in August 1991 to three years' imprisonment. He had previously been jailed in the early 1980s for "illegal religious activity"—preaching without a permit.

Evangelist Billy Graham was given a warm official welcome when he visited China in April 1988. Xu Yongzhe, an itinerant evangelist from China, was denied permission to speak to Graham. Xu had hoped to share with Graham news of the thousands of house churches in rural China which despite government repression had grown from two hundred to over three thousand groups in the past years. Xu and a number of his co-workers were arrested for their efforts to make Graham aware of this.

When U. S. Secretary of State James A. Baker was preparing to visit China in November 1991, the Puebla Institute, an international lobby for religious freedom, delivered to him a list of eighty-one Catholic and Protestant leaders known to be deprived of liberties by the government Public Security Bureau. After Baker met with Chinese officials, two political prisoners were released, but none of the religious leaders were freed. Authorities even prevented some regular worshipers from attending the government approved church which Baker visited while in China.

Also in 1991, the Switzerland-based Christian Solidarity International human rights organization reported that at least eighty-four church leaders were under arrest in China, with many being tortured. The organization said, ". . . Christians are being singled out, having been subjected to beatings, imprisonments, and heavy fines on account of such 'crimes' as holding 'illegal' gatherings, 'maintaining contacts with overseas organizations,' and for the 'illegal distribution of Bibles.'"

In mid-September of 1991, government soldiers reportedly raided a church of about two thousand members, beating preachers and shocking them with cattle prods.

The Marxist government tolerated Christianity only to a degree. The government courts tourism, business, and student exchange, and does not want to be embarrassed by publicity resulting from arrests of Christians and others who do not hold to Marxist ideology.

What is the future for Christianity in Earth's most populous nation where more martyr blood has undoubtedly been shed than anywhere else in modern times? If the limited openness to the West continues and blossoms, millions more Chinese will be exposed to Christianity. How deep this will penetrate and how far the Communist government of China will allow the gospel to spread are matters of prayer concern for all believers.

In 1985, the Chinese government permitted the return of the cremated remains of martyr Bill Wallace to Knoxville, Tennessee from where he had departed on a Sunday afternoon, fifty years before. A memorial service was held for the slain missionary in the church named in his honor, the Wallace Memorial Baptist Church.

Said Pastor James McCluskey: "As long as the sun rises, as long as the moon gives its glow, as long as spring flowers push their way through the earth, Bill Wallace will continue to remain as an influence and an inspiration."

So it was in the past for the countless other Chinese martyrs in China during this twentieth century. Examples of such recent Chinese martyrs are:

Bishops Shi Chunjie, Liu Difen, and Joseph Fan Xueyan whom the Chinese government killed while they were in prison in 1991 and 1992.

In 1994, Lai Man Peng, a 22-year-old Chinese Christian evangelist, was taken from a house church meeting by agents of the Public Security Bureau. Later, in front of his own congregation, he was beaten with truncheons and so badly injured that after he was released he collapsed and died on his way home.

On May 13, 1994, Yan Weiping, an administrator of the Diocese of Yixian, Hebei, was arrested by China's security police while he was conducting a service in a private home without government approval. Yan Weiping was a prominent member of the world's largest underground church, the Catholics who remain loyal to Pope John Paul II, and who shun the Chinese government's officially approved Catholic Patriotic Association. That same evening, he was found dead in a street in Peking. Local Christians believe that Yan had been pushed out of a window after he had been beaten to death. No autopsy was performed on Yan Weiping.

The priest's death coincided with the arrest and torture in mid-May of another underground Catholic. Wang Qing, a seminarian in Baoding, Hebei Province, was arrested in the home of a Catholic family in Baoding and then tortured. It has been reported that he was hung in mid-air by his hands for three days, beaten, and force-fed, suffering severe injuries.

These incidents continue a recent pattern of torture and abuse of underground Catholics and Protestants in China. In 1998 Peter Hu Duo had his legs broken in police beatings in Hebei on December 20. On December 24 in Xushui county, a mob torched a prayer meeting place, blindfolding and beating three Catholic lay leaders who then required hospitalization. In November, police beat a Protestant woman in Henan so brutally that she suffered brain damage.

Nina Shea has commented: "Over the past half year (that is 1998) in China we have observed a pattern of atrocities in which authorities are employing the most barbaric forms of torture even to the point of death against Catholic priests and other Christians. In its attempts to eradicate Christian worship outside its control, China's government is resurrecting practices associated with the darkest days of the communist regime. For the sake of international human rights, the United States must raise its voice in protest against this escalating martyrdom and persecution of Chinese Christian leaders."

# PART TWO

# Martyrs
# of Japan and Korea

# 3

# Manchuria and Japan

## *"Let No Christian Come"*

Conflict between Christianity and the national Shinto religion was inevitable in Japan and its occupied territories. The Japanese emperor was regarded as the divine incarnation of the Sun Goddess. Shinto tradition said she was born from the right eye of the male creator and was the grandmother of the first emperor. Each successive emperor had been her living incarnation.

Shintoism was weak when the first Christian missionaries, Roman Catholics, arrived in the sixteenth century. For a while they met with enormous success. They baptized 150,000 converts in thirty years and had almost made Japan into a papal state with a full-blown inquisition when Shinto devotees of the Sun Goddess raised an army and struck back. In 1638 the Shintoists massacred thirty-seven thousand Catholics in one city.

Throughout the Empire this inscription was posted: "So long as the sun shall warm the earth, let no Christian be so bold as to come to Japan; and let all know that the King of Spain himself, or the Christian's God, or the Great God of all, if he violate this command shall pay for it with his head." For the next 250 years special police squads hunted down suspected Christians and tested their loyalty to the emperor by demanding that they step on a crucifix. Those who refused paid a dire price. Some were burned to death, others buried alive.

A trade treaty with the United States opened the door for Protestant missionaries in 1859. Protestant success brought renewed Shinto reactions. Between 1868 and 1873 some two thousand Christians died in prison. Then in a turnabout, evangelical Christianity flowered again under the leadership of keen Japanese believers. By 1884 many Japanese leaders, having viewed the changed lives of national Christians and social and industrial advance in "Christian" America, were suggesting that Japan be declared a Christian nation.

Again there was a resurgence and counterattack from Shintoism. The first persecutions of the twentieth century occurred in occupied Korea and Manchuria.

## The Manchurian Martyrs

The great Manchu dynasty that ruled China for so long had come from Manchuria. In 1905 the province was divided between Russia and Japan, with Japan occupying the southern half.

Presbyterian missionaries had won thousands of Manchurians to Christ. There was a strong network of churches when the Japanese took control and ordered reverence and submission to the emperor as the incarnation of the Sun Goddess. The Christians of Manchuria were willing to obey civil authority, but they would not reverence the emperor as a deity. When this became known, Japanese soldiers marched on Christian villages, burning homes and massacring hundreds.

Dr. S. H. Martin, a Canadian Presbyterian doctor, interviewed survivors from the Manchurian village of Norabawie and filed this report to his mission board in Toronto:

> At daybreak . . . Japanese infantry surrounded the main Christian village, and starting at the head of the valley, burned immense stacks of unthreshed millet, barley and straw, and then ordered the people to vacate their homes.
>
> As each son and father stepped forth he was shot, and though perhaps not dead, heaps of burning straw were placed over them. If they struggled to escape the flames, they were bayoneted. The Japanese soldiers then set fire to the houses. . . .
>
> I have names of, and accurate reports of, thirty-two villages where fire and willful murder were used—in one village the dead numbering 145. I saw the ruins of a house which was burned with women and children inside. At Sonoyung four men were stood up near an open grave and shot. . . .

## Later Manchurian Martyrs

Small shrines were required to be installed in church buildings. Evangelist Kim, a Presbyterian minister, steadfastly preached that no one could have two masters—he must choose between the emperor or Christ. He was arrested, tortured, and released seven times. The eighth time he was given the famous "water cure." While he was stretched out on a bench with his head hanging back, water was poured from a kettle down his nostrils. Near strangling and half insane, he finally consented to sign a paper signifying his approval of Shinto shrine worship. After his release, he was racked with remorse. He went to Presbyterian missionary Bruce Hunt and confessed that he had lied.

"What will you do now?" the missionary asked.

"I must write back to the police station and say that I do not approve of shrine worship. I expect they will arrest me again."

This time, according to the later recollection of Presbyterian missionary John Young, Kim was kept in a cramped cell until he was too weak to stand. Believing he was about to die, the police called a friend to get him. The friend took him to the home of Dr. and Mrs. Roy Byram, missionaries of the Independent Board for Presbyterian Foreign Missions. He regained his strength and began preaching again. His ninth incarceration was the last. He died in prison in 1943.

Another courageous Manchurian Christian was Miss An, a Sunday school teacher. When a close friend was arrested in the spring of 1940, Miss An went to the police station hoping to secure her friend's release. Instead she was questioned about her loyalty to the emperor and imprisoned. By November she was critically ill. She was released and taken to the mission dispensary, jaundiced and little more than skin and bones. A few days later, as Dr. Byram was entering her room, she suddenly rose up and declared, "I go into the presence of my Father." Then she fell back on her bed and died.

Manchurian martyr Mr. Ni, Young relates, was a country evangelist and worker in secret schools where believers were educating their children free from Shinto influence. He too was arrested, and steadfastly refusing to compromise, later died in prison.

In 1933 two brothers, eleven and twelve years old, in Ogaki, Japan, refused to accompany their class on a trip to the Grand Shrine of Ise to worship the Sun Goddess. The boys were backed up by their parents and members of the Mino Mission Church. Mobs threatened to destroy the church. Patriotic rallies were held in pagan temples, and posters were displayed throughout the area, declaring: "Stand against the Mino Mission" and "Protect the Structure of Japan." The leading national newspaper headlined:

THE MINO MISSION REFUSES TO RECOGNIZE ANY
OTHER GOD THAN THE GOD OF THE BIBLE.

The boys were not harmed, but pressure increased on Christian schools. In one school police ordered that a stained glass picture of Christ be covered with a curtain while a Shinto pledge of reverence was read before a picture of the emperor.

Parts of the Bible and hymns speaking of Christ as Supreme Lord were banned from churches. Small shrines were even installed in church buildings. Ministers who refused to cooperate were jailed. Dissident church organizations were dissolved.

## The Sufferings of Japanese Pastors during World War II

During World War II, a minority of Japanese Christians who refused to bow at the shrines and acknowledge the emperor as supreme lord fared much worse than the interned missionaries. They were branded traitors for honoring the "religion of the enemy." Scores of unyielding pastors were jailed and questioned mercilessly by teams of interrogators.

The largest mass arrest occurred on July 26, 1942, when forty-two Pentecostal pastors were rounded up by civil police. They were charged with teaching that when Jesus returned, every knee would bow to Him. The police correctly assumed this meant the emperor would have to bow to Christ as his superior.

Toyozo Abe, the general affairs chairman of the group, refused to sign an incriminating statement and was imprisoned for 288 days. During this time he saw the sun only twenty minutes. He was not put on trial until July 1944, when he was tried with twelve other leading pastors. He and five of the twelve were sentenced to three years in prison and the others given lesser terms. In other proceedings over fifty additional Pentecostal preachers were given long prison terms. Two of these died in jail, two succumbed after release, and several others emerged with health broken by torture and long confinement.

Thankfully the war ended in 1945, preventing any more Japanese Christian martyrdoms.

## Japan after the War

General Douglas MacArthur, Supreme Commander for the Allied Powers, saw clearly the danger in racist Shintoism. One of his first acts was to declare separation of church and state "to prevent misuse of religion for political ends, and to put all religions, faiths and creeds upon exactly the same legal basis." MacArthur also denounced "the doctrine that the emperor of Japan is superior to the heads of other states because of ancestry, descent or special origin," or that the Japanese people and the islands of Japan were superior to other peoples and lands for the same reasons. Shinto teaching was excised from textbooks.

Sparked by the preaching of Jake DeShazer, an American serviceman who had been captured and ill-treated in Japanese prisons during the war, and by the conversion of Mitsuo Fuchida who had led the attack on Pearl Harbor, thousands of Japanese professed Christianity. But the uptrend in conversions continued only five years, then began steadily dropping. Japanese Christians today number about 950,000, divided about evenly between Protestants and Catholics, fewer than during the time after the first Christian missionaries came to Japan.

According to government polls, only 30 percent of the population claim to have any real personal religious beliefs. They label Christianity as a foreign religion, unworthy of Japan. There may yet be another age of martyrdom in this ancient stronghold of pagan Shintoism.

# 4

# Korea

## *The Land of Morning Calm*

A Korean proverb says: "He that is born in the fire will not faint in the sun." Perhaps this explains why Indiana-sized South Korea with thirty-four million people is today the most Christianized nation in Asia and the Christians of Korea are among the most loyal, devoted followers of Christ in the world. Prayer meetings are routinely held at four and five o'clock before the people go to their work. It is not unusual for one third of a congregation to spend Sunday afternoon evangelizing their neighbors.

Korea, like other Asian nations, is steeped in antiquity. Korean legend carries back to 4300 B.C. The earliest recorded date is 1122 B.C., when five thousand Orientals rebelled against Chinese rule. They fled to the mountainous peninsula that is now Korea and organized the new state of "Morning Calm." For the next three thousand years the "Hermit Nation," as it was called, was a punching bag for China, Mongolia, and Japan. Not until 1876 did Korea emerge from isolation when Japan forced a trade treaty on it. Treaties with other nations followed, and by 1900 all of Korea's ports were open to western commerce.

There can be no accurate accounting of Korean Christian martyrdom in the twentieth century. Thousands died during the long Japanese occupation from 1910 to 1945. Many more were undoubtedly murdered by Communists in North Korea after the country was divided at the close of World War II. And at least five hundred pastors were killed during the savage Korean War of the early 1950s.

## A "Missionary Manual"

In the early nineteenth century Korean diplomats at Peking had met missionaries and brought back the Catholic faith to Korea. In 1835 Catholic missionaries began secretly entering the country. The new faith spread rapidly despite frequent persecutions led by Buddhist priests. In 1846 the Korean Catholic hierarchy and ten thousand communicants were savagely put to death by bitter anti-foreign religionists. A great fear spread across the land. Koreans did not dare even whisper the names Jesus or Mary.

The signing of a trade treaty between Korea and the United States in 1882 opened the door for Protestants. The first missionaries were medical doctors, appointed by the Northern Presbyterian Board. Evangelists and educators followed quickly after.

The pioneer missionaries adopted in 1890 a developmental policy suggested by Dr. John L. Nevius, a visiting missionary from China. The Nevius method, far advanced for that day, called for complete self-support and control by the national church. Churches were to be started in homes and led by tradesmen pastors. Nationals were to build whatever church buildings they could afford. Missionaries were to train Korean leaders and medical specialists at the behest of the church. The Korean evangelical church was thus guaranteed a solid footing.

By 1907 Korea was the missionary marvel of that time with over one thousand self-supporting Presbyterian churches serving an evangelical community of 120,000. That year an evangelical revival of Pentecostal proportions swept across Korea. Church after church witnessed mass prayer meetings, confessions by backsliders, and conversions of hardened sinners. Thousands were empowered by the Spirit to face a coming trial by fire unmatched even by the Boxer scourge in China.

## Shinto "Evangelism"

In 1910 Japan forcibly annexed the country as a colony and set out to convert the Koreans to Shintoism. The Koreans rebuffed the Shinto missionaries and continued turning to Christianity in great numbers. The Japanese responded by arresting the most prominent Korean Christians on a charge of conspiring to murder the colonial governor. Three were tortured to death.

## Fiery Trials

Resentment against heavy-handed Japanese rule boiled over in an independence demonstration in March 1919. Koreans took to the streets in major cities, crying for freedom. The most influential leaders were Christians.

The Japanese retaliated with brute force. Churches and mission schools were burned. Travelers were stopped at roadblocks and asked their religion. Those confessing Christ were killed on the spot. Thousands of pastors, Bible women, and other church officers were rounded up like cattle and herded into smelly, freezing jails. Christian nurses attempting to help the injured were arrested. One pastor was imprisoned because he refused to stop praying for the sick.

Christian men, pressured to sign confessions, were tortured in indescribable ways. As Nathaniel Peffer reported in an effort to arouse the world's conscience:

> Men and boys were trussed and suspended from the ceilings so that their weight hung on the shoulders. Thus they were raised and lowered til unconscious. They had their fingers pressed over red hot wires. Their naked flesh was lacerated with sharp hooks and seared with hot irons. Toenails were torn from the flesh with pincers. Men were placed in a tight box and then screwed up. They were tied up, their heads forced back, and hot water or a solution of water and red pepper poured down their nostrils. Slivers of wood were shoved far under their fingernails. They were flogged until they had to be taken to hospitals, where big slabs of gangrenous skin had to be cut off. In many cases they were flogged to death. And some kinds of tortures were unprintable. This was not done once or twice, but repeatedly for days and nights, hours at a time, until the victim confessed, whether he had anything to confess or not. There are cases where men have said yes to anything, ignorant even of what they had admitted.

## Repression before and during World War II

The new Japanese militarists in power brought fresh repressions in the thirties. Korean church leaders who had studied in the United States were placed under house arrest. In 1937 Christian schools were ordered to have their students worship at a shrine of the Sun Goddess. About three thousand Christians were imprisoned, of whom about fifty were martyred.

## Methodist Martyrs

The martyrs in the Korean Methodist Church included the Rev. Jonggeun Kang, who resisted worshiping Japanese gods, which the conquering empire insisted on during World War II. Jonggeun Kang died under torture on June 3, 1943. Christians continued to be killed even after the end of the Second World War. Another Methodist, the Rev. Enyoung Kang denied the anti-Christian policy proclaimed by communist North Korea and was put to death in prison on October 25, 1950.

After Pearl Harbor more restrictions were imposed. Use of the Old Testament was forbidden in worship. The New Testament was censored to exclude all references to Christ as

Lord and King. Christian families were pressured to give their children Shinto "baptism." Many church buildings were confiscated. Clergy were drafted for war work.

## The Red Menace

Announcements that Japan had surrendered brought Koreans pouring into the streets shouting, "*Iayu haebang Mansei!* Hurrah for our freedom and independence!" Christians sang with fervor hymns that had been banned, such as "All Hail the Power of Jesus' Name." For the first time in thirty-five years they were free to worship and witness as they pleased.

Not for long. Soviet troops remained in North Korea, forcing a division of the country into Communist and free zones. In 1948 two separate governments were established, and Communist persecution began in the north where Christianity was strongest.

Upwards of five million refugees fled the "socialist paradise" for the south where a Christian, Syngman Rhee, was president. After the curtain closed, the blood of Korean martyrs again began to flow.

Thousands upon thousands of faithful Christians are believed to have been killed or herded into forced labor camps. As in Communist China, iron censorship and banishment of non-Communist foreigners prevented the free world from ever knowing the extent of the bloodletting. Only a trickle of escapees lived to describe the horror.

## Murders in Communist "Paradise"

One was Chulho Awe, a mining executive who traded the highest professional honor in North Korea for the life of a fugitive when he declined to join the Communist Party. In *Decision at Dawn* (Harper and Row, 1965), Awe tells of slipping back to Pyongyang, the capital, to see how his Sangjung Presbyterian Church had fared. He found furniture smashed, pews toppled over, files strewn over the floor. A choir member led him to an execution ground outside the city where corpses were stacked like cordwood. In the stack they found the bodies of the pastor and the ruling elder.

## The Incredible Love of Pastor Son

Communist troublemakers infiltrated South Korea, sparking local rebellions in which many Christians died for their faith. Two of those martyred were Tong-In and Tong-Sin, the sons of Pastor Son, the minister of a Presbyterian church near Soonchum.

Tong-In, the eldest, had been thrown out of school by the Japanese for refusing to worship at a Shinto shrine. After World War II, he had gone back to high school where he was elected president of the campus YMCA. In October 1948, a wild Communist uprising exploded in the area and young Communists seized the school. A nineteen-year-old Marxist pointed a pistol at Tong-In and ordered him to renounce Christ. Tong-In replied with the gospel message, pleading for the Communist to accept Christ.

Suddenly Tong-Sin, the younger brother, rushed up. "Shoot me," he shouted, "and let my brother live."

"No," objected Tong-In, "I am the elder. If you must kill someone, shoot me."

The Communist killed them both. When Pastor Son was brought to identify their bodies, he said only, "Their shining faces are as lovely as flowers."

The uprising was quickly put down and the murderer of the two brothers caught and put on trial. Pastor Son found him with his hands tied behind his back, awaiting the death sentence. He hurried to the military authorities. "Nothing will bring back my boys now, so what is to be gained by killing this one. I am willing to take him and try to make a Christian of him so he could do for God what Tong-In and Tong-Sin left undone."

The military officers were momentarily stunned. Finally, they reluctantly agreed to the proposal and Pastor Son took the murderer of his boys home.

The young Communist's parents were overcome with gratitude. "Let us feed and clothe your daughter in return," they begged. The pastor's sixteen-year-old daughter was hesitant to go. But after her father told her, "It is the best Christian witness you can make," she agreed.

## The Martyr Who Died Twice

Another martyr to the Communists during this time was Sung Du, a young Christian teacher. Before World War II, Sung had disappointed the missionaries by yielding to Japanese pressure and worshiping at the shrines. Five years after the war ended, missionary Arch Campbell ran into the teacher's younger brother and asked what had happened to Sung Du. "Oh, he repented before God with bitter tears," the young Korean said. "He promised God that he would die before denying the faith again. And he kept his promise. He died twice."

Campbell requested an explanation. The younger brother, Sung Ho, explained that Sung Du had gone to seminary and prepared for the ministry. After being ordained, he had taken a church near Suyang-Ch'on. Then the Communists came and put him to work as slave laborer in a mine. Because he refused to work on Sunday, they beat him so badly they thought he was dead. "They carried my brother out and threw him in the river," Sung Ho lamented. When they turned away, some of his church members jumped in and pulled his body out. They took him back to the village and were preparing for his funeral when they found he was still alive. Many months later he was well enough to preach again.

But then the Communists came back and arrested him again. This time they shot him and made sure he was dead. So he died twice to make up for the time when he was unfaithful.

## Brave Pastor Im

On June 23, 1950, the North Korean Communists invaded the south and pushed the South Korean Army and a few American soldiers to the southeastern tip of the peninsula. The United Nations pronounced the invasion aggression and authorized UN member nations to help defend South Korea. In slow, bitter fighting, UN forces drove the Communists back into North Korea where the Chinese Communists entered the fighting. The result was a cease-fire agreement fixing a buffer strip at the thirty-eighth parallel just north of Seoul.

One of the many prisoners freed during the UN advance into North Korea was Pastor Im. He had a heartbreaking story to tell. When the Communists first took over, he said, they had ordered the pastors to insert Marxist propaganda into their sermons. Those who refused were pulled from their homes at night and beaten. Some were never seen again.

The day of Pastor Im's testing came. "If you do not teach what we say, you will die," a Communist official warned.

"You may destroy my body, but not my soul," the brave preacher retorted.

"If you do not care for yourself, then think of your family. They will be killed also."

Pastor Im hesitated. Then he said, "I would rather have my wife and babies die by your gun and know that they and I stood faithful than to betray my Lord and save them."

The preacher was taken away and kept in a dark prison cell for two months where he was never allowed to shave or change clothes and was fed only a bowl of slop each day. He kept up his courage by reciting Bible verses he had memorized long before. One verse that gave him comfort was John 13:7: "What I do thou knowest not now; but thou shalt know hereafter."

When the UN troops arrived in September 1950, Pastor Im was put with Communist prisoners by mistake. They refused to believe that he was a pastor. "All you Communists lie," they said.

Accepting the situation as God's will, he began witnessing to the Communist prisoners. Many were converted. Months later American missionaries, who had stayed in Korea as chaplains, heard about the prison camp preacher and investigated. They obtained permission for him to organize evangelistic services in prison camps all over South Korea. By the summer of 1951 thousands had accepted Christ. Upwards of twelve thousand were rising each morning for dawn prayer meetings. But Pastor Im never saw his family again.

## Forgiveness beyond Measure

Another who lost his family was Kim Joon-gon. The first Christian in a Buddhist family, Kim was persecuted by the Japanese for refusing to worship at a Shinto shrine. When World War II ended, he came out of hiding and enrolled at the Presbyterian seminary in Seoul. When the Communists attacked in 1950, he took his wife and young daughter and fled to Chunnam Island where his parents lived. There he was trapped again when Communists took over the island.

He lived from day to day while Christians were being arrested and martyred around him. In October 1950, he was arrested and accused of friendship with American missionaries "who came to make Korea a colony of the United States." When Kim denied this, the Communists dragged him to a place where several other Christians lay dead and naked. Still he refused to make false charges against the missionaries or deny his Lord.

They allowed him to go home. That night his wife showed him the white clothes which she had prepared for their expected martyrdom. Then she prayed that they might be prepared to die.

About two o'clock in the morning the Communists came for Kim, his wife, and his father. They were taken to a "people's court." There an angry crowd shouted, "Christians! Capitalists!" The louder the people screamed, the harder the Communist soldiers beat them. Kim's father died first, begging, "Have pity on my son," as he fell. Kim's young wife fell next, crying, "Good-bye, I'll see you soon in heaven." Finally Kim sank to the ground unconscious.

Kim revived as dawn was breaking. Tears stung his eyes as he looked on the bruised, still bodies of his dead wife and father. He noticed that the ropes which had bound his hands were loose—from the beating, he believed. Wriggling free, he managed to stumble to the house of a woman he knew.

Instead of hiding him, she called the Communists. One advanced toward him with a long sword. "I have killed 300 Christians. Kim Joon-gon will be number 301."

"No," the woman suddenly screamed. "Not in the house. Kill him outside."

Kim was pushed outside where his accusers debated about pushing him over a cliff into the sea. As they argued, a group of villagers came up the road crying. They had heard about the violence and begged, "Don't kill him. He has taught us only good." While the Communists hesitated, a troop ship appeared on the horizon. "Americans!" one shouted. "Go to headquarters immediately." With that the soldiers took off running, leaving Kim to escape death again.

Twenty days later South Korean troops captured the island and rounded up about a hundred Communists, including the ones who had killed Kim's wife and father. At a quick trial Kim told of the killings. But when the South Koreans prepared to execute them, he asked that mercy be shown. "Spare them," he said. "They were forced to kill."

"But they killed your wife and father," the South Korean commander said. "Why do you want them to live?"

"Because the Lord to whom I belong would have me show mercy."

At Kim's behest and because President Syngman Rhee had said Communists who repented should be forgiven, the captives were freed. News of what Kim had done spread across the island. Repentant Communists came to hear him preach and many accepted Christ.

The following year Kim took his little girl to the mainland where he served as principal of a high school and pastored a large church. In 1957 he received a scholarship to Fuller Theological Seminary. There he met Dr. Bill Bright, founder and director of Campus Crusade for Christ. He returned home to head up Campus Crusade's work in South Korea.

## Disappearing Christians

Since 1953 about 300,000 Christians have "disappeared." Anyone found with a Bible may be shot.

It is estimated that 400 Christians were executed in 1999 alone. In October 1999, two Christians were shot to death in Chung Jin prison. After much torture they had revealed the names of several Christian co-workers. However, they did not deny the Lord even when martyred.

In December 1999, two Christian women were shot in Hae San on a fabricated charge of illegal smuggling. Two other Christians were also murdered in Ham Buk Province. One had his teeth broken because he continued to preach the gospel as he was being carted off to be executed.

# PART THREE

# Martyrs of Southeast Asia

# 5

# Thailand

## *A Hard but Open Field*

Ancient Siam. Pagodas and bells. Enchanting land of mystery. Never burdened with colonial rule, Thailand is led by one of the oldest royal monarchies in the world. *Thai* means "free." Of Mongol descent, Thais are notably friendly and peaceful.

Although officially Buddhist, Thailand has long been a western political ally and admits missionaries. Dutch missionaries were the first, in 1828. They were followed by British, French, and German representatives. Yet Christian work was agonizingly slow. Presbyterians waited nineteen years to baptize their first convert. Congregationalists gave up without baptizing a single Thai after eighteen years.

The reluctance of Thais to accept Christ stemmed mainly from family and community pressures. To convert to a foreign religion was seen as mockery of the national heritage. The traditionally friendly Thais did not object, however, to the social work of the missionaries.

One of the first believers was Nin Inta, a Buddhist scholar of Chiengmai Province. He accepted Christ after missionary friends foretold an eclipse a week before it happened.

When Nin Inta's conversion was followed by seven others, the governor of Chiengmai took action. Two of the seven, Noi Su Ya and Nan Chai, were arrested. When they confessed to having abandoned Buddhism, a death-yoke was hung around their necks and a small rope passed through their ears and hung over the beam of a house. After being tortured all night, they were asked if they wished to deny Christ and return to Buddhism. "We do not," they said, and bowed in prayer. The death sentence was pronounced, and they were taken to the jungle and clubbed to death.

The hostile governor died; his successor was less harsh. More converts were baptized.

83

The next crisis occurred when two Thai Christians asked to be married by missionaries without first participating in the traditional feast to evil spirits. Relatives appealed to the magistrate and he forbade the marriage. The missionaries promptly sent a petition to the king in Bangkok, who responded with a proclamation of religious liberty in 1878.

Since that time there has been little official persecution of Christianity in Thailand. The Thai church has grown steadily, though not spectacularly. Today the Protestant community numbers about 150,000 and receives aid from some four hundred missionaries.

## Tribal Christians Die

Much of this growth has taken place among thirty spirit-worshiping tribes in north and south Thailand. And it is among these tribes that Christians were martyred for Christ in the twentieth century. As in China, most have been victims of banditry, terrorism, and border skirmishes.

Documentation on killings of tribal Christians is hard to come by. In one of the worst known incidents, in May 1955, Burmese soldiers intruded across the border—looking for fleeing Chinese soldiers, they claimed. When they discovered a box of Scripture portions in a Lahu village which they thought was Chinese literature, they shot and killed a missionary's language teacher and one of two Lahu preachers in the village. The frightened tribespeople moved away.

## "The Lord Giveth and the Lord Taketh Away"

The first missionary casualties were recorded in 1952. In April, Paul and Priscilla Johnson of the C&MA were conducting services in the village of Ban Dong Mafai, some fifteen miles from their station at Udorn, Thailand. Attendance had been good. One man had accepted Christ and two others had been baptized. On that fateful Friday, the eighteenth, Priscilla had seen seven village children pray to receive Christ.

The evening services were held under an open shelter. The Johnsons' two youngest children, ages five and two, were sleeping in a nearby Thai house. Their seven-year-old was in the C&MA school for missionary children at Dalat, Vietnam. Priscilla was playing the little pump organ and Paul leading the song service. Three hymns had been sung and one of the local Christians was leading in prayer when gunshots shattered the calm.

Priscilla was hit in the chest by shotgun pellets. She ran a short way to a clump of banana trees where she collapsed and died. Paul was hit in the abdomen and fell to the ground but remained conscious. "Give us your gun and valuables," the bandits demanded. Paul had no gun, of course, but they took his watch, camera, and keys to the Land Rover. Then they proceeded to the house where the Johnsons were staying and looted their baggage while the two frightened children looked on. The nine or ten armed bandits got the Land Rover started but could not find the brake and finally ran away on foot.

Paul, still conscious, somehow gave instructions in starting and driving the vehicle to a local man who had never driven before. They went directly to the Thai Army hospital where Paul was given the best emergency treatment available.

The news spread quickly. Government officials, upset and concerned, brought gifts and apologies. The next day R. M. Chrisman, a missionary colleague, arrived. He took custody of Priscilla's body and arranged for the care of the children and the evacuation of Paul to a better hospital in Bangkok. The first words he heard Paul say were, "The Lord giveth and the Lord taketh away. Blessed be the name of the Lord."

The doctors in Bangkok performed an emergency colostomy and gave blood transfusions. For three more days Paul hung between life and death, conscious much of the time. Early Wednesday morning, April 23, he sang with a clear voice a prayer for his fellow workers and Thai Christians left behind: "Bless Them, Lord, and Make Them a Blessing." A few minutes later he lapsed into unconsciousness and died.

## An "Extraordinary" Christian

The next missionary martyr in Thailand was Lilian Hamer, a cheerful young woman with close-cropped brown hair who was not "one whit afraid" in the remote tribal area where she served as a nurse.

Lilian was a member of the China Inland Mission, which with many China evacuees, was easily the largest missionary agency in Thailand. An English girl, she had been working in a cotton mill when converted in a Methodist youth meeting. "I wanted to be an extraordinary Christian," she said later.

Stirred by the martyrdom of John and Betty Stam (see pp. 48–50) Lilian felt a call to China. By the time she had completed nurse and midwifery training, World War II was on and the CIM could not take her. Finally in 1944 she got to China under the auspices of the British Red Cross and was accepted by CIM after the war ended. She was appointed to a missionary hospital in Tali, China, where she was drawn to the poor and neglected hill tribespeople who came to the hospital for treatment. When forced out by the Communists, she willingly accepted the assignment to serve with the Lisu tribe in Thailand.

Living conditions in her new area were hard and rigorous. She was always on call for the sick. She struggled with opium addicts and prayed for demon worshipers. Although she dropped exhausted at the end of a day, her sleep was frequently disturbed by tribespeople dancing around a "spirit" tree for hours on end. But when a friend wondered, "Must you really give all your life to this?" she replied, "The Lord Himself faced the cross because He could not give less than all."

Sometimes she had a missionary partner; often not. In 1959 she was living at a new location known as "demon people." One night a cobra got into her room, a symbol of the enemy she faced. She battled the snake with a stick and won. In her last report she quoted from an old poem: "The handles of my plough with tears are wet. The shears with rust are spoiled. And yet, and yet, My God! My God, keep me from turning back."

On the morning of April 18 she decided to go down to the plain. She walked with two Thais, but along the way they stopped and she went on ahead. A short way on she followed the trail between two trees. As she passed, a figure stepped from behind one and confronted her with a sawed-off shotgun. A few minutes later the carriers came upon her body, slumped against a tree. They noticed that before dying she had managed to cover her feet—a last gesture of identity with the people.

Today there is a small bamboo and grass church only two hundred yards from the tree where Lilian Hamer's blood reddened the earth. The whole countryside knows the spot where she died. The tribespeople. The headman. The old witch doctor who planned the killing. And the tribal believers who walk by her grave on their way to worship the God for whom she laid down her life.

## "Except a Corn of Wheat . . . Die"

Roy Orpin heard of Lilian Hamer's death shortly after telling his parents, "I've been accepted by OMF [Overseas Missionary Fellowship, formerly China Inland Mission]. Maybe I'll leave my bones in some foreign country."

Orpin, a New Zealander, was engaged to marry a young Englishwoman he had met at the New Zealand Bible Training Institute in Auckland. Both had been deeply moved by reading about the death of John and Betty Stam and by the more recent martyrdoms of five young Americans in the Auca jungle of Ecuador. They were married in Thailand, April 27, 1961. At the reception they sang a duet, "Calvary," the last stanza of which seemed to hold special meaning:

> So much more may we united
> Bear Thy Name to men oppressed,
> Break to them the Bread of Calv'ry
> Bless their souls as we are blessed.

After a short honeymoon, Roy took his bride, Gillian, to the shanty house he had prepared in the Meo tribal village of Namkhet. They arrived at night to find the house a shambles. Both had lived in tribal villages for a few months before their marriage. They made the best of the bad situation and settled down for the night. The next morning they ate their first meal off an upside-down pig trough.

Violence escalated in the area during their first year of marriage. They heard of three Thai opium traders being robbed and killed while begging for their lives. Roy stumbled across the bodies of two more murder victims while hiking to another village. Fearing for his safety and that of his now-pregnant wife, he said, "I had no peace until I remembered 2 Corinthians 10:5, 'Make every thought captive to obey Christ.' What havoc uncontrolled thought can play."

As Gillian's time approached, they decided to move to Bitter Bamboo, a village where a few struggling Christians desperately needed instruction and encouragement. Gillian went to a regional town where there was a missionary hospital while Roy worked on the new house and moved their household goods. As he was making his last trip before leaving to join her, three young robbers suddenly appeared and demanded his valuables. When he had emptied his pockets, they told him to go on. When he was a few steps away, they shot him in the back.

Critically wounded, he was rushed to a government hospital. Gillian came and sat by his bedside from Wednesday through Saturday when he worsened. "Say for me the chorus 'Jesus! I am resting, resting,'" he whispered. Slowly, her lips close to his ear, she recited,

> Jesus! I am resting, resting
> In the joy of what Thou art;
> I am finding out the greatness
> Of Thy loving heart.

"How good God is," the young missionary whispered again. A little later his kidneys failed and he was dead at age twenty-six.

The funeral was on May 20, less than thirteen months after their wedding. A few days later little Murray Roy was born. After a short recuperation, Gillian returned to live with two single women missionaries who had shared the Meo work.

The timing of Roy's death seemed symbolic of John 12:24: "Except a corn of wheat fall into the ground and die, it abideth alone: but if it die, it bringeth forth much fruit." The Meo were then planting their grain. A few months later came a bountiful harvest, both in the fields and in the hearts of Meo tribespeople. Twelve families expressed their intention to follow Jesus and to burn their pagan charms.

## Minka and Margaret

A dozen more years passed before the next missionary martyrdoms occurred in Thailand. The war from Vietnam spilled over into Laos and Cambodia. Communist terrorists were now operating in North Thailand. In South Thailand, Muslim "liberation" groups fought frequent hit-and-run battles with Thai police. Adjoining Malaysia had become an independent Muslim nation in 1955. The Muslim activists in south Thailand were demanding independence for four predominantly Muslim provinces or annexation to Malaysia where conversion of Muslims was forbidden.

Two veteran OMF nurses, Minka Hanskamp and Margaret Morgan, ministered to lepers in this troubled southern area. Part of their job involved washing the feet of patients, cutting away rotten flesh, and tending to ulcerated sores emitting a nauseating stench.

Minka, a six-foot Hollander, had grown up in Dutch-controlled Java where her parents were missionaries. While interned by the Japanese during World War II, she had worked in a prison camp hospital. After the war ended, she moved to New Zealand where she volunteered for missionary service. She entered Bible school at age thirty-four and was accepted by OMF two years later in 1958.

Her partner, Margaret Morgan, came from a Welsh mining village and took nurse's training at the Bristol (England) Royal Infirmary. Two years younger than Minka, she began serving in south Thailand in 1965.

Every two weeks the two nurses traveled to the town of Pujud to hold a leprosy clinic. On April 20, 1974, the day of Minka's sixteenth anniversary with OMF, they were called aside by strangers who said they had come to take them to treat some sick patients in the mountains. At first the nurses did not realize the men were terrorists. Margaret suggested that Minka accompany them while she continued the clinic. They were gruffly ordered to pack up their medicines and get in the waiting car.

Ten days later the area OMF representative, Ian Murray, received two letters. One was from Minka and Margaret stating they were in the hands of the "jungle people," and they were well and "still praising." The second letter was from their captors. The Muslims demanded that OMF pay a half million dollar ransom and that the society write an official letter to Israel, protesting denial of Palestinian rights. Mission policy since China days had been never to pay a ransom for kidnapped members. To have done so would have put a price on every missionary's head. The missionaries could not meet the second demand because it was against mission policy to become involved in political issues.

A meeting was set up between Thai officials, Ian Murray, and representatives of the kidnappers. Murray stated that OMF was in Thailand only for religious purposes and that the missionaries worshiped the One Creator God, as Muslims did. "He is a God of mercy and forgiveness, as well as a God of judgment," he added. "He wants to forgive you, but that depends upon your response to Him." The spokesman for the group listened politely, but agreed only to speak to a higher-up in behalf of the captives.

A few days later a police unit was ambushed in the area. Thai military activity was intensified. Then word came that the Muslim gang had no quarrel with OMF but with the United States and British governments for supporting Israel against the Palestinians. They demanded that the "Christian world stop any support to Israel against the Palestinian people."

Introduction of these demands brought international publicity. Thai military pressure increased. The occasional letters that had been coming from the nurses assuring that they were all right stopped. Conflicting rumors spread. One story said they were kept in chains. Another reported they had been shot.

Early in March 1975, a Malay came forward to confess that he had shot them. The gang, he said, had argued over their fate. The chief had concluded that to keep the respect of underlings they should shoot the missionaries. The informer said the nurses had been calm when told they were to die, saying only, "Give us a little time to read and pray." "They were good people," the man added. "Good."

The missionaries did not want to believe the story. But doubts were dissipated on March 20 when news reached them that the skeletons of two women had been found in the jungle. One was tall enough to be Minka and there were identifying dentures and bits of clothing and hair. Both had been shot in the head and had been dead five or six months.

The remains were recovered, positively identified, and buried May 15. The funeral was attended by hundreds of Christians and many Buddhists and Muslims as well. Many sobbed openly. A former bandit killer testified before the mourners that he had become a Christian after Minka had taken his ulcerated foot on her lap to treat it. A leprosy patient recalled how Minka and Margaret had tenderly taken him from a little shack where he had been quarantined from his village and cared for his sores. After the funeral, the missionaries and native preachers received more inquiries about Christianity than ever before in the difficult southern provinces.

## Death on the Trail

Banditry and political terrorism continued in the more remote tribal areas of Thailand. Some missionaries moved in closer to population centers while others chose to remain in isolated hill stations.

Peter and Ruth Wyss worked with the Akha people, one of the least advanced tribes in the north, while their three children remained in school in their native Switzerland. In March 1977, they received a visitor from home. Samuel Schweitzer, a Christian businessman, had made a trip to Japan and arranged a stopover to see OMF work in Thailand. His parents had served before retirement with CIM in China.

Schweitzer spent several days with Peter, helping prepare a house in a village for two single women missionaries. They had much in common. Among other things, both were forty-two and both had three children. On the afternoon of March 15, the businessman figured how much money he would need for the trip home and gave Peter his remaining traveler's checks and currency. Peter took this as an answer to his prayer for aid to the salaries of tribal pastors. Then after telling Ruth, "We'll be back soon," they left for the final trip to the new house.

Ruth became concerned when they did not return by the following afternoon. But, as she testified later, "The Lord gave me John 14:15 through 18 and with these words also a deep peace came into my heart that I could only praise Him for all the good things He had put in my life."

Still expecting them to return, she did not fix breakfast herself the next morning. Schweitzer was due to leave for the regional airport later that day.

The day wore on and finally she and a missionary friend, who had providentially happened along, set out by jeep to discover what had happened. They found Peter's motorcycle at the place where he always left it before beginning the climb to the new house. Part way up the path they met two tribesmen. One said he had seen Peter's body. The tribesmen tried to keep Ruth from going, but she was adamant and ran ahead to the spot. Schweitzer's body was discovered nearby.

The murders had to be reported to the police. Then Ruth had to endure long hours of questioning. She knew of no reason why her husband and his friend should have been killed, unless their assailants had meant to rob them. After that she had to tell tribal and missionary friends and prepare for the funeral. "Yet even in those darkest moments," she recalled later, "the words sounded through my mind: 'I will send you another Comforter' and I knew that He was right there with us, although it was still impossible to comprehend what had happened."

Following the funeral, Ruth Wyss flew home to Switzerland to be with her children. There she began working on curriculum for the Akha Bible School, expecting to return to Thailand within a few months.

## Preparing for the Worst

The murders of Peter Wyss and Samuel Schweitzer did not end the killing of Christians in Thailand. Many Thais were killed by Communist guerrillas and in clashes with Cambodians.

On October 24, 1981, Dutch missionary Koos Fietje was encouraging a small group of Thai Christians as he enjoyed a snack with them in a Thai home in central Thailand. Suddenly a man stuck a sawed-off shotgun through the wall slats and fired, hitting the thirty-eight-year-old Dutch minister in the face with five pellets, killing him almost instantly. The assassin fled into the darkness.

Just twelve days before, Koos Fietje's wife, Colleen, had written a letter reporting that rocks had been thrown onto the roof of the house where they were holding services and that Thai believers had been shot at on their way home in the darkness. This along with the persecution of two Christian school teachers, suggested to other missionaries a growing opposition to the gospel among the local people.

Affiliated with Overseas Missionary Fellowship, Koos and Colleen had been working with Koos's brother Bill and family and with the David Robinsons in building up believers in neighboring villages. Twelve new believers had been baptized, drawing the attention of Buddhists in the area.

After Koos's death, missionaries stayed at their posts. OMF General Director James Taylor called Koos "the kind of pioneer and evangelistic missionary of whom we can never have too many. He had a boldness in the preaching of the gospel that had a Stephen-like quality about it."

## Trusting in God While Preparing for the Worst

Thailand is a troubled, but fruitful field for the gospel. With Communist governments in neighboring Laos and Vietnam, and a volatile political climate in Cambodia, the future of Thailand appears uncertain. The Thai capital of Bangkok has become a cesspool of sin and disease. Thousands of prostitutes service tourists coming from Japan and other Asian countries. The infectious disease called AIDS threatens to become a plague of death.

Christianity, still very much a minority faith, continues to grow. Some churches are reported to be memorizing the whole New Testament, with books assigned to individuals. The only certainty of the missionaries and their Thai brothers and sisters is in Christ and His plan for the future.

# 6

# Vietnam

## *The Books Are Still Open*

Vietnam is now only a bad memory for most westerners. Americans would like to forget the dragon-shaped country in Southeast Asia where over fifty-six thousand Americans died. The terrible war which ended in a Communist victory has obscured the suffering and martyrdom of Vietnamese Christians and foreign missionaries. Their sacrifice is the least known story of Vietnam.

Since 1911, when the C&MA's R. A. Jaffray established a base at Da Nang, evangelical Christians have never known a time in Vietnam when they were not persecuted. First it was the haughty French colonial government which confined Jaffray and his colleagues to the large cities. This proved to be a blessing in disguise, for the missionaries then sent their first converts to evangelize the towns and countryside. Indigenous congregations sprang up from Hanoi to the Mekong Delta.

When Japanese invaders swept across Indochina (Vietnam, Laos, and Cambodia) in 1941, most missionaries refused to leave and were placed in internment camps. Many evangelical pastors went underground and continued to serve their flocks despite threats from the new imperialists.

Peace came only briefly at the close of World War II. A new phase of war began in 1946. Ho Chi Minh and his Viet Minh Communist guerrillas launched their war of "liberation" against the French who had returned in 1945. The fighting lasted eight years and ended with French withdrawal from Vietnam and partitioning of the ancient country along the seventeenth parallel, running through a demilitarized zone.

## Christians Were Caught in the Middle

Not one C&MA missionary died in Vietnam from hostile action during the French-Indochina War. Most of the missionaries were Americans who were considered neutrals by both sides. But tens of thousands of Vietnamese died along with thirty-five thousand French soldiers.

The Vietnamese evangelicals were caught in the middle and often held suspect by both sides. The result was a trail of martyrs' blood up and down the country, among them the following documented examples:

*Item.* Pastor Phan Long and three deacons were shot by French soldiers and their bodies thrown into the Bau Rau River near Da Nang.

*Item.* Nguyen Van Tai, pastor at Ma Lam in central Vietnam, was chased and shot by Communist Viet Minh guerrillas on the road between Phan Thiet and Ma Lam.

*Item.* Nguyen Thien Thi, pastor of Thanh Qui Church in central Vietnam, and his wife and son were seized and bound by the Viet Minh in the home of a layman, then led into a field and executed.

*Item.* Trinh Ly, a pastor near coastal Nha Trang, was murdered by French soldiers at the Nha Trang railroad station. Later his wife was shot near Dalat.

*Item.* Mr. So, a zealous layman at Phong Thu, was killed by French soldiers while on his way to church with Bible in hand.

*Item.* Tranh My Be, pastor at Choudoc, south of Saigon, was seized by the Viet Minh and buried alive standing up. The shock killed his wife.

Scores of other pastors and laymen were killed. Many churches were burned and bombed. Christians who left their homes and fled to the jungles returned to find their household belongings stolen. Of pastors in one area it was said, "When they have not clothes enough they curl up on a heap of straw. One of them has only a coat and a Bible left, but keeps on living with his flock."

After the French admitted defeat, peace again proved illusionary. The Communists in North Vietnam placed restrictions on Christian activity. Thousands fled south. The Communist Viet Minh resurfaced in the South as Viet Cong and began terrorizing villages in the countryside. Headmen who refused to pay tribute and cooperate were killed. Christians suffered not so much because of their religious affiliation but because they had strong moral principles and abhorred violence.

## Death on the Highway

Missionary linguists with the Wycliffe Bible Translators were now moving into tribal locations. The international organization founded on the faith principles of the old China Inland Mission was committed to translating Scripture into over two thousand Bibleless minority languages, over thirty of which were spoken in South Vietnam.

Elwood Jacobson, a Minnesota farm boy of Norwegian descent, was typical of the intrepid Wycliffe pioneers. He had been challenged for full-time Christian service by Dawson Trotman, founder of the Navigators, a ministry that emphasized Scripture memorization and training young Christians to be "spiritual reproducers." Two statements from Trotman haunted Elwood: "If the dying seed of Adam can produce such a race as mankind, what can living seed—the Word of God—produce?" And, "Nothing is yours until you give it away. Giving is the essence of love." One Thursday after seeing a Wycliffe film, he wrote in his diary, "I wonder if this is the thing for which God is preparing me. May You lead me in Your chosen path."

The "chosen path" led Elwood to Wycliffe's Summer Institute of Linguistics, to marriage to Vurnell Newgard, a brown-haired nurse he met through Inter-Varsity Christian Fellowship, and ultimately to Vietnam. A quiet, studious man, he had calculated well the dangers in the war-torn country. Of the German martyr Dietrich Bonhoeffer, Elwood once had written Vurnell: "He had to make the decision . . . whether he would remain in Nazi Germany or escape. He remained and paid for his witness with his life. Life is so short and there are so many things to be done that we really need to choose between the better and the best."

Elwood and Vurnell arrived in Saigon with a new baby, Kari. There they met a young Filipino, Gaspar Makil, whom Elwood knew from Wycliffe's jungle training camp. Gaspar was the first Filipino Wycliffe member.

Gaspar had fought with Filipino guerrillas against the Japanese in World War II and once helped rescue an American missionary from a prison camp. After the war he studied engineering at Southern Methodist University in Dallas, where he was influenced by Inter-Varsity Christian friends "to submit my life to total abandonment to Jesus Christ, that He might lead according as He pleased." Later he wrote his sister Emma, "I do not pray for long life this side of the grave. How you live that life is the thing that matters, not how long. That life is Christ's." Gaspar also attended Moody Bible Institute, where he met and married Josephine Johnson, a girl with deep conviction. Shortly after their arrival in Vietnam, Josephine doubled their family by giving birth to twins, Thomas and Janie.

While waiting for his and Vurnell's assignment, Elwood was "Mr. Fix-it" at the Wycliffe group house in Saigon. No job was too menial for him. "Every work has its place," he wrote in his diary, "and there is time for all that God wants us to do." So it was natural for Elwood to drive the Makils to their location near Dalat where Elwood intended to help another translator with a language survey. Vurnell and baby Kari went along, making seven in the Land Rover. The date was March 4, 1963.

Sixty-six miles out of Saigon they came upon a roadblock. Assuming at first it was a South Vietnamese army checkpoint, they got out and showed identification. Their suspicions were aroused when the "soldiers" began taking things from their vehicle.

Suddenly a truck loaded with real government soldiers rolled into view. A warning shot zinged overhead. More shots rang out around the Rover. Elwood was shot in the head by a Viet Cong and died almost instantly. Gaspar was also killed. His twin son and daughter were wounded. Vurnell, Kari, and Josephine escaped unharmed.

The Viet Cong vanished into the woods. The government soldiers rushed Josephine and her two babies to a first aid station from which they were taken to a hospital. Little Janie died at eleven o'clock that night. Her brother, who had received a bullet in the thigh, recovered.

News of the attack on the unarmed missionaries brought quick apologies from the Viet Cong. "We thought they were government workers. We didn't know they were missionaries," agents told people in surrounding villages.

An avalanche of letters poured in on Wycliffe. Young people wrote of making deeper commitments to follow Christ. A South Carolinian said, "He [Elwood] gave his all for Christ. The Lord Jesus has been showing me how necessary it is for me to give my all to Him."

Both widows remained in missionary service. Vurnell later married another Wycliffe member and continued in Vietnam. Josephine transferred to Wycliffe's Philippine head-quarters in Bukidnon Province and took charge of preschool children for busy translators who were accomplishing what she and Gaspar had dreamed of doing.

## Christians Buried Alive

Two years of escalating war passed. Christians in remote tribal areas suffered most. For example, the language helper of Wycliffe members Dick and Sandy Watson, and a native evangelist were seized by the Viet Cong and buried alive. The Communists charged in propaganda that the two had been serving as "American imperialist agents."

## Ambush at the Pass

Curly-haired John Haywood went on ahead of his Swiss fiancée, Simone DuBois, to help with the World Evangelization Crusade's (WEC) orphanage and Happy Haven Leprosarium at Da Nang. John had served in Britain's Royal Army Medical Corps, then worked in London's Bermondsey Medical Mission where he had met Simone. He was one of the hardiest in the Vietnam missionary corps, often disregarding personal danger to accompany Dr. Stuart Harverson to remote tribal villages where they confronted exorcisers who charged the sick for making sacrifices to appease demons. "I am not out here for thrills," John wrote home. "I have a job to do, and I can best do it while I am alive. There are just not enough hours in the day for the work I have in hand."

Terrorism became more personal to John when the Viet Cong slipped a bomb into the bathroom of his close WEC friends, Roy and Daphne Spraggett, at isolated Cam Phuc. The bomb exploded at midnight, hurling Roy and Daphne to the floor. Daphne was not seriously injured and their two-year-old daughter was not hurt at all. Roy suffered a broken collarbone, damaged hearing, and serious burns. When he heard about the bombing, John went to salvage what he could of the couple's belongings. Then he drove to Saigon and stayed with Roy day and night in the hospital for more than a week.

John and Simone were married on a golden May day in 1965 in Da Nang. They honeymooned in Hong Kong where they studied three months at the British Leprosarium. When they returned to Vietnam, John took over as director of WEC's Happy Haven Leprosarium.

The war continued to escalate. Trips to and from the leprosarium, located at Marble Mountain outside of Da Nang, became more hazardous. But John and Simone were happy and looking forward to the birth of their first child.

On January 8, John kissed Simone and left in the WEC Volkswagen Microbus for the old Vietnamese capital of Hue where he was to pick up a load of pigs and chicks for the leprosy patients. He either failed to notice or ignored a risk factor—the Microbus had just been repainted and new lettering had not been inscribed to identify it as belonging to a mission hospital. It is known that he reached the famed high "Pass of the Clouds" that overlooks the foaming China Sea, and fell in behind a convoy of South Vietnamese army trucks loaded with rice. There was an ambush. American Marines later found his bullet-ridden body in a metal culvert running under the road.

Gordon Smith, the senior missionary who had married John and Simone, preached the funeral. "Jesus said, 'I am the resurrection and the life,'" the veteran WEC worker quoted. "He promised, 'He that believeth in me, though he were dead, yet shall he live.' John is not dead. He is alive, and one blessed day we will see him again." Three days later Jacqueline Edith Haywood was born.

## The Massacre at Banmethuot

January 30, the eve of Tet, the Vietnamese New Year, the "year of the monkey"—the signal for unprecedented Communist attacks from the DMZ to the Delta coast. Thousands upon thousands died in suicide charges. In city after city missionaries huddled in bunkers only yards away from the fighting. Amazingly, no missionaries died, except in one place—Banmethuot. Here occurred the most terrible missionary massacre of the war.

Ten missionaries began Tet at Banmethuot. Ruth Wilting roomed with Betty Olsen, another nurse who had come to help in the medical work. Born of missionary parents to Africa, Betty had been only sixteen when her mother died. The years immediately following were confused for her. She rebelled in school and irritated missionaries by her attitude. On one visit back to Africa she was asked to leave by the missionaries.

Though she had announced her intentions to go to the mission field, she felt constantly defeated. Her conscience bothered her about things for which she'd asked over and over for forgiveness. Marriage prospects dimmed. Depression increased until she was contemplating suicide. In a desperate move, she made an appointment at the church she was attending in Chicago to talk with a young youth counselor. He agreed to talk only if "you really want God's best for your life." Betty said she did. As Betty recalled later:

> He showed me that I was bitter toward God about the way He had made me. I realized I didn't like myself and in rejecting myself, I had rejected God's handiwork. He asked, "How can you serve God if you aren't satisfied with the way He made you?"
>
> He showed me from Scripture how God had prescribed exactly how I was to look, even before I was born. He explained how God could make His strength perfect in bodily weaknesses and how He was not finished working on me yet. I realized then that God's goal was to develop inward qualities in me so that I would reflect the beauty of Christ.

This interview and others with Bill Gothard, who later developed the famous Basic Institute of Youth Conflicts—"based largely on the questions Betty Olsen asked," he says—turned the red-headed nurse in a new direction. She became a warm, caring person and in a few years was accepted by the C&MA for Vietnam.

The nurses shared a house on the Bible school grounds. Ed and Ruth Thompson, veteran transferees from Cambodia, lived in one of the three Italian-style villas in the main compound across the highway. They were studying the Vietnamese language in Banmethuot while a house was being built in Quang Duc where they intended to work with tribespeople who had once lived in Cambodia. Ed was famed as a tiger hunter. At six foot three, he towered over the diminutive tribespeople who affectionately called him, "The Giant."

Bob and Marie Ziemer lived next door to the Thompsons. Ohioans, they had been in Vietnam twenty-two years. Once, while home on furlough in Toledo, Bob had been asked to take the pastorate of his home church, one of the largest in the C&MA. "No," he said. "God wants me in Vietnam. We're needed more there." Bob was now just about finished with his translation of the New Testament into the Raday language and was also teaching in the Bible school.

Leon and Carolyn Griswold, father and daughter, occupied the third house. Leon had attended the C&MA's Nyack College in 1919 and talked of becoming a missionary. Growing family and business commitments kept him and his wife from going. "Go in our place," they encouraged Carolyn. "We'll pray for you and maybe visit sometime." Carolyn, a willowy brunette secretary, reached Saigon in 1953 and became the belle of the foreign community. Her single girl colleagues called her *le papillon*—"the butterfly." Upon moving to Banmethuot, she became immediately popular with tribal teenage girls who constantly came to her for beauty hints. Meanwhile, Carolyn's parents moved from New York to retirement in Florida. After her mother died, her father volunteered to help with office work at Banmethuot and came to live with his daughter in 1966.

Hank and Vange (Evangeline) Blood, the other two missionaries at Banmethuot, were members of Wycliffe. Hank and his brother Dave, both civil engineers from Oregon, had come to Vietnam for Wycliffe in 1951. Dave and the Wycliffe girl he had married, Doris, were working among the Chams, who spoke one of the oldest known languages in the world. Hank and Vange were assigned to a Mnong-speaking group near Banmethuot. Viet Cong pressure had forced them to move into a Raday tribal settlement which adjoined the C&MA Bible school. Shortly before Tet, Hank returned to the Mnong village for a short visit. While there he escaped marauding Viet Cong by hiding in a pigpen. Back with Vange, he wrote his widowed mother, "I have a feeling the Lord is going to do something special."

Monday evening of Tet week, the Banmethuot missionaries went to bed with the distant pop-pop of firecrackers set off by the celebrants sounding in their ears. About one in the morning the pops grew louder—artillery and small arms fire. About 3:30 the Griswolds heard loud raps on their door. They opened it to be confronted by Communist soldiers who ordered them upstairs. A few minutes later the house blew apart in a violent explosion.

There was nothing the others could do. The missionaries were caught in a crossfire between Communist attackers and government soldiers. Bullets whined between the houses. After daylight the Thompsons and Ziemers saw three or four Vietnamese tanks in front of the tribal church shooting at Communists.

Ignoring the danger, Bob and Ed ran to the Griswold house and began pulling away wreckage. They rescued Carolyn, still alive but unconscious, and carried her into the Ziemer house. When they got to her father, he was already dead. The firing slackened, allowing Ruth and Betty to cross the highway and join their C&MA co-workers. The nurses determined that Carolyn's right leg was broken and she was in shock.

Later in the morning they saw a U.S. Agency for International Development agriculturist friend, Mike Benge, approaching in a jeep. "Go back! Go back!" Ed shouted. The warning came too late. The missionaries watched helplessly as Viet Cong ran from hiding places and ordered Mike down into the tribal village.

Tuesday night and Wednesday was more of the same. The C&MA people huddled in the Ziemer house. Once, with bullets flying around them, the nurses ran to the clinic behind the church for medicines and blood plasma for Carolyn. The Bloods remained in their house in the village below.

Wednesday night they saw two North Vietnamese soldiers blow up the Thompsons' house. Fearing that the Ziemer house would be next, the C&MA missionaries took refuge in an open garbage pit in back. Carolyn was left lying in a servant house.

At dawn Ruth and Betty tried another run to the clinic for more medicines. Instead of returning, Betty tried to start a car hoping to get Carolyn to a hospital. Communists closed in and took her to a house in the village where they had other captives.

The Ziemer house suddenly exploded. North Vietnamese swarmed over the grounds. Bob Ziemer jumped from the garbage pit and ran toward the soldiers, hands in the air. They riddled his body with bullets. Ruth Wilting came running toward the bunker amidst a hail of bullets. She fell mortally wounded into the pit, crying, "Lord, help me, so I can help the others." The Communists advanced on the makeshift bunker. Ed Thompson lifted his huge hands, crying, "Mercy! Mercy!" The attackers opened fire. He fell across his wife, also mortally wounded, in a last desperate effort to shield her body.

Only Marie Ziemer and Carolyn Griswold were still alive. Marie was bleeding profusely on her left side. The Communists ordered her out of the hole. They then bound her wounds and took her to a house in the village filled with about fifty prisoners. Here were Betty Olsen, Pastor Ngue of the Raday Church, Hank and Vange Blood and their young children, and about fifty other tribal captives. Shortly, Marie and Vange were told they and the Blood children were free to go. Vange had only time to kiss Hank good-bye before he and Betty and the Raday captives were marched away.

Marie and Vange staggered up the hill with the Blood children. They were met by a Raday church leader who took them and Carolyn, barely alive, to an area hospital. From there they were flown to a hospital in Nha Trang where Carolyn died seven hours later.

The martyrdom of the Banmethuot Six triggered an avalanche of deepened commitments to Christ from families and friends. In one of the many memorial services, Dr. Nathan Bailey, president of the C&MA, said it all to students at Nyack College:

> The missionaries at Banmethuot were not drafted. They chose to be there and stay there. They were all veterans. The romance and the glory of the missionary call had long since departed. They had lived in the midst of war for many years. They had watched three of their comrades being led away into the jungle, never to be seen again. They knew they were vulnerable. They chose to be faithful, even unto death.

## Vietnam under Communism

What of South Vietnam under Communism since? Happenings bear a remarkable parallel to events in China after the Red conquest there. Virtually all foreign missionaries who sought to remain were forced out within a year. They were told that the Vietnamese church no longer needed their help. Church educational and social ministries were taken over by the government and evangelistic activity was discouraged and hindered. Religious services were confined to existing church buildings.

By 1978 about sixty Protestant pastors and some two hundred Catholic priests were reported to be in prison. One priest was accused of plotting against the government. Counterfeit money and weapons, believed to have been planted, were displayed as evidence.

As conditions worsened, many Vietnamese Christians crowded into open boats and sought to flee to Malaysia, Thailand, Hong Kong, and the Philippines. Many of these "boat people" were drowned in storms while others were murdered by pirates. Still, many managed to escape and were placed in refugee camps. Thousands were accepted as immigrants to the United States where they now worship in their own churches. By the late 1980s, immigration procedures had tightened and neighboring countries were sending Vietnamese refugees back to their homeland.

In Vietnam, many pastors and lay leaders were sent to "reeducation" camps for indoctrination in Communism. Some were imprisoned for "preaching against the revolution." In 1987, two noted evangelical pastors, Ho Hieu Ha and Nguyen Hey Cuong, were sentenced to eight years in prison for this "crime." Their churches were confiscated by the government. One was later converted into a Communist Youth League Center.

These two pastors and another evangelical minister, Le Thien Dung, were subsequently transferred from a labor camp to Chi Hoa prison in Ho Chi Minh City, formerly known as Saigon, where they were released on condition that they seek resettlement in the United States. One declined, declaring his intention to remain in Vietnam and minister to his scattered flock, and two agreed to go.

In 1991, Doan Van Mieng, vice president of the tiny Evangelical Church of Vietnam, sent a letter to David Moore of Overseas Ministries, saying, "We have experienced the valley of weeping, the shadow of death, the furnace of fire, and the den of lions. But in every place, the Lord has been with us."

Mieng paid special tribute to nineteen foreign missionaries and relief workers (four with Wycliffe, one with the Mennonite Central Committee, and fourteen associated with the Christian and Missionary Alliance) who had lost their lives in Vietnam during the past thirty years. Listed among the nineteen martyrs were the kidnapped Daniel Gerber, Archie Mitchell, and Dr. Ardele Vietti, whose fate has never been determined.

The Communist Vietnamese government is now attempting to put a better face before the world. Some foreign Christian workers have been permitted to return for short visits. In 1995, diplomatic relations were restored between Vietnam and the United States. With the collapse of her chief foreign backer, the Soviet Union, Vietnam desperately needs outside economic aid. Some observers expect to see a greater loosening of restrictions on Christian activities. There is speculation that some American prisoners of war may still be alive in Vietnam and Laos.

Resistance to the Communist infrastructure in the south is said to be strongest in the tribal areas where one third of the evangelical believers are believed to live. Some pastors remain in reeducation camps, even as others continue to minister in unauthorized churches.

The books are still open in tragic Vietnam. The Communist government continues to view Christianity as an ideology which must be controlled and, where necessary, suppressed. There may be more martyrs in this land which has become only a bitter memory to many Americans. As a church elder said at Ceo Reo as the Communist North Vietnamese were advancing, "How many times can you die? My life is in God's hands."

# 7

# Laos

## *"Land of a Million Elephants"*

Laos, fabled "land of a million elephants," is a little larger but less populated than Minnesota. It was once the center of a great Buddhist kingdom, later a part of French Indochina, then an independent nation; and since 1975, following South Vietnam's fall to Red control, a Marxist state.

## "His Love Inflames Me"

As in Vietnam, evangelical Christianity came late to Laos. The pioneers were Mr. and Mrs. Gabriel Contessee, sent by Swiss Brethren. While a young architectural student, Gabriel had been invited by an English biscuit maker to study for the mission field at Livingstone College in London. There he learned of twenty-five million people in Indochina without a single messenger of the gospel.

Gabriel and a companion reached Saigon on September 4, 1902, and proceeded up the Mekong River. Fifty-nine days later they completed the last leg of their journey by dugout canoe. "His love inflames me," Gabriel wrote his mother, "preparing me for this service."

Slowly the two foreigners became accepted by the local people as they learned the language from a Buddhist monk. They baptized their first convert, a sixty-year-old man, on Easter Sunday, 1905.

When reinforcements arrived, Gabriel returned to Switzerland to marry Marguerite Johnson, a girl he knew only by correspondence. He brought her back to Laos, and they started a school.

A cholera epidemic, which had started in Tibet, swept into Laos. Thousands died. Many more fled to the forest in terror. The missionaries, refusing to flee, plunged in to help alleviate the suffering. Marguerite was the first to become ill, then Gabriel. Quinine, the standard remedy, could only slow the disease. Gabriel, not yet thirty, scribbled his last testament: "I am violently ill. I am ready to go. Thank you, Jesus, for saving a sinner such as I."

A few hours after he died, Marguerite succumbed. They were buried side by side in the corner of a field.

The Christian Missions in Many Lands, as the Brethren work is known in English, grew to over one thousand members. The Bible was translated into Lao, and a leprosarium was opened.

## Two Die, Two Escape

In October 1972, the first missionary murders occurred. The incident happened at Keng Kok, a town of about three thousand in northern Laos. Mr. and Mrs. Leslie Chopard of the Brethren mission had started work here in 1965. By 1972 they had four new associates assisting them in evangelization, literacy, agricultural aid, construction projects, and care of tubercular patients. The newcomers included two single men and two single women. Canadian Lloyd Oppel had come from the University of British Columbia to help with construction workers. Sam Mattix, a native of Washington State, had training in tropical medicine. Beatrice Kosin, also from Washington, was an experienced school teacher and her partner, Evelyn Anderson, a registered nurse from Michigan.

In the early morning hours of October 28, 1972, North Vietnamese soldiers advanced into Keng Kok and surrounding villages. The Chopards managed to flee into the jungle. The young women lived in the section of town first overrun by the Communists and had time only to hide under their beds. They remained concealed in their locked house while North Vietnamese roamed the neighborhood searching for them for two days before they were discovered.

News of their capture quickly reached the leaders of the local Lao Brethren assembly. The Laotians risked their lives by going to bargain for the missionaries' release. The negotiations were unsuccessful. The two American women were shot and dumped in their house, then the house was set afire.

About 5:30 a.m. on the day the women were captured, Lloyd and Sam were warned that the Communists were coming. They tried to flee but ran into a contingent of North Vietnamese. By six o'clock they were tied to fence posts by the side of the road. When the sun rose higher, a man began digging a hole between them—a hole shaped like a grave. Were they to be buried alive?

They saw a Christian man, Mr. Pi, bicycling towards them. Sam began singing, hoping Pi would realize they were all right and go away. When he greeted them several times, they pretended not to know him. Finally he put his hand on Lloyd's shoulder and said, "God be with you, brother." Then after doing the same to Sam, he rode off.

A half hour later he returned with two other Lao Christians. They boldly began challenging the Communists: "Why did you take these men captive? They're Christians. They run the Jesus Hospital. They don't carry guns."

At first the soldiers appeared to pay no attention. Then they moved in with guns pointed. The Lao believers simply knelt down near the missionaries. One embraced Sam. Another wrapped his arms around Lloyd. They prayed and wept together. A North Vietnamese officer came up and ordered the Laotians to leave. They tried to reason with him. He cocked his gun and shouted, "Go! Go!" Only then did they walk away.

After darkness fell, the Canadian and the American were pushed into a truck. A little farther on they were put out and then marched for forty days to Hanoi where they were imprisoned with American G.I.'s. They were released a few days later with the American prisoners.

The familiar pattern of pressure and persecution followed the Communist takeover of Laos. Missionaries were ordered out. Foreign support funds were cut off. "Uncooperative" Laotians were sent to "reeducation" camps. Christian activity was confined to religious services inside recognized church buildings. Excuses were found to close some of the churches.

Yet escaping refugees indicate that the Lao believers, though scattered, remain true to Christ. The number who have died or been imprisoned is unknown.

The future of Laos is tied closely to its Communist big brother, Vietnam. As goes suppression of religious freedom in Vietnam, so will go persecution in Laos.

# 8

# Cambodia

## *Dictatorship of Death*

The recorded history of Cambodia goes back to A.D. 100. From A.D. 802 to the 1400s the Buddhist Khmer "God-Kings" ruled over a great empire from their capital at Angkor Wat, a city of dazzling temples. Catholic missionaries entered in the sixteenth century, but by 1970 there were only one thousand Catholics in the country. The C&MA began work in 1923 and was the only Protestant mission in the country until 1960.

Chief of state Prince Norodom Sihanouk ordered all North American missionaries out in 1965 after South Vietnamese planes bombed Viet Cong forces fleeing into Cambodia. National pastors were jailed for preaching without authorization. Two French Alliance missionary couples were the only missionaries allowed to live in Cambodia during this period.

General Lon Nol's coup in March 1970 brought the Americans back. The following month President Nixon sent American troops into Cambodia to drive the Communists from the sanctuaries which Sihanouk had permitted. Student antiwar leaders reacted by touching off mass demonstrations on U.S. college campuses, forcing the end of the American incursion.

The campus activists proclaimed their beliefs from safe campus havens. C&MA and OMF missionaries proved their compassion by moving their families into the ravaged country. Assisted by food and medical shipments from World Vision, the missionaries and leaders of the small Khmer evangelical church launched one of the most significant ministries of mercy in modern times. Cambodian officials responded by granting permission for World Vision to build a Christian hospital which would be operated by C&MA missionaries—an unprecedented action in the almost-solid Buddhist country.

107

## The Harvest Comes

In April 1972, Cambodian evangelicals took the bold step of renting a thousand-seat auditorium for a week's evangelistic crusade led by Stanley Mooneyham, president of World Vision, ignoring warnings of a possible Buddhist riot or Communist bombing. They were not sure the auditorium would be filled. But two hours before the first meeting hundreds were gathered outside the gate. Every seat was taken, and many left disappointed.

Mooneyham preached and asked those who wished to accept Christ to stand up. About two-thirds of the audience stood. He thought they might have misunderstood, so he explained more carefully the Christian message. When he gave a second invitation, about five hundred immediately came to the front.

More Cambodians became Christians that week than in the past thirty years. Among them were government officials, diplomats, and educators. More prominent Cambodians accepted Christ in the months following. One was Men Ny Borinn, president of the national Supreme Court. "I feel like I have become a torch, and I want to go around lighting candles," he said. Another was the author of the Cambodian national anthem.

Before the nation fell to the Communists, the Cambodian church was one of the fastest-growing churches in the world. From three hundred believers in 1970 the church multiplied to an estimated ten thousand in 1975. In Phnom Penh three congregations multiplied to twenty-six during this time.

## Cambodia Falls

The church kept multiplying until missionaries foresaw the entire nation turning to Christ if the Communists could be held back. But after the U.S. Congress forbade further American participation in the war, the little country was doomed. The enemy took over much of the countryside and encircled and blockaded land and water entry into Phnom Penh. Supplies could be brought in only by air as the Communists tightened the noose.

Most of the twenty-five missionaries remained long past the time they were urged to leave by their embassies, some until the last possible moment. They bade their Cambodian friends good-bye, expecting to see them again only in heaven.

## Genocide!

The Communist Khmer Rouge took over Cambodia on April 21, 1975, renaming the nation "Democratic Kampuchea." "Dictatorship of Death" would have been more appropriate. Reliable estimates by world news organizations say that at least two million Cambodians may have been killed in purges. Marxist leaders predicted another three million might be liquidated to complete the building of their "pure society." This in a country the size of Oklahoma with only seven million population at the time of the Red "liberation." In ratio of murders to population, Hitler, Stalin, and Mao Tse-tung must take a bloody back seat to the Cambodian Marxists.

The Communists clamped strict censorship over the country. Still the world got the story from refugees able to escape into Thailand and from a few outsiders allowed to remain in the country. Over a million Cambodians were driven out of the capital, including some twenty-five thousand hospital patients. Thousands died by the roadside. Refugees reported entire villages emptied of people taken out to be shot, stabbed to death, or bulldozed alive into mass graves. Every educated person in the country and every soldier above the rank of private was put to death. Family units were broken up, Bibles confiscated, prayer forbidden. The survivors were told that the new Angka "organization on high" was their only source of true wisdom for the future.

Eyewitness stories of the massacres were printed in *Time, Newsweek,* and other respected journals. This time there were no American peace marches against bloodshed in Cambodia. Most of the ones who had protested so vociferously against the U.S. "invasion" were as silent as the graves in which over a million Cambodians were buried. Missionaries and others who knew personally many of the Cambodian martyrs could only weep as they moved among the few Cambodian refugees who had managed to escape into Thailand.

It is probably correct to assume that most of the ten thousand Protestant believers counted in Cambodia before the fall were martyred. Among these were twelve Cambodian Gideons, who distributed a million Scripture portions before the Communist takeover.

## "Pray for Cambodia"

More than a year after the fall of the capital, Phnom Penh, the widow of Chhirc Taing, a colonel in the defending army and an important church official, received a letter written by her husband before his execution. He told of the meeting of the Cambodian church leaders when they knew their position was indefensible. Together they had read John 13 and then washed each other's feet and quietly talked about the future, realizing they were about to die. In his last words to his wife who was safe in Scotland studying, the lay leader pleaded, "Tell Christians around the world not to forget to pray for Cambodia."

The murderous Khmer Rouge government, headed by the cruel dictator Pol Pot, who can only be compared to Adolf Hitler and Joseph Stalin, fell to Vietnamese invaders in 1979. Vietnamese troops remained until 1989. Cambodia has since entered a critical new phase. Since 1998 there has been no further warfare. The restored monarchy may not survive.

Only two of twenty-five pastors reportedly survived the Khmer Rouge period. Christianity is presently tolerated. At most, there may be no more than three hundred Christians in the entire population.

Southern Baptist missionaries Bruce and Gloria Carlton are among the few foreign missionaries serving in Cambodia. The Carltons see a "spiritual darkness" hovering over the land. "There's an evil that pervades this country," says Bruce. "I just feel it. I don't know how to describe it. The Bible talks about principalities and powers of darkness; they rule this land."

# PART FOUR

# Martyrs of South and Central Asia

# 9

# Tibet

## *Roof of the World*

Tibet—remote and foreboding. Mysterious roof-of-the-world kingdom of high mountain plateaus and hidden valleys. Even before it became a vassal state of Communist China in 1951, Tibet was one of the most resistant nations to the gospel in the world.

Antoine de Andrade, a Portuguese Jesuit, was the first Christian missionary to enter the Buddhist kingdom. Eight years later, in 1634, he was dead with symptoms of poisoning. A few others tried to introduce Christianity into the isolated Buddhist kingdom during the next century. Most paid with their lives. Finally in 1745 the last mission station, run by Capuchin friars, closed and no further attempts were made until the nineteenth century.

In 1898 two Dutch missionaries, Dr. Susie Carson Rijnhart and her husband, set out for Lhasa, the capital from which the Dalai Lama, the Buddhist head of state, ruled. Mr. Rijnhart and their baby were murdered along the trail. Dr. Rijnhart somehow escaped and after weeks of wandering through the high Himalayas reached a mission outpost across the Chinese border, wearing dirty sheepskin clothes and almost black from exposure. Upon arriving home, she was asked if it would not be a cross to return to Tibet. "No," she replied. "It would be a cross not to return."

## Chain Reaction

Dr. Rijnhart's story became one of the most stirring missionary sagas of the early twentieth century. She later married another missionary, and they returned to Tibet and established a church of baptized nationals—the first evangelical church in Tibet.

The challenge of her story raised up a small force of new recruits. Dr. Zenas Loftis, from a church in Nashville, Tennessee, volunteered "for the most difficult field in the world where the need is the greatest." When he reached the foot of a high snow-covered mountain in Tibet, he saw the grave of a martyred missionary. Unable to sleep that night and heeding a premonition, he rose in the middle of the night and wrote in his diary, "Sleep on, thou servant of the Living God, if it be Thy will that I, too, should find a grave in this dark land, may it be one that will be a landmark and an inspiration to others, and may I go to it willingly if it is Thy will."

Dr. Loftis was soon in the midst of a smallpox epidemic. His own vaccination did not hold. On the second day of treating patients he caught both smallpox and typhus. In six weeks he was dead.

The announcement of his death at his home church drew a quick response. Young Dr. William M. Hardy declared, "I'll go and take his place." Dr. Hardy was joined by more missionaries and the Tibetan work grew rapidly. A number of Tibetans were converted as a result of Dr. Loftis's death.

## Never Give Up

The intensifying of banditry in the area forced the missionaries out until finally there were no Protestant missionaries residing in Tibet and only one remaining on the China-Tibetan border. This was William E. Simpson, the twenty-nine-year-old bachelor son of one of the four remaining missionaries serving in rugged western China.

Associated with the Assemblies of God, Simpson had arrived with his parents in the bleak border country when he was a year old. He grew up with the Tibetans and Chinese, ate their food, spoke the local languages, and braved their hardships. He faced tragedy when his baby sister died and later when his mother died on a trip home. After education in the United States, he returned "home" to Tibet, knowing well the risks and privations involved in missionary work on the border.

Marriage for young Simpson was out of the question. One year he traveled thirty-eight hundred miles on horseback, planting the gospel seed among Tibetans. He won the friendship of Tibetan rulers and was permitted to lease a plot of land for a mission station in Labrang, Tibet, where other missionaries had tried and failed to establish permanent work. From Labrang he became a familiar figure riding among wild herdsmen and sharing with them his message of love. He spent many nights under the stars in their camps. One Christmas the only presents he received were fodder, fuel, and a few pears from a Tibetan.

His converts were few, but he pressed on. At the end of one lonely, exhausting trip, Simpson wrote the Assemblies' Foreign Mission Department:

All the trials, the loneliness, the heartache, the weariness and pain, the cold and fatigue of the long road, the darkness and discouragements, and all the bereavements, temptations and testings, seemed not worthy to be compared with the glory and joy of witnessing to this "glad tidings of great joy."

On June 25, 1932, as William Simpson and a Russian traveler were moving some baggage to Labrang, a horde of Muslim army deserters swooped down upon them. The American and the Russian were killed instantly. A Chinese tax collector who was traveling with them escaped to notify Simpson's father and direct him back to where the mangled bodies lay. As the father was picking up his son's mutilated body, he noticed a Sunday school paper smeared with blood lying nearby. The printed words, "IN REMEMBRANCE OF ME," seemed a fitting testimony of why the young missionary had died.

## The Zeal of Sundar Singh

Another zealous missionary to Tibet in the early twentieth century was Sundar Singh, a world famous Indian evangelist. The son of a wealthy landowner of the fanatical Sikh Hindu sect, Singh was reared to be a Hindu priest. In 1904 at age fifteen he became a Christian after having a vision of Christ. His family pronounced him "dead." A relative tried to poison him.

Singh became close friends with Charles Andrews, a noted evangelical English missionary. He studied the Bible intensely and took a vow of poverty. He was known to pray four hours at a time and fast for days. Once he tried to fast for forty days after the manner of Christ. He traveled to Europe, America, Australia, and various Asian countries, preaching to large audiences. His books were translated into numerous languages.

Beginning in 1912 he evangelized several months each year in Tibet, Nepal, and other regions along the Himalayas. In 1929 he made his last trip to Tibet and disappeared. How he died remains a mystery.

## A Closed Land

After Sundar Singh's disappearance and William Simpson's martyrdom, only an occasional missionary ventured into Tibet. The foreboding land remained closed to any type of permanent Christian work. When the Communists sent in a brutal occupation force in 1951, there were probably no more than a few hundred Christians. Most of these were likely killed in the genocidal Marxist purges that snuffed out the lives of hundreds of thousands of Tibetans.

The Tibetans surviving today under tyranny are said to live in virtual slavery. Thousands of refugees have trekked into India. Among them is the Dalai Lama, Buddhist leader of the Tibetans, who was recently presented a translation of the New Testament in the Tibetan language. Missionaries and national Christians in India have reported a sprinkling of converts among the refugees, and it is presumed some of these are filtering back into their homeland.

# 10

# India

## *Riots*

The story of Christian sacrifice in India, the world's second most populous nation, is not nearly so tragic or violent as in China.

Modern Christian missions began when William Carey and his family arrived in this vast country in 1793. India was then a part of Britain's vast colonial empire, and British commercial interests did not welcome the Careys. But the British government protected them and later arrivals.

The British did not give up India until 1947 when Mahatma Gandhi's nonviolence campaign finally succeeded. Before leaving, the British carved the land into two nations—Hindu India and Muslim Pakistan—in an attempt to halt religious wars between Hindus and Muslims. The two countries both elected to remain in the British Commonwealth and agreed that violence against Christians and other religious minorities should be strictly prohibited. Disease, not violence, took a heavy toll of missionary lives before and after the British occupation.

## Hindus Fear Christian Advances

Indian Christians suffered far more than missionaries in the twentieth century. Many have been disowned by their families. In northern India hundreds were killed in riots directed against British troops and certain missionaries closely identified with the colonial regime.

117

The greatest Christian advances have been made among the Nagas and other tribal peoples of northeast India with a background of pagan animism. In the 1920s over a hundred thousand were baptized under the direction of American Baptist missionaries.

The Hindu majority of India resented and feared such a large conclave of Christians in one area. After independence, there were incidents of discrimination. It seemed to the tribespeople that they had merely exchanged one colonial government for another. An influential missionary had already encouraged the Nagas and their kinsmen to think of organizing their own nation. A Christian tribesman formed a revolutionary government. The alarmed Indian government banned all foreigners from the area and sent in troops.

The hostilities have continued for several years with many killed on both sides. As a further complication, reports persist that Chinese Communists are supplying arms to the Christian rebels and promising to help establish a Naga nation. The unrest has spread to predominantly Christian tribes along the borders of Bangladesh, Burma, Laos, and Vietnam. There is a tight news blackout on all fronts. No one really knows how many Christians have died in the fighting. Nor is there likely to be any intervention by the United Nations or big powers because of the delicate issues involved. World diplomats pretend that the fighting does not exist.

## The Beheading of Brother Abraham

Recent government concern has centered on extremist Sikhs who want independence for the state of Punjab. Terrorist attacks by Sikhs and responses by government soldiers have resulted in hundreds of deaths.

Radical Hindus have made a number of attacks on native Christians. A pastor, known as Brother Abraham, was bicycling home in Tamil Nadu when he was ambushed. A woman eyewitness working in a nearby field told police that Brother Abraham was call-ing, "Jesus, Jesus, Jesus" as he was chased into a field. There the members of a radical Hindu sect caught him and beheaded him with a sword.

After four of the accused murderers were jailed, local Indian Christians heard that Hindu extremists had attempted to bribe police officials to get the charges reduced. Brother Abraham's wife was asked by police to sign papers that could exonerate the men who attacked her husband. She refused.

Other native missionaries report receiving threatening letters from this Hindu group, which has long opposed Christian activity in India. One native missionary was told that he is listed as seventh to be murdered by the group.

India is a democratic nation, with a large Hindu majority. While religious freedom is officially proclaimed, local government officials are sometimes pressured to overlook or go easy on discrimination and oppression against Christians.

## Assassinations of Catholic Missionaries Increase in India

Between 1990 and 1998 fourteen Catholics are known to have been killed in India on account of their faith.

A Catholic missionary, A. T. Thomas, was killed in the Bihar region on October 28, 1997. He was found decapitated.

Brother Luke Puttaniyil, a brother of the Missionaries of Charity, founded by the late Mother Theresa of Calcutta, was bringing medical and food supplies to lepers in Patna, Bihar, when his car was attacked on a lonely stretch of road outside the town of Novada. When the forty-six-year-old native of the Indian state of Kerala was missed in the colony, a search party went out to look for him and they found his body behind some railroad tracks on March 24, 1998. It was half-buried, his hands and feet were bound, his mouth was gagged with a shirt, and bullet wounds were clearly visible in his back and head.

## Graham Stewart Stains and His Two Sons

A mob of rampaging Hindus burned to death an Australian missionary and his two sons, Philip, 10, and Timothy, 8, as they slept in a jeep in eastern India. According to a police statement, Graham Stewart Stains, a secretary of the Evangelical Missionary Society, and his sons were attacked by activists from the radical Bajrang Dal, a group affiliated with the ruling Hindu nationalist Bharativa Janata Party.

Stains, 58, had been working with leprosy victims in India for thirty-four years. The unrest began after radical Hindus accused Christian missionaries of converting people to their faith.

The following e-mail report came from a fellow missionary of Graham Stewart Stains. It is dated January 24, 1999.

Bro. Sam Varughese called late today and said that a Baptist Missionary and his two children were burned to death as they slept in a jeep. They had been preaching to a leper colony.

Their funeral will be today. He was weeping and very upset, though it was not one of his preachers. Today is also a holiday (the day has already begun there) and he and other Christians were meeting for prayer and to raise the Christian flag.

People there are blaming Christians for all their woes and want to make India a Hindu nation. He doesn't know what may happen.

We need the urgent prayers all over the country for all the Christians in India, especially Sam, his family and his church. Please pass this on to as many people as you can.
Love in Christ, Sandy Snyder

## A Constant Flow of Unsung Christian Martyrs

On June 7, 2000, brother George Kuzhikandum, a Catholic priest, was murdered on the Brother Polus Memorial School Campus near Mathura, Uttar Pradesh. He was beaten with iron rods until he died.

On June 10, 2000, Vijay Ekka, a tribal Christian from the Raigarh District, died while in police custody. Ekka was an eyewitness to the murder of brother George Kuzhikandum. Two policemen have since been arrested and accused of killing Vijay Ekka by beating him and giving him electric shock treatment.

On June 12, 2000, construction workers found the body of evangelist Ashish Prabash in his rented house in Punjab State. The body had multiple stab wounds. Ashish Prabash Masih worked for Campus Crusade for Christ. His main ministry was showing the JESUS film. The Punjab Christian Association believe that the killing was the outcome of a concerted campaign against its community by Hindu nationalists.

On July 25, 2000, a Roman Catholic priest, Father Victor Crasta, and three missionaries were killed when a militant group opened fire on them in Balucherra, north Tripura district.

On September 12, 2000, a Christian preacher was beheaded in Karimnagar. Unidentified assailants tied Mr. Yesu Dasu's hands and then hacked at his neck with an axe several times before he died.

## Anti-Christian Attacks Continue in India

On November 23, 2000, two Christians were killed and four wounded in an attack in Gumla diocese, when men on motorbikes attacked the largely Catholic village.

On November 26, 2000, Protestant missionaries were stoned by more than one hundred people in the district of Kolar for distributing evangelistic leaflets.

On December 2, 2000, a Catholic priest, Jacob Chittinapilly, was murdered in northeast India, when he and a driver were attacked by suspected militants on motorbikes.

According to human rights sources in India there have been more than two hundred cases of anti-Christian violence since Vajpayee's party came to power in 1998.

# 11

# Bangladesh, Pakistan, and Afghanistan

## Muslim-Hindu Wars

When Pakistan was part of India and the British Empire, missionaries and their converts were protected by the colonial government. A referendum held in 1947 revealed two predominantly Muslim parts of the old colonial empire. These two sections became East and West Pakistan. When their borders were announced, one of the greatest cross-migrations in history began, as almost six million Muslims fled to Pakistan from India and about four million Hindus entered India from Pakistan. Thousands died in the rioting and fighting that accompanied the mass movement. India's beloved "apostle of nonviolence," Mahatma Gandhi, was killed trying to stop the fighting.

Mission work established before the separation from India continued in Pakistan. Religious freedom was guaranteed, but Christian teachers were forbidden to give religious instruction to students of another religion attending mission schools. In some isolated areas Christian witnessing was resisted and missionaries viewed with suspicion.

Florida-sized, river-laced East Pakistan was the smaller, more thickly populated of the two sections of the country. It was richer in natural resources, but less developed industrially. The people were short and dark-skinned, and spoke the poetic Bengali tongue. The western section was peopled by tall, light-skinned, long-nosed Punjabis who spoke mainly the Urdu and Sindhi languages.

## Bloody Bangladesh!

In 1971, East Pakistan rose in rebellion against callous discrimination by West Pakistan. In one of the bloodiest "small" wars of history over three million Bengalis in the east were killed—mostly innocent civilians—and some three hundred thousand women savagely raped Nazi-style.

The Hindu minority in East Pakistan was a special target of Muslim Punjabi soldiers from the west. The Hindus scrawled crosses on their homes so the Punjabis would think they were Christians. Many begged Christian missionaries to baptize them and give them shelter.

About 320 missionaries, almost equally divided between Protestants and Catholics, were in East Pakistan when the war started. The missionaries were sympathetic to the Bengali cause. Some risked their lives in "smuggling" relief supplies and medicines to endangered Bengalis. Although some had narrow escapes, no Protestant missionaries were killed. Three Catholic workers were not so favored.

Italian Father Mario Veronese came out with his hands up when he saw West Pak soldiers coming into his hospital, the Red Cross symbol on his arm clearly visible. The invaders shot him in his tracks, then ran into the hospital, shooting at frightened staff members. West Pakistani officials later apologized and claimed it was a mistake.

Another Italian priest was beaten to death with a tire iron after he served tea to West Pak soldiers at his hospital.

A third padre, Holy Cross Father William Evans, was pulled from his boat by West Pak soldiers while on his way to church service. They shoved him into a ditch, slashed him with bayonets, shot him twice, then kicked his body into the river.

Despite their neutral status, upwards of a hundred Bengali Christians were later martyred. At Bogra in the far north, a band of West Pak sympathizers burst into the home of a respected Church of God teacher. Utpal Biswas was too sick to flee and get his family away. They killed him, his wife, two sons, and a daughter who served as a nurse at the nearby Church of God hospital. South of Bogra, West Pak troops invaded Rangamati village, tossing torches into flimsy, dry huts. Occupants fleeing the flames were lined up and executed in the light of the flames. Sixteen Christians perished. Similar atrocities were inflicted in other villages.

The tides of war quickly changed after India entered the war and cut West Pakistan's tenuous supply lines. Within days East Pakistan had become newly independent Bangladesh.

In the years since the terrible war Bangladesh has been plagued by unstable governments as well as by disease and hunger. The brave band of missionaries and the Christian minority (less than 1 percent of the population) continues to serve.

## The Threat of Islamic Law in Pakistan

In May 1991, Pakistan's parliament instituted Islamic law throughout the country. Christians feared this would be a reversal of long-standing legal and constitutional guarantees of religious freedom for the nation's non-Muslim minorities.

In one case, Banto Mashi, a Pakistani Christian in Lahore, was accused by a Muslim of "insulting the Prophet Mohammed." Mashi's accuser tried to stab him at a court hearing in 1992. The punishment for Mashi's crime is hanging, as demanded by Islamic law.

Other examples of persecution are being reported. In civil cases of mixed-religion marriages, judges are imposing Muslim laws governing marriage, divorce, and child custody by the non-Muslim partners. In some instances, Christian parents are being denied contact with their families.

Christian lawyers say the law is an ambiguous document. Jamshid Rahmat-Ullah, a Christian attorney in Lahore, notes that "one clause says that minorities have a right to practice their 'ways of life.' But who is going to define that? A Muslim maulana [clergyman]? Or a Christian church leader?"

The Supreme Court of Pakistan has thus far thrown out every case in which lower courts have called for Islamic punishments. Najam Sethi, editor of the *Lahore Friday Times,* says the "legal structure" in the new law "is there to Islamize the entire legal structure. Right now, the political will is not there. But tomorrow, the supreme court could come under pressure from a fundamentalist [Islamic] regime."

## Nine Christians Butchered

On November 18, 1998, a gang of terrorists killed nine Christians, eight from the same family, in Noshehra, a city in the northeast part of the North Western Frontier Province of Pakistan. They were butchered with a sharp knife. Most of them were discovered with their throats cut.

The murderers used the blood of these slain Christians to write on the wall, "No more black magic." Among those slain was a one-month-old baby boy.

The father of the slain family, Sabir John Bhatti, was involved in praying for the sick. Often Muslims, as well as Christians, would come to him to ask for prayer for healing. This offended some of the extremist Muslim groups, and some Christians in the community believe that the reason for killing the whole family was an attempt to threaten other Christians involved in evangelism and other Christian work among Muslims.

Among the slain, apart from Mr. Sabir John Bhatti, was his wife Ruth, his daughter Shaheen, daughter-in-law Rosina, grandson Mohsin (1 year old), grandson Romi (8 years old), granddaughter Sobia (10 years old), a one-month-old grandson (name unknown), and a young friend visiting the family, Ifzal (14 years old).

## Martyred While Awaiting Trial

Christians who are accused of blasphemy have been known to be killed while awaiting trial. Between 1990 and 1998 at least five Christians were murdered after being charged with blasphemy. Mukhtar Masih was allegedly tortured to death in police custody. Tahir Iqbal was poisoned while in prison. Bantu Masih, Manzoor Masih, and Namat Ahmer were also killed while in custody.

## Troubled Afghanistan

Neighboring Muslim Afghanistan has long been one of the most closed countries in the world to Christian missions. Pro-Soviet leftists took power in a bloody 1978 coup and signed a military treaty with the USSR. The first Soviet puppet was shortly replaced with a stronger regime and Soviet troops were sent throughout the country to put down patriotic opposition. After nine years of heavy losses, the Soviets agreed to withdraw their troops in 1988 and support a neutral Afghan state. Refugees began pouring back into the country from camps in Pakistan.

The new "neutral" government fell under pressure from contending rebel groups in April 1992. All of the factions are Islamic, with the only difference being that some are more hardline than others.

Before the Soviet intervention, some foreign Christian relief workers served in Afghanistan. There may indeed be a few Christians left who have survived the years of savage fighting. They could suffer discrimination, if not outright persecution.

# 12

## Nepal, Sri Lanka, and Myanmar

### *No Mass Murders*

### The Mystery of Nepal

No western missionary is known to have given his life for Christ in Nepal, an indepen-dent buffer Hindu state between China and India where scores of mountain climbers have died trying to scale Mt. Everest and other peaks. Foreigners were not even allowed to enter this mecca for mountain climbers until 1950. Christian social, educational, and medical workers are permitted today only if they pledge not to evangelize. The Wycliffe Bible Translators, which had seventy members working in eighteen Nepalese dialects, were asked to leave in 1976.

There are said to be only five or six hundred Nepalese Christians among a population of twenty-three million. These few either were evangelized illegally within the country, or became believers while outside the country. The Nepalese constitution states explic-itly that "no person shall be entitled to convert another person to his religion." Because of this law Prem Pradham, a Nepalese converted while serving in the Indian army, has served time in seven jails. An unknown number of other Nepalese believers have been imprisoned for evangelizing. Many have been disowned by their families.

There are no records of Nepalese who may have died in prison or from other persecu-tions. Any such incidents would have been hidden before 1950 and would not be reported today by the controlled press.

## Sri Lanka

Sri Lanka (formerly Ceylon) is the island nation off the tip of India. The little West Virginia-sized country was ruled for almost four centuries by three European powers in succession—Portugal, Holland, and Britain. Each promoted its own language and national branch of Christianity. Around 1800 over half of the population professed Christianity.

Since its independence from Britain in 1948, an anti-Christian spirit has been rising. Militant Sinhalese Buddhists promote Sri Lanka as the "Promised Land" for members of their sect living abroad. Their brand of Buddhism, they say, is the patriotic national faith and Christianity is the tool of colonialists. Many professing Christians have returned to Buddhism, including a former premier. Today only 8 percent of the fourteen million inhabitants claim to be Christian.

A hard core of fervent evangelicals, missionaries, and nationals are evangelizing vigorously. Sri Lanka law permits individuals to change their religion. They are opposed by Buddhists and Communist agitators bent on creating conflict.

In 1988 Christian evangelist Lionel Jayasinghe was shot to death by two men in his Sri Lanka home. Police suspected the slaying was done in response to Jayasinghe's successful evangelism outreach among Buddhists. He reportedly led eighty people to Christ in 1987, rousing the anger of many in his village. One villager reportedly threatened the evangelist's life.

Troubled times may lie ahead.

## Suffering and Death in Myanmar

Myanmar (Burma) is another South Asian country which avoided blood purges of Christians during the twentieth century.

Shaped like a kite with a tail, this Texas-sized, predominantly Buddhist country was first visited by Armenian Christians in 1612. In 1685 two French Catholic missionaries opened a small hospital, only to be murdered four years later for spreading Christian doctrine. Protestant missions began in 1813 when Baptists Adoniram and Haseltine Judson arrived. Judson was arrested as a spy and thrown into the death prison at Ava. After months of torture and suffering in a squalid cell, he was asked by a jailer, "How bright are the prospects of your mission now, O foreign animal?" Judson answered, "As bright as the promises of God, my friend."

Judson survived twenty-one months in the filthy jail and upon release moved to Rangoon. His wife died in 1826 from a combination of tropical diseases. Judson then married the widow of a colleague who had given his life for Myanmar. He subsequently lost this wife and several children to the ravages of the Orient. Judson persisted. At his death there were seven thousand Christians and 163 missionaries in Myanmar. By 1900 the Baptist community had grown to almost one hundred thousand, due largely to a "people" movement among the Karen tribe.

Both the missionary force and the national Christian body kept growing in the early twentieth century. There were only scattered, localized acts of violence against Christians.

## The Widow's Plea

One tragic incident involved a young Karen doctor who came to help an American Baptist missionary, Dr. Albert Henderson, at the Taunggyi Hospital that served the Shan tribe. For eighteen months all went well. Then one night the Karen physician was called to aid a woman who had been severely injured by her drunken husband. As he was dressing her wounds, the husband suddenly returned and tried to finish the job. While trying to protect his patient, the doctor was killed by the madman.

When the Shan ruler ordered the murderer executed, the Christian doctor's widow rushed to the palace and begged that the man be spared. Drink, she said, had made him insane. The ruler granted the request.

## "He Showed Us God"

Dr. Henderson had been in Myanmar since 1893. He had laid six colleagues to rest in the little cemetery at Taunggyi. In February 1937, he returned from visiting a sick colleague to find a typhoid epidemic raging in the town. His two associates away, he drove himself day and night to help the sick and dying. One morning his wife Cora noticed he was flushed. She quickly took his temperature and found he had a high fever. Further diagnosis indicated that he too had contracted typhoid.

A medical missionary from another station and his nurse wife came and fought two weeks to save Dr. Henderson's life. Finally he awoke from the coma and smiled at his wife. "It's all right, dear, I'm going home," he whispered. Then he closed his eyes and slipped away peacefully.

Thousands came to his funeral—Christians, Buddhists, Hindus and tribal animists, loin-clothed tribespeople, and members of royal households. One old man sobbed, "He was our beloved father. He showed us God by the way he lived."

## Closed to Missionaries but Still Open for Christ

Japanese troops occupied Myanmar during World War II. They succeeded in cutting the Burma Road, over which scores of missionaries had escaped from China. But the Japanese were too busy fighting and keeping order to mount an antireligious crusade.

After the war Myanmar reverted to colonial status in the British Empire, then in 1947 became an independent state. From 1947 to 1950 the country was wracked by revolts from Communists and rebel Karen tribesmen. Like their tribal cousins in northeast India, the Karen people wanted an independent state. The central government finally did agree to a separate Karen state within the nation. Many Karen tribespeople were killed in the uprising. They died in the political struggle and not because they were Christians.

In the 1960s Burma was spared the agonies of Vietnam, Cambodia, and Laos, by adopting a stance of strict neutrality and maintaining tight control over dissidents. The country is ruled today by a one-party socialist government. Myanmar is now closed to missionaries, but national churches are permitted a wide latitude. The largest body, Baptists, reported 555,063 members in 1998.

General Ne Win dominated the government from 1962 to 1988. Ne Win and a revolutionary force drove Indians from the civil service and Chinese from commerce in Burma. The economy became more socialized and the nation more isolated from the world.

Masses of rioters forced Ne Win from power. Sein Lwin assumed control, but street violence continued. In September 1988, General Saw Maung, a close associate of Ne Win, and associates took control and changed the country's name to Myanmar.

Around eight hundred thousand Chinese live in Myanmar. Only 1 percent of these are believed to be Christians. The Chinese Coordination Center of World Evangelism reported in 1985 that three Chinese Christian pastors had been captured and killed by Burmese Communists. One was taken near the border with China and tortured to death. His wife continued to work in a Bible school established in Lashio, Myanmar.

## Nepal, Sri Lanka, and Myanmar Today

Nepal remains a tightly controlled state where Christian workers are not officially welcomed. Sri Lanka has been the target of ultra-leftist terrorists. Since the mid-1980s, the troubled nation has been kept in turmoil by fighting between the Sinhalese majority and the Tamil minority who want a separate and independent enclave for themselves.

In the early 1990s, Myanmar was a seething cauldron. In 1990 the government allowed the first free, multiparty elections in thirty years. The opposition party won a decisive victory, but General Saw Maung and his cohorts have refused to give up power.

In contrast to Nepal where Christians are a tiny minority, Sri Lanka and Myanmar have substantial numbers of Christian believers. Their challenge is to stand faithful.

# PART FIVE

# Martyrs of the
# Asian Pacific Islands

# 13

## Indonesia, Papua, and Surrounding Islands

### *Cannibalism*

W e crept over the spine of the ridge and looked straight down on the naked savages feasting on enemies they had slain in battle. Suddenly we heard a rustle in the grass. Turning in fear, we saw two painted faces staring at us. We had found the cannibals and now they had found us."

Furloughing missionaries, in the nineteenth century, from the Asian Pacific islands kept congregations on the edge of their pews with such hair-raising tales of narrow escapes from fierce cannibals. They brought chills by telling of martyrs speared to death and eaten by cannibal islanders. They roused young people to their feet, resolving to fill the martyrs' shoes.

Overdrawn? Perhaps missionaries did often omit from their home talks such positive factors as native honesty, willingness to share, and simplicity of life, and did neglect to draw attention to the equally savage crimes of so-called civilized peoples. But cannibalism was indeed rampant. One Fiji chief had 872 memorial stones to mark the number of human beings he had eaten. And infanticide was common. Some tribes killed up to two-thirds of their children after birth. And it was very true that missionaries were more likely to be martyred or die of a tropical disease than live out a normal lifetime. In New Guinea there were once more missionary graves than native converts.

## Into New Guinea

The first twentieth-century missionary martyr in the Pacific was James Chalmers. The son of a Scottish stonemason, Chalmers was challenged in his teens when his pastor read a letter from a missionary in Fiji describing the power of the gospel over cannibals. The minister finished in tears, then looked over his spectacles and said, "I wonder if there is a boy here who will by-and-by bring the gospel to the cannibals?" Young Chalmers vowed he would be that pioneer.

There were already Christians at Rarotonga. As soon as other missionaries arrived, the Chalmers turned down a furlough and headed for virgin New Guinea. "The nearer I get to Christ and His cross, the more do I long for direct contact with the heathen," he wrote. They soon reported, "Several of our new friends wear human jawbones on their arms." Once Mr. Chalmers was surrounded by a mob of painted bandits, demanding tomahawks and knives or else they would kill both him and his wife. "You may kill us, but never a thing will you get from us," he declared. The surprised leader left, then came back the next day to apologize. Chalmers extended a gift of friendship and they were friends thereafter. Invitations to feasts began coming. They accepted some, but declined those where human flesh was served. Jane Chalmers was once offered the gift of a portion of a man's chest, already cooked.

The strain soon showed on Mrs. Chalmers. Two years after coming to New Guinea, she went to Sydney, Australia, for rest. There she died in 1879. Upon receiving the sad news, Chalmers told his friends, "Let me bury my sorrow in work for Christ, with whom my dear wife is. Some of our teachers have suffered and lost their wives, and with them I must be."

By 1882 Chalmers could report "no cannibal ovens, no feasts, no human flesh, no desire for skulls," in the area where he worked. He had become so well known and beloved that when he visited neighboring islands residents invited him to speak in heathen temples that were lined with the skulls of people they had sacrificed and eaten. Often he and his assistants would preach all night and at the conclusion, the congregation would declare, "No more fighting, Tamate, no more man-eating; we have heard the good news and we shall strive for peace."

Again he was urged to take a furlough. "No," he said, "I would rather risk climate and savages, than sea and land traveling." Finally in 1886 he did go and received a hero's welcome in London. He returned to the Pacific two years later with a new wife.

He kept pioneering along the New Guinea coast and among nearby islands. In 1900 he lost his second wife after a fourteen-week illness. He comforted himself in "the sweet will of God" and said, "I cannot rest with so many thousands of savages without a knowledge of God near us." To an invitation to spend his last years in England, he replied, "I am nearing the bar, and might miss resting amidst old scenes, joys, and sorrows."

On April 4, 1901, James Chalmers sailed to Goaribari Island where there were few believers. Three days later, on Easter evening, his ship anchored off the end of the island.

Armed natives paddled out and swarmed over the vessel. Chalmers promised to go ashore the next morning and they left. Shortly after dawn they returned. Another missionary named Tomkins decided to go with him.

The crew waited all day. When the missionaries did not return, the captain dispatched a search party. The searchers were told a grisly story.

Upon coming ashore, Chalmers, Tomkins, and the few native Christians had been invited into a building for a feast. As they entered, men knocked them to the ground with stone clubs. The attackers then cut off their heads and hacked their torsos into pieces for cooking the same day.

The murders of Chalmers and Tomkins shook Europe and America. No missionaries had been lost in the Pacific to cannibals for several years. Scores of young men and women were stirred to volunteer.

## "God Takes the Best"

Five C&MA missionaries at Makassar, the largest city of the Celebes (now Sulawesi), a large island group between Borneo and New Guinea—Mr. and Mrs. Russell Diebler, Mr. and Mrs. R. A. Jaffray, and Canadian Ernie Presswood—were permitted to move to a mountain rest home. Five weeks later Japanese officers came and ordered Diebler and Presswood to accompany them back to the city. Because of his age they allowed Jaffray to remain with the women in the rest home until they were moved in December to a small camp nearby.

Diebler and Presswood were interned with about a hundred Dutchmen in an overcrowded police barracks. "It will be only one night," one of the officers promised. The "one night" for Diebler lasted a year and a half, and for Presswood three and a half years.

During their captivity the men were served only two cups of poorly cooked rice and one bun each day. A Bible student who saw them later reported, "They were so thin. It was enough to make a person weep."

In September the two men were moved to the large Parepare camp where there were other missionaries. For a while they were permitted to hold Sunday worship services at the nearby war prisoners' camp. One memorable sermon was based on James 4:14, "For what is your life? It is even a vapor that appears for a little time and then vanishes away."

In the spring of 1943 Jaffray was brought to Parepare. He was given a small room in the hospital and allowed to take walks with Presswood and Diebler.

Diebler's greatest sorrow was the separation from his wife, Darlene. They had been married only three years when the war broke. Before that they had been apart for about a year while he was preparing the entry into the Wissel Lake area. Presswood had buried his wife three years before in the jungle after only two years of service together.

In August Diebler came down with dysentery, not unusual in the camp, and had to be hospitalized. Then he became suddenly worse. Presswood later recalled, "I had prayed so fervently for Russell, but toward midnight the Lord convinced me that I should no longer pray for him. I surrendered him to our Savior." Diebler began calling for his wife and died a few hours later. The Japanese permitted a funeral which all the interned missionaries attended. "God takes the best," a grieving Catholic priest said. Months later a Dutchman confided to Presswood that he had trusted in Christ at the service.

## "So Hard to Be Brave"

Darlene Diebler did not learn of her husband's passing until three months later. Not until the end of the war, almost two years later, was she able to convey her grief to her parents. "I can't put on paper the heartache that has made me so much older," she wrote.

> I only know about his passing what others have told me. He was unconscious the last few hours, the doctor told me, who attended him, and he kept calling for me. And to think I was only three hours by car from him and couldn't be there. The first night I thought I'd go crazy with grief but God—how precious He has become to me! The heartache is still there, but the terrible hurt has left me.
>
> I took dysentery, tropical malaria, and beri-beri all at once. For six weeks I lived on salt-free rice porridge. How often that verse came to me, "The Lord is my Shepherd, I shall not want." I can't write what we suffered there, but through personal intervention of our Jap Camp Commander, we were finally released after having been told we were to be beheaded as spies—but they forgive us this time! Enough said. . . . After Russell's death and during those weeks in prison, I turned quite gray. O Mummy dear, it is so hard to be brave. I did so love Russell.

## A Missionary Statesman Dies

The young widow also reported that after the war turned against the Japanese and Allied planes began bombing in the area, the prisoners were jammed in trucks like cattle and transported 156 miles into the jungle to a camp of grass huts. Jaffray's health had been failing and here he became much worse. He died on July 28, only a few days before peace was declared.

Said Dr. A. C. Snead, the C&MA Foreign Director, of Jaffray:

> The Christian and Missionary Alliance and the Church of Christ throughout the earth have lost an intrepid pioneer, a great missionary statesman, and a man so filled with the love and grace of God that his whole being—body, soul, and spirit—was devoted utterly to Christ and His service.

## Bayoneted to Death

Besides Diebler and Jaffray, four other C&MA missionaries perished in prison camps in the Dutch East Indies, and two others died afterward.

Pilot Fred Jackson and Mr. and Mrs. Andrew Sande had reached east Borneo just before Pearl Harbor. Jackson replaced George Fisk, the first C&MA pilot, who had gone home on furlough. The Sandes, who had an infant son, were also new workers in the already fruitful east Borneo field. Thousands of Dyak tribespeople had renounced cannibalism and were seeking baptism from missionaries and graduates of the Makassar Bible School.

For several weeks Jackson flew mercy missions at the request of Dutch officials, ferrying sick and wounded to hospitals. When the Japanese took control of the air, he hid the plane and joined the Sandes at Long Nawang where the Dutch had a military base. Here the missionaries lived in a house at the edge of a Dyak Christian village.

All was peaceful until August 19, 1942, when some Dyaks reported foreign soldiers moving around the base. The Dutch officers apparently did not believe the report, for they took no steps to fight or flee. Early the next morning the Japanese attacked when the Dutch were taking infantry practice with unloaded guns.

The Japanese rounded up sixty-nine men, including the two male missionaries, for questioning. Jackson and Sande were kept under close guard but not mistreated during the following week. The women and children were detained separately.

Near the end of August, all of the European men were taken out one by one and bayoneted to death. Two months later the women and children were also brutally murdered.

## No "Situation Ethics"

When the Japanese invaded, John Willfinger and Mr. and Mrs. Richard Lenham of the C&MA fled deep into the Borneo jungle and took refuge with Murut Christians. A bachelor Bible translator, Willfinger had been anticipating his upcoming furlough and a reunion with his fiancée when the war came. The Lenhams were also working on the translation of the Murut Bible.

In July 1942, the trio heard that the Japanese had captured a party of Europeans. They moved to a village in northern Borneo. Here they learned that Jackson and the Sandes had been imprisoned.

They anticipated that the Japanese would learn their location. On September 19, a courier came to the village with a list of names of people for whom the Japanese were searching. Their names were on the list. The messenger warned the tribespeople that they would be severely punished for trying to hide any of the wanted persons.

"Stay. We will take you where you cannot be found," the Murut Christians begged.

The three missionaries mulled over their future. Finally they told the Muruts, "You would have to lie to the Japanese. We would rather go and surrender than cause you to be disobedient to God's Word."

Willfinger explained their decision in a "whomsoever-receives-this letter."

> We feel that we could have successfully hidden, but at the risk of involving those Muruts who have been kind to us, and are desirous of hiding us. But we cringed at the thought of this. Therefore we have decided to go to the enemy, trusting God as to the ultimate results.

He added the addresses of his loved ones, asking the receiver to "kindly send my love to my family and sweetheart."

The three decided to separate. Willfinger wanted to visit several tribal churches in eastern Borneo before surrendering. The Lenhams took the precious Bible translations and struck out for a Japanese post further north. Several days later they walked into a Japanese camp and were immediately interned. Mrs. Lenham managed to conceal the Gospel of Mark, often hiding it in wet clothes on the clothesline when the women's quarters were searched. Mr. Lenham kept Matthew until a guard discovered it. After they were released at the end of the war, he found the translation in a pile of trash. Both Gospels were subsequently published by the British and Foreign Bible Society for the Murut church.

Willfinger completed his last missionary journey and gave himself up for imprisonment. He was executed on December 28. At war's end his Bible was recovered. Inside the cover he had inscribed a poem which indicated the power of his commitment:

> No mere man is the Christ I know,
>     But greater far than all below.
> Day by day His love enfolds me,
>     Day by day His power upholds me;
> All that God could ever be,
>     The man of Nazareth is to me.

> No mere man can my strength sustain
>     And drive away all fear and pain,
> Holding me close in His embrace
>     When death and I stand face to face;
> Then all that God could ever be
>     The unseen Christ will be to me.

Below the poem he had written, "Hallelujah! This is real!"

When the war ended, the circumstances of John Willfinger's death were unknown. Ernie Presswood set out to get the facts after his release. He recovered the body of his colleague and arranged for final burial in a cemetery just off the Borneo coast. Presswood died a short time later and was laid to rest in a Pacific grave.

Still the toll of prison martyrs was not to end for the C&MA. Word came that another internee, Grace Dittmar, had succumbed from privations suffered while trying to escape from Sumatra.

## Nine More Die in New Guinea

There were many other prison camp martyrs besides the seven C&MA missionaries. In Papua (eastern New Guinea), the Anglican bishop, when ordered by British authorities to leave, broadcast this message to his staff:

> We must endeavor to carry on our work in all circumstances, no matter what the cost may ultimately be to any of us individually. . . . We could never hold up our faces again if, for our own safety, we forsook Him and fled when the shadows of the passion began to gather around Him in His spiritual and mystical body, the church in Papua.

The bishop and eight of his staff were executed "as an example" on September 2, 1942, in a concentration camp.

## The Fateful Journey of Erickson and Tritt

A Salvation Army couple, imprisoned by the Japanese, was urging The Evangelical Alliance Mission (TEAM), formerly the Scandinavian Alliance Mission, to send workers to tribes in newly independent Indonesia. Walter Erickson, a young theology student, had asked TEAM for appointment to New Guinea. Erickson had visited the south coast while serving in the U.S. Coast Guard during the war and had traveled to the Wissel Lakes. He could not forget the tribespeople he had met.

Erickson accepted appointment to Indonesia, hoping to enter New Guinea later. He reached Java on a student visa and was warned by the American consul to leave immediately because of dangerous political disturbances. He went instead to the Dutch consulate and procured a visa to western New Guinea.

Erickson conferred with C&MA, Unevangelized Fields Mission, and Missionary Aviation Fellowship personnel already there. They suggested that TEAM locate in untouched "Bird's Head," an area on the end of the island, half the size of Illinois and teeming with unreached tribes. Erickson wangled Dutch permission for a quota of ten missionaries.

Erickson had already made several surveys when Edward R. Tritt, his first reinforcement, arrived. On September 10, 1952, the two set out on foot with five native carriers for the remote Kebur and Karoon regions. MAF's single plane had crashed a year before, killing the pilot, and there was no flight service available.

On October 17 Erickson and Tritt's mutilated bodies were found near the Ainim River. Tritt had died at the place of attack. Erickson had crawled to a cave where he succumbed.

Investigation by Dutch police resulted in a confession of murder by the missionaries' carriers. The hired tribesmen had not wanted to go further for fear of being killed by the unknown tribespeople. The missionaries wanted to press on. While the missionaries slept, the carriers attacked and slashed them to death with machetes.

## Stirred by Sacrifice

The martyrdom of the New Guinea pioneers triggered a flurry of new applications for missionary service. Vernon Mortenson, then responsible for TEAM's recruiting program and later the mission's general director, told the Erickson-Tritt story at the Highland Park Baptist Church in Chattanooga. Afterwards a couple came to him and said they felt God was leading them to New Guinea. Mr. and Mrs. Ronald Hill later joined the TEAM force in the new field. By 1965 there were forty-seven TEAM missionaries in the Bird's Head area, and by 1969 they reported 4,280 baptized believers among former head-hunting tribes.

## "Cannibal Valley"

The missionaries at Wissel Lakes knew of an even more remote valley, first seen by an American scientific expedition in 1938. It was reported to be a tropical Shangri-la of breathtaking beauty, surrounded by high mountains and populated by the most ferocious cannibals of New Guinea. R. A. Jaffray had dreamed of entering this valley through which the Baliem River flowed. After the war C&MA workers had made survey trips near the valley. Then in 1951 Jerry Rose and three Dutch officials crossed a rugged plateau at about twelve thousand feet and descended into the remote region. They were on the trail for sixty-seven days and along the way their guide was killed with arrows. Afterwards Rose moved his bride into the valley.

Rose was married to Darlene Diebler, the widow of Russell Diebler. She became the first white woman to live among the Danis, the principal tribe of the valley. The Danis were cannibals. One of their funeral customs required the chopping off of fingers and bits of ears from relatives of the deceased to be eaten by other mourners.

The C&MA missionaries had their own amphibious plane and by 1955 two other couples had joined the Roses.

## The First Dani Martyr

By 1957 the Word of God had taken root. Newly trained Dani evangelists were going to distant villages where no gospel messengers had ever gone.

In 1961 the C&MA's Tom Bozeman and Dave Martin, a visitor from the Regions Beyond Missionary Union, made a trip to a new mission outpost in a deep gorge. They arrived on Saturday night in time to help two Dani preachers, Selanuok and Alikat, prepare for the Sunday service. Before retiring, Selanuok told them that enemies on the hillside intended to kill the Christians in the village. They prayed and committed the threat to the Lord.

The next morning three hundred villagers were chanting praise to God when Selanuok whispered to the missionaries, "The enemy warriors are coming today to kill me." They again prayed with him. A few minutes later Bozeman looked up and saw a long line of scowling warriors filing down the hillside. They carried spears and bows and arrows. Someone shouted the alarm. The Christians huddled together. "Keep singing! Keep singing!" the Dani preachers cried.

The attackers bounded into the clearing, leaping and shouting war cries. The worshipers scattered in all directions, looking for places to hide. Several men charged Selanuok. One threw a spear. "Jesus! Jesus!" the preacher cried and fell. He was the first Dani Christian martyr.

The missionaries reached the woods and sprinted up a trail. From the village they could hear the shrieks of the wounded and dying. Behind them they could hear men in pursuit. They reached the crest of a ridge and heard voices above. "This way," Bozeman shouted, as he led Martin down a side trail leading toward the river. By this stratagem they escaped.

## The High Cost of Serving

The cost continued high. On December 31, the MAF plane crashed in the Baliem Valley. Pilot Meno Voth, Mr. and Mrs. Gene Newman, and three of their four children were killed. The Newmans were also with MAF. The one survivor, ten-year-old Paul Newman, was only slightly injured. He wandered into a tribal village and was given shelter by some of the same Yali people who had earlier killed two missionaries: Stan Dale and Phil Masters.

By this time there were almost twenty thousand baptized believers in the interior jungles of western New Guinea. The Yali work prospered. Hundreds turned to Christ, including many of the murderers of the martyrs.

Tribal evangelists padded along the rugged trails, opening up new territory in New Guinea. Before leaving home they chanted a vow of commitment: "We are ready to be killed for You, to drown or be crushed in a landslide in Your service. You died for us. Your servant Paul went through great tribulations for You. We are ready to suffer for You." Eight were crushed to death by a landslide in the Wusak Valley in 1969. Their Christian friends responded: "Because our blood has been shed in the Wusak it has become our land, and we will continue to take the gospel there."

## Islamic Fundamentalists

One of the most terrifying examples of the work of militant Muslims is the thousands of Christians who were killed in the 1990s by Islamic fundamentalists on the Maluku Islands (the Moluccas) in Indonesia.

The terrorist Abu Sayyaf Islamic Group kidnapped seventy-five people from the Catholic Claret School in Tumahubong on March 20, 2000. Among those taken were children, teachers, school officials, and the Rev. Rohel Gallardo, the school's pastor and director. The thirty-five-year-old Catholic priest was murdered on May 3, 2000, along with four other hostages. Survivors of this ordeal recounted how Rohel Gallardo was beaten by his captors because he refused to wear Muslim clothes and pray Muslim prayers.

According to another priest, "These Muslims are fanatics who target Christian leaders because they think that without them it will be easier to install Islamic power." One of the demands made by the Abu Sayyaf terrorists was the removal of all crosses from churches.

Following the murder of Rohel Gallardo, the Procurator General of the Claret Missionaries, Santiago Gonzales, said, "We are not afraid. We are ready for martyrdom." In the same spirit, Bishop Romulo de la Cruz responded to the terrorists' demand by saying, "Not one cross shall be removed in any church in Basilan even if the Abu Sayyaf group were to capture the bishop. This is non-negotiable—we are willing to suffer and die for the cross."

On June 1, 2000, on Halmahera Island, "A number of militias came down from the nearby hills and attacked the coastal peoples, shooting at anyone they saw," reported a survivor of one of the terrible massacres in the tormented Indonesia archipelago of the Moluccas. The attack was carried out by Muslim groups against the Christian communities of two localities on Halmahera Island.

"Men, women, and children, were killed in a systematic way. This resulted in fifty dead and over one hundred wounded," explained a representative of the Tobello Evangelical Church.

## East Java

East Java is hailed as Indonesia's "tropical paradise" by the tourist brochures. But between 1997 and 1999, 473 churches were burned down and fourteen Christians died as martyrs.

On October 10, 1996, in Situbondo, East Java, Muslim rioters burned twenty-five churches, two Christian schools, and an orphanage in seven cities. Pastor Ishak and his family were burned to death.

## East Timor

Since 1975, one fourth of the eight hundred thousand people of East Timor, according to Amnesty International, has been exterminated by the Indonesian troops.

The exact number of people who died in the post-election violence in 1999 in East Timor will never be known. The massacres rank among the most horrific killings in the country's history. East Timor descended into violence and anarchy in the weeks following an August 30, 1999, UN-sponsored referendum in which the people voted for independence. Most of East Timor's infrastructure was destroyed by paramilitaries and retreating Indonesian troops.

Among those killed were the pastor, Father Hilario Madeira, and two assistants, Father Francisco Soares and Jesuit Father Tarcisius Dewanto. Father Amaral's sister was killed at Suai. At a memorial service Bishop Belo spoke about the murdered priests: "There are no special qualifications for being a priest. These were ordinary men who served the people and chose to die among them."

By March 1999, some one thousand refugees had already fled to the church compound in Suai. By the August referendum, more than four thousand people were there.

After an April attack at a Catholic church in Liquisa, many priests persuaded people to flee to the mountains because the churches, the traditional places of sanctuary for the Timorese, could no longer offer protection.

Saturnino Amaral, a fifty-year-old catechist, explained the situation in this way: "I fled to the Suai church prior to last year's U.N.–sponsored referendum. I remained there until September 3, when I was chased away by Father Madeira. The priest was carrying a stick and hitting us. He said 'Leave, leave. Go away. You don't belong here.'"

Amaral fled to the mountains, but many others stayed behind. He said Father Madeira was angry. "We thought he had lost his mind. Later we understood he was trying to save our lives. Many people are alive today" because of Father Madeira, Amaral said.

Amaral went on to say that Father Madeira told the people if they did not flee to the mountains "me and all of you will be killed by the militias."

Father Madeira "was not afraid to die because he used to tell us that one day we will live again," Amaral said.

## The Miracle in Indonesia

Western New Guinea came under Indonesia's jurisdiction in May 1963. At this time the Indonesian Communist Party, a million-and-a-half strong and with firm backing from Red China, was laying plans to take over the populous new country. Early in the morning of October 1, 1965, the Communists struck. The scheme was to murder eight top army generals under the pretense of catching them in the act of staging their own coup. The

Communists would then begin a mass annihilation of their enemies all over Indonesia, including Christians.

Miraculously, two of the generals escaped. When the plot was exposed, anti-Communist rioting swept the country. In the ensuing bloodbath, Muslims killed upwards of four hundred thousand Communists. One of the generals emerged as the power in a hardline anti-Communist regime. The new government required every citizen to accept the principle that the nation was built on the foundation of belief in a "Divinity." Evidence of acceptance was adherence to a recognized religion.

There followed a mass turning to Christianity, unprecedented in modern times, marked by hundreds of acclaimed miracles. Within two years the Indonesian Bible Society counted four hundred thousand new believers. In 1974 the largest evangelical group on the Indonesian island of Timor claimed 650,000 members.

Because of the dramatic turn, there have been only minor localized hostilities against Christians in the Indonesian islands since 1965. In one instance a Chinese missionary, Miss Lo, was presumably murdered by ax-wielding bandits in western Borneo.

## The Challenge Ahead

Excluding islands belonging to other nations, Indonesia, the world's largest archipelago, today includes 17,508 islands stretching over three thousand miles from the Indian Ocean to the South Pacific. Indonesia in population is now the fifth largest nation in the world, with over 207 million people. It is classified 90 percent Islamic, but Indonesian Muslims have proven to be more open to the gospel than Muslims in the Middle East and North Africa. Over two thousand tribal groups inhabit Indonesia. Many of these are without a New Testament.

Many heroes of the faith of past generations gave their lives to establish the first beachheads for the gospel in this paradise of islands. They are among the "cloud of witnesses" now cheering believers on.

# 14

## Malaysia and Singapore

### *"Right to Profess, Practice, Propagate"*

Malaysia, a former British possession, is situated on two land masses—the finger-like peninsula south of Thailand and the northern coast of Borneo. A constitutional Islamic monarchy governs twenty-two million Malays, Chinese, Indians, and Pakistanis. The constitution guarantees every person "the right to profess, practice, and propagate his religion." But evangelization of aborigines and persons under eighteen is strictly forbidden. Christian missionaries are also barred from certain "New Villages" which are totally or majority Muslim.

No missionary martyrs have been reported in modern times, but government pressure continues strong. Around 180 missionaries are now registered. A few others have recently been expelled or been refused the renewal of work permits. One of the latter tells of officials coming to his school almost every week and threatening to "take all of us to jail if we continued. Nothing happened but the constant harassment made our lives miserable." This former missionary "knows of" Malaysian Christians who have been imprisoned and not heard from for months or years. One, he says, was recently released after converting to Islam.

### An Oasis in Singapore

The 224-square-mile island of Singapore, population 3.3 million, was federated with Malaysia until 1963. The evangelical minority of Singapore enjoys complete religious

143

freedom for worship, education, and evangelism. Because of its openness, neutrality, and strategic location, Singapore has become a training center for Christian nationals from other Asian countries.

Missionaries and national leaders wish that all Pacific countries were as open as Singapore.

# 15

## Taiwan

### *The Republic of China*

The large cucumber-shaped island off the coast of mainland China was lost by China to Japan in 1895 and not regained until the end of World War II. When mainland China fell under Communist control, two million Chinese followed Chiang Kai-shek's government to the island. Today it is officially known as The Republic of China, but more often is called Taiwan or Formosa. Besides Chinese, there are three other distinct groups in the island country: (1) Nine mountain tribes comprising about two hundred thousand people; (2) Hakkas, who migrated generations before from the mainland, and numbering about eight hundred thousand; (3) Taiwanese, numbering over six million and making up the majority.

Before 1950 the Presbyterians were the only Christian denomination in Taiwan. Because of Japanese opposition, no missionaries worked among the mountain tribes before World War II. The Japanese were sorely afraid of these "wild" headhunters and built a 360-mile fence around the tribal territory. The few Japanese settlements in the mountains remained under constant alert. In one attack 134 Japanese heads were taken.

The mountain people were officially off limits to all but Shinto missionaries. However, a few Japanese Christian workers were given tacit permission to work around the fringes. The pioneer was Inoue Inouke, a young Japanese believer whose father had been killed by the headhunters. Inoue was allowed to do only medical and educational work near the fence. On March 10, 1912, he wrote in his diary:

Mr. Ito had been brought to me badly wounded by savages' attack. I quickly did my best to keep him alive, and I think he is hopeful. I heard that there were eight other Japanese killed this morning.

I sincerely hope and pray that one day these people will hold the Bible and the hymnbook in their hands, instead of these swords to kill people.

## "You Will Not Obey Orders"

During World War II the Japanese troops publicly announced they would massacre all Christians on the island if American troops landed. A minority of church members asked that their names be stricken from the rolls to avoid being placed on an official death list. The rest stood firm. Fortunately there were no landings and a bloodbath was avoided.

The worst persecution during war time was heaped upon a small minority of tribal Christians. Some were arrested, beaten, and imprisoned as spies.

Wiran Takko, an ex-drunkard who had become a preacher, was conducting a midnight clandestine meeting in the mountains when the police suddenly appeared. He and his listeners were beaten severely for believing in the "American God." Once released, Takko went back into the mountains.

At another meeting he predicted that Japan would lose the war to the United States which would then liberate the tribespeople. Again he was arrested and beaten, this time so savagely that he was thrown out for dead. A tribal Christian carried him home and cared for him until he regained consciousness. The third time he was kept in a wooden cage for a year. Once released, he went right back to preaching. The sergeant who arrested him declared, "You will not obey orders, so we will have to kill you." While a grave was being dug, the sergeant asked, "Are you ready to die?" Takko replied, "Yes, yes, I'm ready." The sergeant was so shaken that he released him again.

Takko survived, but another Christian hero named Saka Tani did not. Police broke all of his ribs and every bone in his hands and feet. Upon regaining consciousness, he was beaten again, so severely that he died. Pastor Wu Tien-shih asked his widow if she planned to avenge his death. "No, we should love our enemies," she said. "This is the order of the Lord."

The end of World War II brought liberation and rapid evangelization of the mountain tribes. Within fifteen years the Presbyterians had sixty thousand baptized believers in the hills.

## The Mad Cook

The only American missionary to die from violence in Taiwan was Miss Gladys Hopewell, a Southern Baptist who was found strangled in her apartment on March 11, 1973. A Kentuckian, she had previously served in China before the Communist takeover and later in Thailand. She came from Bangkok to pioneer Baptist student work on Taiwan and had been at the student center the afternoon before her death.

Ten days later the body of a Chinese cook was discovered on the roof of Miss Hopewell's apartment building. Beside him police found an empty insecticide bottle. The cook's wife had worked for Miss Hopewell and he had been sought as a prime suspect. The police decided that he had killed the missionary in a fit of madness and later in remorse committed suicide.

No Christian worker is known to have been killed in Taiwan since this incident. There are now almost six hundred missionaries on the island. Southern Baptists, with eighty-four workers, are the largest mission. Many of the missionaries, like Miss Hopewell, previously served in mainland China.

## The Call of the Martyred Pioneers

The Taiwan Protestant community of around 175,000, including the mountain tribal believers, continues relatively small. The challenge of evangelizing the mostly Buddhist Taiwanese majority remains as a symbol of the larger job to be done in all the isles of the Pacific where so many have given their lives to pioneer the gospel.

# 16

## The Philippines

### *Open Door for Missions*

The vast Philippine archipelago of 7,107 islands (only 10 percent inhabited) forms a triangle reaching from Indonesian Borneo in the south to Taiwan in the north. With seventy-seven million people, the Philippines is the only nominally Christian nation in Asia. This is because it was a Spanish possession for some three hundred years until ceded in 1898 to the United States as part of the settlement of the Spanish-American War. In 1946 the nation became independent, but American influence has remained strong. This has produced an open door for missions. Today eighty-nine independent and denominational agencies are represented by about twelve hundred workers. Wycliffe Bible Translators is the largest with about 150 linguists and support personnel.

In culture, however, Filipino people are akin to other Pacific groups. There are three main families: the aboriginal mountain Negritos (about thirty thousand), the Indonesians, and the Malayans who are regarded as ancestors of the majority of the Filipino people.

The first Protestants had to meet underground. One of their early converts, a Catholic Dominican friar, was put on trial, defrocked, and exiled to Spain. After the Philippines became an American possession, Catholic persecution virtually ended. However, many missionaries succumbed to the diseases of the tropics, including the first C&MA worker, who died of cholera in 1902.

The Philippines was hit hard by Japanese occupation and Allied bombing in World War II. The death toll ran high. About 80 percent of all church properties were destroyed.

## The Mystery of Rufus Gray

Rufus Gray was among a group of Southern Baptist missionaries from China interned in the Philippines. He and his wife had been attending language school when the Japanese overran Peking.

Soon after arriving in the Philippines Gray was taken in for questioning. His wife and friends never saw him again, nor was his body ever recovered.

His hobby was photography and he had taken hundreds of pictures in Peking. The Japanese may have assumed that he was a spy.

## A Family Is Strafed to Death

Thousands of foreign civilians were imprisoned in the Philippines. The actual treatment of missionaries varied from one command to another. Some were permitted to hold services in the camps. Some were closely confined. Some in large cities who pledged cooperation with Japanese were allowed to live in their own houses and carry on a limited ministry.

As in the Dutch East Indies, the Japanese demanded that missionaries located in remote places come out and surrender. An American sergeant saw a family of five walking down from the mountains waving a white flag. A Japanese Zero spotted them and opened fire, killing the whole family. The sergeant helped bury them. He recalled that one of the little girls was still clutching a rag doll.

## The Hopedale Massacre

American (Northern) Baptists suffered the greatest loss of missionaries in the Philippines during the war. Eight of their nineteen workers surrendered and were imprisoned for the duration. Twelve, including the ten-year-old son of two of the missionaries, fled into the mountains on the island of Panay and tried to carry on a ministry among rural villagers.

The twelve set up camp in a mountain-top clearing called Hopedale. The sanctuary was in deep, thick woods and was reachable only by a narrow, winding trail. Here they were joined by eight or ten other Americans—businessmen and engineers—who had been caught in the area after Pearl Harbor.

"We live in a grass hut with bamboo floor," James Covell wrote. "The people around supply us with plenty to eat, and we have a good spring . . . The Japanese came very close one day in February (1942) and we have moved out thrice to hide. . . . Our prospects for freedom and seeing you (relatives) are most uncertain. . . ."

They worshiped in a chapel in "a beautiful, deep, dry gorge with giant trees growing in it." Every Sunday, except when the Japanese came near, they had a congregation of around one hundred—mostly other Americans who were hiding out in the region. The missionaries took turns conducting the services and baptizing those who made professions of faith in Christ. When the missionaries felt it was safe, they made evangelistic visits to nearby villages. One of the twelve, Dr. Frederick W. Meyer, was a surgeon, and he continued to carry on a ministry of healing. "Bed patients are scattered all over the jungle," he wrote. "Plenty of long hikes keep me thin but happy."

Dr. and Mrs. Meyer, from Connecticut and Wisconsin respectively, were serving their fourth term. Dr. Meyer, a graduate of Yale Medical School, had been honored by the highest officials in the Philippines for his devotion to the poor. Both he and Mrs. Meyer were talented musically. Mrs. Meyer had taught music at Central Baptist Philippine College. Dr. Meyer had developed choirs at stations where he had clinics.

James Covell, a graduate of the University of Chicago, was from Pennsylvania and his wife, Charma, was from Ohio. Educators, they previously served in a poor section of Yokohama, Japan, and had been forced to leave in 1939 by the Shinto warlords.

Dr. Francis Howard Rose was also a Chicago alumnus and his wife, Gertrude, held a master's degree from Columbia University. They had taught at Central Philippine College. Dr. Rose wrote, "My religion means only so much as what I am. And by so much, that is, by my way of life alone, may I teach religion which really counts—or I will not teach it at all."

Erle and Louise Rounds, the fourth couple, were graduates of Berkeley Baptist Divinity School. They were traveling evangelists to the mountain tribespeople. Their older son was in high school in Manila at the beginning of the war and was interned at the Santo Tomas Camp with other missionary personnel. Their younger son, Erle Douglas, was with them on the mountaintop.

Erle Rounds had written in one of his last letters before Pearl Harbor:

> We are living in interesting times over here, and I believe the missionaries are going to see real persecution before the thing is over. . . . But it is one of the greatest privileges I can think of to be here as a missionary. . . . We hope to see you all again, but, if we should be denied that blessed joy, we can meet again in the land which is fairer than day. May we strive harder to be worthy of the world which God has given us and of that other land made possible through our Lord Jesus Christ. . . . May God keep a clean wind blowing through my heart.

Jennie Adams, from Nebraska, had served for twenty years as superintendent of nurses at Emmanuel Hospital where Dr. Meyer was on the medical staff. She had led many of her nurses to Christ and considered her Bible class the most important course in nurses' training.

The tenth missionary was Signe Erickson from Pennsylvania, a graduate of Moody Bible Institute and Columbia University. A teacher, she had worked in the Missionary Training School. On weekends she visited isolated mountain villages and slept on the floors of crude huts.

Dorothy Dowell, from Colorado, had been principal of the Baptist Missionary Training School. She was adept at getting letters to missionary friends in the Santo Tomas Internment Camp where the Rounds' son and the Meyers' son were being held. She used code words and signed herself "Dad." The boys knew this stood for the initials of her name. In 1942 she left the mountain to visit Christians in distant villages. She returned just before Christmas, 1943. She had terrible arthritis and had to crawl on her hands and knees the last part of the journey.

Erle Rounds had also been away visiting Filipino churches. He wanted to spend Christmas with his wife and son, and arrived back at the clearing about the same time.

Several months before, Japanese troops in the area had learned where the missionaries were and had decided not to molest them. A fresh Japanese detachment was not so compassionate. They surprised the American Baptists late in December 1943 and lined them and five other Americans up for execution.

The Covells could speak Japanese fluently and pleaded eloquently that they be imprisoned instead. The soldiers were reportedly touched, but said they had to carry out orders from their superiors. The missionaries asked for time to pray and were given an hour. Then they were all shot.

## Tribal Christians Are Poisoned

Excluding the missionaries who died in Japanese prison camps, there have been few martyrs in the Philippines in modern times. In 1965 the spiritual leader and two other members of the Cotabato Manobo tribal church were poisoned after the local witch doctor had predicted that all Christians in the tribe would die. The tiny tribal church kept growing and three years later forty-two new believers were baptized.

## The Risk Takers

Political unrest continues in some areas of the Philippines, particularly on the island of Mindanao. In one incident rebels killed ten students at a Catholic school which had recently been used as a headquarters for government action against the dissidents. In another instance two female Wycliffe translators were kidnapped and held by rebels for several days, then released without harm. Some Protestant and Catholic church leaders blame the government for waging a war of repression against social action groups. They point to several pastors who have mysteriously disappeared.

What is certain is that many evangelical missionaries and Filipino Christian workers are serving at considerable personal risk.

The greatest danger to Christian workers in recent years has come from Communists and fanatical Muslims. During the 1980s more than 150 Filipino church leaders were killed in the conflict between Communist guerrillas and government army troops. In 1990 the Bible League office and affiliate ministries in Manila were shut down after the murder of several pastors and the receiving of death threats from the Communist New People's Army (NPA). One of the League's new converts was murdered and a League worker's home was ransacked.

Communist leaders, said Bible League vice president of ministries David Stravers, "know that when Filipinos convert to Christ they no longer listen to NPA propaganda. So the NPA has been a strong opponent of the evangelistic ministries of churches in the Philippines."

On August 10, 1991, Operation Mobilization's missionary ship, *Doulos,* visited the Philippines. Karen Goldsworthy of New Zealand and Maaza Sofia Siegfridsson of Sweden, both nineteen, joined with other members of the ship's crew in giving an open-air Christian performance in the town of Zamboanga. Suddenly a grenade was thrown. The two young women were killed. Some blamed Islamic extremists for the attack as a response to a negative remark made by one of the ship's crew about Muhammad.

Opposition from Muslim extremists and Communist rebels continues. Since the 1983 assassination of opposition leader Benigno S. Aquino Jr., the country has been in political turmoil. Aquino's widow, Corazon, ran against the dictator Ferdinand Marcos in a bitterly contested campaign in 1984. After allegations that Marcos had won by fraud, Aquino declared herself the legally elected president. Marcos fled the country and Aquino was recognized by the United States and other nations.

Communist terrorism remains a serious threat. Political instability has become a way of life. Many foreign missionaries and foreign workers serve in dangerous spots. Yet there has been no call for withdrawal. The gospel continues to be proclaimed throughout the beautiful islands known as the Philippines.

In April 2000, in the southern Philippines, the terrorist group of Abu Sayyaf kidnapped twenty-nine Catholics from two schools in the province of Basilan. They demanded, among other things, that all crosses should be banished from the island of Mindanao, where they plan to set up an Islamic state. In July 2000, some of these Islamic rebels kidnapped another twenty-one Christians in the province of Lanar del Sur, subsequently slaughtering them inside a mosque.

The islands and peninsular land masses of the vast Asian expanse are not as mysterious or exotic as they seemed at the beginning of this century. The gospel has been advanced at the cost of hundreds of martyrs' lives to tropical diseases, aboriginal violence, and wars. Hundreds of thousands of believers from tribes which once practiced cannibalism and other barbarities now ". . . hail the power of Jesus' name" and live in peace.

And yet the high mission of Zion is far from complete. It will not be until every human ear in the Pacific shall hear the good news that "God so loved the world, that he gave his only begotten Son" for them. The completion of this task will not be easy or without sacrifice. There will doubtless be many more names added to the Pacific "book of martyrs."

# PART SIX

# Martyrs of Nazi Germany and Occupied Europe

# 17

# Nazi Germany
# and Occupied Europe

## *In the Land of the Reformation*

In the year 1927 a young Dutch theological student, Willem ten Boom, wrote in his thesis at a German university that a terrible evil was taking place in the land of Martin Luther. German theologians were tearing the Bible apart, he said, reducing it to a collection of myths and debunking the supernatural by the new method called "higher criticism." German philosophers were talking of breeding a glorious new Aryan super race which would not be contaminated by Jews or weaklings.

## Harvest of Hatred

Eighteen years later the world would see the results of this modern paganism called Nazism and recoil in horror. Millions of Jews, old people, citizens of conquered nations, Allied and Axis soldiers, and brave German resisters would be dead. Many among the latter would be German pastors and lay leaders who, having failed to convince their fellow countrymen and the world of the dangers of Nazism, had joined the internal resistance in a futile attempt to topple a government gone mad.

## Destined for Martyrdom

Above them all one name would stand out, Dietrich Bonhoeffer, of whom a prison medic would say, "In the almost fifty years that I worked as a doctor, I have hardly ever seen a man die so entirely submissive to the will of God."

As we follow Bonhoeffer along his road to martyrdom, we shall see how the monstrous Nazi evil grew and how other brave Christians came to walk the path leading to imprisonment and death.

Bonhoeffer, a handsome blonde youth, was thoroughly German, from heel-clicking to a stiffly bowing handshake. He came from one of Germany's best families; his father was a distinguished psychiatrist. Although his family were only nominal Lutherans, he had a passion for finding the meaning of life. In the humiliating years following World War I, Germany was two-thirds Lutheran and one-third Catholic. Baptists and other free-church Christians comprised only a minute fraction of the population.

Born in 1906, Bonhoeffer was only thirteen when German workers and troops revolted against continuing the First World War. The revolution hastened the end of the war and led to Germany becoming a democratic republic. But then the democracy fell prey to postwar inflation, economic depression, and political chaos. When Adolf Hitler's National Socialist Party came to power on a law-and-order and prosperity platform, Hitler quickly tossed out the constitution and created a dictatorship.

## How Hitler Managed the Clergy

Although Hitler used religious language, he was a closet atheist. He wanted to keep in the good graces of the Catholic and Lutheran hierarchies. His deception was astonishingly successful. In 1933, the year his Nazi party rode roughshod over all parliamentary opposition, the German Lutheran bishops proclaimed: "We German Protestant Christians accept the saving of our nation by our leader Adolf Hitler as a gift from God's hand." They affirmed "unanimously our unlimited fealty to the Third Reich and its leader." In this same year Hitler signed a concordat with the Vatican guaranteeing religious freedom for German Catholics.

The question frequently has been asked, how could German church leaders have been so blind? Among Catholics it was a matter of submission to authority, even though many clergy were frightened by the specter of Nazism. Among Lutherans it was an erosion of spiritual authority, the result of years of debunking the Bible in church universities and seminaries, and of a corresponding lapse into dreary formalism and decadent institutionalism.

## Bonhoeffer, an Evangelical Prophet

Not all had bowed the knee to Baal. The brilliant young Bonhoeffer had, at age twenty-one, opposed some of his professors in his doctoral thesis. Bonhoeffer contended that the "essential nature" of the church could only be understood "on the basis of the gospel" and not by sociological reasoning.

Nor did Bonhoeffer agree that philosophy and theology were complementary disciplines. He held, with theologian Karl Barth, that man was irredeemably sinful and self-centered and could never discover truth through his own thought. Theology, Bonhoeffer said, is rooted and grounded in God who chooses when and how to reveal Himself to man. Bonhoeffer further said that personal revelation must be experienced in "direct recourse to Christ" through the Church, which is Christ in community.

Before Hitler's ascension to power, Bonhoeffer spent a year at Union Theological Seminary in New York. Union was then caught up in the cynicism and reaction of Protestant modernism which utilized the methodology of German higher criticism in the classroom. "Union students," the perceptive Bonhoeffer wrote, "intoxicate themselves with liberal and humanistic expressions, laugh at the fundamentalists, and basically they are not even a match for them. . . . I never heard the Gospel of Jesus Christ . . . of the cross, of sin and forgiveness, of death and life (while) in New York . . . , only an ethical and social idealism which pins its faith to progress."

At the same time a friend in Germany warned Bonhoeffer of a "great tragedy for our church and nation." The new nationalism of Hitler, his friend said, was "combined with a new heathenism that parades in Christian dress." The church was being made subservient to race, nation, and culture.

Bonhoeffer soon returned to Germany and confronted the liberals in his church head on. "The question," he argued, "is not whether we still have a use for God in advanced society. God and the Church exist. They are questioning us. Are we ready for God to use us?"

## The Theologian Becomes a Christian

Shortly after this, Bonhoeffer surrendered himself fully for God's use. He could now say, "I believe that the Bible alone is the answer to all our questions . . . that is because in the Bible God speaks to us." Bonhoeffer, as he reported, "had already preached often . . . and seen a great deal of the church . . . (but) had not yet become a Christian. . . . Then something new entered, something which . . . has changed my life and turned it upside down."

On January 31, 1933, the day after Hitler was named Chancellor of Germany, Bonhoeffer spoke over Berlin radio on "the concept of leadership." He posed these questions: Is the demand for a strong leader the expression of Germany's volatile political situation or is it to meet the requirements of youth? When is leadership healthy and genuine and when does it become pathological and extreme? He was cut off the air in mid-speech.

## The Purge Begins

Four weeks later Communist saboteurs burned the Reichstag (parliament building) as a gift to Hitler. The next morning the Fuehrer announced restrictions, "for the protection of nation and state," against free speech and free press, formation of societies, calling of public meetings, privacy of the mails, and other communication systems. He also proclaimed governmental right to search houses and to restrict personal property beyond previous limits.

On April 1 the government called for a boycott of Jewish shops. Bonhoeffer's ninety-year-old grandmother walked resolutely through the cordon of storm troopers and Nazi youth that stood in front of her favorite store which was operated by Jews, did her shopping, and walked out without being stopped.

The next order demanded a purge of all Jews and part Jews from German civil service. Another order forbade church appointments of ministers with Jewish blood.

The "Aryan restrictions" hit Bonhoeffer like a thunderbolt. His twin sister, Sabine, was married to a Jew, and one of his closest Lutheran pastor friends, Franz Hildebrandt, was Jewish.

## The Lutheran Church Split

Hitler further moved to control the Lutheran church by appointing Ludwig Muller, a clergyman loyal to the government, as his deputy for ecclesiastical affairs. Muller tried to interfere with a committee writing a new constitution for German Lutherans. The committee all but ignored him. Bonhoeffer and a group of reformers calling themselves the "Confessing Church," who refused to exclude non-Aryans, pushed through the election of one of their own as the new national bishop. The government and its loyal clergymen, known as "German Christians," refused to recognize the new constitution and national bishop. The church split.

"We deplore," declared Bonhoeffer, "that state measures against Jews in Germany have had such an effect on public opinion that in some circles the Jewish race is considered a race of inferior status. . . . We protest against the resolution of . . . synods which apply the Aryan paragraph of the state to the church, putting serious disabilities on ministers and church officers who by chance of birth are non-Aryan, which we believe to be a denial of the explicit teaching and spirit of the Gospel of Jesus Christ."

On July 23, three days after Hitler signed the concordat with the Vatican, a national referendum was held in the Lutheran churches. The vast majority voted in favor of the "German Christians" as their official leaders.

The reformers refused to accept this and formed their own Free Synod. They met the next year at Barmen and declared that they represented the true Protestant church of Germany as envisaged by Luther. They subscribed to a confession of faith drawn up by Karl Barth. They proclaimed that "Jesus Christ, as He is testified to us in Holy Scripture, is the one Word of God which we have to hear and to trust and obey in life and death."

Hitler made no immediate move to suppress the rebel minority. He was too busy consolidating his political rule, tightening the screws on other dissenters, and whipping up the youth for a war. And all the while, the majority of German Lutheran pastors were praising him for maintaining law and order and bringing the nation closer together.

Bonhoeffer, representing the Confessing Church, went abroad to alert other Lutherans to the perils of Nazism. "There is no way to peace along the way of safety," he told the Lutheran World Alliance, "for peace must be dared . . . ; battles are not won with weapons, but God. They are won where the way leads to the cross."

## The First Arrests

In the fall of 1934 the first arrests were made of Confessing Church leaders. On October 6 Bishop Theophil Wurm of Wurttemburg was placed under house arrest. A week later Bishop Meiser of Bavaria was confined to his home by armed guard. Their colleagues responded by calling a second Free Synod, which rejected the official German Church and set up an independent government for the Confessing Church under a National Council of Brothers. They asked congregations "not to accept any directions from the existing German church government or its agencies and to withhold cooperation from those who continue to give obedience to this ecclesiastical regime." They urged acknowledgment of "the rule of the Confessing Church and its institutions." Scores of Lutheran congregations became affiliated with the new church. The Nazi government, fearing a rebellion, withdrew the guards around the homes of the two bishops.

Bonhoeffer was appointed to set up and direct one of several new theological schools for the Confessing Church. In the fall of 1935 he began classes in a commodious old country house outside the small village of Finkenwald. The first students refurbished the house themselves and Bonhoeffer provided his personal library for their use. Bonhoeffer maintained a stiff, almost monastic regimen. Each day began and ended with a half-hour of common prayer, with arduous Bible study and theological disciplines in between. Bonhoeffer was a hard but warm taskmaster. He would not tolerate spiritual mediocrity or sloppy study habits, and constantly reminded the students that they were bonded together in love and commitment for "outgoing service."

## "We Have to Fight for the True Church . . ."

Bonhoeffer now took a harder line against the German church. He refused an invitation to participate in an ecumenical meeting because representatives of the official church would be there. "We have to fight for the true church against the false church of antichrist," he explained. "Fighting in this faith we derive no small power from considering the fact that we are fighting for Christianity not only with regard to the church in Germany but in the whole world. . . . All churches," he warned, "may be attacked by the very same power one day or another."

At the next Free Synod he detected that the Confessing Church was softening. He protested that the real issues had been ignored. Not one speaker had defended the church's freedom to teach biblical truth; no protest had been made against a requirement that German citizens take an oath of loyalty to Hitler; and nothing had been said about increased discrimination against the Jews. Forty-eight churchmen, including Pastor Martin Niemoller, joined Bonhoeffer in signing a circular calling upon pastors to stand firm and "submit to the sole rule of our Lord Jesus Christ." The Nazi government, however, was encouraged by the "cooperative spirit" at the Synod and began assiduously courting moderates in the Confessing Church. The new minister of church affairs was successful in soliciting representatives of both the Confessing and the older church to participate in a national committee. Bonhoeffer was incensed. "Between church and pseudo-church there can be no cooperation," he thundered.

The dispute hurt the Confessing Church. Among those departing was one of Bonhoeffer's top students. Undeterred, Bonhoeffer encouraged his former students, who were now pastors, not to compromise. "If we persevere in prayer," he advised in a monthly circular, "then we can have confidence that the Holy Spirit will give us the right words at the time when we need them, and we shall be found faithful."

The government took advantage of the confusion to pass a "Fifth Emergency Decree." Unauthorized church groups were forbidden to appoint and ordain clergy, announce policy, spend money taken in collections, call synods, and train theologians. Bonhoeffer's school and the other new seminaries were now illegal. At Finkenwald Bonhoeffer assembled his students and suggested that any who wished to, could leave. None did.

The young pastors who looked to Bonhoeffer as their spiritual guide stood firm. In 1936 one was arrested, Johannes Pecina, the minister at Seelow. The seminary immediately sent a replacement. When he was arrested, a Finkenwald student was sent.

## Other Brave Christians Speak Out

Early in the summer of 1936 the Prussian Council of Lutheran Churches issued a memorandum to Hitler. The paper, handed in at the chancellery, criticized the oppressive law against the Confessing Church and the discrimination against Jewish Christians. The government tried to suppress the charge but copies were circulated and read aloud by 80 percent of the pastors in the Confessing Church. Also published in European newspapers, it aroused criticism of Hitler abroad.

Hitler and his Nazi henchmen were incensed over the leak. The Gestapo began an immediate investigation. Werner Koch, a student at Finkenwald, and Ernst Tillich, nephew of theologian Paul Tillich, were arrested along with Friedrich Weisler, an employee of the Prussian Council of Lutheran Churches. Koch and Tillich were interned in a concentration camp. Weisler, because he was Jewish, was tortured and beaten to death.

From this time until 1945 there was never a time when some of Bonhoeffer's present or former students were not in prison. The seminary body lived in danger every minute. "We accept every day as a gift from God," said Bonhoeffer.

Dietrich Bonhoeffer himself went to England and then to New York where he was offered the position of pastor to German Christian refugees. "The only thing that makes me hesitate . . . is the question of loyalty to my people at home," he wrote a friend.

## Bonhoeffer Returns to Face the Storm

Bonhoeffer's American friends kept urging him to remain in New York. But the young theologian's face was set. In July 1939, having boarded ship, he wrote, "I . . . made a mistake in coming to America. I must live through this difficult period of our national history with the Christian people of Germany. I will have no right to participate in the reconstruction of Christian life in Germany after the war if I do not share the trials of this time with my people."

With a small group of students, remnants from his illegal seminary, Bonhoeffer secluded himself in a rough-hewn hunting lodge deep in the Pomeranian forest. He was there when the first stories of German brutalities and genocide in Poland began seeping back to the German civilian population.

## The Christians' Dilemma

Bonhoeffer and his Christian brothers faced an agonizing decision: Should they join the cloak-and-dagger, kill-and-be-killed resistance to Hitler that was desperately trying to topple their own government and end the war, or should they continue much as before, secretly teaching and witnessing and encouraging Christian living? They concluded that they should do all they could to hasten the downfall of Hitler. It was better to "consent to the bad," Bonhoeffer said, "knowing full well that it is bad, in order to ward off what is worse. . . ." From this time on Bonhoeffer and his friends were active among the conspirators working for the defeat of Hitler.

## Arrested without a Warrant

Bonhoeffer continued to be watched. On April 5, 1943, the chief investigator for the air force and a Gestapo official confronted the young theologian at a friend's house. They said simply, "Come with us," and took Bonhoeffer away in a black Mercedes. Without a trial or an explanation, he was thrown into Tegel Military Prison.

He put his inmost thoughts in writing, confessing to struggles, weariness, and doubts. But he could say, "I believe that we ought so to love and trust God in our lives, and in all the good things that He sends us, that when the time comes we may go to Him with love, trust, and joy." And, "Through every event, however untoward, there is access to God."

Bonhoeffer was moved to the cellar of the Gestapo prison in Berlin's Prinz Albrecht Strasse. His family and fiancée, Maria, were forbidden to see him, and he was seldom permitted to write. His brother Klaus and two of his brothers-in-law, Rudiger Schleicher and Hans Adam von Dohnanyi, both lawyers, were now also in prison. All three would summarily be executed.

## The Death of a Martyr

On February 7, 1945, twenty of the most important prisoners in Prinz Albrecht Strasse were loaded into trucks. Bonhoeffer's vehicle went to the dread Buchenwald. By Easter Sunday, 1945, the prisoners could hear American guns. Their waiting, for life or death, would not be long now.

One morning they were herded into a van and driven towards the southeast. Unknown to Bonhoeffer, a Nazi official was following behind with an order for his execution.

The next Sunday, April 8, they stopped at a schoolhouse. At the prisoners' request, Bonhoeffer held a brief worship service. He chose as his texts Isaiah 53:5: "By His stripes we are healed," and 1 Peter 1:3: "Blessed be the God and Father of our Lord Jesus Christ, which according to his abundant mercy hath begotten us again unto a lively hope by the resurrection of Jesus Christ from the dead."

The service ended when a harsh voice called, "Prisoner Bonhoeffer, come with us." Bonhoeffer was taken to Flossenberg Prison. That evening he and several other prisoners were formally condemned.

Years later the prison doctor wrote, "Through the half-open door of a room in one of the huts I saw Pastor Bonhoeffer still in his prison clothes, kneeling in fervent prayer to the Lord his God. The devotion and evident conviction of being heard that I saw in the prayer of this intensely captivating man moved me to the depths."

About 5:00 a.m., an escort came for an admiral and two generals who were among those charged with trying to overthrow the government. They were taken from their cells and told of the verdict.

Bonhoeffer was soon removed to join the other condemned men. They were marched to the place of execution and told to strip. One last time Bonhoeffer knelt to pray. Then he stood up. Shots pierced the stillness of the woods. The most famous Christian martyr of World War II was dead.

Three weeks later Hitler and Eva Braun, the mistress he had just married, swallowed poison. Hitler's aides burned their bodies after dousing them with gasoline. Seven days after this Germany surrendered.

It was June before Maria learned that Bonhoeffer was dead. On July 27 his aged parents accidentally heard the sad news. They happened to tune in to a memorial service from London and heard a German saying in English, "We are gathered here in the presence of God to make thankful remembrance of the life and work of his servant Dietrich Bonhoeffer, who gave his life in faith and obedience. . . ."

Many Christians in the occupied countries had died protecting Jews and for opposing other Nazi occupation policies. The toll was especially high in Eastern Europe. Large numbers also gave their lives in France, Belgium, Holland, Norway, Finland, and elsewhere.

## The Martyrs Have Not Been Forgotten

Dietrich Bonhoeffer has been revered by every class of seminary students since his martyrdom was made known. Today, a half-century after the war's end, no other modern martyr arouses more respect and reverence among young theologues than this intellectual and spiritual giant who died rather than compromise his convictions. Other German pastors and priests who died, along with those who survived Hitler's concentration camps, are less known, but in the German Lutheran and Catholic churches, their bravery will not soon be forgotten.

## A Farmer Who Died for His Convictions

Both in Germany and across occupied Europe, many more Christians gave their lives in standing for convictions. Austria, where Hitler was born, became the first neighboring nation to be conquered, falling to the Nazis in March 1938. Among the Austrian Christians who fled to America were the Von Trapp Family Singers, who would later become famous in the award-winning movie *The Sound of Music*.

Franz Jaegerstatter, a thirty-seven-year-old Austrian farmer, deserves special attention. Friends, relatives, and some church authorities told him he was foolish for refusing to take the military oath under Hitler. Jaegerstatter was imprisoned in Berlin's Brandenburg prison where he was later beheaded.

## Brave Father Titus

Hollander Titus Brandsma, a sickly child, fell in love with the Bible and devotional books during his youth. After ordination as a priest, he earned his doctorate in philosophy from the Pontifical Gregorian University and established the Catholic University of Jijegen in the Netherlands. He was then appointed as spiritual adviser to the lay staff members of more than thirty Catholic newspapers throughout the country.

After the Nazi army overran the Netherlands in 1940, German officials ordered all clergy removed as principals or directors of Catholic schools. Fr. Titus fought the oppressors through Catholic newspapers and in classrooms and lecture halls. "The Nazi movement," he declared, "is a black lie. It is pagan."

Fr. Titus's proclamations brought a quick response from Hitler's allies in the Dutch Socialist Party. They considered anyone a traitor who objected to the Nazi occupation, and ordered the priest to toe the acceptable line.

"We cannot serve them," Fr. Titus told Catholic journalists. "It is our duty to refuse Nazi propaganda if we wish to maintain Catholic newspapers. . . . We are not sure if violence will strike, but if it does, always remember God speaks the last word and he rewards his faithful."

At 6 p.m. on January 19, 1942, the Gestapo came to arrest Fr. Titus at the Boxmeer monastery where he was living. "Imagine my going to jail at the age of sixty," he quipped to his arresting officer.

The security men stripped him of his Carmelite dress and whisked him off to the Arnhem prison. The next morning he was taken to the state prison at Scheveningen, where he underwent seven weeks of intensive questioning. Throughout the interrogation, he maintained that he had no other alternative than to be obedient to God. He could not be a party to spreading the evil of Nazism.

Unable to break his spirit, his captors placed him in a barren ten by six feet cell. After almost two months of solitary confinement he was moved to Amersfoort prison where he and other Catholic intellectuals formed what came to be called the "Tiburg Circle" of prayer and ministry.

Nazi authorities offered him release from prison if he would sign papers stating that he would no longer preach or resist the occupation forces. If he did not sign, they said, he would be transferred to the dread Dachau concentration camp. He refused.

Fr. Titus was placed in Dachau on June 12. His clothes were exchanged for a prison uniform. His head was shaved and he was told to answer to Number 30492. Any mention of God or religion was strictly forbidden.

A brave village priest risked his life to smuggle sacramental wafers to Fr. Titus and other Catholics in Dachau. A prison guard suspected that he was receiving the wafers and threw him to the ground. The sacred bread remained safely hidden in Fr. Titus's eyeglass case.

Fr. Titus never gave way to hatred for his captors. He prayed, "God bless Holland. God bless Germany. May God grant that both nations will soon be standing side by side in full peace and harmony."

After numerous beatings, Fr. Titus dragged himself to the prison infirmary where he collapsed on a cot. After four days he lost consciousness. Two days later, he was murdered with a lethal injection.

His testimony is found in a poem written shortly before his death:

> O blessed grief and hallowed pain,
> That lead to Thee, my Savior slain,
> To suffer now a joy will be;
> It brings me, Lord, so near to Thee.

## Maria Skobtsova

Mother Maria was a Russian Orthodox nun who fled to France to escape the Bolsheviks. At the outbreak of World War II Maria made no secret of her hatred of Hitler and all he stood for. It was no surprise, therefore, that the SS broke up her work during a visit to her home on February 8, 1947. Maria was arrested and after a stint in camps at Romainville and Compiègne, was finally sent to the notorious Ravensbrück concentration camp.

In Ravensbrück Maria still carried on caring for all those suffering around her, in answer to her own prayer which she prayed shortly after her arrest: "Lord, I am your messenger. Throw me like a blazing torch into the night."

Prisoner 19263, from Block 27, gave courage, hope, and encouragement to all around her, counseling her fellow prisoners who were suffering the most appalling human misery. She comforted them with the words, "Don't let your spirit's flame die." With her swelling feet, ankles, and legs, and becoming weaker and weaker, Maria became a mother to many of the women prisoners who went to her for a hug.

Somehow, one young girl had managed to smuggle in a prayer book and Maria read aloud the words of the Gospel and Epistle, adding her own short meditation afterwards.

More than one account of Maria's final days exists. One account of her death tells how she became so weak that she was unable to walk and so was callously condemned to death by the Nazis. Himmler had sent orders that all sick people should be killed, in a vain attempt to cover up the inhuman treatment and medical experimentations that had been carried on in these camps.

A second version of Maria's last days is very much in keeping with the tenor of her whole life. Maria exchanged places with a woman who was in a queue of condemned prisoners and went voluntarily to her martyrdom in order to help her companion to live.

What is certain is that Maria's name is on the list of those people who were gassed to death on March 31, 1945, Easter Eve. The next day, Easter Day, the Red Cross arrived at Ravensbrück camp, a day too late for Maria.

## Three Hundred German Catholic Martyrs in Nazi Germany

While much has been written about the supposed weak reaction, if not direct cooperation, of Catholics to the evils of Nazism, it cannot be contested that many German Catholics gave their lives because of their opposition to Hitler. Commenting on the book *German Catholic Martyrs of the 20th Century,* Cardinal Meisner has stated that "the Catholic Church does not have to be ashamed of its role during the course of this century."

During the twentieth century it has been claimed that there were seven hundred Catholic martyrs in Germany, hundreds of whom died under Stalinism. Bishop Moll maintains that there were more than three hundred Catholic martyrs under Nazism, of whom 123 were laymen and laywomen who went to their deaths for their faith, in opposition to the dictatorship. Bishop Moll believes that there was not a single diocese in Germany that did not contribute a martyr.

## Edith Stein

To support his assertion that "Our research revealed how a good part of the laity and clergy carried out an important and convincing battle against the Nazi ideology," Bishop Moll cites several examples of well-known martyrs, such as Edith Stein. Although she was born into a devout Jewish family, after her conversion to the Catholic faith, she became a Carmelite nun and took the name Theresa Benedicta of the Cross. This gifted philosopher had alerted Pope Pius XI to the dangers of Hitler's ideology in a letter she sent to him.

As the Nazi oppression worsened, she moved to the Netherlands for safety. However, on August 2, 1942, she was arrested by the Gestapo at the Carmelite convent in Echt. She and her older sister, Rosa, who had also become a nun, were given minutes to pack. "Come, we are going for our people," she said. They were deported to Poland and arrived at Auschwitz on August 7. Two days later, they were both killed in a gas chamber.

## Bernhard Lichtenberg

Canon Bernhard Lichtenberg, provost of Berlin Cathedral, was an outspoken critic of the Nazis and their anti-Semitism. He organized protests outside the concentration camps, led public prayers for the Jews after the terrors of Krystallnacht, and filed formal complaints against the racist policies of the party. It is hardly surprising that he was therefore arrested and imprisoned for two years. Upon his release he immediately resumed his ministry, both pastoral and social. He was arrested again, sentenced to the Dachau concentration camp, despite his failing health, and died en route in a cattle truck.

A number of laymen and laywomen are cited by name in the book *German Catholic Martyrs of the 20th Century.* Maria and Bernhard Kreulich, a married couple, were killed in March, 1944, for criticizing the Nazis. Nicholas Gross, the editor of *Kettelerwache,* the organ of the Association of German Catholic Workers, was killed in the Plotzensee Berlin jail in January, 1945.

## Hitler's Greatest Folly

There are many lessons to be learned from the Nazi era to ensure that the martyrs did not die in vain. One is that no earthly power can stamp out Christian faith or eliminate the search for meaning. Small independent Protestant churches are growing rapidly in Germany and have sent hundreds of missionaries to other lands.

A symbol of the continuing power of the gospel of Jesus Christ is revealed in the last request of German soldiers, surrounded by counterattacking Soviet troops in Stalingrad. Their last wireless message voiced the plea, "Send us Bibles." German planes responded and flew over enemy lines to drop precious copies of the Book of Books.

# PART SEVEN

# Martyrs of the Soviet Union and Eastern Europe

# 18

## The Soviet Union

### *True Faith Grows Strong*

The trail of martyrs' blood now leads us northeast across the broad expanse of the former Soviet Union, which sprawled over eleven time zones in Europe and Asia. It also covers Eastern Europe as well since after the fall of Nazi Germany near the end of the Second World War, most of Eastern Europe came under the domain of the Soviet Union as the "iron curtain" was pulled shut.

The background for martyrdom in the Soviet Union and Eastern European Communist nations is different from most of the countries previously covered. The populations were "converted" centuries before by "Christian" armies marching from the West. The powerful church establishments which developed tended to see dissent as heresy and as a threat to society. Evangelicals and other religious minorities were, therefore, persecuted even before the conquest by Communism. For a few years after the rise of Communism, the minorities enjoyed relief from persecution while the Marxist rulers were killing and imprisoning leaders of the old national church who refused subservience to the state. Then the Marxists enacted a set of controls designed to confine the activities of the minorities to private worship inside their sanctuaries at times approved by the government. When multitudes refused to comply, particularly evangelicals, the Marxist rulers began to enforce their laws. Depending on the times and the severity of local persecutors, believers were fined, banished to Siberia, imprisoned, and in some instances killed. The persecutors maintained that punishments were not for religious reasons but for crimes against the state.

In the drive to stamp out religion, the Communist leadership sought to avoid dramatic executions. They feared that violent killings of Christians would shock world opinion and that the example of the martyrs would spur church growth. Consequently, most resistant pastors and lay leaders were either exiled to barren wastelands, where their influence was restricted, or confined to prisons until they were broken in health and spirit. Even though death might occur years after he was released, a believer who died as a result of the horrors of a Communist prison was no less a martyr than one who was beaten to death or shot by a firing squad. Understanding this, we will have a broader view of the meaning of martyrdom in the Soviet Union and Eastern Europe.

As recently as 1972, for example, members of the Evangelical Christian and Baptist Church Council in the USSR included in their plea to the UN secretary-general these testaments of evangelical leaders:

> ". . . N. Khmara was tortured to death in prison . . ."
> "I. A. Afonin, a member of the Action Group and father of nine children, died in prison at age 45, in July, 1971."
> "P. F. Zakharov, after insults and torture in prison, died at the age of 49."
> "S. T. Golev, a member of the Council of Churches, elderly and ill, has spent about 20 years in bondage. At present he is virtually condemned to death in prison for his nationwide work for the Council of Churches."

These are only four among the multitudes of Soviet Christians who suffered in the so-called benevolent socialist workers' paradise. According to the official record, they did not die for their faith, but for disobeying the laws of the "people." These laws were never devised or administered by the majority, but by an atheistic bureaucracy intent on reducing religious beliefs to the ashes of legends and myths.

## Martyrs of the Russian Orthodox Church

The Orthodox Church, which in the previous century had sought to suppress the growing evangelical movement, fought back against Lenin's oppression. The newly elected patriarch announced the excommunication of "avowed or secret enemies of Christ." The Communists who had been baptized into Orthodoxy were not named, but it was obvious they were the subjects of the decree. They began a propaganda attack, and warfare soon erupted between supporters of the Orthodox Church and the state. Violent clashes occurred in several cities. Communist-inspired crowds burned Orthodox churches and pillaged monasteries. Clergymen and laymen were brought to trial for crimes against the state. Eleven were condemned to death in Moscow.

In January 1918, Communists began attacking Orthodox churches in the Ukraine. On the evening of January 23, they broke into the Petchersky Monastery and killed hundreds of Orthodox priests. The Orthodox Church later claimed that over two thousand priests and some fifty bishops were killed or deported.

The main target in Kiev, the largest Ukrainian city, was Metropolitan Vladimir. At age seventy he was the oldest hierarch in the Russian church. A widower who had lost his wife and only child to illness, he was known for ministries of charity and was one of the most beloved churchmen of Russia. At 6:30 p.m. five men dressed as soldiers entered his house. They pushed the old priest into a bedroom where they twisted the chain of his cross around his neck and demanded money. Then they took him to a waiting car and drove outside the gates of the monastery to a small clearing. When they stopped, he asked, "Is it here you want to shoot me?"

"Why not?" one of the abductors said with a curse. "Do you expect us to stand on ceremony?"

"Will you grant me permission to pray before I am shot?"

"Be quick about it!" he was told.

Lifting his arms to heaven, the old man prayed aloud, "O Lord, forgive my sins, voluntary and involuntary, and accept my spirit in peace." Then he blessed his murderers with both hands, murmuring, "God forgive you."

Four shots rang out and he was dead.

## "I Will Lift Up My Eyes Reverently to God"

In Petrograd, Metropolitan Benjamin joined with the Communists on a committee called "Help to the Starving." He asked clergymen to raise cash offerings and contribute from church treasuries on a voluntary basis. His appeals helped tremendously.

The Communist Central Committee in Moscow, fearing that the voluntary gifts would raise the prestige of the clergy, ordered their Petrograd comrades to confiscate church valuables instead of accepting them by donation. They further published a letter from twelve self-proclaimed clergymen denouncing the arrangement in Petrograd.

The church valuables were confiscated and Metropolitan Benjamin was arrested and put on trial with others. After several false witnesses had testified and conviction appeared obvious, his defense attorney begged the tribunal of judges:

> Do not make a martyr of the Metropolitan. The masses revere him, and if he is killed for his faith and his loyalty to the masses, he would become much more dangerous to the Soviet power. The immutable law of history should be a warning. Let it remind you that true faith feeds and grows strong on the blood of martyrs. Would you risk giving more martyrs to the restless people?

The presiding judge asked the Metropolitan to speak for himself. The clergyman first expressed his sorrow at being called "the enemy of the people. . . . I am a true son of my people," he said. "I love and always have loved the people. I have dedicated my whole life to them." Then he proceeded to speak in behalf of his codefendants.

"Tell us more about yourself," the judge interrupted.

"About myself? What else can I tell you? One more thing perhaps; regardless of what my sentence will be, no matter what you decide, life or death, I will lift up my eyes reverently to God, cross myself and affirm: 'Glory to Thee, my Lord; glory to Thee for everything.'"

The verdict for Metropolitan Benjamin and the other defendants was guilty. The sentence: death before a firing squad.

Before the execution they were shaved of their long beards and dressed in rags so the executioners would not know they were killing clergymen. Just before the guns cracked, one of the priests, Father Serge, prayed aloud, "O Lord, forgive them for they know not what they are doing." Metropolitan Benjamin merely crossed himself and whispered a prayer before falling under the hail of bullets.

## More Orthodox Martyrs

Russia was now in the throes of a full-scale civil war between the "Whites," who defended the old order, and Communist "Reds." By 1921 more than twenty million people had died in fighting, in epidemics, and from starvation. Had not an American relief commission, directed by Herbert Hoover, given emergency help on a mammoth scale, millions more might have died.

As the Reds conquered, they closed more Orthodox churches and arrested clergymen. Among the Orthodox clergy put to death during the early years of Communist rule in Russia were Bishop Germogen of Tobolsk, Bishop Nikodim of Belgorod, and Bishop Makary of Viazma.

Bishop Germogen and some other prisoners were taken away on a steamer. After they were well underway, guards began ripping off the prisoners' clothing and throwing the prisoners one by one into the Tura River where they drowned. When they came to Bishop Germogen, he prayed aloud. "Hold his jaw!" the commissar shouted. A fist silenced the old man's prayers. Then an eighty-pound rock was tied to his bound hands and after several swings to and fro, he was tossed into the river.

Bishop Nikodim of Belgorod had taken no sides in politics, but in his sermons he had condemned violence, robberies, and murders, while asking his flock to follow the teachings of Jesus. His sermons enraged local Communists. Commandant Saenko, famed for killing hundreds with his own hands, arrested the Bishop. A furor arose among the people, forcing Saenko to return the Bishop to his residence. On that same day Nikodim preached another sermon against violence. He was rearrested by Saenko who declared, "The clergy are ruining the revolution." A priest's wife pleaded for the Bishop's freedom. Saenko shot her himself and ordered the Bishop's execution. Nikodim was disguised in a military overcoat and taken into a dark corner of the prison yard to be shot. Saenko knew that the soldiers would not perform the execution if they recognized the Bishop.

Bishop Makary of Viazma was a learned theologian and powerful preacher. Local Communists first staged a fight at the door of his church so they could kill him when he came out to settle the dispute. Instead the Bishop remained inside and preached a powerful sermon. In the pretended melee one of the Communists was killed by mistake.

After this failure, they had the Bishop and thirteen other clergymen arrested and falsely charged with organizing a White Volunteer Army uprising. Before dawn, the fourteen doomed men were taken to a deserted spot and lined up with their backs to a freshly dug pit. As an executioner moved to the first in line preparing to shoot him through the forehead, Bishop Makary whispered, "Go in peace." The gun fired and the priest fell backwards into the grave. The Bishop comforted each of his colleagues in this manner. Finally he stood alone. The stars were now fading and the eastern sky was alight. The executioner lifted his gun, then hesitated and lowered his hand. His face hardened. He clenched his teeth. He lifted his hand again and fired. The Bishop, who had been serenely gazing into the brightening sky, tumbled backwards to join the others.

Throughout this period, 1917–1929, the Russian Orthodox Church, because of its power, influence, and connections with the old tsarist regime, was the main object of the Communists' war on religion. At the beginning of the period there were over fifty-four thousand Orthodox churches and more than thirty-seven thousand parochial schools. All of the schools were closed or transferred to state jurisdiction. There is no accurate record of the number of churches closed or of the number of clergy and lay leaders killed, just as there is no accounting of the millions of civilians brutally murdered by Communists during this time. Today only an estimated seven thousand Orthodox churches remain.

## Orthodox Martyrs from the Monasteries

Between 1917 and 1922, Russian Orthodox monasteries were ransacked and many monks martyred.

A sailor, Dibenko, took a seventy-five-year-old Archimandrite Radion from his monastery at Spasovsky and scalped him, before cutting his head off.

A novice, Ivan, hiding himself in the monastery's loft, lived to recount the following attack on the Alexandro-Svirsky monastery and the martyrdom of five of its brothers and the Superior Eugene:

When the monks refused to hand over the keys to the rooms so that their treasures could be taken they were forced to dig their own graves in the courtyard of the monastery. When this was completed they were told to line up on the edge of the graves so that they could be shot. As it was the third day of the Pascha, the monks requested that they should be allowed to sing "Christ is risen", a short Paschal hymn. They were refused permission but started to sing anyway as the young soldiers fired their rifles.

The last member of the Solovky monastery, Archimandrite Benjamin, lived as a hermit in a poor peasant's hut on the outskirts of Archangel. The communists sealed its windows and doors and then set fire to the hut with Benjamin inside it.

On June 27, 1918, the Rev. Gregory Nikolsky was taken out through the gates of his own monastery, the Mary Magdalene monastery, by the communists. They forced Gregory to open his mouth, and then shouted, "We will also give you the Sacrament," and then killed him by shooting him in the mouth.

The Rev. Athanassy, a priest from Spasov Skete monastery, was taken out to be executed by a Red soldier. Athanassy knelt to pray, crossed himself, and then stood up to bless the soldier, who then fired two shots into the pastor's head.

The Rev. Mil from Poltava Krestovozdvizhensky monastery was interrogated many times. The Red soldiers found him so obstinate that they "were forced to spend thirty-seven roubles on him," the price of a bullet. On July 4, 1918, with two others, he was shot in the forest. When his body was examined it revealed the extent of the terrible tortures this martyr had bravely endured during his interrogations.

The Red soldiers decided to take over Spaso-Preobrazhensky monastery. They rounded up twenty-five monks and Prior Ambrose. They were commanded to bring in firewood and told that they would be burnt at the stake. When the Reds realized that the White Volunteer Army was nearby, they took the priests to the local railway station. Commissar Bakai started the massacres of these martyr-monks and shot Prior Ambrose. Seventeen of the monks were killed outright as they were shot, but the eight other monks, who were not fatally injured, pretended that they were dead as they were shot in the dark, and later were able to escape.

## Extermination of the Catholic Church

Next to the Russian Orthodox Church, the Latin-rite Catholics suffered most under Lenin's rule. When the Communists came to power, about 1.5 million Roman Catholics lived in the territory of the old Russian empire. Most were of Polish, Lithuanian, Belorussian (White Russian), German, and French origin. Before the 1917 Revolution, Roman Catholics were suspect to most Russians because of their allegiance to the foreign Vatican. After the Revolution, their churches, schools, and priesthood were virtually wiped out. Key leaders were arrested and given long prison sentences or sent to remote labor camps. Many died from disease and malnutrition in the camps. Some were executed.

Contrasting figures tell the grim story of Russian Catholics. In 1917, 980 churches; in 1934, only three "showcases" open. In 1917, 912 priests and monks; in 1934, only ten remaining. In 1917, 504 schools and institutions; in 1934, none.

The much smaller body of Eastern-rite Catholics (Uniates) was also virtually annihilated. Other religious minorities with hierarchal structures were substantially dismantled.

## How the Free Churches Fared

The Baptist groups flourished from 1917 to 1929. Because they lacked an organized superstructure and were mostly of the working class, the Communists either did not fear them as a counterrevolutionary force, or perhaps felt that, given enough time, the Baptists would slough off their religious lives and become active participants in the new order. For whatever reasons, Russian Baptists were not the target of a general persecution during this period.

The "golden decade" of Russian evangelicals ended in 1929. The year before leaders had reported to the Baptist World Congress in Toronto exciting new developments and prospects for greater successes. The following year most of them were either in prison or in exile.

## Tightening the Screws

This new attack on religion was undergirded by the Law on Religious Associations, decreed in 1928. Under the following specifications a Communist official could find a reason to arrest almost any Christian:

A religious group could hold activities only after registering with a government committee for religious matters. Registration was often denied on flimsy pretexts.

The registration committee could remove any members it desired from the executive body of a religious society.

Religious groups could not organize activities or classes for children, young people, and women. Sunday school classes, sewing and prayer groups, reading rooms, libraries, excursions, and children's playgrounds were also forbidden.

Clergymen were restricted to areas in which members resided and could only preach in designated prayer buildings that had to be leased from the government.

Voluntary offerings could only be collected to maintain prayer buildings and premises and to pay clergy salaries.

Under these and previous laws, organized religion was practically shut down in the Soviet Union and thousands of known church leaders were imprisoned. This time the evangelicals did not escape.

*Harvest Field* reported eyewitness accounts of the terrible suffering now prevailing. In 1930 a believer wrote:

Chapels in all of Russia have been taken from the believers by the thousands. . . . The banished are "fetched" at night without previous notice and are . . . placed in cattle cars. . . . The sick are carried out in their beds. The old and the children die enroute.

. . . Many of our brethren have ended their thorny path in Arctic regions. Where there are believers, there spring up small groups, and baptismal services are held by night. There

179

are Christian workers who look for a still greater spiritual awakening in Russia. Is the day of labor in Russia really over, in regard to spiritual works, and has the night set in?

## Under the Iron Heel of Stalin

Lenin was dead and the dread Stalin in power. The country was now officially the Union of Soviet Socialist Republics (USSR), originally comprising Russia, Belorussia, Transcaucasia, and the eastern Ukraine. The eastern Ukraine had been forcibly annexed by a brutal Communist invasion while other world nations refused to intervene. Other "republics" were annexed in the twenties. More would be swallowed up in the thirties and forties to make the USSR the largest nation on earth.

Stalin had become Party Secretary in 1922. In 1929 he became Premier as well and gained iron-clad domination of the Communist apparatus. He began stepping up efforts to industrialize the nation and collectivize all farm land. He increased his secret police, clamped tight censorship over all publications, and enlarged the system of concentration and forced labor camps which had been established earlier.

The next twelve years of Stalinism were brutal beyond description. Millions died in blood purges and famines created by manipulations of food supplies. Hundreds of thousands were sent to prison camps from which they never returned. They were jammed like cattle into unheated, unventilated railway cars. On every car was the inscription: VOLUNTARY SETTLERS FOR SIBERIA.

## The Penalty for Believing

In village after village residents were called to mass meetings and confronted with the question: "Are you with the godless [the Marxists] or the believers?" Those who signified that they stood with the believers were marched to central loading places and shoved into cattle cars for shipment to Siberia.

A survivor described a trip of horror for a missionary who translated the diary into English for *Harvest Field.*

At Omsk ten thousand believers and others were brought on five hundred sledges . . . in temperatures forty degrees below centigrade.

Priests, preachers, and ministers of other denominations were driven thus, but the majority were innocent peasants. . . . The first night was spent under the open sky. Many of the aged and women and children froze that night. Others had frozen hands, feet, or faces. There were screams and sobs that cannot be described. One father . . . could not stand it any longer. Snatching a rifle from a Red soldier, he shot his family and himself.

The howling of the wolves awaiting their prey was terrible to hear. In this way we marched four days. The dead were not buried but the wolves devoured them. Only on the tenth day did we arrive at our destination. Snow and interminable forests surrounded us.

Many never reached the place, especially the children. The erection of barracks was begun. The food was unfit to eat. . . . The dying were not cared for nor taken away—we did not know what became of them.

Daily we turned to our Savior. Those who had no hope in Christ sank into a state of depression.

## Faith That Overcame

The wife of a prominent pastor, who was later martyred, managed to smuggle out this account of following her husband on another forced march:

For almost three months I followed him from town to town, from prison to prison. Once I drew near to a very long line of banished men, possibly a thousand. . . . Thin and haggard, pale and exhausted, they tried to keep in line. Some of them fell, but they were drawn forward by force. Beside them walked their wives and children, heartbroken, but not permitted to help them in any way. The men carried on their shoulders small bundles containing their few belongings.

The road led up a mountainside. I thought of our Savior climbing up Calvary's mountain. All the time I was scanning every face, trying to find my poor husband. At last, just as we came to the station, I caught a glimpse of him in the crowd. He looked very, very sick and had to be supported by a guard.

He saw me, too, and raised his eyes to heaven, giving me an unspoken message that I would meet him there. Just at that moment, he was roughly pushed by a Red guard into a railway freight car. Of course, I could not be admitted to see him.

Can you imagine the scene on that station platform with hundreds of women and children sobbing convulsively and wringing their hands in distress, some of them falling to earth in a dead faint? I ran from the place as from a cemetery, for I felt sure that I would never again see my husband on earth. It was only the Lord who gave me strength to bear the awful grief. Praise be to the Lord!

When I returned home, I knew that my next real danger was the loss of my children. The government had threatened to take them from me . . . I was ordered not to leave my home, and was taxed 500 rubles because my husband was a presbyter [church leader]. Now we are awaiting confiscation of our goods because we can't pay the tax.

We are expecting every day to become beggars or prisoners, but we thank the Lord that we are free from any fear. We thank Him for everything.

After some time, word came that my husband went to be with the Lord. With my husband gone and my children constantly threatened, of course I had rather be in a place where God is worshiped and where the teachings of the schools are different. Sometimes it seems to me that the believers in Russia will have to face the arena of the early Christians.

A short time later *Harvest Field* received word that this pastor's widow had joined her husband in heaven. Exactly how she died and what happened to her children is not known.

## Massacres in the Ukraine

During the Stalin era all of the Soviet Union was a prison of fear where no one could be sure of tomorrow. Ukraine, where Stalin's police killed or took away millions, suffered the worst.

Ukrainian horror began when millions of farmers were ordered to report to city factories to help the progress of industrialization. To feed the swollen urban population, Stalin clamped impossible agricultural quotas on Ukrainians who had been allowed to remain on their farms. The quotas were set deliberately high to ensure widespread famine. The farmers were required to turn over to the government up to 80 percent of their production. For most this was impossible, so lying became a way of life. For example, a family that was required to turn in three hundred eggs a year for each laying hen would hide some of the hens when inspectors came around. Devout Christians could not readily lie and were, therefore, likely to miss their quotas.

For them, as well as those caught cheating, the dread NKVD (Soviet secret police) came in black cars, often in the middle of the night. Many were herded into river barges which were then sunk. Others were shipped to labor camps and did not see their families again for years, if ever.

## Minister Martyr

Pastors in Ukraine and elsewhere were special targets for the NKVD and other police. The story of young Pastor Arseny is dramatically related by S. Prokhanoff in his book *In the Cauldron of Russia: 1869–1933,* published by the All-Russian Evangelical Christian Union in 1933.

Prokhanoff recalls that the young man first visited him in Leningrad in 1932, announcing, "The Lord has called me to preach the gospel in Siberia." This was at a time when millions of political prisoners were being shipped to Siberia. Prokhanoff promised to help with prayer and support.

Arseny went to a city in central Siberia. Upon his arrival he was told the atheists were arranging a series of antireligious debates. "I will go there and defend the faith!" he immediately responded.

For three nights he spoke with such eloquence that he was frequently interrupted by applause. At the end of the debates he was given an ovation.

The next day an atheist visited his landlady. "Tell Arseny not to come any more to our debates. Otherwise something will happen to him."

The landlady informed the preacher early the next morning. He listened gravely, then said, "Whatever may happen, I will go to the debates and will fulfill my duty."

Eyewitnesses reported that he spoke with special power and his face shone like that of an angel. The audience gave him a resounding ovation as the debates closed. When the applause died down, three young men came and took him away. The next morning Christian brothers found him dead in the snow near the railway station. They noted that he was in a half-kneeling position with his New Testament in his hands. He had been shot while praying.

## Letters from "Hell"

During this time of repression, perhaps unequaled since the persecutions of Christians in the first century under the mad Emperor Nero, letters continued to leak to friends outside the Soviet Union. Some of those published in *Harvest Field* indicate the heartbreak and agony of the Russian people under Stalin.

> A woman wrote the Russian Missionary Society: Save, oh save us! Have pity on us! Women, young women, and children are being arrested and hundreds sent into exile. Men are sent to other places. (March 2, 1930)

> A church leader reported: We have divided into groups of ten. In case one is shot or imprisoned, the next in rank steps into line. One of our pastors who stood for Christ in a Communistic gathering was watched and followed by the secret police. While he was preaching in his own pulpit, they entered and arrested him. Later our congregation received a note saying, "If you wish to find the body of your pastor, go to a certain cemetery." We found him shot dead with his Bible on his breast. They had offered him a large reward if he would renounce Christ, but he chose death with Christ. (November, 1931)

> Another Russian evangelical wrote to a missionary: Our conditions here are becoming worse and worse, and we are facing death. We have absolutely nothing to eat. My husband is in bed, suffering from swollen legs because of starvation. Sometimes we get a little something to eat and we mix it with grass, trying to satisfy our hunger. People are falling down from starvation like sparrows in the frost. (December, 1933)

Only eternity will reveal the depth and extent of suffering among evangelicals imprisoned by the Stalinist regime because they chose to obey God in matters of faith rather than man. Many died in prison or in Siberian exile. Some, incarcerated during the late twenties and thirties, may have lived through the trauma of the terrible camps. The stories of two dynamic leaders serve to illustrate the bravery and sacrifice of those who died.

## Terror in the Labor Camps

Nikolai Odintsov, born in 1870 and ordained in 1909, was the best known Baptist preacher of his time. He preached in the mountains of the Caucasus, in bustling Moscow, in historic St. Petersburg, and in far eastern Russia where churches were hundreds of miles apart. In 1926 he was elected chairman of the Federal Baptist Union and in 1928 was a delegate to the World Baptist Congress in Toronto. He was editor of *The Baptist* in 1929 when that journal was closed by the government.

That same year the Baptist Bible School and the local and Federal Baptist Unions were forcibly shut down. Then Odintsov's closest assistant was arrested. The veteran preacher, teacher, and journalist felt he would be next. Quoting from the apostle Paul's farewell statement to the elders of the church at Ephesus, Odintsov told his associates, "'Bonds and afflictions await me. But I do not consider my life of any account as dear to myself, in order that I may finish my course, and the ministry which I received from the Lord Jesus, to testify solemnly of the gospel of the grace of God'" (Acts 20:23, 24, NASB).

His arrest did not come until the night of November 5, 1929. A co-worker arrested with him reported that he vigorously defended the Word of God in bouts with questioners. After serving a three-year sentence in Yaroslav prison, he was exiled to the village of Makovskoye in remote eastern Siberia. His wife visited him there in 1937 and reported to the believers at home that he was very weak physically but strong in spirit. He sent greetings to his brothers and sisters in Christ and anticipated that he would soon be with the Heavenly Father. "He often said to me," Mrs. Odintsov told them, "'I want to go home.'"

The following year he was placed in an unknown prison. He died there soon afterwards. Some of his letters from prison live on. In one long epistle he wrote, in part:

> I shall not describe the terrors which the prisoners are experiencing, as that is a matter for a specialist-historian or a simple honest man. I shall say only one thing: there is no terror like it! Can one imagine the bestial look of the hand-picked convoy escorts, who, making use of the right granted them, can shoot sick men who collapse and hunt down with vicious dogs the prisoner who falls on the road? . . .
>
> My body is tired and weak, my work for the Lord here in the camps is unbearably hard, and the repressions I suffer often hold me for long periods on my bare plank bed, which represents my bed of ease.
>
> I have grown weak in body, but not in spirit. Jesus, the Lord, upholds me. . . . Nothing atheistic has adhered to me. "I have fought the faith." I have refused to betray God. "Henceforth there is laid for me a crown of righteousness, which the Lord, the righteous judge, will give me on that day" (2 Timothy 4:8). I have always avoided every injustice. With this my earthly life will be finished. . . .
>
> What else will there be? The Lord knows! Eternal glory to Him! Rejoice, dear brothers and sisters, as I REJOICE! Your brother . . . to the end of his days has not forgotten you all. May the name of our God and of his Son our Lord Jesus Christ be blessed and glorified. Amen! Hallelujah!

## Peter Vins

Peter Yakovlevich Vins, a minister of the gospel during the 1930s in Siberia and eastern Russia, was the first of three generations to be imprisoned for the sake of the gospel. Vins was participating in the assembly of the Russian Baptist Union in Moscow in 1930 as a representative of Baptists from the eastern part of the USSR when he was first arrested. Advised by the secret police to back the candidacies of two "ministers" chosen by government agencies to be members of the administrative board of the Russian Baptist Union, Vins had refused.

The government candidates were elected anyway. One later proved himself to be a traitor when he helped the government shut down the Baptist Union. In that time the churches were plagued by many apostates whom Communists maneuvered into leadership positions with the purpose of destroying Christianity from within.

Peter Vins was arrested and, after three months of investigation, sentenced to three years in the Svetlaya Bay labor camp. His two-year-old son, Georgi, had just begun to talk and often prayed, "Jesus, bring Daddy back."

Peter was released in 1933 and a year later, when his passport was restored, moved to the town of Omsk where the Baptist church had been closed. After working all day, he would visit believers at night, encouraging and strengthening them from God's Word, and teaching them to minister to fellow members of Christ's body who were suffering. Though all meetings, including those in homes, had been forbidden, by 1936 there were one thousand believers in Omsk.

Because of his activity among the believers at Omsk, it was inevitable that Peter would be arrested and tried again. This became the pattern of his life during these years. Believers all over the Soviet Union were in the same predicament. Forbidden to assemble for worship, they could only minister to one another through prayers and home visitation, and in sharing of material goods. Arrests continued; thousands more were taken away to the camps.

After a new wave of arrests began in Omsk, little Georgi Vins noticed his parents cutting a Gospel into parts and sewing sections into a coat collar lining and into trousers. He knew the departure of his beloved father was again at hand.

## A Family's Last Look

This time the father was put in a cell on the fourth floor of the Omsk prison. The family took parcels for him to the prison gate. For a while they were able to walk along the streets that surrounded the prison and see him waving his arms from a window. Noticing workmen building boxes over the windows on the lower stories, they knew this pleasure would shortly be taken away. One day they arrived and saw that the workmen were close to Peter's window. They stood and looked lovingly for a long time at the familiar figure waving to them from above. Then the workmen closed the window and they were left only with the memory of the wave of his hand and the faint outline of his face.

Lydia Vins and young Georgi never saw him again. Mrs. Vins made repeated inquiries about his fate. Finally she was told he had been sent to a closed camp for socially dangerous people for ten years. Prisoners at that camp were denied the privilege of correspondence so they had no further contact with him. They subsequently learned that he had died on December 27, 1943, at the age of forty-five. After his death, Mrs. Vins continued filing petitions that his case be reconsidered. Finally on Christmas Eve, 1963, a new hearing was held in the Omsk regional court, and Peter Vins was declared posthumously rehabilitated.

## Why Persecution Eased

In 1939 Stalin signed a nonaggression pact with Adolf Hitler. Then, in a series of brutal, imperialistic moves, the Soviet Communists forcibly annexed neighboring Latvia, Lithuania, Estonia, western Ukraine, the eastern half of Poland, and even a slice of territory from little Finland. Western democracies did nothing.

In 1941 German armies suddenly attacked the Soviet Union. Russia entered the war on the side of the Allies. Facing a long siege, Stalin ordered his underlings to stop persecuting the churches and to court the support of church leaders in the name of national unity. When the war ended, the nation was so weakened that unity continued to be pursued. Cooperative church leaders were permitted to travel abroad to world church conferences. Moscow needed them to combat claims in the West of religious persecution in the Soviet Union and to soften criticism of postwar Communist takeovers in eastern European countries as well as Communist spying and infiltration in other nations.

## Khrushchev's Crackdown

Wily Nikita Khrushchev took power in 1956. When he denounced Stalin as a despot and took a softer line in foreign policy, Christians hoped that persecution in the Soviet Union might be over. Then suddenly in 1959 the Khrushchev government initiated a new wave of repression against the churches in order to demonstrate to other Communist powers that the Soviets had not betrayed the world Communist movement. A target date of 1980 was set for the eradication of all religion in the country.

Once again the government-controlled press began attacking church leaders. Old laws were again rigidly enforced. Clergy were forbidden to instruct children, and youth under eighteen were ordered to stay away from churches. Some laws, which had seemed unrelated to religion, were applied to Christians. Most common was the so-called antiparasite law, which related to persons whose work was considered socially unfit by government officials. This law was used against full-time religious workers.

During the next five years ten thousand more Russian Orthodox churches were closed to services and the buildings taken over by the state for public use. Under pressure from the government, a rump synod of Orthodox bishops issued new *Regulations* forbidding

186

Orthodox priests to serve on parish councils. In separate government actions Communist sympathizers were named to parish councils by local Communist committees under existing laws. Priests who refused to follow desired propaganda lines were fired. Three objecting Orthodox bishops were sent to prison. Another objector, Metropolitan Nikolai of Krutitsy, president of the Council of the Orthodox Church for Foreign Relations, was dismissed from office. Shortly afterwards he died mysteriously.

## The Pochaev Monastery Massacre

The worst single atrocity against Orthodoxy during Nikita Khrushchev's era occurred on November 20, 1964, when the KGB and other police attacked the Pochaev Monastery. A later protest filed by the Spiritual Council of the Monastery to the Supreme Soviet (national legislature) of the USSR gave this report:

> They broke into cells, removing the doors, seized the monks and rampaged through the churches and living quarters of the monastery. The following were arrested and sentenced: priest-monks Valerian Popovich and Vladimir Soldatov and priest-deacon Gavriil Uglitsky. Monk Mikhail Longchakov, because of his age, was accorded the "indulgence" of confinement in a mental hospital instead of being imprisoned. . . . Many monks had to go into hiding in conditions of considerable difficulty in order to evade further arrest and imprisonment. . . . Many others died prematurely and passed on to eternal life before their time. Yevlogi died after torture outside the monastery, as did Abbot Andrei and a number of others. Some who remained alive lost their good health.

## Communist Strategy against Evangelicals

The government applied a similar strategy against Baptist evangelicals. Although details are still not known, it can be logically presumed that Party officials persuaded certain leaders of the All-Union Council of Evangelical Christians and Baptists in the USSR to issue regulations designed to check the growth of evangelicals.

## Tortured to Death

Among the cities especially hard hit was Kulunda in western Siberia. There the target was an "illegal" Baptist congregation which Communist officials had refused to register. This meant they could neither legally assemble nor obtain a building for their services. They could not meet outside in the bitter cold, so they met secretly in private homes.

Though they could not openly evangelize, they had private ways of witnessing. One convert was Nikolai Khmara. At forty-five he was transformed from a chronic drunk to a glowing believer. He became such an active witness that within six months he and three others were arrested for religious activities and for failing to conform to the *Statutes* of the official All-Union Council. He was sentenced to three years imprisonment. His pastor received five years. Two weeks later his dead body was returned to his wife. Burn marks were on his palms, toes, and the soles of his feet. A sharp instrument had punctured his stomach. His legs and ankles were swollen and his whole body was covered with bruises. A rag was stuffed in his mouth. His wife removed it and stepped back. His tongue had been cut out. Plainly, he had been tortured to death.

The persecution in Kulunda and other localities convinced the "reformed" Baptists that another purge was in process. Yet they would not give their persecutors victory. They banded together in prayer and mutual support and launched an action unprecedented in the Soviet Union.

## The "Suicide" of Pastor Moiseyevich

Ivan Moiseyevich had once predicted, "I must die for the faith." In 1974 he was in poor health and living in forced exile in cold Siberia. Though a medical commission recommended that he should be returned to a warmer climate, Communist bureaucrats blocked his transfer. In January 1975, his family received a telegram reporting his death. His sons and several close friends flew to the Siberian town of Nyagan where his body had been embalmed. They were met by an official who claimed Moiseyevich had hung himself.

His family reported in the *Bulletin* of the Council of Baptist Prisoners' Relatives:

> Knowing our father's powers of endurance and his deep faith in eternal life, we did not believe that he had done it himself. . . . We tried to discover who saw him last . . . but we were unable to because the two men who shared a room with our father had suspiciously disappeared, no one knew where, although we tried for the next two days to find them.

Their suspicions increased when they examined the body and noted that his hands and his legs below the knees were almost black, and his face white. They wangled permission to ship the body home to Odessa by air freight. But because of bureaucratic stalls, they were unable to leave for two weeks. Police were waiting when they landed and kept constant watch over the coffin. Twenty-five minutes after they reached the dead man's house a group of Communist doctors arrived and ordered that the coffin not be opened. The travelers were told by neighbors that Communists had been watching their house almost every night for the past two weeks.

The body was transferred to a new coffin on February 13 in the presence of relatives and three of the doctors. The relatives wanted to examine the body for marks of violence, but the doctors refused, claiming that an epidemic might result. When relatives and friends began filing by to view the body, the doctors kept hurrying them along. Afterwards the room was closed so no one could look at the body.

A thousand mourners gathered for the funeral. The services were accompanied by a church band and evangelical hymns while Communist functionaries looked on sourly. One of the sons spoke about his father's life and death. Altogether eight sermons were preached.

After the burial, local police continued to harass the martyr's family. Early in March his eldest son, Pyotr, age twenty-seven, died suddenly in the night from a heart condition.

"Summons to the authorities continue both in the family of Ivan Moiseyevich and in the church," the Council noted at the close of their report. The report continued:

> But praise God that the spring countryside and our beloved work on the land, together with our prayers to God, help us all to bear the cross laid upon us. We are convinced, beloved brothers and sisters, that as we believe in the power of the cross of Christ, so the Lord will manifest His power in us through Him. Please, beloved, pray for the continuing life of our church and for the sorrowing family of Ivan Moiseyevich. "Grace be with all who love our Lord Jesus Christ with love undying. Amen" (Ephesians 6:24).

## The Strange Case of Private "Vanya"

Another martyr of the seventies was Private Ivan "Vanya" Vasilevich Moiseyev. The parents of Vanya were told that he had died from drowning. His coffin was delivered to them welded shut. A Communist officer attended the funeral to see that the lid remained closed. Despite the officer's protests, the parents insisted on seeing their son's body. A crowbar was passed through the crowd. The officer fled in fear. When the coffin was opened, the family saw their son's bruised, blackened face and body. He had been stabbed, burned, and beaten—tortured to death.

Investigators from the Council of Baptist Prisoners' Relatives carefully compiled evidence from Vanya's letters home, a tape recording he had made, and the testimony of soldiers who had known him. They soon pieced together what had actually happened.

Vanya's crime had been praying and witnessing. His first punishment was to stand outside in the cold for five days without food. When he refused to be quiet about his faith, he was ordered to stand for twelve straight nights in subzero weather. He survived this.

Determined to break him, his commanding officer, Colonel Malsin, tried interrogations, beatings, and prison. He could not be broken. He was put on trial for attending unregistered religious meetings during recreation time, and for distributing literature containing falsehoods and slander against the Soviet Union. "I have one higher allegiance," he testified, "and that is to Jesus Christ. He has given me certain orders, and these I cannot disobey."

The court sentenced him to prison. He was taken back to jail and beaten repeatedly. Colonel Malsin finally sent him to the dread KGB. The "treatment" they administered in a soundproof room ended his life. His murder was later confirmed by Colonel Malsin. Ill and stricken by remorse, the officer told Vanya's parents, "I was present when your son died. . . . He died hard, but he died a Christian." The true circumstances of his death are recorded in a book titled *Vanya,* by Myrna Grant.

Vanya's family received many letters testifying of the spiritual impact of his martyrdom. Typical was this statement from a discharged soldier: "Our dear brother will be in our hearts eternally. He suffered much torture, but he was faithful to Christ to the end. He left us an example of how to strive for the crown of Christ."

## An Analysis of Persecution in the USSR

The martyrdom of the preacher and the soldier indicated that violence against believers had not ceased in the Soviet Union. But these and other killings, along with less violent persecution, did not mean that believers all over the Soviet Union were the victims of such oppression. Peter Deyneka Jr., former director of the Slavic Gospel Association, noted that imprisonments and beatings were "basically limited to areas where tourists do not go. In trying to woo third world nations, the Soviets are attempting to show more humaneness in places where visitors do go."

Deyneka continued as one of the most knowledgeable persons in the West on Christianity and Communism in the Soviet Union and Eastern Europe. The Slavic Gospel Association, which his father, an immigrant from Ukraine, founded, includes workers who are active in radio broadcasting and the printing and distribution of Bibles in the area. He cautioned that "while sensational stories of martyrdoms and imprisonments are true, the majority of Soviet evangelicals are able to carry on their worship and witness in meaningful ways." But he added:

> Persecution in the Soviet Union is not just imprisonment. Every Christian there experiences psychological, economic, and educational pressure. One of the most fearful pressures which all Christian parents face is the possibility that their children will be taken away. Some children are taken away and put in atheistic orphanages because of stringent Christian teaching in their homes. Because of this every Christian mother wonders every day if it could happen to her children. This psychological pressure is real. The Communists use these and other experiences to keep Christians on edge with nervous tension.

## Pastor Nikolai Kharpov Dies a Martyr's Death

In 1982, Pastor Nikolai Kharpov joined his wife who had died shortly before his arrest two years earlier. The sixty-eight-year-old Kharpov was serving his twenty-eighth year in concentration camps for his ministry as an evangelist and Christian writer and poet. His body was returned to his family. Five hundred attended the funeral services, which were secretly photographed, with the pictures sent to Georgi Vins in America for publication in the *Prisoner Bulletin*.

## The Toll of Orthodox Martyrs

Russian Orthodox Patriarch Aleksy II estimated three hundred Orthodox bishops and eighty thousand priests, monks, and nuns had been executed, and uncounted millions of laity left to die in labor camps, during the long dark night under Marxism.

Stalin, he noted, had reduced fifty thousand Orthodox parishes to three hundred. "Despite the terrible persecutions and horrors, the church and faith managed to survive," he said in an interview. "I consider it a miracle of God's grace." The total of Orthodox churches now open, he said, was nearing twenty thousand.

## Disturbing KGB Secrets Revealed

For many years stories had circulated that a few high-ranking leaders in the Russian Orthodox Church had served as agents with the KGB. In March 1992 two new Russian Parliament members said KGB files showed this to be true. One of the Parliament members, Rev. Gleb Yakunin, an Orthodox priest, recalled that he had spent five years in prison for his religious activities.

Bishop Basil Rodzianko of the Orthodox Church in America came to the defense of his Russian colleagues. "All that Father Gleb [Yakunin] says is true and genuine," he said. "But he himself is very naive." Bishop Rodzianko said the Russian Orthodox leaders in question had only "used their position [with the KGB] to protect the church, to keep it all through the years of Communism."

Yakunin disagreed, saying the Orthodox leaders had collaborated to advance their careers, not the interests of the church. As late as 1989, the files provided by Yakunin showed the KGB was still receiving information from church officials upon return from trips abroad. During those visits, they promoted the Communist Party line in meetings with officials of such groups as the World Council of Churches, which had a record of overlooking human rights violations in the Soviet Union while criticizing such violations in the West. Yakunin said he and other clergy had asked Patriarch Aleksy II, worldwide leader of Russian Orthodoxy, to "remove at least five or six people who everybody knows about, the most hated, most odious personalities," who collaborated with the KGB. "But so far, nothing has been done."

191

## Triumph of the Martyrs

Over eighty-five years have passed since the Communist overthrow of the freely elected Russian government on November 7, 1917. The second revolution, bringing the restoration of liberty and religious freedom, has now begun.

Bathed in blood, schooled in suffering, and smothered by regulations from an oppressive atheistic government, the subjugated church of believers in the former Soviet Union has not only survived, but triumphed.

Lenin and Marx are dead and so is their damnable ideology that brought untold suffering to millions. All praise be to God!

God lives and so does the faith of His people.

## Chechnya

After the fall of the Soviet Union, Chechnya attempted to break away from Russia, triggering a bloody and rather unsuccessful incursion by Russian troops. Chechnya remains a contested territory.

Pastor Aleksandr Kulakov took over the leadership of Grozny Baptist Church after the previous pastor was abducted in October 1998. He disappeared after boarding a bus on March 12, 1999, and was never seen alive again. A member of the Grozny Baptist Church discovered his disembodied head on display in a market place later in March. Beheadings and the public display of the victim's severed head by armed groups are not an infrequent occurrence in Chechnya. This is an age-old practice designed to instill fear in the population.

# 19

# Eastern Europe

## *The Struggling, Growing Church*

Besides the Soviet Union, the Communist empire in Eastern Europe once included Estonia, Latvia, Lithuania, Bulgaria, Czechoslovakia, Hungary, Poland, and East Germany. Moscow claimed the first three—Estonia, Latvia, Lithuania—as constituent republics of the Soviet Union, but their annexation by the Soviets in 1940 was never recognized by most of the free world. Thus in this section, they are treated as separate national entities. The remaining five served as political satellites of the Soviets. Three other Communist East European countries—Romania, Yugoslavia, and Albania—pursued a political line somewhat independent of the Soviet Union.

In a secret agreement made in 1943 at Teheran, Churchill and Stalin decided that, after World War II, Central Europe would continue in the democratic western sphere, whereas Eastern Europe would be under the auspices of the Soviet Union. America's Roosevelt opposed this trade-off, as did his successor Truman, but the Churchill-Stalin pact prevailed. Thus all of Eastern Europe was virtually surrendered to the ideology of despotic Marxism, allowing the people no voice in their future.

Religious faith was viewed as an enemy to be vanquished. The ultimate intention of these Communist governments was to stamp out faith and produce a generation of pure Marxists. Meantime, the governments had to deal with the churches that held favor with much of the population. Although they sought to contain church growth and curtail church influence, these governments did permit temporary accommodations with the powerful religious establishments, so long as the power of the state over life and conscience remained explicit in the constitution. No religious group or individual, however, could be allowed to act against the best interests of the state. The constitution might call for separation of church and state, but the state was always prosecutor, judge, and jury over the activities of any church.

The East European Communist countries sought to avoid religious martyrdoms that would arouse world opinion. Imprisonment of religious dissenters was acceptable, but the charges were always non-religious in nature. The illusion of religious liberty under communism had to be perpetuated. The effect of this policy was the persecution of believers and resistant churches, resulting in the martyrdom of many professing Christians.

## LITHUANIA—MARTYRS BEFORE COMMUNISM

The greatest persecutions occurred in the three Baltic countries later claimed by the USSR. Lithuania, bordered by Poland, is the southernmost of the three.

Most Lithuanians were converted to Catholic Christianity in the fourteenth century. For the next four centuries the land was self-governing and a bulwark of Catholic faith. Then from 1792 until 1915 the little country suffered under Russian rule.

The tsarist government closed all Lithuanian Catholic convents and monasteries and shipped thousands of priests and nuns to Siberia, where many died as martyrs. Determined to stamp out the spirit of the conquered nation, the Russians suppressed the Lithuanian language. Any Lithuanian heard talking in his mother tongue was punished. Desecration of Catholic churches by Russian occupation forces provoked frequent riots. Thousands of civilians died in the two worst occurrences, in 1830 and 1863.

### Russian and German Brutalities

Germany occupied Lithuania during World War I. Near the end of the war the country again became independent and remained free until Communist troops invaded in 1940. After a mock election, the Soviets proclaimed Lithuania a Soviet Republic of the USSR. The Soviets attacked religious institutions which had been revived during the period of independence. They seized Catholic schools, churches, and other church property. Thousands of Lithuanians were arrested, including most of the country's religious and political leaders, and deported to labor camps in the Soviet Union. When Germany turned on the Soviets and marched into Lithuania, the Russians massacred 5,740 Lithuanian prisoners. Among them were fifteen priests.

The German occupation was no less cruel. About two hundred thousand Lithuanians, Jews, and Catholics died in concentration camps in Lithuania and Germany during World War II.

## Cruelties under Communism

The Soviets recaptured Lithuania in 1944. During the next dozen years some three hundred thousand Lithuanians were either killed or exiled to Siberia and other parts of the USSR. Families were broken up—fathers were sent to one concentration camp, mothers to another, and children were separated from both parents.

Between 1945 and 1956 almost every priest in Lithuania was ordered to submit to interrogation at one of 480 "centers of terror" set up across the country. Soviet Communists demanded that each priest sign a "loyalty" oath to spy on his own parishioners, make reports to the police, and help organize a puppet church independent of the Vatican. Clerics who refused were either shot or shipped to Siberia.

After Stalin's death, persecution was less savage, but Lithuania remained under the heel of tyranny. "Uncooperative" bishops and priests continued to be exiled or put under house arrest. Smaller, scattered congregations of "reform" Baptists were treated more harshly, with scores of pastors being arrested and imprisoned.

## Martyrdoms Continue

In 1980 five priests in Lithuania and two in adjoining Latvia were brutally attacked. Two of the five died. One in Latvia was checked into a psychiatric ward of a hospital.

On August 8, 1980, sixty-three-year-old Father Leonas, who had signed a human rights letter to the Presidium of the Supreme Soviet, was murdered in church. The next day, another supporter for human rights in Latvia, Father Leonas Sapoka, was found dead. His body showed that he had been tortured to death. No arrests were ever made.

In July 1983, four of the five Catholic bishops in Lithuania were permitted to go to Rome for a visit with church leaders. But pressures at home continued.

Communist authorities kept a watchful eye on potential religious subversives—pastors who dared object to political harassment and onerous rules. Catholic Father Juozas, a founding member of the Committee for the Defense of Believers' Rights, was on this list. Once arrested and imprisoned for a year for teaching religion to children, he had been kept under surveillance by the secret police and repeatedly threatened for more than twenty years. He was reported killed in an automobile accident, February 5, 1986. The underground *Chronicle* of the Catholic Church in Lithuania called the crash "a carefully planned and executed act of violence."

## LATVIA AND ESTONIA—PAWNS OF MOSCOW

The story of religious persecution and martyrdom in these two small Baltic countries is tragically similar to the Lithuanian experience, except that 50 percent of Latvia's 2.3 million people and 70 percent of Estonia's 1.3 million population were Lutheran according to the religious census taken in 1971.

Like Lithuania, Latvia and Estonia have ancient cultural, linguistic, and religious identities. Both were occupied by tsarist Russia in the eighteenth century, regained their independence at the end of World War I, and were annexed by the Soviets through mock elections in 1940. After annexation, thousands of Latvian and Estonian Lutherans died as a result of imprisonment in Siberian labor camps.

## Martyrs among Baptists

Both countries also have sizable Baptist minorities. Baptist work was initiated in Latvia in 1860 when a visiting German Baptist challenged a group of seekers to study believers' baptism in the New Testament. Nine of the seekers became convinced and journeyed to the German city of Memel to be baptized in a Baptist church there. By 1875 there were thirty-five Baptist churches in Latvia with twenty-two hundred members. As Baptist work continued to grow, Latvian leaders became active participants in the Baptist World Alliance. During Latvia's period of independence, 1918–1940, many prominent foreign Baptist preachers visited the small country and preached in the large church at Riga. Estonia has likewise been a fertile field for the Baptist witness.

Under Communism, thousands of Latvian and Estonian Baptists were deported to Siberia where many died. Some returned home broken in health after years of confinement. Baptist churches in both captive nations, legal and illegal, were reported crowded despite the government restrictions which prevailed across the Soviet Union. In the city of Tallinn, Estonia, Baptists were permitted to meet in the Lutheran cathedral.

In Latvia and Estonia the light of the gospel continued to shine in the 1980s. All of the atheist crusades, discrimination, and persecution emanating from Moscow could not put it out. When the Moscow hard-liners made their ill-fated coup attempt in August 1991, both Baltic nations declared independence.

## BULGARIA—THE MOST "RUSSIAN" OF THE SATELLITES

A mountainous, Tennessee-sized country on the Black Sea, Bulgaria was never officially a part of the Soviet Union. But it was often called "Little Russia" because its rulers adhered so slavishly to the Soviet system. The dreary tale of suffering and martyrdom for religious faith under Marxist dictatorship continued here.

Bulgaria is deeply rooted in Christian tradition and influence. The Bulgars adopted Christianity as their state religion in 865 A.D. When Christendom split in 1054 between East and West, the Bulgarian church sided with the Byzantine-rite Eastern Orthodox Church. Later the Bulgarian church became a distinctly national movement. Today 85 percent of the population of 8.8 million holds some Orthodox identity. The remaining Bulgars who profess Christian faith are divided among Roman Catholics, Arminians, Pentecostals, Baptists, and smaller groups.

For almost five hundred years—from around 1400 to 1876—Bulgaria was under Turkish control. In 1876 a nationalist revolt provoked bloody massacres by Turkish soldiers. Russian troops intervened to defeat the Turks, but other European powers forced a withdrawal and Bulgaria remained in the Turkish empire. Full Bulgarian independence did not come until 1908.

## Martyrs to Stalinism

In 1948 the repression began, reflecting a Stalinist trend all across subjugated Eastern Europe. The puppet Bulgarian government forced the leader of the Bulgarian Orthodox Church to resign, then pressured the ruling Orthodox Synod to take a pro-Communist line. In 1949 state officials prodded the Orthodox clergy to hold special services in honor of Stalin's seventieth birthday. Pastors who objected or failed to follow instructions were arrested and sent to labor camps.

In this same year a new law put all church activities and appointments of clergy under the control of the state. The theological faculty at the University of Sofia was compelled to add Marxism to its curriculum. More Orthodox pastors were arrested and put on trial. Some were executed.

Persecution of smaller church bodies was even more severe. All churches with connections to denominations outside Bulgaria were ordered shut down. Only after these churches cut links with their foreign brothers and sisters were they allowed to resume worship services.

Also in 1949 fifteen prominent leaders of Baptist, Pentecostal, Methodist, and Congregational churches were arrested and charged with high treason, espionage, unlawful foreign exchange transactions, and attempts to undermine the government. The government press claimed that all made "confessions of guilt" and, after being sentenced to terms ranging from one year to life, thanked the judge for such "mild punishment." Protests were lodged with western governments and in the General Assembly of the United Nations, but to no avail. The only response of the Marxist regime was to make more arrests. Among others taken into custody were the Roman Catholic Bishop of Nikopol, Monsignor Eugene Boslov; the head of the Catholic seminary at Plovdiv; and two other priests. It is assumed that all four were executed.

# CZECHOSLOVAKIA

## Cardinal Stepan Trocta

Under Dubcek's liberal government Trocta was made a cardinal in 1969. In 1974 he was subjected to prolonged and brutal interrogations. He died after a cerebral hemorrhage, and was immediately declared a martyr by the Czech Catholics.

## Milan Gono

Cardinal Trocta had secretly ordained a number of people, one of whom was Milan Gono. Gono was arrested in March 1979 for engaging in so-called "unauthorized priestly activities." In July 1979 he died in prison, as a result of falling off scaffolding, according to the authorities. But the doctor who carried out the post-mortem discovered that Gono had been dead before he fell. Gono's prison warder corroborated this. Gono had been interrogated as the authorities tried to make him divulge the names of other people who had been secretly ordained. Gono died as a result of these severe tortures.

## Father Premysl Coufal

Father Coufal was secretly a Catholic priest and so was frequently harassed by the secret police. In January 1981 he was given an ultimatum by the secret police. He was given until February 23 to cooperate with them. This would have meant divulging names of other secret priests. On February 24 Coufal's friends found him dead in his flat. While the authorities claimed that Coufal committed suicide by gassing himself, his friends who found him discovered that his head had been very badly wounded.

# CATHOLIC POLAND—NATION OF DEATH

More people have died as martyrs to freedom and faith in Poland than in any other European country, excepting the Soviet Union. Over six million Poles died under the Nazi occupation during World War II. Many priests and pastors were among them. After the Communist takeover, thousands more were imprisoned or killed by Communist police and officials. Yet today no Eastern European nation is more stubbornly resistant to foreign tyranny than the beleaguered Poles. The Marxist rulers were thwarted again and again in attempts to completely communize Poland.

Next to Italy, Poland is the most Catholic country in Europe. Over thirty million Poles are Catholic. The next largest religious body, the autonomous Polish Orthodox

Church, has 553,000 adherents. Eastern-rite Uniate Catholics number 280,000; Lutherans report 80,000; and the Polish National Catholic (Old Catholic) Church claims 54,000. There are smaller numbers of Methodists, Baptists, Calvinists, and other Protestant communions. Jews are reduced to a minority of around five thousand. In 1939 there were 3.4 million. Of these, only ninety thousand survived the genocidal slaughter by the Nazis and most of them emigrated to Israel.

## A Nation Was Baptized

Poland's Catholic legacy dates from 966 when the state's first ruler, Mieszko I, professed faith. Following his command, the entire population of the new nation was baptized. In the centuries following, Poland continued as one of the most tightly knit Catholic countries in the world. Today, the most common greeting in the Polish countryside is still, "Blessed be Jesus Christ." Before Communism collapsed, Cardinal Stefan Wyszynski, the Catholic primate of Poland, the most powerful man in the country, was the only churchman in Eastern Europe who could make the national Communist Party boss blink.

From 1772 to the end of World War I Poland was divided under Prussian, Russian, and Austrian control. A Polish republic was formed in 1918. Pianist Ignace Jan Paderewski served as the first prime minister.

## The Tragedy Begins

The modern tragedy of Poland began on August 23, 1939, by the stroke of a pen, when Hitler's Joachim von Ribbentrop and Stalin's Vyacheslav Molotov signed the Nazi-Soviet Pact, dividing Poland between the two totalitarian powers. Eight days later the Nazis staged a Polish "provocation" and invaded Poland from the west. The Russians moved in from the east the same month.

The Communist attackers executed fifteen thousand Polish army officers and deported another 1.7 million Poles. Many of the latter were sent to Russia and trained in Communist strategy, then sent back after the war to aid in the capture of Poland.

## The Nazi Death Camps

After the break between Stalin and Hitler, Nazi armies swept across Eastern Europe and deep into the USSR before being turned back. Because of its proximity to Russia, intense nationalism, and large Jewish population, Poland was turned into a vast death prison. Names of such death camps as Auschwitz and Treblinka are still sounds of terror to Polish survivors.

Catholic priests numbering 3,644 and an unknown number of Protestant ministers died in Polish concentration camps or were shot to death near their residences. Those in the death camps were forced into the gas chambers along with the laymen. In labor camps they were used like work animals. When no longer able to work, they were killed. At the Oswiecim Camp, which held thirty thousand prisoners, prison laborers were not expected to survive over six weeks. In this camp Jews and Catholic priests were given the hardest jobs. They were harnessed daily to huge rollers designed to smooth out walkways within the compound. Many fell in their tracks and were roughly pushed out of the path of the rollers to await the corpse collectors.

One hundred twenty priests were incarcerated in the Dzialdowo Camp. The oldest was eighty-three-year-old archbishop Antoni Julian Nowowiejski, the bishop of Plock. Because of his position, appeals were made to high authorities for his release, but he was never permitted to go free. He died there in May 1941.

## Dying for Another

Many clergymen died trying to protect fellow inmates. One of the most celebrated Catholic martyrs is Father Maximilian Kolbe. While in Auschwitz, he was an inspiration to hundreds of unfortunates. One day the names of some prisoners scheduled for execution were called out. One of these pleaded that he was married and had children.

At that moment a smaller man, wearing wire rimmed glasses, came forward, without asking anyone's permission. The Franciscan stood to attention in front of the Deputy Commandant. "What do you want, Polish pig?" screamed the Deputy Commandant.

The little man replied, "I would like to die in the place of this man. I am a Catholic priest, whereas he has a wife and family." They allowed prisoner 16670 to be a substitute for Francis Gajowniczek. The ten condemned men were left to starve in an underground cell, although the sound of praying and singing of Christian songs could be heard from under the ground at Block 13. One by one the men died, as they were deprived of water and food. They were so desperate for fluid to drink that they even drank their own urine. By August 14 four prisoners were left alive. Then the moment came for a lethal injection of phenol to be administered in the left arms of the four men, including Kolbe. Kolbe prayed and gave his arm to his executioner.

## A Priest Is Murdered

An uproar occurred in 1984 when a popular and beloved Warsaw priest, Fr. Jerzy Popieluszko, was murdered by three employees of the Ministry of Interior Affairs, the government agency which handled religious affairs. The government agents later confessed that the murder had been planned during regular meetings at the Ministry and that the cars and instruments used in the murder were government property.

Captain Grzegorz Piotrowski, the leader of the murder squad, told a court that they had merely hoped to "scare" the priest. On the day of the murder the three agents took with them a bottle of vodka and a tape recorder for use in fabricating a conversation between Father Popieluszko and an imaginary husband who was to have attacked the priest after allegedly discovering that his wife had been sexually involved with the pastor. One of the agents was to play the role of the aggrieved husband, another to tape the exchange, and the third to force the priest to drink the vodka. They then planned to leave the priest drunk in a forest and distribute the tapes with the contrived conversation. Apparently, the priest did not cooperate, for he was found beaten to death from heavy blows. The public outcry led to a trial during which the methods used by the Ministry of Interior Affairs to persecute and intimidate church leaders were exposed.

## The Defeat of Marxism

On December 9, 1990, Lech Walesa was elected president of Poland. Outgoing president Wojciech Jaruzelski apologized for "each harm, pain, and injustice" suffered by Poles during his nine years as president.

In 1991 the new democratic government called for privatization of government-owned industries and businesses, and declared an end to official harassment of churches.

Poland is now free. Catholic and Protestant churches are growing. Christian programs are broadcast on a regular schedule. Bibles and Christian literature are freely distributed. Churches conduct their own affairs without fear of intimidation.

## ALBANIA—PUBLIC WORSHIP IS A CRIME

The human spirit does not soar in Albania, land of the "Sons of the Eagle." The Maryland-sized mountain country, bordered by Greece, Yugoslavia, and the Adriatic Sea, became the most repressive police state in Eastern Europe, and also the poorest. In this predominantly Muslim nation, Stalinism reigned supreme. Government leaders denounced the Soviet Union for tolerance of religion. No church or mosque was allowed to be open in Albania. No public expression of religion was allowed. After World War II, any Albanian clergyman who did not escape was martyred, imprisoned, exiled to a collective farm, or inducted into Communism.

## Executed for Baptizing a Child

Father Shtjefen was first sentenced to death in 1945 on a charge of spying for the Vatican. His sentence was subsequently commuted to life imprisonment, and eighteen years later he was released. He served as a parish pastor for a short time; then when the Marxist government ruled all religious practices illegal, he took a clerk's job in a cooperative. For defending the destruction of his church with his fists, he was returned to prison where he carried on his ministry secretly. In 1973 a woman prisoner begged him to baptize her child. The baptism was discovered. Charged with "subversive activities designed to overthrow the State," he was executed by a military firing squad.

After his death the official Vatican newspaper *L'Osservatore Romano* published an article decrying the sad fate of Roman Catholic Christianity in Albania:

> Places of worship either no longer exist or have been transformed into dance halls, gymnasia or offices of various kinds. . . . The church of the Stigmatine Sisters has become a lecture hall, the one of the Institute of the Sisters is used as the headquarters of the political police. The national sanctuary of Our Lady of Scutari, "Protectress of Albania," has been pulled down. On its ruins there now rises a column surmounted by the red star.

## Albania in History

Albania, like other East European captive nations, has a storied past and the legacy of a valiant struggle for freedom.

As ancient Illyria, it was engulfed by the Roman Empire in 167 B.C. Christianity came early to the mountain province, but the mountainous tribes were never really conquered for Christ. Albania was successively a part of the Byzantine, Serbian, and Turkish Ottoman empires. Under Turkish rule 70 percent of the population (now about 3.3 million) became Muslims through coercion or economic bribery. Many of these took only a Muslim public name, while retaining their Christian name for private use.

## The World's First "Atheist Nation"

After the Sino-Soviet split, Communist Albania sided with China on grounds that the Soviets had become soft on Marxism. The closing of the country's 2,169 churches and mosques was part of a "cultural revolution," China style, in which bands of young hoodlums were turned loose to terrorize the population. The Albanian Communists claimed that their youth had "created the first atheist nation in the world."

## The Red Record of Martyrdom

From 1945 on, clergymen and lay leaders were arrested and tried on various charges. For centuries, the Catholic clergy had taught and worked with all the people without religious distinction. It was this religious tradition the new government sought to shatter. By the end of 1946, almost half of the Catholic clergy were imprisoned, all foreign clergy were expelled, and twenty priests and religious leaders were put to death.

In the 1940s, Enver Hoxha, the then general secretary of the Communist party and head of the government, directed all his efforts toward fomenting resentment against the Catholic church leaders. The church, however, stood firm and united in opposition to the government's plan to establish a new church organization, severed from Rome, which would enable the Communists to spread their atheistic teaching throughout Albania.

## Hoxha's Plan

Enver Hoxha attempted to establish a Catholic church severed from Rome. His plan began to take shape in May 1945 when he expelled the Apostolic Delegate to Albania, Archbishop Leone G. B. Nigris. Then, hastily summoning the Metropolitan Archbishop of Shkodra, Primate of the Church, Gasper Thachi, and the Archbishop of Durres, Vincent Prendushi, a nationally famed poet and writer, he demanded that they separate from Rome, establish a new national church, and give their allegiance to his new regime. In exchange he offered the government's "conciliatory attitude" and material help in maintaining the Church's institutions. Both prelates bravely refused and paid for this stand with their lives. Thachi died in 1946 while under house arrest. Prendushi was sentenced to twenty years at hard labor and died in prison in 1949 after enduring horrific tortures. Most other Catholic bishops were "liquidated."

The government's onslaught then turned against the priests. In March 1945 the distinguished poet and humanist, Father Lazer Shantoja, was mercilessly tortured and shot.

In May 1945 the Catholic Bishop of Lezha, eighty-year-old Venerable Luigj Bumci, who headed the Albanian delegation at the Paris Peace Talks in 1918, died under house arrest after uninterrupted harassment.

In December 1945, Father Ndre (Andrew) Zadeja, poet and writer, was tortured and shot without trial.

During a mock trial on January 30, 1946, the Jesuit Vice Provincial, Gjon Fausti, rector of the Pontifical seminary, another Jesuit, Daniel Dajani, two Franciscan fathers, Gjon Shllaku, and seminarians Mark Cuni and Gjergj Bici were sentenced to death along with thirteen laymen. Their executions took place on March 4, 1946, outside the Catholic cemetery in Shkodra, and their bodies were thrown into a common grave. Their last words asked for pardon for their persecutors and gave praise to God and Albania. They shouted, "Long live Christ. Long live Albania." Exactly one month later all Jesuit institutions were closed and the order was outlawed.

In February 1946, the Franciscan Anton Harapi was executed after mock trial.

In May 1946, the Metropolitan Archbishop of Shkodra and head of the Catholic church in Albania, Gasper Thaci, died while under house arrest as a result of continual harassment and humiliation for not accepting government pressure to cut ties with the Vatican.

In January 1947 the Sigurimi, the Albanian security police, planted a cache of arms and ammunition in the main Franciscan church in Shkodra. When these weapons were "discovered," many Franciscan priests and brothers were arrested, tortured, and executed.

In February 1948, the forty-four-year-old Bishop of Sappa, Gjergj (George) Volaj was executed after being brutally tortured.

In March 1948, Abbot Frano Gjini, substitute Apostolic Delegate in Albania, was executed after being tortured and following mock trial, along with seventeen other clerics and lay people.

In February 1949 Metropolitan Archbishop of Durres, author and poet Vincent Prendushi, died in prison after suffering horrific torture.

Between 1951 and 1965, dozens of priests and other people were executed, imprisoned, or sent to forced labor camps in southern Albania. Among these were Fathers Ded (Dominic) Malaj, Zef Bici, Nikol Mazrreku, Andrew Lufi, Tom Laca, Gjon and Engjel Kovaci, Anton Suma, and Konrad Gjolaj.

The worst year was the 1966 cultural revolution. The first targets were churches and monasteries. At Shkoder the Catholic Franciscan monastery was set afire. Four monks were killed. The rest were forced to stand in their underwear and watch the building burn. Then they were driven through screaming mobs of Albanian "Red Guards" and taken to prison. At the city of Fier, Red Guards stormed the Catholic church. They broke and trampled upon priceless treasures and crosses, chopped the pews to pieces, then beat and abused the resident priests.

In the spring of 1971, only fourteen Catholic priests, among 203 priests listed in 1939, were known to be alive. Twelve of the fourteen were in concentration camps and two were in hiding.

In April 1979 the titular Bishop of Shkodra, Ernest Coba (Cho-ba) died in a labor camp as a result of the savage beatings he had received from police. He had been originally arrested for celebrating mass on Easter day.

The forty years of the Albanian government's campaign of persecution against the Catholic Church have resulted in the arrest and death of two archbishops, five bishops, an abbot, sixty-four diocesan priests, thrity-three Franciscans, fourteen Jesuits, ten seminarians, and eight nuns.

## Orthodox Church Persecution

The elimination of the leaders of the Orthodox Church in Albania was carried out by murder, execution, imprisonment, and torture. The Albanian regime killed, imprisoned, or sent to labor camps the majority of the hierarchy of the Orthodox Church.

Orthodox Christians suffering in this way included: Visarion Xhuvani, Archbishop of Elbasan; Bishop Irine of Apollonia (Pojan); Bishop Agathangjel Cance of Berat; Bishop Irine, Deputy Metropolitan of Korca and Gjirokastra; Papas Josif Papmihaili, as well as many priests and deacons. The head of the Albanian Orthodox Church, Archbishop Kristofor Kisi, was deposed and sent to prison where he died after much humiliation. He was replaced by the government with Pais Vodica, an archimandrite and Communist agitator.

## ROMANIA—DEATH, BUT NOT DESPAIR

Room Four in Romania's Tirgul-Ocna Prison was known as the "death room." When Abbot Iscu, the saintly head of a Lutheran monastery, was put there, no one had yet left alive. With him was a motley group of dying men. Vasilescu had been the overseer of a slave gang working on the ill-conceived Danube-Adriatic canal project. Filipescu, an old socialist, kept up hope that the Americans would come and set the prisoners free. Bucur, a police sergeant, kept raging that the doctors had put him in the room to satisfy their personal hatred. There was also General Tobescu, a former chief of police; Moise, a Jew; two Communist guerrilla refugees from Greece; Valeriu Gafencu, a member of the Iron Guard who had been in prison ten years; a farmer named Aristar whose nightly prayer was, "God smite the Communists"; Badras, who had given refuge to a Romanian nationalist fleeing from the secret police; and Richard Wurmbrand, a Lutheran pastor. Some of the prisoners were near death from beatings. Some suffered from tuberculosis and other illnesses brought on by years of maltreatment and torture.

## Memories of Horror

In his weakened condition Abbot Iscu recalled for his fellow prisoners the terrible slave camps at the canal project where thousands had died from Communist brutality. The canal had been forced on Romania by the Soviets who wanted a more efficient means of transportation to drain the satellite of its farm produce. Engineers who warned that the Danube would not supply sufficient water for both the canal and its irrigation tributaries were shot as "economic saboteurs." Moscow's planners said it must be built.

The abbot had been in one of the penal colonies strung along the canal route. Each of the twelve thousand prisoners in his string of barracks had been forced to move eight cubic meters of earth a day by hand. They pushed wheelbarrows up steep grades while guards rained blows on them from behind. Disease was rampant. Many men froze to death. Often, prisoners hoping to be shot deliberately ran into the forbidden area around the camp.

Christians were put in a so-called "Priest's Brigade." If one so much as made the sign of the cross, or closed his eyes to pray, he was beaten. There was never a day of rest, no Christmas, no Easter. The Lutheran clergyman knew that under the pressure, some had turned informers. One was Andrescu, an Orthodox priest, who reported a young Catholic priest, Father Cristea, for closing his eyes in prayer. "The political officer called Cristea out and asked if he believed in God. Cristea replied, 'When I was ordained, I knew that thousands of priests had paid for their faith with their lives. I promised to serve God, even if I had to go to prison or die. Yes, lieutenant, I believe in God.'"

"What happened to Father Cristea?" one of the men in Room Four asked the abbot softly.

"He was locked for a week in the place where you stand and never sleep; then beaten. When he again refused to deny his faith, he was taken away. We never saw him again."

## Forgiveness for the Dying

It happened that Vasilescu had been the overseer of Abbot Iscu's brigade. A common law criminal, he had been promised special privileges for assuming this position. "It was join the torturers or be tortured," he told his prison mates. A part of his training had been to shoot cats and dogs, then jam steel spikes into the heads of animals still alive. In the room of the dying he now listened to Abbot Iscu's whispered prayer and heard his words of comfort.

Vasilescu was also dying. Guilt-stricken, he confessed to Pastor Wurmbrand the terrible punishments he had inflicted on the abbot. The Lutheran pastor assured him that God's forgiveness knew no limits. But Vasilescu could find no peace. One night he woke up gasping for breath. "Pastor, please pray for me. I'm going," he rasped. He dozed, then woke again, and declared, "I believe in God." Then he began to cry. Abbot Iscu had overheard. He asked two prisoners to move him to Vasilescu's bed.

"You were too young to know what you were doing," the abbot told his former torturer. "I forgive you. And if I and other Christians can forgive, surely Christ will forgive, too. You have a place in heaven," he assured.

That night both died. Richard Wurmbrand, the only member of the group who survived, wrote later in his shocking narrative of prison life, "I believe they went hand in hand to heaven."

## The Sufferings of Richard Wurmbrand

Wurmbrand's books—translated into forty-five languages—are among the most shocking indictments of Communism ever published. Arrested for engaging in an underground ministry to both Romanians and Soviet soldiers after the close of World War II, Wurmbrand was imprisoned and tortured for fourteen years. He was subjected to the worst tortures imaginable. He describes one experience:

A hood was pulled over my head and I was forced to squat with my arms around my knees. A metal bar was thrust between my elbows and knees and set between trestles, so that I swung head down, feet in the air. They held my head while someone flogged the bare soles of my feet. Each blow sent an explosion of agony through my whole body. Some fell on my thighs and the base of my spine. Several times I fainted, only to be revived by buckets of icy water. After each drenching a voice would say that if I gave just one of the names they wanted, names of secret enemies of the state, the torture would stop. When at last they took me down from the spit, I had to be carried to my cell, my feet a mass of dark red pulp. (From *Christ in the Communist Prisons,* p. 38)

During his long captivity Wurmbrand led many men to Christ, some through tapping a secret code on the walls. He saw scores of other clergymen, including some informers, and a number of former high officials in the Romanian government. Some of these were Communists, deposed and imprisoned in purges.

## Wurmbrand's Testimony

Wurmbrand was released in 1958. After resuming his underground work, he was rearrested in 1959 and sentenced to twenty-five years in prison. In 1964 a general amnesty provided for his freedom. He was in danger of a third arrest when Norwegian Christian friends paid $10,000 to the Romanian Communist authorities for his release. He subsequently came to America and in testimony before the U.S. Internal Security Subcommittee in May 1966, bared his body above the waist to show the scars from his captivity.

COMMUNIST EXPLOITATION OF RELIGION HEARING
Before the
SUBCOMMITTEE TO INVESTIGATE THE ADMINISTRATION OF THE INTERNAL
SECURITY ACT AND OTHER INTERNAL SECURITY LAWS
of the
COMMITTEE ON THE JUDICIARY UNITED STATES SENATE EIGHTY-NINTH CON-
GRESS, SECOND SESSION
TESTIMONY OF REV. RICHARD WURMBRAND
COMMUNIST EXPLOITATION OF RELIGION

Friday, May 6, 1966
U.S. Senate, Subcommittee to Investigate the Administration of the Internal Security Act and Other Internal Security Laws, of the Committee on the Judiciary, Washington, D.C.

The subcommittee met, pursuant to call, at 10:20 a.m., in room 318, Old Senate Office Building, Senator Thomas J. Dodd presiding. Also present: Jay G. Sourwine, chief counsel; Benjamin Mandel, director of research; Frank W. Schroeder, chief investigator; and Robert C. McManus, investigations analyst.

*Senator Dodd*
I will call this hearing to order. We have as our witness today Pastor Richard Wurmbrand, who is a refugee from Rumania.
... Did you have any fellow Christians like you imprisoned?

*Reverend Wurmbrand*

We had hundreds of bishops, priests, monks in prisons; my wife who is near me, she has been with Catholic nuns. My wife tells that they were angels; such have been put in prisons. Nearly all Catholic bishops died in prison. Innumerable Orthodox and Protestants have been in prison, too.

. . . One Sunday morning in the prison of Pitesti a young Christian was already the fourth day, day and night, tied to the cross. Twice a day the cross was put on the floor and 100 other cell inmates by beating, by tortures, were obliged to fulfill their necessities upon his face and upon his body. Then the cross was erected again and the Communists swearing and mocking "Look your Christ, look your Christ, how beautiful he is, adore him, kneel before him, how fine he smells, your Christ." And then the Sunday morning came and a Catholic priest, an acquaintance of mine, has been put to the belt, in the dirt of a cell with 100 prisoners, a plate with excrements, and one with urine was given to him and he was obliged to say the holy mass upon these elements, and he did it. And I asked him afterward, "Father, but how could you make this?" He was half mad. He answered to me: "Brother, I have suffered more than Christ. Don't reproach to me what I have done." And the other prisoners beaten to take holy communion in this form, and the Communists around, "Look, your sacraments, look, your church, what a holy church you have, what fine is your church, what holy ordinance God has given you."

I am very insignificant and a very little man. I have been in prison among the weak ones and the little ones, but I speak for a suffering country and for a suffering church and for the heroes and the saints of the 20th century; we have had such saints in our prison to which I did not dare to lift my eyes.

I am a Protestant, but we have had near us Catholic bishops and monks and nuns about whom we felt that the touching of their garments heals. We were not worthy to untie their shoelaces. Such men have been mocked and tortured in our country. And even if it would mean to go back to a Rumanian prison, to be kidnapped by the Communists and going back and tortured again, I cannot be quiet. I owe it to those who have suffered there.

. . . Nobody enters in the Rumanian secret police without being beaten, without being tortured. I have been not the worst tortured. The proof is that I am alive. So many died. Nearly all our Catholic bishops have been so handled that they have died, and in that time the Russians were in our country, they decided that the Catholic bishops should be killed. I have seen Catholic priests, heroes trampled under the feet and tortured to death. Under our eyes they were killed.

. . . This is a list of 150 Baptist pastors of Russia who have been recently deported to Siberia. I have the names , the addresses, the names of their wives, of their children. They have not all arrived to Siberia, because of the tortures many died.

*Senator Dodd*

These were Rumanians?

*Reverend Wurmbrand*

No, no, Russians. And I give it to the Senate.

*Senator Dodd*

We don't have any more questions. Do you have anything more you want to say, Pastor?

*Reverend Wurmbrand*
I want to say something. I owe it to those with whom I have been in prison. I have told you so many sad things. I don't wish to end with this note. I must tell you that in these great tortures and this great suffering, Christians have shown themselves as saints and as heroes, and if I am allowed to conclude with just one scene which I have seen myself.

It was at the canal. With us, 150,000 men and women have been arrested to build a canal. Beaten, tortured, hungry, without anything, they had to build a canal.

*Senator Dodd*
Build a canal?

*Reverend Wurmbrand*
Yes; a canal, the Danube Canal. My wife has worked and shoveled the earth. At this canal, there was a religious brigade of 400 men, bishops, priests, peasants who loved Christ, sectarians and so on, all who were for religious motives in prison.

Over this brigade criminals have been put, and to the criminals it has been promised that they will be released if they torture these Christians. This promise has never been kept. But imagine a criminal who is sentenced for life, if he knows that he has such a hope. If they saw you in this brigade making a cross as it is a habit with us in Rumania, or folding your hands or saying a word about God you were beaten to death.

And now a Sunday morning the political officer of the prison comes, the whole brigade is gathered, and just at random he sees a young man. He calls him, "What is your name?" He says the name. "What are you by profession?" He said, "A priest." And then mocking the Communist said, "Do you still believe in God?"

This priest knew that if he says yes, this is the last day of his life. We all looked to him. For a few seconds he was silent. Then his face began to shine and then he opened his mouth and with a very humble but with a very decided voice he said: "Mr. Lieutenant, when I became a priest I knew that during church history thousands of Christians and priests have been killed for their faith, and notwithstanding I became a Christian and I became a priest. I knew what I became. And as often as I entered the altar clad in this beautiful ornate which priests wear I promised to God, 'If I will wear the uniform of a prisoner, then also I will serve Him.' Mr. Lieutenant, prison is not an argument against religion. I love Christ from all my heart."

I am sad that I can't give the intonation with which he said these words. I think that Juliet when she spoke about Romeo, she spoke like that. We were ashamed because we—we believed in Christ. This man loved Christ as a bride loves the bridegroom. This man has been beaten and tortured to death. But this is Rumania. Rumania is a country which is mocked, which is oppressed, but deep in the hearts of the people is a great esteem and a great praise for those who have suffered. The love to God, the love to Christ, the love to fatherland has never ceased. My country will live. With this I finish.

*Senator Dodd*
Your testimony has certainly been very impressing.

Wurmbrand has been criticized for attacking Romanian religious leaders, particularly Orthodox prelates who accommodated themselves to Marxist restrictions. But his descriptions ring with authenticity and his courage in resisting inhuman treatment cannot be denied. And the repression of Christianity by Romanian Communists is well-documented by many others besides Wurmbrand.

## A "Roman" Nation

Oregon-sized and located on the southeastern tip of Europe, Romania is the only European country which traces its ancestry and language back to the Romans. The Romanian language is closely related to Latin, the official language of the Roman Empire.

Christianity came to Romania as early as the fourth century. In the ninth century, the Romanian church joined in the Byzantine defection from Rome. The Romanian Orthodox Church has since been the established faith of Romania and today claims 90 percent of the country's twenty million people.

In centuries following, Romania, like other East European nations, became a pawn of European politics and wars. For almost four centuries the region belonged to the Turks. The Turks ruled Romania through vassal Greek Orthodox Christian princes, so Islam made no real inroads in Romania.

## Persecution of Baptists in the 1920s

Romania became independent in 1877 under a monarchy closely allied with the Orthodox Church. The next three largest Christian bodies, Roman Catholic, Hungarian Reformed, and Lutheran, were benignly tolerated because of their size. Baptists and other small evangelical groups were severely persecuted. The worst persecution occurred in the 1920s when many Baptist churches were confiscated and pastors imprisoned. During this harsh Fascist period, no Baptist worship services, burials, or weddings were permitted. The oppression eased from 1928 to 1937, then during 1938 and 1939 all Baptist churches were closed. Pressure from the Baptist World Alliance brought relief.

## "Cleanse Your Hands, You Sinners"

Freedom for Romanian evangelicals was short-lived. Under Stalin's pact with Hitler, Romania was divided among Russia, Bulgaria, and Hungary. The fascist Iron Guard movement tried to involve the Orthodox Church in political terrorism. Premier Armand Calinescu, the leading Iron Guard opponent, was murdered. The night before, nine Orthodox fanatics had kept a prayer vigil lying across a cold church floor, their bodies forming a cross. Hitler's protégé, General Ion Antonescu, seized power and ruled behind a young figurehead king.

Nazi and Orthodox fanatics ran amuck. Iron Guard agents kept a constant check on churches of minority groups. One Sunday, Wurmbrand noticed a group of strangers in the green shirts of the Iron Guard slip quietly into the back of his church. He saw revolvers in their hands and thought he might be preaching his last sermon. He spoke on the hands of Jesus—how they had fed the hungry, healed the sick, and been nailed to the cross. Then he raised his voice so the intruders could hear clearly. "But you. What have you done with your hands? You are killing, beating, and torturing innocent people. Do you call yourselves Christians? Cleanse your hands, you sinners!"

The Nazi agents waited with guns drawn as the congregation filed out. Wurmbrand surprised them by slipping behind a curtain and running through a secret exit to a side street. They ran forward, shouting, "Where's Wurmbrand?" But he had escaped.

Hitler's legions swept across Europe and invaded the Soviet Union. Thousands of Romanian evangelicals were murdered or herded into concentration camps with Jews. Wurmbrand's wife was Jewish. Her entire family was arrested. She never saw them again, but later met and forgave the man who issued the orders to kill them. Wurmbrand himself was arrested, beaten, and imprisoned by the Nazis three times. When the war ended, he was well equipped to face Communism.

## Communists Court the Clergy

A Moscow-guided Communist minority gained control of a coalition of Romanian political parties. They took over the government through "free" elections and forced the monarchy to abdicate. The Soviets had another satellite.

Communist Party boss Gheorghe Gheorghiu-Dej moved to win the support of the Orthodox clergy. Gheorghiu-Dej had been raised in a devout Orthodox home. During imprisonment under the Nazis, he had discussed religion with many incarcerated Christians. He escaped shortly before the Russian soldiers arrived pushing the Nazis west, and would have been killed by the Nazi dictator had not an Orthodox priest given him shelter.

Gheorghiu-Dej spoke at a meeting of Orthodox priests, which Wurmbrand attended as an observer. He assured the Orthodox clergy of his willingness to forgive and forget their subservience to Nazism. The state, Gheorghiu-Dej promised, would continue to pay clerical salaries from tax revenues. Communism and Christianity, he declared, could complement each other. All persons would enjoy complete liberty of conscience in the new Romania. Most of the audience cheered, and a spokesman promised that they would cooperate with the state.

Sabrina Wurmbrand was seated beside her pastor-husband. "Go and wash this shame from the face of Christ!" she demanded of him. Wurmbrand pleaded that he would probably be taken away. "I don't need a coward," she replied. Wurmbrand asked permission to speak. The organizers invited him forward, apparently anticipating a unity speech from the representative of the Swedish Church Mission and the World Council of Churches.

Wurmbrand began by saying it was the duty of pastors to glorify God, not fleeting earthly powers, and to support the eternal kingdom against the vanities of the day. As he continued, someone suddenly began to clap. The clapping erupted into waves of applause. "Stop! Your right to speak has been withdrawn," the Minister of Cults, a former Orthodox priest, ordered.

"My right to speak comes from God," Wurmbrand declared. He kept speaking until his microphone was disconnected. From that time, Wurmbrand's days of freedom were numbered.

The Romanian Communists proceeded on course. Many properties were nationalized. A new government department, the Ministry of Cults, became responsible for paying clerical salaries and confirming appointments to church offices. Father Justinian Marina, the priest who had sheltered Gheorghiu-Dej from the Nazis, was made an Orthodox bishop and control of the church was put in his hands.

## The Martyred Bishops

Party leaders now demanded that Roman and Greek Catholics break with Rome. The Greek Catholics, numbering 1.5 million, were ordered to merge with the Orthodox Church. Their monasteries and seminaries were closed and parish churches delivered to the Orthodox Church. The Romanian Catholic hierarchy paid a terrible price for protesting. All six bishops were arrested. Four of the bishops subsequently died in prison. Fifty priests were killed, two hundred disappeared, and four hundred were imprisoned or put in forced labor camps. A minority of Orthodox priests protested against the forced assimilation of Greek Catholics. They were treated in the same ruthless fashion.

Article 27 of the Communist-devised 1948 constitution specified: "Under state control the Romanian Orthodox Church is autonomous and unified in its organization." Between 1958 and 1963 Orthodoxy felt the hot breath of this control. Some fifteen hundred priests, monks, and laity were arrested. Half of the Orthodox monasteries were controlled and two thousand monks forced into "useful work."

## Church Growth in "New" Romania

The worst times appear to be behind as Romania enters a new era. With the restoration of religious freedom, church membership is reportedly showing a rapid rise. The Romanian Baptist Union is now the largest Baptist group in Europe with 1500 churches. Josef Ton, the "Georgi Vins" of Romanian Baptists, raised money in the West to expand two training schools for ministers.

# VOICES FROM EASTERN EUROPE AND
# STATES OF THE FORMER SOVIET UNION

Two powerful messages come from Christians who suffered during decades of living behind the iron curtain of Communism.

One message is addressed to believers in the democratic West: Don't take your freedom for granted. Use opportunities which you have learned to take for granted to evangelize people. Be aware of Communist plans and strategies. Don't be beguiled by peace and freedom talk from China and other countries, still under the heel of Communist rulers.

The second message is presented to Communist leaders in power in these countries and western Marxists who never seem to learn from history: You have not and you will not produce a "new man" through Marxism. You mistakenly assume that man is perfectible and will become honest and altruistic in a system working for economic equality. The record shows that functionaries of Communist societies are like sinners everywhere: greedy, proud, full of vice and selfishness.

You have assumed that matter is all that matters. That man is flesh and bone, a creature of instincts and desires, devoid of eternal spirit. You have seen that man cannot live by bread alone, that he hungers for the presence of God; that he cannot find meaning in life apart from God's presence and direction.

You have discovered that your ideal of the new man is best exemplified by the Christian believers. They are honest, chaste, disciplined, unselfish, and hardworking, while the serfs of your system lie, cheat, steal, and seek release in alcoholism.

You will never change the world's social order with Communist man. The world can only be changed by new men in Christ. It is these new men and women whose blood you have taken in your futile quest for Utopia. Recognize this, repent, and look to the Savior for forgiveness and the power to live righteously before the last door closes before you forever.

# PART EIGHT

# Martyrs of the Middle East

# 20

## The Middle East

### *Troubled Lands of the Bible*

### The First Christian Martyr

And when they had driven him out of the city, they began stoning him, and the witnesses laid aside their robes at the feet of a young man named Saul. And they went on stoning Stephen as he called upon the Lord and said, 'Lord Jesus, receive my spirit!' And falling on his knees, he cried out with a loud voice, 'Lord, do not hold this sin against them!' And having said this, he fell asleep" (Acts 7:58–60 NASB).

Stephen was the first of many thousands who would perish in the historical land of the Bible that extends from present-day Turkey south across the ancient land of Canaan and into North Africa. The history of the early church courses with the blood of Christian martyrs who died rather than acknowledge the divinity of Roman emperors.

### When Christianity Became Respectable

With the conversion of the Emperor Constantine in the fourth century, Christianity became, in effect, the official religion of the Roman Empire. Entire ethnic and national groups converted. The new respectability resulted in enormous growth, but at the expense of true spirituality. "Christian" soon became a status of birth and political affiliation. From that time to the present, the persecution and killing of "Christians" in the Middle East

217

must be seen from three perspectives: (1) persecution of evangelical Christians by official church bodies aligned with political and nationalistic forces; (2) persecution of believers by Muslims who see Islam as encompassing the total social, political, and religious order; (3) persecution and pressures by Jews.

## ARMENIA: THE MASSACRES

Armenia, regarded as the first nation to accept Christianity, was converted early in the fourth century. A desert and mountainous country, the ancient land was sandwiched between the Russian, Turkish, and Persian empires. It was often made a buffer state for these and other rival civilizations.

In the nineteenth century Protestant evangelical missionaries brought the gospel to the Armenians with stirring freshness. This precipitated an evangelical renewal movement within the staid old Armenian church. The patriarch became alarmed and banned Bibles and books imported by the missionaries. Several evangelical Armenian leaders were imprisoned. From their prison cells they asked their supporters to continue working for reforms from within the established church.

At that time much of Armenia was under a Turkish Muslim government. The Turks distrusted the Armenian church hierarchy and sympathized with the evangelicals, although conversion of a Muslim to Christianity was punishable by instant death. This law was suddenly lifted in 1856 and complete religious liberty declared. The evangelical movement took on new zeal. Scores of Muslims became Christians. Among them was the secretary to the ruling sultan. The opportunity proved to be short-lived. In 1864 the Turkish government began rounding up and sentencing to prison Muslim converts to Christianity.

Turkish fears of an Armenian uprising continued. From 1895 to 1896 government soldiers killed up to one hundred thousand Armenian civilians. Then in 1915, under the cover of World War I, the Turks accused the Armenians of helping Russian invaders and launched a genocidal action that ranks as one of the most terrible barbarities in history.

In the spring an attempt was made to kill every Armenian within Turkish borders. Lawyers, doctors, clergymen, and other intellectuals were rounded up and charged with subversion. Many had their heads placed in vises and squeezed until they collapsed. April 24 was the day set to kill the rest of the Armenians. Thousands of children were pushed alive into ditches and covered with dirt and sand. Many more Armenians were stoned or hacked to death. Some had their jaws ripped apart. Women and girls, some as young as twelve were stripped naked and raped before being slaughtered. Some persons were branded on the chest and back with red-hot iron crosses. Evangelicals died alongside members of the established church.

As many as six hundred thousand may have died on that fatal April 24, the day still observed as Memorial Day by the descendants of the Armenian survivors. When the Turkish soldiers saw they could not kill all of the Armenians in a single day, they began

218

driving the crowds into the desert. Those who fell by the wayside were killed. Only the strongest escaped into Russian territory where American relief camps had been set up.

## LEBANON AND SYRIA: CONFLICTS

The dominant church in Lebanon is the Maronite Church, named for John Maron, a church leader who, in the seventh century, led a break from the official Roman Catholic Church over a doctrinal dispute about the nature of Christ. The Maronites were brought back into the fold of Rome in the twelfth century by Catholic crusaders from Europe.

Evangelical work in Lebanon began in 1819 with the arrival of two missionaries of the American Board of Commissioners for Foreign Missions. Today there is a large body of Presbyterians in Lebanon, as well as in adjoining Syria, plus churches affiliated with the Baptists, the Christian and Missionary Alliance, the Church of the Nazarene, and other groups.

Thousands of Maronites have been killed in clashes with Druzes and Muslims. In 1860 the Druzes, an offbeat sect of Islam, killed hundreds of Maronite Christians, arousing a military response from Catholic France. French troops took control of the area which comprises present-day Lebanon and Syria.

Under a government of like faith, the Maronites became the dominant religious group in Lebanon and Syria. Evangelical missionaries were allowed broad liberties in spreading the gospel, but Maronites who became evangelicals were persecuted. Usually this persecution involved banishment from home and community and loss of employment. Occasionally a convert was imprisoned on a trumped-up charge. A few were killed.

### "Kiss the Coals!"

One of the most notable Lebanese converts to evangelical faith in the early twentieth century was Asaad Shidiak, a Syrian, and former secretary to the Maronite patriarch. The astounded patriarch first tried persuasion, then offered the convert the bribe of promotion, and finally threatened him with excommunication. When Shidiak remained steadfast, angry relatives had his marriage annulled and asked the patriarch to deal with him severely. The patriarch had him thrown into jail where he was later chained before an icon and a pot of burning coals. "You may choose to kiss the icon in token of repentance or kiss the coals!" he was told. He pressed the burning coals to his lips, and then with scorched and blackened lips was returned to his cell.

The torture continued. Finally they built a wall around him in his cell, leaving only a small opening through which he could breathe and reach out for food. There, after prolonged suffering, he passed into the presence of God.

## Prayer amidst Death

Night after night evangelical believers and missionaries huddled in their homes while war between the political factions raged around them. Many inspiring stories and testimonies of God's protection are related in *Flowers from the Valley of Terror*, a book published by Baptist Publications in Beirut.

Wrote Chassan Khalaf, an instructor at the Arab Baptist Theological Seminary in Beirut:

> We spent many long sleepless nights. . . . How the building shook and swayed from the force of the blasts, and how the shrapnel rained on the balconies of our apartment, falling like hailstones on a tin roof. From time to time we heard cries of distress from neighboring buildings or the siren of an ambulance speeding by, carrying the injured. And in the mornings we saw the death notices filling the walls of the narrow streets and new pictures of those who died in battle the night before. . . .
>
> In this atmosphere of dryness and death the only soothing factor was a prayer meeting that we held by turns every night in various homes. We met around the Lord Jesus, listening to a reading from His words and pouring out our hearts before Him in thanksgiving and intercession and petitions for help. God the Father of our Lord Jesus Christ showered these meetings with a deluge of mercies and kindnesses and assurances of His care for His children. Fountains of hope exploded in the deserts of our hearts, and praises flowed out of our mouths to the Father of mercies and the God of all comfort. How we were encouraged when we would remember that we had brothers in neighboring Arab countries and in the world who were praying for us continuously. We felt that we were members of one body with them. If a member of that body suffers pain his brother feels it with him.

## A Martyred South African

Kentleigh Torrente, a thirty-four-year-old South African serving in Lebanon under Youth With a Mission, was in his second term of ministry when shot by Syrian forces on October 13, 1990. Torrente was believed to be the first western missionary killed in Beirut during the past fifteen years.

## "TOLERANT" EGYPT

Among the Arab countries of North Africa and the Middle East, Lebanon has the largest proportion of "Christians" among its population. However, the largest Christian minority group in the Middle East is the Egyptian Coptic Church. With around three million members, the Coptic Church dates its origin to the first century when John Mark, the author of the second Gospel and Paul's sometime missionary companion, reportedly established a congregation in Alexandria. There is also a sizable Coptic Evangelical Church, established by Presbyterian missionaries in Egypt.

Since the early 1980s, severe restrictions have been placed on Christian activities. Presidential permits are required for building new churches. Some congregations must wait for years for permission to make small repairs. Hundreds of church-building permits are pending. Some requests go back as far as ten years. Fifteen existing churches in the Coptic neighborhood of Old Cairo have been put under government control. The Christian periodical *El Keraza* has been banned. No Christian holds any of the 160 top government positions outside the Egyptian cabinet. No Christian serves as a university president, college dean, or police commissioner.

Radical Muslims speak so harshly against Christians that soldiers are stationed outside many Egyptian churches to protect worshipers from extremists.

One of the worst outbreaks of violence in recent years came in a small Coptic Christian village, 130 miles south of Cairo on May 5, 1992. According to a report in the *New York Times*, local Muslims attacked when a Christian refused to sell his house to a Muslim who had demanded that he do so.

The attackers waited for the Christian farmers to enter their fields. When the farmers arrived, one group of attackers opened fire, killing at least six Christians instantly. Another radical Muslim group burst into the home of a Christian doctor and stabbed him to death. A third group forced their way into a school and started shooting. Altogether, thirteen Christians were killed. One woman who witnessed the attack told a *Times* reporter, "They were like mad dogs, running and shooting." Another man said, "People are terrified. The Muslim militants do what they want in our villages and the government does nothing to stop them."

Since 1992 hundreds of Coptic Christians in Egypt have been killed by Muslim extremists.

## Armed Muslims Murder Coptic Christians

On February 12, 1997, twelve Coptic Christians were shot dead as they listened to a sermon in the Church of Mar Girgis in Abu Qurqas, which is nearly 150 miles south of Cairo. Over two hundred bullets were fired from automatic weapons by three masked gunmen. Christians had not been previously attacked while they were in a church.

On February 15 three Christians were killed in a sugarcane field in a village close to Abu Qurqas. On March 13, nine Coptic Christians were shot dead by three Muslim gunmen who were disguised as police officers. This happened 350 miles south of Cairo in a village called Nag Dawoud.

## Young Christian Men Murdered

On August 14, 1998, two young Christian men were killed in the village of Al-Kosheh. The local Coptic bishop reported that the consensus of the village was that the killers were three Muslim men who were known to police. The police made no effort to arrest them but over the following week they rounded up nearly 1,200 Christians, including men, women, and children. It was reported that while they were detained they suffered many kinds of abuse, both verbal abuse and physical abuse. Their tortures included electrical shock treatment, whippings, beatings, and being hung from their feet for many hours. In this way the police hoped to obtain false confessions about the murders of the Christians.

Eleven-year-old Romani Boctor was suspended from a spinning ceiling fan for several hours in an attempt to get his father to confess to the murders. A fourteen-month-old baby was beaten in front of her mother to get the mother to confess to these murders.

## Twenty-one Christians Killed

Violence and mayhem between Christians and Muslims erupted between December 31, 1999, and January 2, 2000, leaving twenty-one Christians dead and 260 of their homes and businesses destroyed or looted in Al-Kosheh and the surrounding villages in southern Egypt.

Christians were ordered by police to stay in their homes and shut their windows and doors. Reports suggest that police stood idle while groups of armed Muslims were allowed to enter the Christian areas. Many of the victims were told to renounce their Christian faith, and when they refused they were executed with automatic weapons or knives.

Adel Ghattas Fahmy, a twenty-two-year-old deacon at the local Coptic Orthodox church, was one of the victims of this massacre. After the Sunday service in his church, Adel was approached by four armed men. They dragged him to a nearby field and ordered him to renounce his Christian faith and to embrace the Islamic religion. Adel refused. So he was forced to kneel down before being shot in the back of his head. Adel had a younger sister, Maysoun, who was just eleven years old. Maysoun was made to lie down next to her brother's dead body and then was also shot and killed.

## U.S. State Department Annual Report
## on International Religious Freedom for 2000

The following testimony was provided by Joseph Assad, Middle East Research Director of the Center for Religious Freedom, Freedom House before the House Committee on International Relations, Subcommittee on International Operations and Human Rights, on September 7, 2000.

> I am appearing here both as the representative of the Center for Religious Freedom and as a Coptic Christian born and raised in Egypt, who has witnessed firsthand the problems facing the Middle East's largest religious minority. I return to my native Egypt frequently.

My last visit was in July, 2000, in order to investigate the facts surrounding the Al Kosheh massacre of last January.

I have been asked to concentrate my remarks on the situation of Christian Copts in Egypt. Egypt is a pivotal country. It is the cultural and intellectual center of the Arab Middle East and it is the home of the region's largest community of Christians—a community larger than all other Christian communities in the region combined.

The Copts, while usually having some freedom of worship, are threatened in varying degrees by terrorism from extreme Islamic groups, by the abusive practices of local police and security forces, and by discriminatory and restrictive Egyptian Government policies.

While neither the Constitution nor the Civil and penal codes prohibit Christians from speaking about their religion or evangelizing, some Christians have been arrested for publicly sharing their faith on charges of violating article 98(f) of the penal code, which prohibits citizens from ridiculing or insulting "heavenly religions" or inciting sectarian strife.

Another prominent concern of the Copts is that vulnerable young Christian women and girls are targeted by some extremist Muslim groups and are pressured to convert to Islam, sometimes with the cooperation of local police. Pastors who have worked with such girls have been threatened and assaulted by extremists. Pastor "Youssef," an Assemblies of God pastor in Upper Egypt, saw his eleven-year-old daughter killed in 1996 in a deliberate automobile accident which he attributes to his efforts in bringing back to Christianity girls who have been forced to convert to Islam.

In addition to the long-standing problems faced by the Copts, this past year Egypt has witnessed several severe setbacks for religious freedom . . . The most egregious of these occurred in the southern Egyptian village of Al Kosheh in one of the worst massacres of Coptic Christians in Egypt's recent history."

Coptic leader Pope Shenouda III charged the Egyptian government of not doing enough to stop the violence, and demanded answers for why the police withdrew from the area minutes before the massacre began. The Pope usually refrains from public comments about the difficulties the Christian community faces, and indeed is restricted under Egyptian law from criticizing the government. The fact that he spoke out on this issue indicates the seriousness of the Copts' concern.

In July, as part of a Center for Religious Freedom team, I spent three weeks in Egypt documenting and investigating Al Kosheh, where 21 Christians were killed and dozens were injured after they were attacked by rampaging Muslims in early 2000 . . . While in Egypt, our team interviewed the families of victims and dozens of eyewitnesses. They gave us a firsthand description of the attack. Nine of the dead Copts were killed in their own houses, which indicates they were hunted down as they sought to escape. Three of the dead were females, one an eleven-year-old girl, and four were under the age of sixteen, and one was 85. One man was reportedly asked to renounce his Christian faith. When he refused, his arm bearing a Christian tattoo was cut off and he was stabbed to death. A mob then burned his body. His mother was an eyewitness to these events. While there was destruction of property in Al Kosheh by both Muslims and Christians, all those murdered were Christians.

The massacre in January 2000 cannot be understood apart from events in Al Kosheh in 1998. The murder of two Copts in August 1998, allegedly by five Muslims, was followed by the arrest, abuse and sometimes torture over the next six weeks of about 1000 Copts by local Egyptian police. Many reliable observers believe that the arrests were intended to portray the murders as within a religion so as to avoid further sectarian violence. The government continues to deny that discriminatory police brutality occurred in Al Kosheh in 1998, and arrested clergy, including local Coptic Bishop Wissa, and members of the human rights groups who reported publicly on it. No police officer has been penalized for the well-documented mass abuses and incidents of torture in Al Kosheh in 1998. The only conviction in connection with the 1998 Al Kosheh abuses was that of a Christian for the original double murder in August 1998.

There can be little doubt that the failure of justice for Christians after the police dragnet and abuse in 1998 left the Coptic community vulnerable to further assaults by possibly sending a signal that the Christian community could be attacked and driven from their homes with impunity. In other words, the 1998 Al Kosheh events set the stage for the massacre of January 2000.

While Al Kosheh was the most drastic example, it was not the only example of violence against Coptic Christians during the period covered by this Report. In August and September 1999, there were three separate attacks on Coptic orthodox clergy. On September 2, Father Aghnatious Al Mohariky was shot and killed by two Muslim brothers in a field belonging to a monastery in Al-Kosiya. Another priest was also shot and killed in the nearby city of Asyut, and, in Al-Mahalla, Father Istaphanous Sobhi was seriously injured after being repeatedly stabbed in his chest and stomach shortly after conducting a mass at his church.

## "CLOSED" ARAB COUNTRIES: PERSECUTIONS

Other Arab countries tell a different story. With few exceptions during recent years, evangelical missionaries have been unable to enter as Christian workers in Syria, Iraq, Saudi Arabia, Kuwait, the two Yemens, Oman, Qatar, the United Arab Emirates, Iran, and the North African Arab nations of Morocco, Algeria, Tunisia, and Libya. The two hundred or so full-time foreign "missionaries" residing in some of these countries are there as teachers, nurses, doctors, and practitioners of other "helping" occupations. Their freedom to witness to Muslims varies from country to country.

Libya, North Yemen (Sanaía), and Saudi Arabia are perhaps the most difficult. Southern Baptist medical workers in Yemen, for example, are forbidden by the Muslim government to hold public services or to directly evangelize patients. In Libya four young evangelists from the United States were imprisoned for distributing Arabic gospels. After special appeals, the Libyan ruler, Colonel Muamimar al-Qaddafi, issued a personal command ordering their release and deportation.

Pro-western Saudi Arabia permits "Christian" ministries only in foreign communities. A Saudi Arabian national Christian, Abdul Kareem Mal-Allah, was beheaded in 1992 for "insulting" God by speaking negatively of the Prophet Mohammed.

## Repression in Iran

Christians, with 0.4 percent of the population, are recognized as a minority in neighboring Iran. Since the downfall of the government of Shah Mohammed Reza Pahlavi, Iran has been governed as a Muslim theocracy in which Christians are declared a protected minority.

Many Christians have fled to the West because of political restrictions. Some Episcopalians, with Muslim ancestry, have suffered martyrdom and imprisonment. Nevertheless, some churches have grown.

The severest repression in Iran, as well as in other Muslim countries, has come upon Muslims who have become Christians. One of these was Hosein Soodman, an ordained fifty-five-year-old Assemblies of God minister. When Soodman's church in the city of Mashad was closed by the government in 1988, Soodman conducted private services for a while, then moved to a church in Gorgan, a city north of Tehran. Soon after arriving, he was arrested by Gorgan police, blindfolded, and taken away for questioning. He was then ordered to return to Mashad.

At Mashad he was rearrested and reportedly accused of spying, a charge friends dismissed as preposterous. "He was harmless, a meek man, who will be remembered for his quiet spirit," one said.

He was then subjected to public mockery for his faith and ordered to pray aloud repeatedly. His captors permitted his blind wife to visit him only twice during his final imprisonment and denied them a final meeting before his execution.

Fellow pastors went to the prison where he had been held and learned that he had been hung on December 3, 1990. Authorities took the delegation to an isolated grave where they said Soodman was buried. After hearing the news, his wife suffered a nervous breakdown. She and her four children, ages ten to fifteen, were taken into the homes of fellow Christians.

Several other Iranian believers have disappeared since Soodman's martyrdom and are feared dead.

## Bahram Dehqani-Tafti

Bahram Dehqani-Tafti, the son of the Anglican bishop, was shot. In the Shah's day, Bahram's father was the first Iranian to be made a bishop in Iran. After the revolution, that made him an enemy of the state. Bishop Hassan Dehqani-Tafti was forced to leave Iran, but his son, Bahram, was detained. The bishop is convinced that his son died as a result of his Christian faith. He had been bundled into a car and shot.

The following prayer was written by Bishop of Iran, on the martyrdom of his son.

O God
    We remember not only our son but also his murderers;
    Not because they killed him in the prime of his youth and made our hearts bleed and
    our tears flow,

Not because with this savage act they have brought further disgrace on the name of our
country among the civilized nations of the world;

But because through their crime we now follow thy footsteps more closely in the way
of sacrifice.

The terrible fire of this calamity burns up all selfishness and possessiveness in us;
Its flame reveals the depths of depravity and meanness and suspicion, the dimension of hatred
and the measure of sinfulness in human nature;

It makes obvious as never before our need to trust in God's love as shown in the cross
of Jesus and his resurrection;

Love which makes us free from hate towards our persecutors;
Love which brings patience, forbearance, courage, loyalty, humility, generosity, greatness
of heart;

Love which more than ever deepens our trust in God's final victory and his eternal designs
for the Church and for the world;

Love which teaches us how to prepare ourselves to face our own day of death.
O God

Our son's blood has multiplied the fruit of the Spirit in the soil of our souls;
So when his murderers stand before thee on the day of judgement
Remember the fruit of the Spirit by which they have enriched our lives.
And forgive.

*Hassan Dehqani-Tafti*

## Bishop Haik Hovsepian

Bishop Haik Hovsepian, an Armenian pastor, disappeared from the streets of Tehran
on January 19, 1994. The authorities reported his death to his family on January 30. Haik
was a man of God who believed in the God-given right of a person to believe according
to his conscience. He loved the people of Iran whether Christian or Muslim. He gave his
life for their religious freedom.

He did not believe in succumbing to government pressure and chose instead to "tell
the world" about the plight of Iranian Christians. He said: "If we go to jail or die for our
faith, we want the whole Christian world to know what is happening to their brothers
and sisters."

Also in 1994, the sixty-two-year-old leader of the Presbyterian church, Rev. Tateos
Michaelian, was murdered after taking over Bishop Hovsepian's position as chairman of
the Protestant Council of Ministers.

## Rev. Mehdi Dibaj

Rev. Mehdi Dibaj, who was born into a Muslim family, became a Christian when he was a young man. On December 21, 1993, an Islamic court in the city of Sari condemned him to die. The conviction was based on the charge of apostasy. Dibaj was accused of abandoning Islam and embracing Christianity. Once news of Rev. Dibaj's death sentence reached the international Christian community, their initial reaction of disbelief was followed by prayer and action.

Mehdi Dibaj has also been quoted as saying, "I have always envied those Christians who were martyred for Christ Jesus our Lord. What a privilege to live for our Lord and to die for Him as well. I am filled to overflowing with joy; I am not only satisfied to be in prison . . . but am ready to give my life for the sake of Jesus Christ."

One of the people who worked very hard to overturn the death sentence handed out to Rev. Dibaj was Bishop Haik Hovsepian-Mehr. Bishop Haik shared the news of Rev. Dibaj's death sentence as well as other violations of religious freedom of Christians in Iran with the world. Due to the world's reaction, Rev. Dibaj was released on January 16, 1994.

Five months after the release from prison, Rev. Mehdi Dibadj was abducted mysteriously and suffered martyrdom in June 1994.

## Pastor Mohammed Bajher Yusefi

Mohammad Bagher Yusefi was the seventh Christian leader to be killed in Iran since the 1979 revolution. At the beginning of the revolution the Anglican Church, which was mainly made up of converts from Islam, was attacked.

Yusefi was a thirty-five-year-old pastor who had converted from Islam at the age of twenty-four. After attending Bible school, he entered into full-time ministry and became pastor of the Assembly of God churches in Sari, Gorgan, and Shahr in the province of Mazandaran.

Pastor Yusefi, affectionately known by his flock as "Ravanbaksh" (soul giver), was killed on Saturday, September 28, 1996. Pastor Yusefi had left his house in Sari at 6:00 a.m. to spend time in prayer, but he never returned. The Iranian authorities notified the family later that evening that his body had been found hanging from a tree in a nearby forest.

## PERSECUTION IN ISRAEL

## Nurse of Gaza

Only one evangelical missionary is known to have been killed in Israel in the 1970s. This was Miss Mavis Pate, a dedicated forty-six-year-old Southern Baptist missionary nurse, serving in Gaza. A short, dark-haired woman with an infectious smile, Nurse Pate had only been a full-time missionary eight years.

She had served on the famous hospital ship *S.S. Hope* on its maiden voyage to the South Pacific in 1960–1961. At her missionary appointment service in 1964, she recalled, "God has his way to deal with us, and with this obstinate one, it required that He send me approximately halfway around the world and leave me there for about a year, to see the need that existed and to help point out to me my part in meeting that need. . . . On the basis of that . . . I made the commitment to foreign mission service."

She served first in East Pakistan (now Bangladesh) and Thailand. In 1970 she was transferred to the Baptist hospital in Gaza to serve as operating room supervisor and director of the nursing school. Here on the narrow strip captured by Israel in the Six-Day War of 1967, she and other missionaries were in one of the most dangerous areas of the world. The staff frequently heard gunfire around the hospital, and victims were often brought in for emergency treatment.

Nurse Pate was especially touched by the plight of the 360,000 Palestinian refugees living in camps on the narrow segment of land. Total population of Gaza, including the refugees, was then 420,000. She visited homes in the refugee camps and shared her faith in Christ. Her prayer list in one of her first letters home included the request "that we all may be truly surrendered to His will, willing tools in His hand, channels for His blessings, more Christlike than manlike."

Sunday evening, January 16, 1972, Nurse Pate left with missionary Ed Nicholas and his three daughters on the short trip to Tel Aviv where the girls were enrolled in school. She went along to refill some oxygen tanks for the operating room, and to drive a new car back to Gaza. They left the hospital just after 6:00 p.m. traveling north in the hospital's Volkswagen Microbus. There was little traffic at this time because of the danger of commando attacks from refugee camps along the highway. But the missionaries felt their neutrality would be respected.

Just outside the Jabalya camp, hidden Palestinians opened fire with automatic weapons, spraying the side and back of the Microbus with fifty rounds of bullets. Ed Nicholas was wounded in the leg and side. One of his daughters caught a piece of flying shrapnel in the foot. Miss Pate was hit in the head and several other places.

Israeli soldiers patrolling nearby heard the shooting. They rushed the Americans to an Israeli first-aid station. From there Ed Nicholas and Mavis Pate were flown by helicopter to the regional medical center in Beersheba for special treatment. Miss Pate lived for about three hours after the attack and died while doctors were working on her. Nicholas and his wounded daughter recovered.

News of the tragedy brought an immediate outpouring of sympathy and sorrow. Israeli Defense Minister Moshe Dayan came from Tel Aviv to offer assistance. Israeli television presented a five-minute editorial in Arabic and an interview with missionary doctor Jean Dickman. Dr. Dickman gave a clear testimony of the assurance that followers of Christ had in such a tragedy. And in Gaza scores of Palestinian Arabs came to the hospital expressing sorrow and regret at the accident. It was generally felt that the Microbus had been mistaken for an Israeli army vehicle.

At the funeral on Tuesday morning in the church at the hospital compound, the sanctuary overflowed with Arabs, Jews, United Nations relief workers, embassy representatives, fellow missionaries, and newspersons. Miss Pate was laid to rest in a quiet garden area on the hospital grounds.

## The Meaning of a Life Laid Down

An Arab student nurse wrote a poetic tribute. "She went, but just her body. For she still lives in our spirits. She planted the seeds of hard work, honesty, and faithfulness in us and these seeds will become the trees of love and peace."

The executive director of Nurse Pate's mission board assessed her death from another perspective. Said Baker J. Cauthen in a eulogy:

> We know how urgently a missionary nurse is needed, and how radiantly a life like this shines forth in its Christian testimony. We recognize, however, that the Lord of the harvest knows more than we do about the affairs of His work. He sometimes sees fit to let his choicest servants seal their testimony by laying down their lives in the line of duty, and out of it God has a way of bringing sustained advance in the work of his kingdom.
>
> Her silent grave will be a permanent witness to the high calling of God. Missionaries will look at it and remember the great extent to which missionaries go in order that the love of Christ may be shared. Non-Christian people will look at it and be reminded of the love of God that sent the Lord Jesus into the world for our redemption, and has continued sending his messengers forth to make that redemption known.

Meanwhile, the ministry of love and reconciliation by Christian missionaries and nationals goes on in the troubled Middle East. The work continues to be slow and the responses varied.

# PART NINE

# Martyrs
# of Sub-Saharan Africa

# 21

# Northeast Africa

## The Sudan, Ethiopia, Somalia

### THE SUDAN—"DESOLATION OF DESOLATIONS"

The worst fate a nineteenth-century British civil servant could suffer was being sent to the Sudan. One European traveler called it "a desolation of desolations, an infernal region, a howling waste of weed, mosquitoes, flies, and fever, backed by a groaning waste of thorns and stones—waterless and waterlogged. I have passed through it, and have now no fear for the hereafter." Yet the Sudan, extending along the upper Nile from Egypt to Uganda, over three times the size of Texas and the largest country in modern Africa, was considered important in Britain's sphere of influence.

Ethnically Sudan was then, and is now, two nations. In the more advanced north, two-thirds of the population comprised Arabic-speaking Islamics, descendants from mixed marriages of brown-skinned Nubians and blacks. Beyond a great unexplored marsh, the south was populated by nomadic black animistic tribes who spoke a variety of unknown languages.

The Nubians claimed descent from Cush, grandson of Noah, further asserting that the Ethiopian whom the evangelist Philip had baptized, had come from a city north of Khartoum, the capital of the Sudan. (In Greek, the language of the New Testament, "Ethiopian" meant only "burnt face.") But it was not until the sixth century that the Nubians were converted by Byzantine Catholic emissaries. Islam sprang up in the Middle East later and by the fourteenth century the faith of Mohammed had replaced

233

nominal Christianity. Catholic missionaries returned in 1848 when the Sudan was under Egyptian rule with aid from the British.

## Missionaries Are Expelled

Even before independence there was trouble between northern Sudanese Arabs and southern tribal blacks. The southerners could not forgive the northerners for slave-raiding expeditions in the past. The northerners blamed the missionaries for keeping this hostility alive. They noted that the missionaries had included the history of the slave trade in their school curriculum. After guerrilla attacks began on northerners in power, missionaries were blamed for aiding southern rebels, interfering in politics, and working against the unity of Sudan. Another contention was that the missionaries were undermining the Islamic faith. Impartial observers said the missionaries were not guilty. Before independence, they said, tribal feuding in the south and enmity against the north had been waning because of Christian influences.

The fighting escalated into full-scale civil war between the government, composed mostly of northerners, and southern Anya Nya (meaning "the venom of the Gabon viper") rebels. All mission schools were nationalized, Friday replaced Saturday as the day of worship, and severe restrictions were put on the activity and movement of missionaries. Finally, in 1964, the Muslims in power expelled all missionaries, 503 Catholics and 104 Protestants. The missionaries left behind the graves of sixty-four colleagues, most of whom had died from diseases peculiar to the harsh Sudanese environment.

## Communist Intervention

An ominous new presence entered the war on the side of the north. Soviet advisers flew support missions. Soviet arms, supplied through Egypt and Algeria, were shipped via the Nile. Sudanese pilots went to Moscow for training.

Despite numerous incriminating reports, the Soviets denied intervention. In one instance a missionary pilot from the Congo landed across the Sudanese border in Juba by mistake. At the airfield he met two Soviet pilots who proudly showed him the interior of their helicopter. When local authorities realized who the visitor was, they hustled the missionary back to his plane.

All of the facts added up to one conclusion: for the first time, Russians were fighting and bombing Africans.

# Christians Perish in Sudanese Genocide

Armed with Soviet arms and supported by Russian advisers, the north was overwhelmingly superior to the south. Over a half million southerners died by guns, bombings, starvation, and disease. The Sudanese government claimed this was an exaggeration.

Numerous atrocities inflicted against Christians were recorded:

A southern Catholic priest, Father Bagriel Dwatuka, was whipped while he hung from a rope, then salt was rubbed into his wounds. He and others who were whipped were made to say "thank you" at the end of each whipping.

Pastor Gideon Adwok, who served a thriving church in the upper Nile region related to the Sudan Interior Mission, was charged with aiding the rebels. His accusers claimed that he had used church money for helping tribal fighters. He was killed without being given an opportunity to defend himself against the charges.

Southern Christian schoolboys who protested cruel treatment by Arab teachers were rounded up by soldiers and some had their teeth pulled out by pliers. Reports came from other schools telling of southern native teachers and students being killed.

Educated southerners, many of whom had studied in mission schools, were imprisoned and tortured. At one prison metal balls were used to push eyes out of heads to get confessions. In another torture, red chili pepper was dumped into a bag, then the victim's head was forced into the bag and held there until his eyes were inflamed and he could no longer breathe. Other victims reported having flesh sliced off their bodies. Some had their flesh roasted with hot irons.

Southern Sudanese civil servants and political leaders were special targets. Paul Debior, a southern Sudanese Christian, had served in public office for over twenty-five years. He was murdered by soldiers in his own home.

Almost every Christian house of worship in the south was destroyed. The most notorious incident was the reported massacre of a Christian village, Banja, on the Sudan-Congo frontier, July 26, 1970. Survivors told a Norwegian journalist that a Sudanese military patrol had burst in on the people while they were at prayer. They tied up the pastor with his hands behind his back. Then the soldiers scoured the village, killing everyone they saw. The rest were kept in the church, tied to chairs with thick rope. The commander reportedly told them, "We're shooting you in your church. Let your God come and save you." Then the soldiers emptied their guns on the helpless people and the building was set afire. Only fourteen persons in the village managed to reach a hospital to tell the story. The Norwegian heard their stories and took a television photographer to the scene to record the grisly evidence.

Protests of this and other mass killings were sent in vain to the United Nations.

## Muslim Persecution

Food shortages continued to plague the Sudan, aggravated by a huge emigration of refugees from neighboring countries. Militant Muslims in the north waged a virtual civil war against Christians and animist populations in the south. The government declared the nation an Islamic republic. After sixteen years in power, President Nimeri, a tolerant Muslim, was overthrown in 1985 in a bloodless military coup. Democratic elections were held the next year, but then the elected government was overthrown in 1989 by Muslim military who seemed bent on turning the country into an intolerant Islamic state.

Millions of southern Sudanese Christians and animists were displaced or subjected to terrible repression. The government closed many churches and declared Christianity a "foreign organization" even though Christianity predates Islam by centuries. Worship services were forbidden without the issuance of a certificate. Dozens of pastors were killed and numerous churches burned.

One massacre followed the driving of twenty-five Christians of the Dinka tribe from their prayer service by a mob of Muslims wielding sticks, spears, axes, and guns. That evening, several Dinka were murdered and dozens of homes burned.

Early the next morning hundreds of Dinka were crowding into rail boxcars for safe evacuation when Muslim hordes began an attack. The unarmed people pleaded in vain for mercy. Burning mattresses were heaped on innocent victims. Others were shot, mutilated, and clubbed to death. By nightfall, more than a thousand Dinka were dead.

With the advent of the nineties, starvation prevailed in many Sudanese localities. Conversion to Islam was made a necessary prerequisite for Christians seeking food and shelter in displaced camps. Arrests, beatings, and executions became common.

The surviving Sudanese Council of Churches addressed an open letter to President Umar Hassan al-Bashir in December 1991, calling for cancellation of the policy that "aims at destroying Christianity in the Sudan." The Council charged that the government was trying to control all public expressions of Christian faith and even trying to prevent Christians from feeding victims of war and starvation.

In 1991 the government decreed that public school students must pass Islamic studies to become eligible for higher education. In 1992 the government imposed Arabic as the national language of school instruction.

At the close of the twentieth century Sudan ranked as one of the worst examples in the world of Christians being persecuted, bombed, and murdered by Muslims. Government (Muslim) forces bombed civilian and humanitarian targets in southern Sudan (which is nearly all Christian) at least 113 times in 2000.

## *Jihad* Declared

The NIF (the National Islamic Front, the current military regime) declared a *jihad* (holy war) against the religious and ethnic minorities that resist forced Islamization. It is estimated that two million people have died in the conflict and five million out of the eight million people that live in southern Sudan have been displaced since the fighting began in 1983.

The NIF seals off areas by road and air and government forces move in. Units are often sent in to "depopulate" the area. Mines are often sown on important roads and paths. People and livestock are taken or killed and structures are destroyed. People are forcibly relocated to "peace camps" where the young are taken away from their parents and sent to other camps for indoctrination by Islamic fundamentalists.

## End of the Century Martyrs

On Tuesday, February 13, 2000, three weeks after the Sudanese government declared a cease-fire, government bombs fell on Holy Cross School in Kauda, Sudan, in the Nuba Mountains. Fourteen children and a twenty-two-year-old teacher were killed outright, and seventeen other students were wounded, some critically. The survivors of the attack carried eighteen wounded children, some with limbs blown off, to a nearby German medical facility, one of many such makeshift medical facilities operating in hazardous locations throughout Sudan. A videotape recorded the aftermath of the slaughter. Five of the wounded children later died of their injuries. A three-foot-wide crater marks the spot where one bomb fell near the classrooms. Most of the victims were part of a first-grade class studying English outside under the shade of a tree.

Local eyewitnesses were appalled to see the government plane drop eight more bombs on two villages close to the school. "The bombs landed where they were supposed to land," declared Dirdiery Ahmed, an official in the Sudanese embassy in Nairobi. Sudanese government officials claimed that the school was part of a military camp.

Bishop Macram Max Gassis of El Obeid, whose jurisdiction includes the Nuba Mountains, and who founded Holy Cross School, testified about this evil attack before the U.S. Commission on International Religious Freedom, and said:

And as so often before, the forces of Khartoum have targeted the most vulnerable and most precious of our resources—our children. We do not have gold; we do not have money to invest in banks. Our capital investment is our children. They are the future of the Church, they are the future of the country.

On February 7th and 8th, two Russian-built Antonov bombers targeted the heavily populated areas around Kauda. The Catholic Church has set up the only well-established school in the area, with more than 360 students. 14 of these students were killed outright in the raid, and the number of wounded is yet to be fully determined. Truly, this is a slaughter of innocents, an unbridled attempt to destroy the Nubas' hope and indeed their future by destroying their children.

The Bishop believes that the Khartoum regime will not rest until the Christian and animist population of Southern Sudan is wiped out. He has said:

> I have time and time again told the world that the National Islamic Front regime in Khartoum has been, and is conducting a campaign of genocide aimed at exterminating the Christian, African, and non-Arab populations of Sudan in order to establish a uniform Arab-Islamic fundamentalist state in the heart of Africa. This terrible, heart-breaking incident is yet another piece of evidence, if more were still needed, that the war in Sudan is a religious and ethnic war launched by Khartoum and aimed at the destruction of my people.

In total, one teacher and nineteen children were killed, in addition to dozens of other children who lost limbs or were maimed as a result of this attack.

On August 7, 2000, eighteen bombs were dropped near a UN relief mission at Mapel in Bahr el Ghazal. This is just one example in a series of intentional bombings on civilian targets. This seems to be part of the northern government's effort to kill off the southern population by depriving them of food and medical care.

On November 3, 2000, the Khartoum government bombed humanitarian aid organizations linked to the UN-organized Operation Lifeline Sudan (OLS). Both Norwegian Church Aid Ikotos and the Ngaluma displaced camp were bombed, during which five people were killed.

On November 20, 2000, at least three children were murdered and twenty-four were enslaved when PDF (Popular Defense Force) forces raided the Gog Nhom elementary school in Aweil West County. On the same date eighteen people were killed when bombs were dropped on an open market in the rebel-controlled town of Yei in southern Sudan.

## Testimony on Religious Freedom in Sudan

Commissioner Nina Shea presented the following report to the U.S. Commission on International Religious Freedom, Congressional Human Rights Caucus, on September 28, 2000.

> The U.S. Commission on International Religious Freedom has found that the government of Sudan is the world's most violent abuser of the right to freedom of religion and belief. As it prosecutes its side of a 17-year-old civil war—a war that ignited when the regime in Khartoum attempted to impose Sharia, or Islamic law, on the non-Muslim south and in which the Commission has found that religion continues to be a major factor the government of Sudan is carrying out genocidal practices against its religious and ethnic minorities. Such practices include aerial bombardment, scorched earth campaigns, massacres, slavery, forcible conversion, and its most lethal tactic, what Senator Frist has termed "calculated starvation.". . . As

238

a direct result of the conflict, some two million persons have been killed, mostly Christians and followers of traditional beliefs in south and central Sudan.

# Persecution of Christians and Traditional Believers

The U.S. Commission on International Religious Freedom also produced the following report in 2000.

### Violation of Religious Freedom

Since the NIF-backed coup of 1989, discrimination and serious violations of religious freedom increased dramatically. Non-Muslims in Sudan, both Christians and followers of traditional beliefs, in essence have become second-class citizens subject to a wide range of violations, including . . . forcible conversions to Islam and religious coercion, restrictions on religious institutions, harassment of religious personnel, and persecution.

In spite of the government's rhetoric claiming that it respects the rights of followers of the "revealed religions," Christians of all denominations and backgrounds in Sudan are subjected to repression, discrimination, and persecution. These include restrictions on operations of their churches and on church personnel, harassment, and persecution. The government has not allowed the building or repair of churches in Khartoum since 1969. According to Bishop Macram Gassis, a total of 750 Christian schools have already been confiscated by the government. The government rarely grants building permits to Christian institutions, while permits for mosques and other Islamic institutions are readily attainable. Numerous churches and church properties have been bulldozed or confiscated on the grounds of not fulfilling rigid requirements, or of any other pretext supplied by Sudanese authorities. In June 1999, the government served eviction notices on the Episcopal bishop and all other church personnel of the Episcopal diocese in Omdurman, and ordered them to vacate the headquarters. After ecumenical demonstrations, the government returned the headquarters. Government authorities confiscated the Catholic Club in Khartoum. In some areas, such as the province of Damazin, Christian preaching has been outlawed altogether. The government also intimidates and harasses Christian leaders critical of the regime by charging them with both ordinary and security-related crimes. For example, in 1998, a military court tried Fr. Hilary Boma and Fr. Leno Sebit, chancellor of the Archdiocese of Khartoum, along with 24 others for "conspiracy and sabotage." The government released Boma and Sebit in December 1999, following international pressure. . . .

There are reports of individuals being forcibly or otherwise coercively converted to Islam. Forcible or coercive actions have occurred among the Nuba of Southern Kordofan and the Gamk of the Ingessana Hills in Southern Blue Nile, and elsewhere in the south such as Bahr al-Ghazal. Much of this religious coercion takes place in so-called "peace villages"—a cynical euphemism employed by the government officials to describe camps for the mostly non-Muslim Sudanese who have been forcibly removed from their homes and villages by government or government-backed militia forces.

239

## Muslim-Dominated Government

With twenty-five million deprived people, the Sudan is potentially rich in agriculture, oil, and other products. Seventy percent of the people are Muslims, 18 percent are pagan animists, and only 5 percent are Christians. The Muslim-dominated government appears bent on stamping out all expressions of Christian faith.

# EMPIRE OF ETHIOPIA—LAND OF MANY MARTYRS

It is possible that more Christians have died in the twentieth century in this ancient, fabled land than in any other nation of black Africa. Yet Ethiopia has the longest history of political independence and is the only country in black Africa with a Christian heritage.

Until 1974 Ethiopia was ruled by a line of monarchs claiming descent from King Solomon and the Queen of Sheba. Most modern historians disagree, holding that the ancestors of the Ethiopians came across the Red Sea from Saba (biblical Sheba) many years after the queen's death, conquered the black Hamites, and established the kingdom of Axum (present Ethiopia). The Axumites were converted to Christianity in the fourth century and established a national church under the ecclesiastical jurisdiction of the Coptic Church of Alexandria, Egypt. For the next fifteen hundred years the Ethiopians remained landlocked and "slept . . . forgetful of the world, by whom they were forgotten," according to historian Edward Gibbon.

## Mad Emperor Orders British Missionary Flogged

The first foreign missionaries in the nineteenth century were hardly welcomed. Johann Ludwig Krapf and his wife were driven out. Britisher Henry Stern was flogged and imprisoned at the personal command of Emperor Tewodros II (Theodore), whose mad homicidal acts provoked British retaliation. Theodore subsequently committed suicide.

Ethiopia's feudalistic class structure became known to the outside world. The Amharas, members of the established Coptic Church, ranked at the top. Comprising only a quarter of the population, they owned vast tracts of land and held thousands of slaves. The Gallas, numbering 50 percent of the people, toiled as peasants. Most of the rest of Ethiopia's people, the wild tribes, had never seen an outsider.

The Swedish Evangelical Mission began the first Protestant work among the Gallas. The Swedish missionaries were forbidden to evangelize members of the established church, the Amharas. This mission carried on alone for almost sixty years until in 1920 the United Presbyterians opened their first station. The Sudan Interior Mission (SIM) arrived in 1927. It would become the largest and most influential foreign work in Ethiopia and would suffer the first missionary martyrs.

## The First SIM Martyrs

On May 15, 1936, news came that two SIM missionaries, Tom Devers and Cliff Mitchell, had been killed in the Kassi Desert west of Addis Ababa. Mitchell's wife and child and Devers' fiancée were already in Addis Ababa. Fearing that their loved ones were in danger, the two men had been on their way there with a large group of Amharas when ambushed by two hundred fierce Arussi tribesmen. Tribal custom required a male Arussi to emasculate another man as proof of his manhood. The missionaries and Amharas had been killed with spears and then mutilated.

Allen Smith, the last missionary to see Mitchell and Devers alive, wrote a moving tribute to the two martyrs. He recalled that Mitchell had been translating the Gospel of John into the Gudgi dialect:

When the Italian bombers visited Yirga Alem, Cliff never took refuge in our bombproof shelter without bringing with him his manuscript of John and his Bible. I have seen him, when the planes were almost overhead, run into the house to fetch the manuscript, fearing that firebombs would be dropped and the precious papers thus destroyed. The work was almost completed when he left Yirga Alem, and he took it with him on the tragic journey to Addis. . . .

I have heard him speaking of Christ by the bedside of a dying Darassa, to a company gathered in a Gudgi hut before high Amharic officials, and to Greek traders. He had a message that was positive, and its never-changing theme was "Believe on the Lord Jesus Christ and thou shalt be saved."

Tommy Devers was one of the joyful type. In some ways he reminded me of Peter. He was irrepressible and bubbled over with the joy of the knowledge of sins forgiven, and of a Mansion on high where the King reigns in glory. . . . No native ever heard an unkind word from Tommy. They loved him.

Mitchell's wife and Devers' fiancée were not harmed in Addis Ababa. Their response to the sad news was best expressed by Mrs. Mitchell:

There are times when one's faith is at stake, except that God graciously turns our eyes from the greatest sorrows in this life unto Him, the Author and Finisher of our faith, and we realize all that is entailed by the words, "My flesh and my heart faileth, but God is the strength of my heart and my portion forever."

Mitchell and Devers were the first SIM martyrs, but they were not the only missionaries to die as a consequence of the Italian invasion during World War II. Dr. Robert Hockman, of the American United Presbyterian Mission, had remained to help the Red Cross. He died while attempting to remove the detonator from a bomb.

## The Seed of the Church

The Italians had tried to stamp out the church. Hundreds of Wallamo believers who refused to kiss crucifixes extended by Italian Catholic priests had been jailed. On one occasion fifty Wallamo leaders had been clapped in prison. Each received one hundred lashes and one was given four hundred. None of the leaders could lie on their backs for months. Three of them died.

Certain Amharas, whom the Italians used to administer the tribal areas, had done their share of persecuting the evangelical believers. An Amhara lieutenant governor named Dogesa, had ordered Wandaro, a zealous Wallamo preacher, to stop evangelizing. Wandaro merely replied, "I will suffer for my Savior."

The Amhara official then ordered Wandaro to have his congregation tear down their church and await the coming of soldiers. They complied. Dogesa arrived with the soldiers. "Sing the song the missionary taught you," he demanded. The Wallamos sang about the coming of Christ to take them to a place where there would be no more trouble or pain. The singing only made the governor furious. He ordered all of Wandaro's church members jailed.

He released every one the next morning except Wandaro. He took the pastor to the marketplace and shouted to the people. "See, the preacher is bound. His church is broken down. Don't go there again."

"Listen, everybody," Wandaro shouted loudly. "Believe on Jesus for salvation. This rope on me is not the final rope."

Dogesa called on the townspeople to beat the pastor up. Bystanders rained blows upon Wandaro, but not enough to kill him. The governor sent Wandaro back to the jail. Again he was lashed and beaten. Between every lash of the whip, Wandaro preached. Wandaro was beaten several more times while his family and friends stood by helplessly. For a year he was held in prison. Wallamo Christians brought food and clothing to him and the other church leaders. Their love for the prisoners deeply impressed the guards and other observers.

When Wandaro was finally released, hundreds of Christians welcomed him home. And when Dogesa asked Wandaro to help harvest his ripened grain, a hundred singing Christians swarmed into the field. Dogesa and his friends marveled at such faith and love.

Dogesa then arranged a meeting with an Orthodox Coptic priest. "We will hear from both you and the priest," he told Wandaro. But before the meeting could take place, Dogesa collapsed in his home and died.

## The Book of Acts in Ethiopia

Postwar Ethiopia was still a troubled country. Bandit hordes continued to roam the back country. In remote areas only the local laws of the tribes prevailed.

The Wallamos were now sending out missionaries to distant villages where the gospel was unknown. Two of those who answered a call from God were a husband and wife team, Omochi and Balotei. They had only one small child, having lost their firstborn to illness at age three.

They left their home village and took only their animals and the few possessions they could carry. Climbing steep, stony mountains and fording deep, swift streams, they finally reached their destination after two weeks. The hut which Omochi had built on an earlier trip was waiting for them. After three weeks, Omochi had to return to their home village on business. The morning Balotei expected him back, he was killed by roving bandits.

The elders at his home church heard first. They dispatched a messenger to break the news to his wife. Before they arrived, Balotei was awakened by a voice asking, "What would you do if your husband did not return?" She replied, "Lord, he belongs to You and I am Yours. You can do what You wish with Your own."

"He is not coming," the messenger replied sadly. Balotei walked resolutely back into her hut. She knelt and prayed for guidance.

The news that the evangelist had been killed spread rapidly through the village. It was tribal custom for neighbors to weep profusely at the occasion of a death, jump high in the air, and throw themselves to the ground. The villagers came to Balotei's hut to show their sympathy by such mourning. As each group came she asked, "Why are you weeping?" Each replied, "Because your husband has been killed." And each time Balotei replied calmly, "I have already told you of One who died for you. Not once have you wept because of His death for you. Why do you now weep for my Omochi? He didn't die for you. Jesus did." Through this many heard the gospel.

After a few days elders from her home church arrived and urged her to return home. "No," she declared. "When God called Omochi, He called me too. I will stay until God tells me to leave." She became one of the Wallamos' most effective tribal evangelists.

During the 1950s and 60s the Ethiopian tribal churches doubled and redoubled in size. There were occasional incidents of banditry, but no large-scale persecutions. The rich spiritual harvest, the stability of the Selassie government, and Ethiopia's strong pro-western stance caused western mission groups to give Ethiopia top priority. By 1972 almost six hundred Protestant missionaries were ministering in the country of less than thirty million population.

## A Kidnapping and a Killing

The biggest political trouble spot was the northeastern province of Eritrea where a guerrilla war for Eritrean independence was heating up. The Eritrean guerrillas first ignored foreigners. Then in early summer, 1974, perhaps to grab world attention, Eritrean nationalists seized an American oil company helicopter. Landing near the American Evangelical Church hospital in Ghinda, they kidnapped a pregnant missionary nurse, Mrs.

Deborah Dortzbach, twenty-four, of Freehold, New Jersey. They shot a single Dutch nurse, Anna Strikwerda, to death, apparently because she resisted capture. Mrs. Dortzbach's sponsors, the Orthodox Presbyterian Church, speculated that she was taken to provide medical assistance to the guerrillas. She was released after several months.

## Another Disciple Named Peter

Other Christian lives were lost through isolated acts of hostility. Peter Isa, an Ara tribesman, had been won to Christ at age nineteen by a Wallamo evangelist. He attended the SIM Bible School at Bako and married a fellow student. After graduation in 1973 the couple went to the spirit-worshiping Bunna tribe. They faced hostility from the beginning. Some Bunnas seemed afraid of the gospel they brought. Others mocked their efforts. After three and a half years the Bunnas began to accept them. A few even became Christians.

Peter frequently left his wife and children at home to make trips to distant villages. On one trip in November he stopped at the mountain home of people he knew. He shared lodgings with a Bunna stranger. The next morning the stranger said he was going the same way as Peter. Spear in hand, he accompanied Peter down into the valley.

Two young herdsmen watched them from a high meadow. The boys saw the Bunna grab Peter by the shirt and attempt to take his small packet of food and medicine. When Peter pulled back, the stranger plunged his spear into Peter's abdomen, then drew a knife and slashed his throat. The attacker stripped the body of clothing and walked away.

Word spread rapidly. Several young Bunnas gathered to dance and sing in celebration of the killing of the Ara preacher. Missionary Charlie Bonk notified the police. He found the body and buried it where it lay.

Peter's young wife wept uncontrollably when she first heard what had happened. Her youngest child, she told the missionary, had stood in the doorway each morning, announcing, "Daddy! Here comes my daddy!" Then the mother gained her composure. When neighbors arrived, she told them, "I'm sitting with God. My heart is at rest."

There were seventeen other evangelists in the area. Bunna believers begged them to stay. They did. Two more families of Christian workers arrived in Bako to take Peter's place. "When I heard that Peter had been killed," said one of the new evangelists, "I was afraid to come. But God's voice continued to tell me to preach to these people. So here I am."

## A Good Samaritan Is Murdered

During the 1970s Ethiopia was also hit with severe droughts. Hundreds of thousands of people starved to death.

One of the short-term workers who came to assist the career missionaries in famine relief was Dr. Douglas Hill, a twenty-six-year-old bachelor from Australia. Dr. Hill worked with two Canadian nurses, Judy Fraser and Mary Amalia, among the Somali people in the hot Ogaden Desert. They treated emaciated children, fed the starving, brought many who were dehydrated from intestinal diseases back from the edge of death, and set up mass inoculations. They traveled in the stifling heat from one desert village to another, working almost from dawn to dusk, then camping out at night.

A vibrant Christian, the Aussie medic was on a three-week stint. He had only five days to go when he and the nurses and Mohammed, a native helper, pulled into the remote little settlement of Merkman. As in other places, the entire village turned out to welcome them.

They had stopped, but the motor was still running when a mad Muslim came charging through the welcomers with a knife. An instant later Dr. Hill was lying on the ground, bleeding. In the confusion the assassin got away. Dr. Hill, whom the veteran Mary Amalia described as "one of the finest Christians I ever met," was dying. A village woman had placed her shawl under his head and now stood over him weeping. "You came in peace," she wailed. "We said peace to you. And now you are dead."

Somehow the nurses got his body in the Land Rover and headed toward the town of Bokh, an hour's drive away over a desolate stretch of gravel road where there was a small Ethiopian army base. En route, a rear wheel came loose. They stopped, jacked up the vehicle, and tightened the lugs. Farther on, the motor stalled. They ground the starter, checked possible trouble spots, and even tried pushing. Exhausted from the debilitating heat, they prayed: "Please, Lord, make it start." Mary hit the starter once more. The engine rumbled into life.

They reached Bokh. But their friend was dead. "Perhaps the Lord is going to reap a great harvest among the Somali people," Mary said in reflection. "The good seed had to be planted. Pray the Lord of the harvest for messengers who will follow in Doug's footsteps."

## Advancing by Blood

Evangelical Christianity kept advancing in Ethiopia. But the killings also continued.

One of those slain in 1977 was Tesfaye Argew, a convert from the Orthodox Amharas. His family and neighbors had cast him out for accepting the evangelical faith. He found a place with tribal Christians, married a young woman of the Goojee tribe, and trained for the ministry in the SIM-related Dilla Bible School.

Tesfaye and his wife, Kibabush, went to an unevangelized Goojee village, even though he was warned that the Goojees there would probably kill him because he was an Amhara. His wife was then one of the few Goojee converts to Christ. The majority were still animists and prone to raiding and pillaging other tribes around them. Goojee wives proudly wore a coin in their ears to indicate their husband's reputation as a murderer.

Tesfaye and Kibabush and their two small children settled in a tent. They opened a school for village children and Goojees began affirming their belief in Christ.

Their third child, a baby girl, was born on August 19, 1977. Nine days later Goojees from the village were involved in a fight with government forces. Tesfaye and his family tried to flee to a safer place until the trouble died down. Along the road, a strange Goojee sprang from the bushes. He killed Tesfaye and mutilated his body.

Kibabush screamed and ran in terror, carrying two of her children, and holding on to the hand of the oldest, a five-year-old boy. The murderer's teenage son caught the boy and killed and mutilated him according to the custom of his tribe. Kibabush hid in the woods with her babies for two weeks. It was two more weeks before the missionaries learned what had happened.

## Bandits Kill Veteran Missionary

The government made no overt threats against foreign missionaries, but strong pressures were applied to make their work difficult. The greatest danger for the foreign workers seemed to be in frontier areas. On March 21, bandits attacked the SIM station at Kelafo, near the Somali border, and robbed and assaulted the missionaries. Ethiopian police intervened and after a siege of several hours succeeded in driving the bandits away. The missionaries were given sanctuary by local authorities and then evacuated out of the area.

Five days later in the middle of the night, the same bandits attacked the refugee center at Godi where United Presbyterian missionaries were staying. Dr. W. Don McClure and his wife, Lyda, and their son Don had left the station a few days earlier because of fighting in the area. They had returned in a mission plane to pick up some of Dr. McClure's belongings when the attackers closed in. The senior McClures had been in Ethiopia almost fifty years and were among the most admired foreigners in the country. Dr. McClure was both an agriculturist and theologian and was then director-treasurer of the Refugee Relief work in Ethiopia, treasurer of the All-Africa Relief Center, and a teacher in the Orthodox Church's seminary. With the McClures were an Australian couple, Graeme and Pamela Smith, and a number of Ethiopian Christian workers.

The bandits knew the three foreign men by name and ordered Graeme Smith in the Somali language to get five thousand dollars from the safe. The Australian did not understand and when he made no move to comply, the invaders ordered him and the McClures outside to be shot.

A moment later the women heard shots. Dr. McClure died instantly. His son managed to run into the bush. Graeme Smith was hit in the chest and fell to the ground. One bandit saw him move but did not fire, perhaps because he thought the movement was a reflex action. Children and nurses were now screaming and in the confusion and darkness bandits began firing at one another. Finally they ran away.

Graeme Smith was conscious, although a bullet had passed through the midsection of his body. He managed to crawl into the house where the frightened women and children waited. They stayed until daylight, then the Australian staggered outside to search for Don McClure. When he could not find him, they all piled into the station's Land Rover and drove to the clinic. While they were there, Don arrived. He could hardly believe Graeme was still alive. The younger McClure said he had seen the Australian shot and had started to run as they fired at him. He tripped and a bullet whistled over his shoulder, leaving only powder burns. He had dug a hole in the desert and hid until daylight.

Later that morning Dr. McClure was buried in a simple coffin on the compound. That afternoon the survivors flew to Addis Ababa and from there were evacuated out of the country.

# 22

## Former French Africa

### *New Nations*

Thirteen nations became independent in one year, 1960: Republic of Chad, People's Republic of the Congo, Kingdom of Benin, Republic of Ivory Coast, Republic of Mali, Islamic Republic of Mauritania, Republic of the Niger, Republic of Senegal, Republic of Togo, Malagasy Republic (Madagascar), Republic of Upper Volta, Central African Empire, and Gabon. A fourteenth country, the Republic of Guinea, had been expected to be in the group, but had broken ranks and declared independence two years before.

All were former possessions of France, which had ruled a great arc of almost three million square miles stretching from the westernmost side of Africa at Dakar across a vast hinterland to the border of Sudan. Except for Madagascar and for the steamy coast and equatorial region, this French empire was a vast but thinly populated area sandwiched between the Sahara Desert and the rain forest. In recent years the Sahara has been pressing south and the land has been tortured by devastating drought and famine the like of which Africa has never seen before.

### Muslim Power

The religious variances are also greater here than in the southern half of Africa. The northern area is almost totally Muslim. The southern part is animist and Christian, mostly Roman Catholic. Mauritania, where no Christian missionaries are known to work, is practically 100 percent Muslim. Senegal, which has been ruled by Roman Catholics, is nearly 90 percent Islamic.

For these nations independence and separation from the colonial possessor came easier than some others in central Africa because there were fewer whites. There was no official color bar. The people had French citizenship and could send representatives to the French National Assembly in Paris. France's De Gaulle—perhaps because of the bloody war for independence in Algeria—did not drag out negotiations. He asked each colony to vote on its status after independence. A "yes" vote meant they wished to remain in the French "community" with France responsible for foreign relations and national defense. A "no" meant the colony preferred to break all French ties. Only Guinea, which was led by avowed Marxist Sekou Toure, voted no and declared immediate independence.

Still, most of these nations were plagued by problems after independence. Chad, for example, had only two persons with legal training and not a single doctor. Most of the violence resulted from palace rebellions and from guerrilla warfare by northern Muslims trying to take control of their respective countries. The Muslim guerrillas were reportedly armed and financed by radical Arabs from Libya and Algeria, which were, in turn, backed by the Soviet Union.

There was less Protestant missionary activity in French Africa, both before and after 1960, than in areas formerly controlled by the British and Belgians. Work in predominantly Muslim areas was difficult and in some places impossible, particularly since France preferred Catholic missionaries. However, after independence, most of these countries welcomed evangelical specialists in education, medicine, and agriculture, and some admitted evangelists and church builders. Today there are around nine hundred foreign evangelical workers in former French Africa.

Fewer twentieth-century Christians were killed in these former French possessions in connection with their faith and witness than in nations further to the south. In most of these countries no Christian martyrdoms are known to have occurred. The exceptions are Chad, Guinea, the Congo Republic, Madagascar, and Mali where several pioneer workers died from tropical diseases.

## REPUBLIC OF CHAD—TROUBLE BREWS

Before the 1970s the only outsiders who cared much about Chad were the French and about sixty missionaries and their supporters. French generals who served in Chad when it was a part of French Equatorial Africa would say, "The power that controls Chad can control Africa." They saw the great flat basin—supporting only about two million people but twice the size of France and sandwiched between the Sahara and the African rain forest—as a critical land area in north central Africa. The mission supporters were interested in Chad for another reason. It was one of the most fruitful fields in Africa.

Mr. and Mrs. Victor Veary, for example, went to Chad in 1926. In forty-two years their leadership, and that of later colleagues, produced 258 self-governing and self-support-ing churches, 168 chapels and other meeting places, and a total of 42,000 evangelical believers with average Sunday attendance of 62,000. The Vearys came to Chad under the North American branch of the Sudan United Mission. The other large mission in Chad, Baptist Mid-Missions, began work in 1925 and also built up a large body of believers.

## A "Christian" President

Most missionaries associated with The Evangelical Alliance Mission (TEAM) and Baptist Mid-Missions rejoiced when Chad became independent in 1960. The first president, N'Garta Tombalbaye, was a professing Christian. He credited his conversion to a Baptist missionary and had taught in a Baptist elementary school before entering politics. A few old-timers counseled caution. Tombalbaye had once been disciplined by his home congregation for "unchristian behavior," and there was also concern over his lack of educated leadership.

Tombalbaye came from the Sara tribe. The Saras and other tribes in the south had a background of animistic spirit worship. Residents of the northern desert were Muslims. Antagonism between south and north had run strong for centuries.

The new government was hardly installed when rebel activity began in the north. President Tombalbaye moved quickly to establish dictatorial powers. Then to appease nationalists, he launched an "authenticity" crusade. Step one called for the replacement of all "Christian" names with African names. Muslims were allowed to retain their Koranic names, but the rebellion continued. On top of that, a terrible drought began in 1968, lasting over six years. It killed thousands of Chadians, destroyed their herds of cattle, and dried up vast areas of pasturelands.

Tombalbaye survived several attempts on his life. In 1973 he arrested and imprisoned his army commander on charges of plotting his overthrow.

## A Return to Paganism

Suddenly, in a presidential decree, Tombalbaye announced step two in his "authen-ticity" campaign. All tribesmen must submit to "Yondo," the old pagan initiation rites that called for sacrifices to ancestral spirits, circumcision, and an animistic "rebirth." The secret ceremonies also involved floggings, facial scarring, mock burials, drugging, and gruesome tests of stamina, such as crawling naked through a nest of termites. The president said it was for the sake of national unity.

Enforcement was centered in Christian villages where the Baptist missionaries had concentrated their efforts. Some said Tombalbaye's special target was the church that had excommunicated him when he was young.

## The Cost of Courage

Reprisals upon Christians who refused began immediately. Houses were ransacked, lives threatened. The children of some Christians were forcibly taken to initiation camps. A courageous pastor who refused to let his sons go was shot. The son of an evangelist who had helped translate the New Testament into the Sara language was reported killed.

After the Baptist missionaries left, the persecution intensified and spread to congregations related to TEAM. Tombalbaye set up a state church under the name Evangelical Church of Chad. The top officials were two pastors who had been disciplined by Baptists. In one area government officials ordered the dismissal of the leading pastor without consent of the people. Regional political committees were set up, which included a pastor in each district, to enforce the pagan initiation. The committees also directed self-accusation meetings where punishment was meted out on the spot. "Comrade" replaced the title "Monsieur." Chinese and Russian Communists were seen in the capital.

Evangelicals outside Chad were now alarmed. The Association of Evangelicals of Africa and Madagascar investigated and authenticated at least fifty martyrs. Some Chadians estimated hundreds had perished rather than obey the government order.

## Christian Protestors Suffer Agonizing Tortures

One evangelist who objected to the rites was jammed into a tall, narrow tom-tom drum. The skin was sewn back over the drum and a hole cut in the side to feed him. He was kept alive in the confining space for almost three weeks before he died.

A pastor was fastened in stocks and had all his fingers broken. He sent thanks to his fellow Christians for their love and said that he expected to die "any day now." Many others were put in stocks, beaten, or killed simply because they refused to drink chicken blood offered to idols, or to be subjected to fetish practices.

A number were buried alive with a leg exposed above the ground as a warning to others. Some were buried with their heads left above ground and exposed to heat and insects. Neighbors were told they would get the same punishment if they dug the victims up.

## PEOPLE'S REPUBLIC OF THE CONGO—INTRIGUE

This small, hot, New Mexico-sized country straddles the Equator and lies across the Congo River from much larger Zaire (formerly the Belgian Congo). Unlike Guinea, Muslims in the People's Republic of the Congo number less than one-half of 1 percent of the population. The remaining 99 plus percent are divided about equally between Christianity and tribal religions. Roman Catholic missionaries, working under French protection, have had fantastic success. Protestant missionary societies have paid more attention to Zaire. The exception is the Swedish Evangelical Covenant Mission which has built up an evangelical constituency of over fifty thousand. More recently, the United World Mission has also been able to enter this troubled country.

Christian martyrs are hard to classify here. There has been no national vendetta against Christians; however, many Christians have died in political rebellions and purges.

Around 1900 much blood was shed by brutal overseers of foreign companies granted concessions by France. Shocking reports reached Europe, prompting the French government to appoint a commission of inquiry. The findings were so upsetting and blood-curdling that the government refused to publish them. But Paris did change some policies.

## Catholic Reformers Are Executed

The abuses continued. In 1927 Andre Matsoua, a Congolese Catholic teacher, organized an aid society to lift Africans to equal status with the French. French administrators saw the society as a political threat. Matsoua and other leaders were put on trial. Several were executed. Others were exiled or imprisoned. Matsoua died in prison in 1942. Many Congolese refused to accept his death and continued to believe that he was in Paris negotiating with Charles de Gaulle and would return to liberate them from French rule.

France gave the Congolese French citizenship. This helped, but the mysticism of Matsoua continued to pervade the country.

## A Catholic Priest Becomes President

Matsoua's successor was Fulbert Youlou, a Congolese Catholic priest. When he ran for a seat in the French National Assembly, the Roman Catholic bishop in the Congo ordered Catholics not to vote for him. Youlou lost this election, but rapidly gained power and was elected the first president when the French Congo gained full independence in 1960. Fierce rioting resulted and in 1963 the priest was deposed.

## Winnie Davies

The last European in the hands of the Simbas, the Congo Rebels, was Father Alphonse Strijbosh, a Dutch Roman Catholic missionary, freed by the Congolese Army on May 27, 1967. He was able to give his eyewitness account of Winnie Davies' death, when she was killed, aged 51.

Miss Davies practiced as a midwife in the Rebel Camp in which General Gaston Ngalo had ten wives. Along with Alphonse Strijbosh, Winnie Davies was captured by the rebels when the hostilities began in 1964. In 1964, during this uprising the following four missionaries were also killed: Jim Rodger, Bill McChesney, Cyril Taylor, and Muriel Harman.

Winnie Davies' health went into severe decline as she was forced to accompany the rebels who were "on the run" from 1965 to 1967. On May 27, 1967, as General Ngalo tried to escape from the Congolese soldiers, he had Winnie Davies killed. She had two visible knife wounds, one to her face and the other to her throat. Alphonse Strijbosh saw her in this condition about fifteen minutes after she had been killed, with blood still seeping out of her mouth.

## A Marxist Coup

Youlou's successor, Alphonse Massamba-Debat, lasted five years before being overthrown by Major Marien Ngouabi. The new president established a one-party Marxist state. The little country became a Communist stronghold and in 1975–1976 served as a staging center for Cuban troops fighting in the Angolan civil war.

Ngouabi was killed by assassins on March 18, 1977. Four days later members of his family killed the Catholic archbishop of Brazzaville, the capital, in reprisal. Shortly after this the previous president confessed to plotting Ngouabi's death and was executed.

An eleven-man military junta took over and declared themselves supreme over the Marxist political party and the government. One of their first acts was to restore diplomatic relations between the Congo and the United States which had been broken twelve years before.

However, Marxism was not renounced and opposition parties were not legalized until 1990.

## ALGERIA

Algeria became independent in 1962, after a century of French rule. In Algeria the GIA (the Armed Islamic Group) are committed to install an "Islamic Republic" similar to those found in Iran and Saudi Arabia. In 1994, this group declared its intention to eliminate Jews and Christians from Algeria even though, in theory, the government allows small Christian and Jewish groups to practice their faith.

On May 20, 1996, the Armed Islamic Group beheaded seven French Trappist monks after holding them captive for two months.

In October 1996, the Armed Islamic Group are believed to have killed Bishop Pierre Clavier of Oran.

On December 30, 1997, four hundred people in isolated villages in the Relizane region were killed by Islamic extremists on the first night of Ramadan. Most of the victims had their throats slit or were decapitated.

# 23

# Former British West Africa

## *Born in Sacrifice*

The libertine John Newton traded for slaves along these swampy shores before he was "preserved, restored, pardoned and appointed to preach the faith he long had labored to destroy." His hymn "Amazing Grace" is sung today by thousands of descendants of the Africans he bought and sold.

Some two centuries after Newton, American author Alex Haley visited the village of Juffre, ancestral home of Kunta Kinte of Haley's epochal book *Roots*. Juffre was declared a national monument of Gambia, a former British colony on the coastal bulge of West Africa.

In the years separating "Amazing Grace" and *Roots*, hundreds of missionaries sailed into the calm harbors of Africa's Atlantic coast, bringing the gospel of Christ to black tribal peoples steeped in ancestor worship, fetishism, and witchcraft. Today in five new nations once controlled by Britain—Gambia, Sierra Leone, Ghana, Nigeria, and Cameroon—as well as in Liberia, millions of black believers sing praises to the Savior whose love was brought to them by brothers and sisters, both black and white, from Europe and North America.

## LIBERIA

### Liberia's "Prophet" Harris

In the twentieth century Liberian Christians began taking the gospel to neighboring territories. The most famous Liberian missionary was William Wade Harris, a Methodist

255

convert. Obeying a vision, in 1913 he moved to the Ivory Coast. Clad in a white gown and turban and carrying a large cross and Bible, he preached against idolatry, and urged repentance and faith in Christ. By the time Methodist missionaries reached him, he had won nearly one hundred thousand converts. Hundreds of congregations from "Prophet" Harris's ministry exist today in the Ivory Coast.

## Civil War

By 1980 Baptists, numbering about fifty thousand, were the largest denomination in Liberia.

The worst violence against Christians came in July 1990 when government troops barged into St. Peter's Lutheran Church in the central section of the capital, Monrovia. The invaders murdered some six hundred men, women, and children who had taken shelter there.

In another incident, the SIM mission's Radio ELWA was caught between warring armies and heavily damaged. The trouble began when rebel chief Charles Taylor of the National Patriotic Front used the ELWA transmitter to announce his shadow government. Government troops responded by blowing up the missionary station.

In September 1990, the murderous Doe was captured and tortured to death by rebels from the Independent Patriotic Front of Liberia faction. A cease-fire was declared February 13, 1991. Heads of regional African states began peace talks which they hoped would lead to a permanent, peaceful Liberia. It was estimated that nearly half the population of Liberia had been displaced by the violence. Many churches were also destroyed in the inter-factional fighting.

The fighting between factions continued. Missionaries who chose to stay put themselves at great risk. This risk was highlighted in October 1992, when five Catholic nuns were brutally murdered.

Said Southern Baptist missionary John Carpenter: "We are going to see a more purified, stronger church than ever before."

## NIGERIA—TRIALS AND TRIUMPHS

In the twentieth century, Nigeria, the most populous nation in Africa today, was one of the most fruitful mission fields in the world. The influence of Christianity in Nigeria is immeasurable. Practically all of Nigeria's leaders were educated in mission schools. The smoothness with which Nigeria attained independence, the efficiency of its government in contrast to some of the other new African nations, and the prosperity of its economy were due in large part to the ministries of foreign missionaries and the leadership of astute national church leaders.

## Koranic Law

In northern Nigeria about twenty regional states, including Zamfara, Sokoto, and Kano, have introduced or are considering introducing Koranic law. This is a direct threat to the 40 million Christians in Nigeria. In February 2000, clashes in the city of Kaduna and the state of Abia resulted in more than one thousand people being killed, the majority of whom where Christians.

Peter Yakubu from the Diocese of Kaduna states that the extremists offer 100,000 naira (about a thousand dollars) for every priest who is killed. Among the estimated two thousand people who were killed during this fighting were three parish priests, eight seminarians, 148 evangelists, and 38 Protestant pastors from various denominations. The Baptist Theological Seminary was also destroyed and four student evangelists were killed.

On May 22, 2000, Muslim youths torched the First Baptist Church and Christian homes in Kaduna, during which eleven people were killed, as well as many others injured.

More than two hundred people were killed in fighting in Kaduna, Nigeria, during the week of May 21, 2000. It is clear that a number of Christians were deliberately targeted and murdered in cold blood. A former Muslim who was ordained a Catholic priest in 1999, the twenty-six-year-old Reverend Clement Ozi Bello, was one such victim. His lifeless body was discovered in an area of Kaduna where there had been no fighting. While he was sitting in his car the priest was dragged from it, tied up, and had his eyes gouged out before being killed and left dead in the road.

In addition to the Rev. Clement Ozi Bello, the dead included Rev. Aniya Bobai of the Evangelical Church of West Africa, and Rev. Bako Kabuk, along with Pastors Paul Chikira, David Maigari, and Adamu Seko of the Nigerian Baptist Convention.

## Africa's Most Populous Nation

With some 130 million people scattered among 426 language groups, Nigeria is Africa's most populous nation and the potential superpower of Africa. Militant Muslims want to impose Islamic controls on the entire nation. As the scene keeps changing, opportunities for Christian ministries abound.

## GHANA—BORN IN SACRIFICE

Christianity in Ghana (formerly the Gold Coast), as in Nigeria, was born in sacrifice. Four pioneer missionaries of the Basel mission landed at Accra in 1827. Three died within a few weeks. The fourth survived until 1831. Three more arrived, but again in a few weeks there was only one man left alive.

The first Methodist missionary, Joseph Dunwell, arrived in 1836 and lived six months. Two couples followed, the Wrigleys and Harrops. The Harrops and Mrs. Wrigley died within a month. Stricken himself and in agony, Mr. Wrigley sent a last plea for help. "Come out to this hell," he begged, "if it is only to die here." He did not live out the year.

Successors of both missions and representatives of later agencies did succeed in planting a solid core of Christianity on Ghanaian soil.

## The Dark Shadow of Marxism

In 1957 Ghana became the first black African colony granted independence by Britain. Political firebrand Kwame Nkrumah was elected president. Nkrumah had studied in a Roman Catholic mission school, as well as in France, Britain, and the United States. While living in Philadelphia, he had become embittered at racial segregation and discrimination.

Although Nkrumah termed himself a Marxian socialist, he also called himself a nondenominational Christian and not a Communist. By 1961 he had made himself into a cultic messiah "equal to Moses, Christ, Marx, Lenin, and Ghandi." He fostered guerrilla warfare in neighboring countries and conducted purges of political opponents. The Christians who perished in these purges died primarily because of their identification with groups opposed to the dictator.

Nkrumah's Christian profession to the contrary, Ghanaian church leaders did feel threatened. Several leading missionaries, including the Anglican bishop of Accra, were expelled. Church attendance plummeted.

In 1966, while Nkrumah was visiting in Peking, Ghanaian military officers took power. Seven of the eight coup leaders were practicing Christians. Unable to return home, Nkrumah landed in Guinea where dictator Sekou Toure proclaimed him his coruler. Nkrumah's popularity waned in socialist Guinea. He was never able to return home.

Further coups occurred in 1972, 1978, 1979, and 1981. The last successful coup leader, Jerry Rawlings, remained in power, although a new constitution allowing for multi-party politics was approved in 1992. Ghana is today a secular state with considerable religious freedom. However, some members of the military government have shown hostility to Christianity and made efforts to impede the spread of the gospel.

The Ghanaian government has required all religious groups in the country to register with the National Commission of Culture. Some cultic groups have been banned for actions believed to "undermine the sovereignty of Ghana" and "not conducive to public order." Some large churches have refused to register, stating that the government does not have the right to regulate religion. Leaders of these groups could go to prison.

Fifty percent of Ghana's population is classified as Christian, with 17 percent Muslim and 31 percent belonging to traditional African religions.

# REPUBLIC OF SIERRA LEONE—THE "HUT TAX REBELLION"

This South Carolina-sized colony that became known as "the white man's graveyard" was the earliest Protestant mission field in West Africa. The first two missionaries were sent by the Baptist Missionary Society in 1795.

Christians in Sierra Leone were never a target for intensive persecution. However, there was one tragic missionary massacre in a violent tribal rebellion against British assumption of authority over tribal lands in the interior.

In 1896 the British governor at Freetown arbitrarily proclaimed the hinterland region a British protectorate. Administrators were appointed and members of the Frontier Police Force sent into areas where hitherto only missionaries and traders had gone.

The chiefs of the various tribal domains felt humiliated. Slave owners themselves, they had long resented the colony of freed slaves established at Freetown. Many had lost runaways to the colony. Now former slaves were coming back as Frontier Police to harass and arrest their former owners.

The chiefs had been unhappy with the missionaries for a different reason. Some of the young people educated in the mission schools had come to despise their illiterate and pagan elders. And Christian converts were questioning the custom of polygamy. Some of the chiefs claimed as many as three hundred wives.

The last straw was a British property tax based on the size of native huts for administration of the "protected" areas. Chief Bai Bureh, a chief of the Temne people in the north, refused to pay. The Frontier Police began forcibly collecting the taxes, plus sizable commission fees. Temne warriors sprang on the police and the fight was on. A few weeks later the Mende chiefs in the south joined the rebellion, vowing to push the whites into the sea.

Bai Bureh and neighboring chiefs protected missionaries and traders in their territories on the grounds that they were guests. But they could not prevent the killing of Reverend W. J. Humphrey, the principal of Fourah Bay College in Freetown, which had been established to train Africans for the Anglican priesthood.

## The Rotifunk Massacre

No European was safe in Mende country. Friendly chiefs, knowing of the danger, had to force some reluctant missionaries into canoes. However, the concerned chiefs were unable to get to the American United Brethren's Rotifunk station in time.

An African who escaped told the grim story:

> We started to walk to Sierra Leone [the original colony at Freetown], but had gone only half a mile when we met warriors who blocked the way. The Reverend Mr. Cain tried to frighten them by firing a revolver over their heads, but seeing they were determined to do mischief, he cast his revolver away and said that he would not have anybody's blood on his hands.

The natives then seized the party and Misses Hatfield, Archer and Kent, stripped them of their clothing, dragged them back to the mission home in front of which the "war boys" cut down the Reverend Mr. Cain and hacked him to death, and then treated Miss Archer and Miss Kent the same way. Miss Hatfield, who was very ill, was thrown on a barbed wire netting, and finally her throat was cut. Mrs. Cain escaped to the bush with a native girl, but the warriors went out seeking for them and afterwards killed them.

Before the year's end British forces, with their superior fire power, had put down the "Hut Tax Rebellion" as it was called. They imprisoned Bai Bureh and hung twenty-nine other dissident chiefs. Bai Bureh and those chiefs are national heroes in Sierra Leone today.

Partly because of conflicts with British colonists and partly because of Islam's close identification with tribal customs, only 10 percent of Sierra Leone's population is Christian today, compared to 30 percent Muslim, with most of the remainder identifed as animists. However, Christian mission agencies have been giving more attention to Sierra Leone in recent years. About 185 missionaries are now in the country. The Wesleyan Church has the largest representation among eighteen agencies.

## CAMEROON—NO MARTYRS UNTIL 1978

Cameroon, lying just south of Nigeria, has a checkered history of colonialism but has experienced less violence than any of its neighbors. It belonged to Germany before World War I, then after the German defeat, was apportioned between victorious Britain and France. French Cameroon became independent in 1960. Part of British Cameroon voted to join Nigeria. The remainder joined independent Cameroon.

Baptists, Lutherans, and Presbyterians built up strong constituencies in Cameroon. But it was during World War I, while the missionaries were absent, that the church grew most rapidly. Today about 33 percent of the fifteen million people, scattered among a melange of two hundred tribes, are Christians. The North American Baptist General Conference has the largest missionary force—about sixty—in the struggling country.

Missionaries and national evangelists have pushed steadily into the interior taking the gospel to tribes who still practice witchcraft and make animal offerings to dead ancestors. There has always been the risk of confronting fanatics steeped in ancient pagan rituals such as human sacrifice. Yet not until May 1978, did the first martyrdoms occur.

The victims were fifty-nine-year-old Ernest Erickson and his wife, Miriam. Natives of Minnesota, they had served in Cameroon for thirty-four years as representatives of the small nine thousand member Lutheran Brethren Church of America. Details of their deaths are still not known. But from the condition of their bodies, other missionaries speculated that they might have been victims of spirit worshipers.

Whatever the dangers and the consequences to health, missionaries and African Christians will continue ministering in the independent nations of West Africa. They are spurred on by brave pioneers of the past who risked all for the sake of the gospel.

# 24

# Former
# Portuguese Possessions

## *Trail of Martyrs' Blood*

The trail of martyrs' blood widens in Angola and Mozambique. In these two former Portuguese possessions, thousands upon thousands of Christians have perished in the twentieth century.

## Seeds of Trouble

Portugal was the first of the European colonial powers in Africa and among the worst. Tiny Portuguese Guinea on the western bulge of Africa was claimed in 1446, Mozambique in lower east Africa in 1483, and Angola in lower west Africa in the 1500s. Portugal hoped to exploit rich lodes of gold and silver. These and other metals were found, but the greatest riches came from slaves. The cruel traffic in human cargo persisted long after foreign pressure forced Portugal to pass a law abolishing slavery in 1869. Only the name was changed. Under a new "contract labor law" African adult males were required to work for Portuguese employers who could deduct from their paycheck the cost of fines, rent, overdue taxes, or any other cleverly devised charge. Employers could also send their contract laborers to neighboring countries. In this way hundreds of thousands were sent to toil in South Africa's sweltering mines. They were given no choice. Any African not under contract could be arrested for vagrancy.

After World War II, Portugal, a "Catholic" nation, defined her African colonies as provinces to which citizens could immigrate and buy land. On paper, any African could become a Portuguese citizen by learning the Portuguese language and adopting the culture of the mother country. In reality, few Africans could. Portuguese settlers always ended up with the best land.

So it was that disease, immorality, drunkenness, and ignorance pervaded the colonies. For instance, as late as 1955 there were only six secondary schools for almost five million people in Angola, which covers an area nearly twice the size of Texas.

In all of this, church and state were intertwined. At the height of the slave trade, Catholic bishops blessed cargoes of chained Africans departing for Portuguese Brazil. Catholic institutions were provided labor pools. A single monastery in Luanda, the capital of Angola, had at one time twelve thousand slaves.

Catholic authorities tried to block the entry of Protestant missionaries. Not until 1939 were the first evangelical workers allowed to enter Portuguese Guinea. Today only a half dozen serve there. Missionaries managed to enter Angola (1878) and Mozambique (1880) earlier. The evangelical witness met with huge success in these colonies. But in both countries the Church developed through chafing restrictions and, at times, bitter persecution.

## MOZAMBIQUE—FREEDOM CRIES OUT

Mozambique was stirred by the independence fever that swept Africa in the 1950s and 1960s. Mozambique nationals pressed Portugal for promises of freedom. But the Portuguese dictator felt the African provinces were too valuable to relinquish.

The Vatican had a concordat with Portugal and until 1970 the Catholic hierarchy gave no official attention to the rebels in Mozambique, Angola, and Portuguese Guinea. Suddenly in June 1970, Pope Paul received in special audience the leaders of the movements. Portugal instantly protested, but the die was cast. A year later members of the White Fathers Catholic missionary order denounced their church in Mozambique for its identification with Portuguese rule. Portuguese authorities immediately ordered them out of the country.

From this time on the Portuguese government began arresting church leaders, Catholic and Protestant, suspected of rebel sympathies.

### Suicide or Murder?

On December 12, 1972, the wife of Jose Sidumo, an arrested Presbyterian church elder over sixty years old, went to a detention camp to try to locate her husband. She was told to come back the next day. Then she was told he had hung himself in his cell on July 21. But prison authorities refused to disclose where he had been buried. A few days later the Portuguese governor-general of Mozambique denied the suicide story and claimed the elder had died of natural causes.

A few days later a report leaked out that the president of the Presbyterian church in Mozambique, Pastor Manganhela, age sixty, had committed suicide on December 11 following six months of isolation and interrogation by the security police. People who knew him refused to believe the story, and some Portuguese authorities agreed with them.

## PEOPLE'S REPUBLIC OF ANGOLA— OPPRESSION AND EVANGELISM

Angola is the tragedy of Mozambique and much more; it is a history of more than four centuries of oppression by Portugal, seen in 70 percent illiteracy, rampant disease, abject misery and discrimination, and religious intolerance by the state-aligned Catholic Church.

But Angola was blessed with more evangelical mission work than Mozambique. English Baptists arrived in 1878 and by 1961, when guerrilla warfare began, they had opened 250 preaching-stations. The American Board of Commissioners for Foreign Missions arrived in 1880, but won fewer than three hundred converts in the first twenty-five years. After 1914 the growth rate picked up and by 1961 they had fourteen hundred places of worship and thirty thousand members. Methodists attained about the same growth during this period. The Plymouth Brethren opened 145 assemblies and 350 preaching places. Canadian Baptists, the United Church of Canada, the African Evangelical Fellowship, and the South African General Mission came later than the three largest mission groups, but also found Angolans responsive.

### The Mysterious Death of an Angolan Believer

One of the first Angolan Protestant martyrs, a former witch doctor named Chiteta, was reported by T. Ernest Wilson, a Plymouth Brethren missionary. A member of the wild Chokwe tribe, Chiteta built a grass hut near the house where missionaries lived. After attending services for several weeks, Chiteta and his wife Chambishi stood up publicly and announced they had accepted Jesus as Savior and Lord.

A few days later one of Chiteta's legs suddenly became swollen for no discernible reason. Also a piece of bone broke through his five-year-old daughter's hand. He took this for the power of witchcraft and immediately removed some hidden fetishes from his hut. The next Sunday he carried the bundle to church and publicly dumped them in the flames. He told the missionary, "There is a saying among the Chokwes, 'Throw away the honeycomb and the bees will leave you.'"

The missionary left on a trip. When he returned, Chiteta and his family were gone. Neighbors told him that they had taken sick and some men had carried them back to their home village.

The next morning the missionary and three African believers walked the twenty-four miles to the village. When he asked the old men in the palaver house about Chiteta, they pointed to a grass hut. There the missionary found the ex-witch doctor. His body was naked and mutilated and he had been dead for several days. Through further questioning, Arnot learned he had been poisoned.

When villagers refused to help make a coffin, the missionary and his African companions tenderly wrapped the decaying corpse in a blanket and buried it in a grave in the forest. The village headman would not even accompany them to the grove. "The dead man followed the teaching of the white man and this is what has become of it," he declared.

Where were the dead man's wife and children? Again, the missionary inquired and was told she had been married off to a crippled pagan as payment for an unredeemed debt. One of the children, a four-year-old girl, had been poisoned. Others would die, the villagers predicted, because they had insulted the spirits of their ancestors and become Christians. Before the affair was over, several other members of Chiteta's family did die under mysterious circumstances.

## Christian Casualties

Most Protestant suffering resulted from Portuguese repression. Over two hundred thousand Angolan refugees, fleeing Portuguese repression in the north, flooded into western Zaire. British Baptist missionaries, who established relief centers, heard harrowing tales of civilians being strafed and bombed by Portuguese planes and attacked by soldiers who showed no mercy to the aged, the infirm, or children.

A Protestant pastor was killed for no other reason than that he was a minister in the Cuanza Norte District. "Before killing him," his horrified daughter reported, "they tortured him by cutting off his limbs." She had escaped by hiding in the bush.

A nineteen-year-old girl told British Baptist missionaries that her father, Vemba Mateus, a teacher-evangelist in the village of Kidilu, and many other church leaders and teachers had been arrested in March 1961. Her mother and ten children, she said, escaped into the forest and had had no word of her father since.

T. Ernest Wilson, the Plymouth Brethren missionary mentioned earlier, recalled that a disgruntled native teacher, who had been dismissed from his post in a mission school for misconduct, had spitefully told Portuguese authorities the Christians in his village favored Angolan independence. Eight church leaders were arrested, beaten, and tortured to extract confessions. When it was clear they could not be made to submit, they were lined up on the edge of a pit and shot, one by one, through the neck. As the shots rang out, one of the younger men started to sing in his tribal language,

> Be not dismayed whate'er betide,
> God will take care of you.

Methodists were made special targets. For example, Reverend Filipe Antonio de Freitas, an Angolan clergyman, was slain at his home near Quessua Mission Station. In reporting his death, the Methodist bishop said he did not know how many Angolan Methodist workers had lost their lives in the fighting in the area.

# 25

## Former
## British East Africa

### *Curtain on Colonialism*

Legendary land of Livingstone and Stanley; safaris and big game hunts; cockney accents under pith helmets; British administrators in tailored white suits shuffling papers under high ceiling fans; four o'clock tea on shaded, expansive lawns, served by immaculate house servants; and Sunday morning church services with croquet in the afternoon. This was British East Africa for most whites before black revolutionaries unceremoniously rang down the curtain on colonialism forever. This vast area of mountains, lakes, and steaming jungles, twice the size of Texas, became Tanzania, Kenya, and Uganda.

### KENYA—CRUCIBLE OF CONFLICT

The story of Kenya is tragically different than that of mainland Tanzania. The clashes between Europeans and Africans have been violent and bitter. Christians have suffered immensely, although only two missionaries have been murdered.

#### A Brutal Missionary Murder

In 1930 an elderly, deaf AIM missionary, Hilda Stumpf, was found choked to death. First, reports said she had been killed by a thief. Then the real facts came out. She had been brutally mutilated in a fashion that pointed to the work of circumcision fanatics who enforced the barbaric practice of female circumcision.

## The Christian Martyrs

The immediate incident which provoked the Mau Mau insurgency was the eviction in 1949 of sixteen thousand Kikuyu squatters from "British" land. Stories spread of a secret Mau Mau society, in which members took an oath to expel Europeans from the country.

The Mau Maus claimed that 90 percent of all male Kikuyus took the oath. Pressure was put on all to join the anti-white, anti-Christian crusade. Mau Mau organizers swept into the villages rounding up the men. They ordered them to swear on the sacred oath stone that if called upon, they would join in the killing of Europeans. Many professing Christians yielded. Many did not. Some of those who refused were beaten and their houses torched. Some were martyred. Many more cut ties with churches and missionaries for fear they would be killed.

A respected Christian chief was shot while traveling in his car. Another chief, who tried to break up a Mau Mau meeting, was hacked to pieces. Still another was assassinated as he lay in a hospital bed. Altogether, almost one thousand Christians lost their lives for standing against the Mau Maus.

## A Missionary Is Murdered

The recent murder of a missionary was not linked to a political movement. Ralph and Lynda Bethea, affiliated with Southern Baptists, were robbed and beaten on a lonely stretch of road one night just before Easter in 1991. They had seen many Kenyans accept Christ in the city of Mombassa.

Lynda was beaten the most severely. Her last words to her husband were that he should take care of their four children. Of her attackers, she said, "They just need Jesus."

In that spirit, missionaries and national workers continue to serve Christ in Kenya.

## REPUBLIC OF UGANDA—NERO'S ROME REVISITED

Rivers of blood. Bodies floating like logs amidst hungry crocodiles. Execution cells littered with human eyes and teeth, the gory residue from the sledgehammering of prisoners. Innocent civilians, whose only crime was to belong to an unfavored tribe, screaming in agony as their sex organs were ripped away.

This was Uganda, dark domain of "Big Daddy" Idi Amin, the "Nero" and "Hitler" of Africa, who is credited with killing one hundred thousand people in six years out of a population of only twelve million. The victims included political opponents; members of tribes that he saw as a threat to his despotic rule; residents of any city or village viewed with the slightest suspicion; and Christian lay leaders and clergy who dared criticize misuse of authority and suggest that the fat, swaggering dictator would one day be judged by God.

## Christian Martyrs under Amin

All along, many devout Christians had been killed. One of the first was Chaplain Ogwang of the Ugandan army, murdered in the coup that overthrew Obote. Another well-known Christian killed was Francis Walugemebe, mayor of the fourth largest town in Uganda. Walugemebe was dragged from his house by Amin's hired killers on September 22, 1971. When he asked to call the president, a soldier mutilated him, then dumped him in the back of a jeep and drove him away to be finished off.

Still another Christian leader murdered was Benedictor Kiwanuku, whom Amin had made chief justice in June 1971. The respected judge was literally butchered in 1973. Still alive, he was thrown in his car and burned to death.

An evangelist was killed in 1972 for innocently reading over the radio a reference to Israel from the Psalms. The chairman of an evangelical church, Joseph Kiwanuka, after escaping to Kenya, was kidnapped by Amin's agents and brought back to Kampala for execution. According to Dr. Kefa Sempangi, a Christian leader who eluded Amin's agents and emigrated to the United States, Kiwanuka "died with hands lifted to Jesus, refusing to deny his Lord as the murderers demanded."

## A Month of Horror

Amin's bloodiest month, February 1977, merited a *Time* cover story, "The Wild Man of Africa." News media around the world joined in reporting the most shocking massacre yet. Typical was a grisly cartoon in *The Des Moines News and Register* showing a smiling Amin, beribboned with a row of clinking skeletons.

The so-called provocation for the massacre was a short-lived army rebellion in which seven men had been killed and another wounded. Before the month was over, Amin's trusted hirelings had killed thousands of soldiers and civilians. In the village of former president Milton Obote, Amin's men reportedly killed every civilian they could find.

But the most sensational act was the killing of the Anglican archbishop of Uganda, Janani Luwum, along with two former cabinet ministers. It was the archbishop's death and Amin's clumsy cover-up that aroused the loudest outcry in many world capitals.

The macabre bloodletting sent thousands more Ugandans fleeing across the eastern border into Kenya to join refugees from Amin's previous bloody tantrum. Among those escaping were the martyred archbishop's widow and children, three black Anglican bishops, and thousands of other Christians. Best known of the three bishops was Festo Kivengere, an evangelical leader of world renown. Bishop Festo went on to New York and told the terrible story to trusted church leaders and editors.

## Bishop Festo's Story

On Sunday, January 30, Bishop Festo had preached to a crowd of thirty thousand in a western Ugandan city. His topic: "The Preciousness of Life." In the audience were Ugandan governors, Muslim sheiks, and officers of Amin's dread State Research Bureau—killers in sport shirts with authority to kill as they desired. The bishop concluded his sermon with a direct speech to government authorities. "God entrusts governments with authority," he declared. "But authority has been misused in our country by force."

"When I sat down," he later recalled, "every Christian was trembling, thinking that I was going to be whisked away. I wasn't."

Instead of coming for Bishop Festo, Amin's operatives in Kampala, the capital, roused Anglican Archbishop Janani Luwum out of bed at 1:30 a.m. the following Saturday. While eight soldiers pointed guns at his stomach, others ransacked every room of his house. Amin would later claim arms had been found near the Anglican prelate's house. The real reason for the shakedown were the calls from Archbishop Luwum, Bishop Festo, and other churchmen for morality and decency in government.

The invasion of the Anglican archbishop's residence resulted in a long, signed protest to Amin. The archbishop and fifteen bishops said:

> We are deeply disturbed. In the history of our country such an incident in the Church has never before occurred. . . . Now that the security of the archbishop is at stake, the security of the bishops is even more in jeopardy.
>
> This is a climax of what has been constantly happening to our Christians. We have buried many who have died as a result of being shot and there are many more whose bodies have not yet been found; yet their disappearance is connected with the activities of some members of the Security Forces. Your Excellency, if it is required, we can give concrete evidence of what is happening because widows and orphans are members of our Church.

The archbishop delivered the letter to Amin in person on February 12 and told him he had not been involved in any overthrow plot. Amin countered by summoning the prelate to hear the reading of a document attesting his guilt.

After exchanging courtesies over afternoon tea, Amin charged that the document had been written by ex-president Obote. He read the fabricated evidence before the archbishop and a carefully selected audience of supporters. When he came to the archbishop's name, the audience shouted on cue, "Kill!" Amin replied that the archbishop and two accused cabinet officers would be given military trials.

A few hours later, Uganda Radio announced their deaths in an automobile accident. Newsmen were shown pictures of a wrecked car, which Amin claimed was the death vehicle.

Bishop Festo and other refugees told the true story. Archbishop Luwum and the two cabinet members, both devout Christians, were led through an underground passage to the torture chamber. In the torture room they met four other condemned prisoners, awaiting their execution. The guards permitted the archbishop to hold a short prayer meeting. He laid his hands on each prisoner, prayed for them, and encouraged them in Christ.

Then the archbishop and the two cabinet ministers were roughly shoved into a Land Rover and driven to a private lodge outside the capital. They were never seen alive again. The next day, February 17, the official announcement was made that one of the cabinet members had tried to subdue the driver of the vehicle. The Land Rover spun out of control and the three prisoners were killed in the crash. The severely injured driver was taken to a hospital in Kampala. The story was widely disbelieved. The alleged driver, a Major Moses, was seen walking around in apparent good health the next day. Further leaks and rumors gave a strange twist to the incident.

## The Bizarre Murder

According to the pieced-together accounts, Amin came to the lodge and asked Archbishop Luwum to sign a prepared confession stating that he had plotted to overthrow the dictator. After several refusals, the archbishop was stripped and forced to lie on the floor.

At Amin's orders, two soldiers began whipping the archbishop mercilessly. Instead of agreeing to sign the confession, the archbishop prayed for his tormentors. Amin flew into a frenzy. Screaming obscenities, he struck the archbishop, then ordered the soldiers to perform certain obscene and sacrilegious sex acts with the churchman. When Amin grew tired of watching, he drew his pistol and shot the archbishop twice in the heart. Death occurred instantly.

Family members and church officials were denied the archbishop's body. They were not even permitted to view his corpse. Instead, Amin's soldiers took the remains to Luwum's native village for burial. Relatives there were told to bury him immediately, but they insisted on summoning a pastor to officiate. When the Anglican priest arrived, the coffin was opened and the bullet holes discovered.

## Bishop Festo's Escape

Bishop Festo had been among those trying to get the body. On Saturday, February 19, he was warned by friends that Amin intended to get him next. Festo and his wife drove to their home town in eastern Uganda. There they were told that Amin's agents had checked on their house four times that day. Festo had planned to preach in his home church the next day, but after a tearful prayer meeting, he and his wife decided they should try to get across the border into Kenya. They drove to the end of the road, then followed a guide on foot five miles through the mountains. At 6:30 a.m. they stepped across the border.

Meanwhile, a story spread in Kampala that Amin had prohibited services in Uganda on Sunday. Nevertheless, forty-five hundred worshipers packed the Anglican cathedral in Kampala for a thanksgiving service. Afterwards, they went outside and gathered around the open grave that had been dug for the martyred archbishop next to the plot of Bishop Hannington who had been martyred in 1885.

The archbishop's grave had been purposely left open. His appointed successor began reading about the resurrection of Christ. When he voiced the assurance of the angels to the women on the day of Christ's resurrection, "He is risen," the crowd burst into a song of spontaneous praise. In Nairobi, Kenya, a crowd estimated at ten thousand participated in a second memorial service for the murdered archbishop of Uganda.

## Selective Condemnation

One of the participating bishops at Archbishop Luwum's memorial service in Nairobi blasted the selective condemnation of the World Council of Churches in Africa. "It is very well to condemn white regimes in southern Africa and turn a blind eye elsewhere. But the time has come for the church to be the church, otherwise we are doomed." Kenyan church leaders subsequently declared in a statement: "We confess that we have too often kept quiet when we should have identified ourselves with the suffering and persecuted peoples of the Continent of Africa and Uganda in particular."

Archbishop Luwum's murder and sweeping purges that followed in the Lango and Acholi tribes did bring widespread condemnation on the erratic Amin. The Vatican found Amin's wrecked-car story "unswallowable." The World Council of Churches' executive committee lashed the Ugandan dictator for "inhuman behavior." Billy Graham deplored the "cold-blooded murder" of the archbishop. President Jimmy Carter said Amin's actions had "disgusted the entire civilized world."

Amin reacted to Carter by ordering Americans in Uganda not to leave and to appear before him on February 28, 1977, bringing their chickens and goats. When they came, Amin praised them and asked them to keep up their good work for Uganda. Fearful that Amin might again reverse himself, many left the country anyway.

## The "Martyrs" Who Became Martyrs

During that bloody month of February, the Protestant churches had been preparing for the June centennial celebration of the coming of Christianity to Uganda. As part of the celebration, a group of talented young Ugandan Christians were producing a play about the first martyrs of Uganda. A week after the archbishop's death, they themselves became martyrs. Their bodies were found a few miles outside Kampala.

The celebration went ahead as planned. Twenty-five thousand Ugandan Christians came into the capital in June for two days of festivities. Most camped outside the Kampala Cathedral at night, singing, praying, ignoring Amin's agents who circulated through the crowd. On June 30 they formed a procession behind church leaders and gospel bands. Singing and holding crosses aloft, they marched through the streets of Kampala as a testimony that the Ugandan church could not be silent. In the procession were many reclaimed backsliders who had renewed their commitment to Christ after the death of Archbishop Luwum.

# 26

# Former
# British Central Africa

## *Zimbabwe/Rhodesia, Zambia, Malawi*

Friday night, June 23, 1978. British Pentecostal missionary Ian McGarrick slept soundly in his quarters at the Emmanuel Christian School in the Rhodesian town of Vumba, near the western border of Mozambique. The 250 black students rested uneasily in their dormitories. They knew something McGarrick did not know. A short while before, about twenty black guerrillas had crept onto the school grounds. They wore knitted caps, spoke English and the Shona tribal language, and identified themselves to the students as members of Robert Mugabe's outlawed Zimbabwe African National Union (ZANU). "The school is being closed," they said. "Stay in bed and no harm will be done you."

The students later claimed they heard nothing from their dorms. Not until the next morning did they alert McGarrick. He quickly began looking for the other missionary personnel at the school—four children and nine adults. All were missing.

### A Grisly Discovery

McGarrick was walking anxiously past the soccer field when he saw the horribly mutilated bodies. Three of the children, all under nine years of age, lay in a cluster, pajamas stiff with dried blood, faces bloody and disfigured. One of the little girls had the purple imprint of a boot on her face and neck. Nearby he came upon a husband and wife. Roy Lynn, his hands tied behind his back, was dead. Lynn's thirty-six-year-old wife, Joyce,

273

her face battered beyond recognition, lay with her left hand touching the battered head of their week-old infant, Pamela. The baby had apparently been killed by a single blow to the head. A short bloodstained log lay nearby.

McGarrick spotted the bodies of another missionary couple, Peter and Sandra McCann, both only thirty. A few feet away he found the ravaged corpses of two single women missionaries, Wendy White and Catherine Pickens, and a little farther on, two other single women. One woman, her hair in curlers and clutching a scarf, had an ax embedded in her back. Some of the women were only partially clothed and presumably had been raped. Only Mary Fisher was missing.

Stupefied by grief and horror, McGarrick ran to call the Rhodesian police. They drew up in a cloud of dust, leaped out, and followed the missionary to the soccer field. A trail of blood took them to the cricket field where they located Miss Fisher. Still alive, she was taken to a hospital in Salisbury, the capital, 120 miles away. She later died of injuries, making her the thirteenth fatality of the horrible attack.

The Rhodesian government flew in troops and reporters. The troops crossed the border into adjoining Mozambique and searched the scenic Vumba mountains for the killers of the Britons. Reporters came and took pictures of the carnage and hastily interviewed McGarrick and some of the students. McGarrick, who by this time was beyond tears, noted that the missionaries and the children had been scheduled to move to the fortified town of Umtali on Sunday.

## A Toy on a Coffin

Five days later the funeral of the martyrs was held in the Umtali municipal hall. Some five hundred mourners, mostly whites, crowded into the building. They saw the eight oak coffins of the adults and three small white ones of the children. Each coffin bore a single wreath. Tiny Pamela Lynn shared a coffin with her mother. The mourners watched Rachel Evans, age eight, place a yellow toy owl on the coffin of her sister, Rebecca. Rachel and her ten-year-old brother, Timothy, had been in a boarding school in Salisbury.

Leaders of the Elim Pentecostal Church, which has headquarters in Cheltenham, England, presided at the services. One of them, Reverend Ronald Chapman, declared, "We do pray God will be merciful to those who perpetrated such an act of shame, that they might know grief and repentance and God's mercy."

## Denials and Charges

Already a bitter controversy was raging. Guerrilla leader Robert Mugabe, a former teacher in a Roman Catholic mission school, strongly denied that his men were responsible. He claimed to have witnesses that would implicate black soldiers of the Rhodesian army in the murders. A World Council of Churches editor came to Mugabe's defense, charging that Rhodesian soldiers had previously dressed like guerrillas to attack defenseless civilians. The Rhodesian government called such claims "completely without foundation" and blamed the guerrillas. The hunt went on for the alleged murderers.

The slaying of the nine missionaries and four children marked the worst atrocity of the Rhodesian guerrilla war. Altogether during a two-year period, thirty-six European and American missionaries and children were killed, along with hundreds of white and black civilians.

## The First Missionary Martyrs

The first missionary killings occurred near Bulawayo in southwestern Rhodesia. The retired Catholic bishop of Bulawayo, seventy-five-year-old Adolph Schmitt, and two nuns were shot to death on a lonely road.

Hitherto, missionaries and black church leaders had experienced more trouble with the white government than with dissident African political groups. Some missionaries, mostly Catholics and Methodists, had been deported for speaking against white minority rule and other policies of discrimination. There was little fear of the black guerrillas. Many of the guerrillas had attended mission schools and received medical aid from mission hospitals. There seemed no reason for an attack on the hands that had educated and cared for them.

This attitude began to change after the Bulawayo killings and similar tragedies that followed. In February 1977, for example, two Jesuits, four Dominican nuns, and one lay brother were murdered at St. Paul's Mission, thirty-five miles north of Salisbury. Government investigators blamed terrorists from Joshua Nkomo's Zimbabwe African People's Union (ZAPU). Ironically, the slaughter came just after Prime Minister Smith had announced plans to deport Irish-born Roman Catholic bishop Donald R. Lamont. The bishop had been convicted of aiding guerrillas by failing to report a rebel request for aid at a mission.

In a second raid about this same time, guerrillas marched four hundred students from the Manama Swedish Evangelical mission school across Rhodesia's southern border into Botswana where many were put on planes for training camps in Zambia. Black Lutheran leaders from southern Africa, meeting in Botswana, "thanked" that nation for receiving the young "refugees."

Through the rest of 1977 and into 1978 guerrilla attacks increased. Some six hundred civilian whites and two thousand blacks were killed. Frightened whites began leaving Rhodesia at the rate of one thousand a month, while thousands of blacks fled into slum camps around Salisbury. Most missionaries at rural stations remained at their posts.

## Bloody June

Then came bloody June 1978, when twenty missionaries and dependents died violent deaths in Rhodesia, compared to sixteen killed during the previous eighteen months.

The June victims included, besides the Pentecostal casualties at the town of Vumba, two German Jesuits, two Catholic Marianhill brothers, two Salvation Army workers, and a Southern Baptist missionary.

The German Jesuits, Fathers Gregor Richert and Bernhard Lisson, were located at St. Rupert's, a remote mission hospital in central Rhodesia. Black staff members reported that three gunmen came to the station and took the foreigners away. The black staffers heard gunfire but did not see the shooting. Afterward the gunmen returned and told them, "We have shot the two whites." The gunmen were presumed to be from Joshua Nkomo's Zimbabwe African People's Union. St. Rupert's is one of sixteen stations operated by German Jesuits in Rhodesia. Monsignor Helmut Reckter, leader of the group, said after the killings, "All our stations have white personnel. We have no plans to withdraw anyone."

The Catholic Marianhill brothers, one Swiss and one German, were shot while sleeping on the veranda of the Embakwe Mission near the Botswana border.

The young Salvation Army workers, twenty-five-year-old Sharon Swindells from Northern Ireland and twenty-eight-year-old Diane Thompson from London, were killed at the Usher Institute, a World Vision-sponsored boarding school for girls, about one hundred miles from the Botswana border.

Southern Baptist missionary Archie C. Dunaway, the only American to die during the month, was a veteran of over thirty years of service in Nigeria and Rhodesia. A maintenance supervisor of the Baptist hospital at Sanyati, he was also a well-known and well-liked area evangelist. He was bayoneted to death by four intruders and his body carried or dragged to the spot where it was found. The guerrillas took his wallet, glasses, boots, pen, and watch, but left his wedding ring.

Fellow missionaries brought the ring to Mrs. Dunaway at the Salisbury airport as a gesture of support when she was departing for home. She blamed her husband's death on "outside terrorists, Communists who wanted to make an example of Archie, to scare us away." His murder, she said, "does not represent the feelings of the Christian Africans. The only thing that sustains us now is our love of the Lord. It's such a loss. Archie and I were together thirty-three years."

Dunaway's body was flown to Nashville, Tennessee, where he was buried beside the remains of another Baptist missionary, eighty-one-year-old Mansfield Bailey, who was a medical missionary in China until forced out by Japanese invaders in 1937.

The loss of so many personnel in one month forced some missions to tighten security to minimize future risks. Southern Baptists, for example, began traveling only between 8:00 a.m. and 4:00 p.m. Some went out from Salisbury in the morning to their rural posts and returned at night. After guerrillas shot down a Rhodesian passenger plane and brutally murdered some of the injured survivors, safety precautions were further tightened.

## The Missionaries Carry On

April 21, 1979, formerly white-dominated Rhodesia held its first election in which all blacks were eligible to vote. In this election, Bishop Abel Muzorewa's United African National Council gained a bare majority control of the black-dominated parliament. Independence was finally achieved and a cease-fire accepted by all parties. Rhodesia officially became the Republic of Zimbabwe in 1980.

Under new leadership, Zimbabwe moved towards becoming a socialist state. The government officially favored Marxist-Leninism, but promised religious freedom and urged the churches to help with national rebuilding.

In the 1980s guerilla warfare continued with white landowners the target of many attacks. Most white farmers posted guards armed with automatic weapons to fend off attackers. Pentecostal ministers at Olive Tree Farm and neighboring New Adam's Farm simply trusted in God.

One night in late November 1987, an armed gang swept in and pulled the Pentecostal missionaries and their children from their beds, bound them with barbed wire, and butchered them with axes. After three hours of mutilation and murder, the attackers set fire to the houses, threw the bodies into the flames, and departed.

The charred remains of sixteen white Christians were found in the ashes of their homes. Five were children. One was only six weeks old. This was the bloodiest massacre of whites since Zimbabwe became independent.

Thirteen-year-old Laura Russell, one of only two that survived, was given a written message, telling "all people from Western or capitalist countries" living in Zimbabwe to get out or die.

An investigation revealed that two weeks before a group of black squatters had moved onto the whites' land. When ordered off, the leader of the evicted band warned, "You won't get another meal." The squatters then sought help from a local gang.

Zimbabwean officials expressed distress. "These were innocent missionaries," declared Home Minister Enos Nkala. "Engaged in production, talking about peace. They were people we so much value."

Zimbabwe borders South Africa. Black Zimbabweans are sympathetic with the African National Congress which now holds power in South Africa. White missionaries and other Christians remaining in Zimbabwe must be careful not to incite attacks from blacks who blame all their troubles upon colonial white rule of past decades. Furloughing Southern Baptist missionary Linda Coleman is one who intends to return. "You cannot live in fear," she said. "You either have to conquer it or you have to leave."

God's work continues in troubled Zimbabwe.

# 27

# Former Belgian Possessions

## *Bloody Massacres*

### THE REPUBLIC OF BURUNDI AND THE KINGDOM OF RWANDA—THE HUTUS AND TUTSIS

A war between Hutus and Tutsis? The few Westerners who read about it in 1972 tended to snicker over the bloody quarrel in Burundi, a little land-locked African country they had never heard of. Yet it was no joke to the families of the two to three hundred thousand killed in less than three months, and to the missionaries who saw the leadership of hundreds of congregations decimated.

The Anglican Church lost thirteen of thirty-five national pastors. All but one of fourteen members of the Baptist executive committee were killed. And in some congregations there were more widows than wives with living husbands. Yet this massacre and other lesser genocides in Burundi and Rwanda were not a religious purge, but the bitter fruit of hatred centuries old.

Adjoining Burundi and Rwanda together are less than two-thirds the size of Maine. But their combined population is over ten times that of Maine, while their economies are among the lowest in the world. Per capita income is around a hundred dollars a year. Increase in the gross national product hovers at zero. This is an area billed as the Switzerland of Africa with enormous potential for tourism.

## Hutus Kill a Brave Pastor

In 1963 an unsuccessful Tutsi invasion from Burundi provoked the Rwandan Hutu army to go on a rampage against Tutsis in Rwanda. Tutsi pastors did not escape the wrath.

One of the bravest pastors was Reverend Yona Kanamuzeyi who ministered to a camp of Tutsi refugees whose homes had been destroyed in previous purges. He had developed a string of twenty-four village churches, centered around a large mother church, to help six thousand people.

On January 24, 1964, a jeep loaded with soldiers drew up in front of his house. They ordered the pastor and a friend, Andrew Kayumba, into the jeep. The pastor anticipated what was coming and told his friend, Kayumba, "Let us surrender our lives into God's hands."

When they reached a military camp, Pastor Kanamuzeyi asked permission to write in his diary. He inscribed, "We are going to heaven," then asked the senior sergeant to please see that his wife was given the diary and the money in his possession. The sergeant replied, "You had better pray to your God."

The pastor stood up and prayed. As his friend Kayumba later recalled, he said, "Lord God, You know that we have not sinned against the government, and now I pray You, in Your mercy, accept our lives. And we pray You to avenge our innocent blood and help these soldiers who do not know what they are doing."

The two prisoners were then tied. One soldier came to take the pastor away, but before leaving, he asked his friend, Kayumba, "Do you believe, Brother?" Kayumba replied, "Yes."

Then the pastor was taken to a bridge. As he walked, Kayumba heard him singing:

> There's a land that is fairer than day
> And by faith we can see it afar:
> For the Father waits over the way,
> To prepare us a dwelling place there.

Shots rang out. The pastor fell, and they threw his body in the stream.

The soldiers told Kayumba to get in the jeep. "We're taking you home," they said. "But remember, if you tell anyone about the killing of the pastor, you, too, will be killed." After the soldiers dropped him off, Kayumba escaped to a neighboring country where he told the story of his pastor's martyrdom.

## "Jesus, I Come"

Many Hutu Christians went to their death expressing peace and asking forgiveness for their executioners. One was Abel Binyoni, the principal of a Quaker mission school and the lay leader of a local church. Before Friends missionaries left Burundi, he wrote them a farewell of thanks and appreciation: "We have nothing that we could return to you for all that you have done to help us. But we know well that our Lord, who is also your Lord Jesus, will not fail to repay you abundantly over and above what you have done for us. . . ."

Abel Binyoni was one of those marked for death in the 1972 carnage. A Christian soldier later reported the details of his death. After he stood up to be shot, he asked if he could sing. Permission was granted and he began,

> Out of my bondage, sorrow and night,
> Jesus, I come, Jesus, I come;
> Into Thy freedom, gladness, and light,
> Jesus I come to Thee.

When he finished the fourth stanza the order came to fire. Deeply affected by his testimony, the squad hesitated for a suspenseful moment, then obeyed.

## THE REPUBLIC OF ZAIRE—THE BELGIAN CONGO

"We will make our fetishes with the hearts of the Americans and Belgians, and we will clothe ourselves in their skins." So thundered Christophe Gbeyne, president of the rebel forces that in 1964 took over Stanleyville (now known as Kisangani), the second largest city of Belgium's former possession. This was no idle threat from the Communist-supported, half-crazed rebel leader. Before the bloody debacle was finished, hundreds of foreigners were dead, including 179 Catholic priests and nuns and thirty Protestant missionary personnel in southeastern Congo. Ten thousand Congolese also fell before the spears, arrows, and guns of the rebels who called themselves Simbas (lions).

The Congolese massacres occurred thirty years ago. Over a dozen books have been written about the martyred missionaries, some by wives whose husbands were killed. Hundreds of articles about the faith and conduct of missionary and Congolese victims have been published.

### Death in the Moonlight

Two missionary teachers, Irene Ferrel and Ruth Hege, had retired for the evening at their school and dispensary in the Kwilu bush. They had heard that Simbas were moving into their area, burning villages, shooting, and spearing every person with ties to Americans or Europeans, seizing and torturing foreigners in unspeakable ways. A few hours earlier they had held a farewell worship service with faithful African workers. In the morning they were anticipating the landing of a helicopter to snatch them away.

Shortly past midnight a gang of young Simbas, crazed from drinking alcohol and smoking hemp, some barely fourteen years old, invaded the lonely station. Hurling rocks through windows and screaming for blood, they rushed into the house, jerked the women from their beds, and dragged them to a grove of trees outside. There was no pleading with them. Dancing wildly about under the bright moon, they began shooting arrows at the Baptist women. A teenager shot an arrow into Irene's neck. Ruth saw her pull it out, take a few steps, and collapse. Also hit, Ruth fell to the ground feigning death, not even moving when a Simba jerked out a handful of her hair. Finally the attackers ran away into the forest, permitting Ruth to escape and tell the story.

## Cruelty beyond Measure

About fifty Protestant and Catholic missionaries were herded into a Catholic mission compound at Buta in the northeast. The arms of thirty-one priests were tied and crossed in back with elbows pressed together. Their feet were bound and their bodies arched. The arm and foot ropes were looped together. The tight bonds evoked cries of agony.

Denied food and water, the priests were untied, stripped, and inspected under a scorching sun. Then they were retied and marched to the river bank where the Simbas cut them to pieces and threw the parts of their bodies into the river. When the job was done, one Simba returned to the mission with a priest's leg. Extending it on a spear, he forced each captive, including the children of the Protestants, to hold it.

## A Missionary "Spy" Is Captured

Young Dr. Paul Carlson and his wife Lois served at an Evangelical Covenant Church hospital in the northern Congo. Their station at Wasolo was called "the forgotten corner" because it was so remote. Dr. Carlson had come out to help in Congo relief for a few months during 1961. Later he and his family returned as permanent missionaries.

Dr. Paul kept Congolese Christians abreast of what was happening. At the annual church conference he told them at communion time that Pierre Mulele had been taught by the Chinese "to hate Christians and shown how to wage war. He returned in 1963 to the Congo to begin doing just what others did long ago in China. . . . Our missionaries worked there for Jesus, but when the Communists took over the government, they sent away all the missionaries." Then he gave reports radioed by other missionaries about the burning of churches and Bible schools. "We do not know what will happen in 1964—and in 1965—until we meet together again. We do not know if we will have to suffer or die during this year because we are Christians. But it does not matter. Our job is to follow Jesus." Then he urged, "My friends, if today you are not willing to suffer for Jesus, do not partake of the elements. . . . To follow Jesus means to be willing to suffer for him."

In August the Carlsons heard that rebels were coming toward Wasolo. They waited until after the wedding of two missionaries at the hospital. Then in early September Paul escorted Lois and their two children across the Ubangi River into the Central African Republic and returned to the hospital alone. Before leaving his loved ones, he assured them he had several escape routes mapped out just in case.

They stayed in touch by radio. Wednesday morning, September 9, Paul reported a "little disturbance" in the town near the hospital. "I'm going to check it out." That afternoon he came on again. "I must leave this evening," he said.

Lois and a woman colleague waited up and watched the stream of refugees pour across the river. Dr. Paul was not among them. Lois remembered a message he had recently taped for their church in California. He had asked prayer for revival in the Congolese church and for wisdom to help the Congolese Christians with their problems. "They do not realize," he had said, "that in this century more people have died for their witness for Christ than died in the early centuries, which we think of as the days of martyrs."

Saturday morning Lois picked up his voice again. "I'm all right. I'm all right," he repeated. "I love you all. Take the children to a school. This may take a long time. I love you."

She hung by the radio. Another missionary came on, calling for Paul. "Where are you? Everyone is gone." Lois heard him answer back, then the other missionary asked, "Can we send a plane or a 'copter?" Paul replied, "Please don't. I am all right now. . . . The Lord is very near."

Once more, on September 18, she heard him say again, "I'm all right." The next report was that he and three Catholic priest friends had been captured by rebels who had burned the hospital and taken them away.

She received a brief letter dated September 24 in which he said, "Where I go from here I know not, only that it will be with Him. If by God's grace I live, which I doubt, it will be to His glory." And another dated October 21 assuring, "I know I'm ready to meet my Lord, but my thoughts for you make this more difficult. I trust that I might be a witness for Christ. . . ."

Five days later the rebel radio announced that a "Major" Carlson, a mercenary, had been captured and brought to Stanleyville and would be tried for spying.

## The Hostages in Stanleyville

By mid-November hundreds of foreigners were trapped in Stanleyville. But only the Americans and Belgians were held as hostages.

"Major" Paul Carlson was the most talked-about captive. Rebel propaganda had made the mild, unassuming missionary medic a monster to the minds of impressionable Congolese. Almost every day he was marched out for execution. He was cuffed and kicked around before jeering mobs, but never shot.

Public facilities had broken down. Young gun-toting Simbas were everywhere, each a law unto himself it seemed. But it was the near prospect of intervention that kept nerves on razor's edge.

On Friday, November 20, Paul Carlson, five U.S. diplomats, and two young American conscientious objectors who had come to help in relief work were moved to the Victoria Hotel. Here they joined Charles Davis and Al Larson along with an assortment of other prisoners.

In the four days they were together, the little group enjoyed a close fellowship. They laughed and kidded one another a little, but underlying everything was the feeling that each day might be their last. "I can't think about the future," Paul Carlson said. "I can just live one day at a time, and trust the Lord for that day."

But they did talk about the future. Paul said he would like to come back to the Congo if his wife was willing. He wanted an airstrip built at the Wasolo hospital. (Less than a year later children in vacation Bible schools of the Evangelical Covenant and Evangelical Free churches collected money to buy a plane for Wasolo. An airstrip was subsequently built.)

Saturday night, November 21, the men prisoners were ordered downstairs. A Simba officer appeared and gave a long harangue about American and Belgian atrocities. He claimed that planes had bombed the town of Banalia, killing most of the women and children there. Then he said, "You're all going to prison tomorrow to be shot. Go back to your bedrolls and wait in the hallway."

Sleep was impossible. Simbas roamed the hallways, frequently stopping to point a rifle at a prisoner and stare. If a man stared back, the Simba would turn away. Sunday morning came and nothing more had happened. The Simbas had only been playing another cruel game.

Or had they? That afternoon the male prisoners were herded into two trucks and a bus. "You're going to Banalia," an officer said. Seven miles outside Stanleyville the bus broke down and the passengers were brought back to the hotel.

## Day of Doom and Deliverance

Tuesday morning, November 24. The prisoners in the hotel were awakened about 6:00 a.m. by the roar of plane engines. "Outside! Outside!" a Simba screamed through the halls. "Run! Run! Hurry!"

At the sound of the planes, missionary hostages and prisoners held elsewhere in Stanleyville were also herded into the streets. Among them were WEC's Muriel Harman, the Cyril Taylor family, and Miss Phyllis Rine who was with the African Christian Mission.

At age twenty-five Miss Rine was one of the youngest missionaries in the Congo. A teacher from Cincinnati, she had signed up in 1960 for missionary service. Before the rebels took over Stanleyville, she had been planning to ride her bicycle into outlying areas of the city and teach about Jesus Christ.

Silver-haired Muriel Harman had been in the Congo thirty-seven years, during which she had taken only three furloughs. A native of British Columbia, Canada, she had spent many of those years with a co-worker among the isolated Wandaka people who had been completely unreached by the gospel. Another missionary would later remember how she had once taken the sheets off her own bed to bind up the wounds of lepers.

Cyril Taylor, forty-five, was a New Zealander. A gifted linguist, he had opened a Bible school just the year before. His wife, two sons, and two daughters were with him in Stanleyville when the American planes dropped the rescue force.

The Belgian paratroopers were floating down like giant snowflakes when the Taylors and Muriel Harmon were pushed into the street and ordered to get into a line. Moments later a nervous Simba sprayed the line with an automatic rifle. Cyril crumpled to the ground—dead. His sons, fourteen and twelve, escaped by falling down and feigning death. Mrs. Taylor and two daughters, three and five, were attacked by a rebel soldier with a machete. They received severe gashes across their heads, but all survived.

Phyllis Rine was among some 250 white hostages driven into the public square. She was fatally hit by a machine gun blast.

## "Paul Died That I Might Live"

Charles Davis ran beside Paul Carlson. "What's happening, Paul?"

"They may be planning to use us as a shield."

They were in the street now and still running. They heard a machine gun cut loose about a block away. Suddenly they were halted at the corner and ordered to sit on the ground. The firing was closer now.

They recognized a Simba colonel named Opepe. He looked like a wild man. "Haven't I been your friend and protected you?" he yelled. "Why are your brothers coming to attack us now?"

The machine gun kept firing. Closer. A Simba guard at the rear of the crowd panicked and fired his rifle. Other guns began firing, shooting into the crowd. The prisoners fell flat on the street and waited for the end. The guns fell silent. About ten prisoners ran for a house. They had to climb over a masonry wall to reach the porch. Paul Carlson was behind Charles Davis and motioned for Charles to go first. Charles leaped and dove over the wall. He turned to grasp the doctor's outstretched hand. A gun cracked five times. Dr. Paul fell back into the street . . . dead.

Some of the other hostages were hit and killed or wounded. Among the missionaries, only the doctor was shot fatally. Charles Davis ran on into the house and huddled among seven other men on the floor of a closet. A Simba ran by and did not see them. Ten minutes elapsed. They heard an American voice. "They're in here." Then two Belgian paratroopers. "You're safe! You're safe!" they called. "Come out."

Charles Davis ran back to the porch and saw his friend's bullet-riddled body. "Paul's dead! Dead!" he sobbed. "I must have cried for fifteen minutes," he later recalled. "By letting me go first, Paul died that I might live."

## "You Shot My Friend"

The missionaries at Kilometer Eight were also awakened by the planes. They ran outside to see. Then they went back for breakfast and devotions as usual.

Two armed Simbas burst into the house while they were praying and turned the breakfast tables upside down. One grabbed a slide projector and shouted accusingly, "Radio transmitter!" Another ordered, "Everybody outside."

The Simbas lined their prisoners up, separating the men from the women. Then they sent the women and children back inside one of the houses, telling the two men, Hector McMillan and Bob McAllister, to stay where they were.

The Simba who escorted the women inside turned back to the door, and then whirled and sprayed the room with bullets. Two of the McMillan boys were hit, but not hurt seriously. The younger children were crying; the rest were praying.

Guns blazed in the yard. Hector McMillan fell, dying instantly. "You shot my friend!" Bob McAllister yelled at a Simba. The Simba shot again. Bob fell to the ground and lay there playing dead. The Simbas left, apparently thinking they had killed both men. Bob got up, and he and some of the women tenderly carried Hector's body into the living room. Ione McMillan called her six sons. "Your father has gone to be with the Lord," she announced. Those in the room knelt with her in prayer.

Some of the women and children fled into the forest behind the station. Others remained to care for the injured boys. Those in the forest waited until almost noon, when suddenly they heard heavy shooting. Abruptly the shooting stopped. Al Larson, who had escaped from Stanleyville, called out that the siege was over.

## The Massacre at Banalia

Before the parachute drop, the prisoners at Banalia had been permitted to do medical work. English missionary doctor Ian Sharpe was too valuable, the rebels said, to be kept in confinement.

The Simbas there waited until the day after the parachute drop into Stanleyville. At 4:00 p.m. they pulled Dr. Sharpe from the midst of an operation. "We will kill your family and allow you to keep helping us in the hospital," they offered.

The British medic shook his head. "We will die together. You may kill me first."

A Simba threw a spear. Others beat the doctor with guns and arrows until he died. Then they killed Audrey Sharpe and their three young children. The Parrys and their two children were next. Then Mary Baker and Robina Gray. The Catholic missionaries were the last to die.

The Simbas threw their bodies into the river.


## "He Is in Heaven"

Angeline Tucker was still separated from her husband in Paulis. She heard via Voice of America that paratroopers had landed in Stanleyville and rescued about a thousand Europeans. Shortly afterwards, the Mother Superior phoned her from the Catholic school where J. W. Tucker and other prisoners had been held. The nun assured her that J. W. was well and in good spirits. There were seventy-two prisoners at the school, she said.

At 9:00 a.m. the next morning, November 25, she called the Mother Superior back. "How are things?" she asked.

"Oh—so-so," the nun replied in a tight voice. Angeline knew something had happened.

"How is my husband?" she asked hopefully.

"*Il est au Ciel*—He is in Heaven," the nun replied softly. "May God comfort your heart to know he was ready to die."

Angeline was still crying when her daughter Carol Lynne appeared. "Mummy, what happened?"

"Honey, I'm afraid the rebels have killed Daddy." The little girl and her younger brother, "Cricky," burst into tears.

The phone connection had been broken. Somehow Angeline managed to call the nun back. "Sister, how did it happen?"

"I don't know all the details, Madam. Only that the rebels came about nine-thirty last night and dragged the men from their rooms. We think they killed about thirteen. We know your husband was among them and some of the priests." Angeline later heard that J. W. and the priests had been stomped and clubbed to death and thrown in the Bomokandi River, twenty-five miles away.

The next morning they heard planes, then after a while gunfire. An hour or so after the planes landed, Cricky looked out the front window. "Mummy," he squealed, "soldiers in the street. They're white!"

One of the Belgian soldiers saw them and several ran into the yard. "Come quickly! Quickly!" they called in French. The grieving family climbed into a truck for the trip to the airport. An officer asked who they were.

"We're Protestant missionaries," Angeline said. "Americans."

"Mrs. Tucker's husband was killed by the rebels two nights ago," the woman beside her whispered.

The Belgian gently put his arm over Angeline's shoulder. "I'm so sorry, Madam. I wish we could have come in time to save him."

## "We Will All Die Together"

On November 27, the Protestant and Catholic women prisoners at Bafwasende were ordered into the yard and made to pick grass. Then the Simbas marched them barefoot to the nearby river to bathe. "Sing," a Simba ordered Dolena Burk and Olive McCarten, who were leading the procession. They began, "Onward, Christian Soldiers." Louie Rimmer, an elderly missionary woman, Laurel McCallum, Jean Sweet, Elizabeth and Heather Arton, and the nuns joined in.

After they got back to the house, fighter-bombers of the Congolese air force, piloted by anti-Castro Cuban mercenaries, buzzed the station. The Simba guards panicked and ran in every direction. "If one of us dies today, ten of you will be killed," one Simba yelled as he ran for cover.

When the planes were past, several rebel soldiers ran into the house screaming, "We've got to kill you now." "Disrobe! Disrobe!" shouted another.

Helpless before pointed guns the eighteen Catholic missionaries and the eight Protestants began undressing. Before they had finished, some of the rebels were already prodding the men toward the river.

"Chester!" Dolena Burk called. "Chester!" The Simbas pushed him ahead, refusing even to let him turn his head.

On the veranda the Simbas separated three nuns from the other sisters. "You nursed in the hospital, so you will not be killed," they told them.

The three refused. "If one dies, we will all die together." But by beatings and sheer force the Simbas kept the three nurses back.

The Simbas pointed at the Protestant women. "You and you and you," they said, indicating Dolena, Louie, and Olive. "Follow the sisters and the men to the river."

They walked a few steps, then the apparent leader of the Simbas yelled for them to come back. The other nuns, also, were brought back.

Dolena stumbled back to the house. At the doorway she heard shots from the river. She looked back at the path to the river bank. Laurel McCallum, Jean Sweet, and Betty Arton and Heather were disappearing from sight. No one was calling them back.

Nothing more happened until evening when Simba guards brought back clothing to the nuns and the three Protestant women who had been spared.

"When will we be killed?" one of the nuns wanted to know.

"Oh, we're done," a Simba replied.

"Did you shoot my husband and the others?" Dolena Burk pressed. The Simba refused to answer.

A couple of days later the survivors saw Congolese women in the area wearing the clothing of those who had been marched to the river. Then the wife of the rebel colonel who commanded Bafwasende stopped at the house and verified that Chester and the others were dead. "My husband told me," the woman reported. "He said the teenage girl could have lived if she had let the soldiers do what they wanted. She was so stubborn."

During the next two weeks the survivors were kept in suspense. Some were slapped around and cursed. Only the intercession of a young rebel captain, Jean Pierre, kept them from being killed. They knew he was risking his life by protecting them.

On December 18 the government mercenaries came and rescued them. The women signed a letter attesting to Jean Pierre's bravery and asked that he be spared. "We'll not kill him," the mercenary officer promised. "But the national army is something else."

That afternoon the women were flown to liberated Stanleyville. While there Dolena Burk heard a radio newscaster say a young rebel captain from Bafwasende had been turned over to the national army and executed.

## "Brother, I'll Die with You"

Bill McChesney, Jim Rodger, and their colleagues faced the final wrath of the Simbas on the evening of November 24 at Wamba. An arriving rebel officer turned livid when he saw Bill McChesney. "Why is this man still free?" he demanded. "Take him to prison at once!"

When Bill was pushed into a truck, Jim Rodger jumped in to accompany his sick friend. During the short trip, Simba soldiers beat Bill mercilessly. Still weak from malaria, Bill could not stand up under the abuse. Jim had to carry him into the prison where they were pushed into a tiny, fetid cell, already jammed with some forty prisoners, including several foreign priests. The Simbas had ripped Bill's clothes from his back. The priests gave him their clothes to contain the malarial chills that wracked his body.

The next morning a glowering rebel colonel came and ordered the prisoners to be moved into the courtyard where local Congolese swarmed around them, screaming for their deaths. After a while the colonel began separating the prisoners by nationality.

Eight Belgian priests and a bishop were put in one group. The bishop had been beaten so badly that he was hardly recognizable. The colonel turned next to Bill and Jim. "You, American?" he snarled at Bill. Bill nodded weakly. The colonel glared at Jim. "What are you?"

"British."

The officer motioned for Bill to stand apart. From signs made to his men, it appeared that he was about to order Bill's death. Jim Rodger stepped beside his friend. "If you must die, brother, I'll die with you."

"He's an Englishman," one of the priests shouted to the colonel. The colonel turned to face Jim. "What is your nationality?" No reply. "Doesn't matter. American—British—they're all alike."

The frenzied mob was permitted to move forward. Clubs and fists rained on the two WEC missionaries. Bill McChesney was probably killed by the first blow. Jim Rodger caught him as he fell and gently laid him on the ground. The mob knocked Jim down and trampled on his body until he was dead. The Belgian fathers were next. Like crazed jungle beasts, the rebel-incited mob beat, kicked, and trampled them until life had fled their bruised bodies. The mob also killed sixteen other foreign civilians before the massacre was over.

Cooler Congolese carted the bodies to the Wamba River and tossed them into the yellow, swirling water to be eaten by crocodiles.

## Burleigh Law's Last Flight

The Congo missionary martyrs were all killed in groups except pilot Burleigh Law. The genial Methodist might have lived had he not insisted on trying to help colleagues in difficult circumstances.

Law dropped a note to missionaries at the Wembo Nyama station, requesting a landing signal. Trapped by rebels, they did not respond, hoping he would fly on. He landed anyway to check on them and was seized. When he refused to turn over his plane key, he was shot by a trigger-happy guard.

Burleigh Law was known and loved in the area. The rebel commander was displeased at the rash action of the guard. One of the young Simbas talked sadly about him. "He was our pilot, you know."

The rebels permitted two missionary doctors to operate with the hope of saving his life. "Why did you land?" his friends asked. He replied, "I just couldn't leave you folks in this situation." Despite transfusions from fellow missionaries, he died on the operating table.

The missionaries he had tried to help later escaped.

## Comparisons with the Boxer Rebellion

Not since the Boxer Rebellion had so many foreign missionaries been killed in one year. Indeed, the Congo massacres of 1964–1965 bear striking parallels to the Chinese Boxer uprisings in 1900. The assailants were whipped into a frenzy by their political superiors bent on controlling the country. The attacks were motivated, at least in part, by a burning hatred of western foreigners and a drive to stamp out Christianity. There was even a Chinese connection, for some of the rebel leaders had been trained and armed by Chinese Communists in the forests of bordering Tanzania. And some had been to China, and to other Communist countries as well, for indoctrination in Marxism. On a different note, missionaries held captive by Congolese rebels were encouraged by reading of the courage of the martyrs in Communist China.

## "No Greater Love"

After the massacres came the funerals and memorial services. Most of the slain missionaries, whose bodies were retrieved, were buried in the Congo. Lois Carlson felt that her husband would have wanted to be buried at Karawa in a little cemetery in the northeast where other missionary personnel were interred. His body was flown there for burial.

Hundreds and hundreds of Congolese, along with many foreigners, flocked to Karawa for the funeral. As Lois and the children approached Palm Lane which led to the church, they saw that flowers and bright-colored leaves had been tied to the trunk of each palm tree. All along the way children stood holding flowers. Still more flowers decorated the arches of the doors. A single bundle of native flowers graced the plain wooden casket. Lois placed beside it a bouquet of red and pink carnations that she and her children had picked for the occasion. A large white bow held the carnations together, and on it was the word "BELOVED," in large, gold letters.

Pastor Zacharie Alengi, president of the Evangelical Church of the Ubangi, gave the funeral message. He recalled the last time he had seen Dr. Paul: "He told us, 'If I have to leave, I won't go far, and I will return to you as soon as possible.' I saw this was love, and I asked myself, 'Why did this doctor choose a place like this?' It came from love and joy."

Later the funeral procession wound to the cemetery, where other missionaries and missionary children who had given their lives to the Congo lay. An honor guard of Congolese soldiers stood at attention. The soldiers presented arms and played "Taps." Palm branches were laid reverently across the coffin. Then the body of "Monganga Paul," (the title of the biography of Dr. Paul Carlson, written by Lois Carlson and published by Harper and Row, 1966) as the people knew him, was lowered into the ground.

The simple grave marker placed under a plain cross, said:

> DR. PAUL E. CARLSON
> THERE IS NO GREATER LOVE THAN THIS,
> THAT A MAN SHOULD LAY DOWN HIS LIFE
> FOR HIS FRIENDS. JOHN 15:13

## Another Missionary Is Killed

March 1977 brought trouble from a new source. Ex-Katangese rebels, trained by Cubans in Marxist Angola, invaded Zaire's copper-rich Shaba Province (formerly Katanga). Seven Methodist missionaries at Katanga were put under house arrest, but allowed to continue their medical and teaching work.

On April 18, the rebels ordered one of the missionaries, Dr. Glenn Eschtruth, to face trial at their headquarters in Angola for "capitalistic crimes." He spent his last night at home setting family and financial matters in order with his wife, Lena, and writing messages to their three daughters. The next morning—his forty-ninth birthday—he wrote on the flyleaf of Lena's Bible, "And we know that all things work together for good to them that love God" (Romans 8:28).

That afternoon the rebels came for him. They ordered the mission hospital and school to be closed and the remaining missionaries to stay in their homes.

Six weeks later government forces recaptured Katanga. Mission planes landed to evacuate the Methodists.

Lena Eschtruth asked about her husband and was told he had never reached Angola, but had been shot about thirty miles from Katanga. Africans led a missionary friend to Glenn's body which was identified by his watch and khaki bag. The Asbury Seminary graduate was buried at the Katanga station.

# PART TEN

# Martyrs of the Caribbean and Latin America

# 28

# The Caribbean and Latin America

## *Catholic by Conquest*

Christian martyrs in "Christian" nations such as Mexico, Colombia, and Brazil? Yes, though there have not been as many as in "pagan" Africa.

Until recent times, in the southern hemisphere the name "Christian" signified little more than adherence to traditional rituals in the Catholic church—baptism, marriage, and burial. The Catholic hierarchy claimed over 98 percent of the population in countries where spiritual ignorance, poverty, immorality, and political oppression reigned. Astute and honest Catholic leaders now say 5 to 10 percent may be a more accurate figure.

The story of how Latin America and most of the Caribbean islands became Catholic by conquest is well known. Little changed after these colonies of Spain, Portugal, and France gained independence. Concordats with the Vatican were retained, making governments, in effect, subservient to intolerant Catholic hierarchies. Inquisitions continued. In Peru alone 120,000 "heretics" were tortured and 189 dissenters burned at the stake.

Early Protestant missionary thrusts were beaten back. Five of the first Protestant preachers in Brazil were killed. In Argentina hostile Indians drove the first missionaries back to their ship, where they starved to death. A pioneer missionary in Peru was imprisoned, then released only after a sensational trial brought international criticism on the government. The first Baptist worker in Cuba, when that nation was still a Spanish colony, was imprisoned and threatened with death.

Reaction to heavy-handed clerical intolerance, leading to the rise of liberal parties, brought some relief in the nineteenth century. But in most countries Catholic opposition to Protestant ministries continued.

Political-clerical alliances, representing the rich and powerful, fought every movement towards civil, political, and religious freedom. The ruling oligarchies opposed Bible translation in the vernacular, banned Bible distribution, and encouraged fanatics to stone, flog, and sometimes murder Bible colporteurs. They even blocked Protestant orphanages and schools for poor children, who otherwise would not receive an education. Such religious and political repression, accompanied by rampant disease and poverty, drove many intellectuals into agnosticism and atheism, and some into Communism. In most Latin American countries this persecution persisted into the 1950s with sporadic outbursts still recurring in remote rural areas.

A new twist to the violence involves the peasant revolts against the conservative governments, resulting in the deaths of a number of Catholic priests who became allied with the Marxist left. Then there is the other end of the spectrum in Cuba where many Catholics have been killed or imprisoned by Castro's Marxist government.

The great majority of evangelical missionaries and national pastors have not been involved in volatile political conflicts, choosing instead to pursue evangelism, church-building, and healing and teaching ministries. Their service in the name of Christ has not been without great sacrifice. Some have been martyred by hostile mobs acting at the behest of fanatical Catholic priests and politicians; some have been speared to death by hostile Indians or killed by bandits; others have been mysteriously slain and their assailants never identified.

# 29

## Cuba

### *Communism in the Western Hemisphere*

F idel is a reformer, a revolutionary, maybe a socialist, but not a Communist." So ran the line that issued from Havana to Castro apologists and liberal clergymen all over the world when Castro and Argentine "Che" Guevara were trying to overthrow Cuban dictator Fulgencio Batista.

The deception was still being repeated in 1959 by thousands of foreign clergymen and other Castro defenders. But Cuban patriots knew Fidel had betrayed the revolution. He was no more than a left-wing dictator.

### A Catholic Leader Is Killed

The Cuban government had prohibited religious processions, but on September 10, 1961, a crowd burst out of the Church of Our Lady of Charity in Havana and began shouting for a march. A guard of militiamen was overwhelmed. Reserves were rushed to the church under the command of the Minister of Interior. They wore Russian military caps adorned with the hammer-and-sickle insignia.

The militiamen charged into the Catholic crowd, firing machine guns and swinging clubs. Dozens were wounded. Arnaldo Socorro, a leader of the Young Catholic Workers' Association, was killed. The next day Castro declared him a "Hero of the Revolution" and announced that he had been shot down by priests.

## Priests and Nuns Are Deported

Castro decreed that religious demonstrations would never again be allowed in Cuba. Any priests who did not pledge loyalty to the government would lose their citizenship and be deported. The pastor of Our Lady of Charity Church was one of the first to go. Father Diego Madrigal was pulled out of bed and shoved aboard a ship with over one hundred other priests. They landed in the United States, and from there they proceeded to countries of their choice. None were permitted back in Cuba.

Over two thousand nuns also left Cuba during this time. Few went voluntarily. Most were expelled. The forced exodus left only about four hundred priests and nuns to serve Cuban Catholics.

Later in the year Castro quit pretending. "I am a Marxist-Leninist and I will be a Marxist-Leninist to the last day of my life," he declared in a five-hour telethon.

## Most Protestants Had Favored the Revolution

Until this time the religious struggle had been mainly carried by Catholics. The Protestant minorities were mostly lower class workers and farmers. They had not been identified with the deposed Batista, as Catholics had been. Protestants had been persecuted in Cuba when the island was a colony of Spain. After independence, which followed the defeat of Spain in the Spanish-American War, they enjoyed more freedom than Protestants were experiencing in most Latin American countries. Church and state were separate in Cuba.

In a society which favored the rich, Protestants sympathized with the announced aims of the revolution. Many cheered Castro's land redistribution policies. But when it became obvious that Cuba was becoming a Communist state, the seeds of discontent were sown. As the government tightened controls, thousands of Protestants joined the Catholics' flight to Florida.

Still the Protestants left in Cuba did not experience overt persecution. They were small and divided. Their churches did not operate large institutions or own large sections of land, as did the Catholics. There was little that Castro's commissars could confiscate from them.

## The Hammer Falls on Protestants

Late in 1963 Dr. John A. Mackay, a prominent leader in the National Council of Churches, visited Cuba and returned saying he saw no religious persecution. His itinerary had been cleverly drawn.

The following March 13 Castro openly attacked certain "Protestant sects" for the first time. This signaled a wave of persecution and government legislation over church affairs, not unlike what had happened in Eastern European satellites of the Soviet Union.

The law limited religious activities to church buildings and to traditional schedules. Special services could not be held on weekday nights with the exception of Wednesday, the customary prayer meeting time. Churches were also ordered to register as associations. Those that refused were fined. Only persons above legal age could become church members. Youth under fifteen, unless accompanied by parents, were forbidden to enter churches. Government spies began appearing in church meetings.

Church construction was stopped and some buildings were confiscated. Around one hundred churches were closed, their furniture and pews confiscated. The Pentecostal Bible Institute of Manacas was closed. The Baptist Seminary in Santiago de Cuba was denied a food quota. Theological students were drafted into the military or sent to labor camps.

Radio preaching and distribution of literature was outlawed. The last shipment of Bibles was confiscated. Circulation of other Bibles and hymnals was forbidden. House-to-house proselytizing was banned.

Protestant preachers fought back. Baptist pastors were especially bold in condemning state interference in church affairs. Using a spy network that included children, the government began amassing a list of the most troublesome Baptists. In 1965 police arrested fifty-three Baptists simultaneously. Thirty-four were tried and sentenced for offenses ranging from espionage to "twisting biblical texts for the purpose of ideological diversionism."

## Executions and Imprisonment

Among those arrested and sentenced were two Americans, David Fite and his father-in-law, Dr. Herbert Caudill. Dr. Caudill was superintendent of the Baptist seminary and Fite was pastor of a Havana church and a faculty member at the seminary.

Convicted of espionage, which they vehemently denied, they were held for four years. Their release largely resulted from a crusade by Fite's pastor-father among American, Canadian, Mexican, Cuban, and Russian diplomats to persuade Castro to let them go.

Fite told of "witnessing more than two hundred executions about one hundred meters from my cell." The firing squad would march into the area, he said, and tie the condemned person to a stake. After the sentence was read, "we could occasionally hear a cry of desperation and then the volley of shots . . . and then the shot of grace."

Another pastor, Benjamin Valdez, was kept in a Cuban prison for twelve years. He told reporters in Atlanta in 1978 that only one Baptist pastor still remained in prison. He indicated some government relaxation against church activities. "The church is able to work from house to house. But in a careful way, you know," he added with a wry smile. Cuban pastors, he said, were not making "big propaganda. But as long as a minister speaks only on religious matters, the government isn't going to interfere." Valdez said he was never physically abused in prison and was able to witness to fellow prisoners. "We won several to the Lord," he recalled.

## Cuba's Prisoners

A slow trickle of released "political" prisoners told their stories during the 1980s. The most dramatic and painful testimony came from Cuban patriot and poet Armando Valladare whose book *Against All Hope* chronicled the physical beatings and psychological torments inflicted on prisoners at the notorious Isla de Pinos. Located near the southern mainland, the prison housed more than five thousand inmates at its peak. Some of the prisoners were common criminals. Others—including a number of Christians—were there because they had dared oppose Castro and his Communist regime.

In excruciating detail, Valladare told of how some prisoners were kept in isolated, darkened cells with doors welded shut and fed a diet that included watery soup laced with pieces of broken glass and a cow's intestine filled with excrement.

Another released prisoner, Jorge Valls, in a book titled *Twenty Years and Forty Days: Life in a Cuban Prison*, told of some prisoners going mad and others maintaining their sanity by religious faith. Christian prisoners, Valls said, bound themselves together in a communal prayer group to resist efforts of prison officials trying to make them make statements and do other things against their morality and beliefs.

## Cuba: The Last Communist Holdout?

Early in the last decade of the twentieth century, Cuba laid out the welcome mat to tourists and loosened restrictions on the printing of Bibles. In 1991 the United Bible Societies received permission to print—in Cuba—one million Scripture selections to be distributed by churches during the Pan American Games in Cuba in August. With the collapse of Cuba's biggest benefactor, the Soviet Union, Cuba faced stringent economic times and desperately needed an influx of foreign dollars. The paling economy has also forced Castro to call home troops from Africa and lighten up on political meddling in Central American countries.

An August 10, 1992 *Newsweek* report on Cuba asked, "Is Castro's regime nearing its final months?" Disillusionment with Castro and communism is said to extend deep into Cuba's Marxist elite. Harvard Cuban scholar Jorge Domingues calls Cuba "a situation without hope."

In 1994, Castro permitted thousands of Cubans to escape on rafts to Florida. When Florida became overwhelmed, the refugee flow was stopped and thousands of Cuban boat people were shipped back to the U.S. base at Guantanamo Bay for more orderly immigration.

There is hope among suffering Christians, hope and expectancy of opportunities for ministry after the fall of communism in Cuba. Under Castro, almost 60 percent of the population have identified themselves as "atheist." As is now happening in the former Soviet Union, many of Cuba's "atheists" will be open to the gospel.

# 30

# Haiti and the Dominican Republic

## *The Island of Hispaniola*

The word Haiti arouses images of frolicking tourists, quickie divorces, casino gambling, cockfighting, and backyard voodoo at midnight. Shadowy secret police wearing dark glasses and gray fedoras, telltale bulges at their hips, whispers of revolution, palace intrigue, and rumors of a torture room painted dark brown so the walls and floor will not reveal the blood splotches—these imaginative pictures contrast harshly with the grinding poverty and wasting disease that abounds in the back alleys and remote countryside of Haiti.

## A History Bathed in Blood

Haiti and the Dominican Republic share the island of Hispaniola—the land Columbus "loved most." French settlers on the western side of the island imported thousands of black slaves from Africa to work on sugar plantations. A century later, in 1791, the blacks rebelled and murdered most of the whites. French troops sent to establish order were crushed by black defenders and wiped out by disease. With independence in 1804 came a long reign of political terror marked by palace purges and power plays between whites and mulattoes. From 1915 to 1934 the United States fully controlled the country. More recently, Haiti had been the private fiefdom of the despotic Duvaliers. First was the father, Francois "Papa Doc" Duvalier, who died in 1971. He was succeeded by young Jean-Claude "Baby Doc" Duvalier. Like his father he served as "president for life." The Duvalier government became one of the most repressive regimes in the world—torturing, murdering, and forcing political dissidents, including many clergymen, into exile, while effectively blackmailing Washington for financial aid against the threat of a Communist takeover.

## An Episcopalian Clergyman Disappears

In 1961, an Episcopalian clergyman, Father Yvon Emmanuel Moreau, joined with five other senators in opposing dictatorial powers for Papa Doc (Francois Duvalier), while speaking for constitutionality, rights, and the dignity of man. Duvalier accused the six of advancing a Communist plot and declared them immediately impeached. Two fled the country. Three took refuge in the Mexican embassy. Father Moreau refused to run, replying,

> I am a believer in democracy and I thought I was doing my job when I criticized what should be criticized to protect the welfare of the people and the country. . . . I have never been involved in any subversive activities and I don't intend to be used now by any group of politicians.

Moreau was arrested and disappeared, as so many Haitians have, never to be heard from, or of, again.

## The Dominican Republic—Haiti's Next-Door Neighbor

The terror is over in the Dominican Republic, as Haiti's next-door neighbor is known, although adult Dominicans still look around cautiously when the name Rafael Trujillo is mentioned. The "Hitler of the Caribbean" was assassinated in 1961. For thirty years previous he and his relatives practically ran the Dominican Republic like a concentration camp. Motorists had to show identification every few miles. Phones were tapped, hotel rooms bugged, and informers seemed to be everywhere, even in families. Each week the balding dictator's procurers selected a group of young girls for the president's bed. Young women and families that resisted sometimes lost their jobs, were beaten, or if they made a big fuss, simply disappeared.

The "Benefactor of the Fatherland," as he termed himself, kept up a front of respectability. He milked the economy to build showplace monuments, jailed Communists, and cultivated U.S. politicians. When Batista was being overthrown, he funneled money to the Cuban dictator. After Castro won, Batista took up temporary exile with his friend Trujillo.

## A Tall Texan

About one hundred foreign missionaries were then in the Dominican Republic. Most had been in the country less than a decade, even though the first missionary, a Free Methodist, had arrived back in 1889. Of the missionaries, best known to the Dominican people was rangy Howard Shoemake, a tall Southern Baptist from Texas. He had been in the country only three years.

Shoemake introduced a television ministry and a unique medical aid program credited with saving thousands of Dominican children from deadly gastroenteritis. Shoemake had a powerful ham radio and during the war sent hundreds of mercy messages for desperate Dominicans. He and his wife also welcomed into their home various political refugees.

The medical program featured clinics at churches in Santo Domingo, the capital, where patients paid a dollar for a doctor's services and received needed medicines free. The medicines came from U.S. drug companies through Medical Assistance Programs in Wheaton, Illinois. Shoemake and other missionaries also cooperated with medical teams of visiting Christian physicians who came under the auspices of the Christian Medical Society.

After the fighting ended, other clinics were set up around the country and staffed by Dominican Christian doctors. One was in Santiago, the Dominican Republic's second largest city, under the direction of Paul and Nancy Potter, newly arrived Southern Baptist missionaries from Missouri.

## The First Missionary Martyrs

Paul, age thirty-three, had been a seminary-trained pastor. He had heard a missionary home on furlough ask, "Why has God called so few to serve the rest of the world and so many to serve the United States?" When a challenge was given for five thousand new missionaries at the Southern Baptist Convention in Atlantic City, he and Nancy offered themselves for service. Nancy was a warm, outgoing young woman who had sensed God's leading through teaching mission study courses at their church. At Cottey College in Nevada, Missouri, she had been selected by the faculty as the student who most nearly approached "the ideal of intellect and spirituality" and who had exerted "the most wholesome influence upon her associates." Paul and Nancy brought with them two lively youngsters, Susan, seven, and David, five.

In their first evangelistic effort in Santiago they won eleven young Dominicans to Christ. When these came to the Potter home for instructions, they brought four friends who wanted to accept Christ.

They soon organized a church. Four hundred Dominicans came to the dedication of the new sanctuary. By 1970, when they left for their first furlough, they had two flourishing churches and three mission chapels.

Near the end of their year at home, Nancy was asked why they wanted to return to such a troubled, impoverished country. "We have seen God's power at work and human lives changed," she said. "Nothing can be more thrilling."

They returned in June 1971, to find that the work had continued to grow under the leadership of fellow missionaries. The clinic was handling almost two hundred patients a week, each patient receiving a Christian witness. They began to think of the possibility of establishing five churches by the end of their next term.

The Potters never reached that goal. Early on the morning of July 7, ten-year-old David discovered their bloody bodies. While the son and daughter had slept, Paul and Nancy had been beaten and stabbed to death.

## Why Were the Potters Killed?

The first martyrdom of missionaries provoked editorials in all the leading newspapers demanding an immediate investigation. The papers took note of their medical services to the poor.

Robbery was one motive considered by investigators. The possibility that they had been killed by anti-American political terrorists was also weighed. A reporter noticed that "Death to the Yankees" had been scrawled on their car. Another theory later surfaced that some members of the Dominican medical establishment had paid to have the Potters killed and their deaths blamed on leftists. These upper-class Dominicans were losing money in patient fees and pharmaceutical sales to the missionary clinic and wanted the clinic closed. The investigation continued for months, but no one was ever arrested. The case is still open.

The churches begun by Paul and Nancy Potter continue to grow. The medical clinics continue to serve thousands of poor Dominicans. With the murders still unsolved, missionary Shoemake expressed the feelings of the Potters' missionary colleagues. "Regardless of the cause of the death of Paul and Nancy," he said, "our attitude must be that of Christ who said from the cross, 'Forgive them for they know not what they do.' The work which they began must be carried on."

## A Harvest of Converts

The commitment of Paul and Nancy Potter and other evangelical missionaries, pastors, and lay Christians in the Dominican Republic contributed to a rich spiritual harvest. The Luis Palau evangelistic crusade in Santo Domingo netted 3,984 Dominicans coming forward for spiritual counsel. Protestants now represent almost 5 percent of the population with 190 missionaries serving in this land which the explorer Christopher Columbus claimed to have "loved most."

# 31

## Mexico

### *South of the Border*

Mexico today is a warm, friendly country where thirteen hundred North American missionaries work in cooperation with a body of more than 1.3 million evangelicals.

Mexico yesterday was far different. As in other Latin American countries, Mexico's native Indian population was forced to renounce their pagan religions and submit to Catholic baptism. It was convert or die in "New Spain" during the sixteenth century. The corrupt church, in league with the Spanish oligarchy, was not challenged for three centuries. Bible colporteurs and later missionaries met with immediate opposition. Evangelical workers risked their lives every time they preached the gospel. They were often cursed, spat upon, and stoned, then chased out of town by a mob. Many were killed by mobs incited by Roman Catholic priests who feared evangelicals as their worst enemy.

### Mexico's Era of Martyrs

The revolutionary fervor was waning by 1940. Easing of restrictions brought an upsurge in evangelical activity and hundreds of new missionaries. The Catholic hierarchy, which had regained much of its old power, became alarmed.

In 1944, the archbishop of Mexico, Luis Maria Martinez, issued a harsh pastoral letter to all priests in the country. "We oppose the continual extension of the Protestant campaign," he said. "We will fight it until we finish. God wills it." Then he called on the priests to "place their efforts at the service of the faith" in vanquishing the "hellish serpent" of Protestantism.

This signaled the beginning of the most intense Catholic persecution against evangelicals ever seen in Latin America, with the exception of Colombia. Scores, perhaps hundreds, of evangelical pastors, evangelists, and lay leaders were murdered by Catholic fanatics. The worst incidents occurred in small communities and rural areas where Catholics controlled law enforcement and the courts. Little protection was provided for the embattled Protestants, and newspapers feared to publish the truth.

The fanatics were careful not to kill foreign missionaries. The missionaries agonized with their Mexican brothers and sisters. But all they could do was write letters to the State Department, which ignored their protests. At that time the State Department opposed the sending of Protestant missionaries to Catholic Latin America.

## The Murderers Are Exposed

A few small stories about the persecution were printed in Mexico City newspapers. But it was not until February 8, 1952, that a major publication, *Tiempo*, published a long documentary covering eight years of savagery.

*Tiempo* called the Catholic war on evangelicals "an unprecedented violence, whose extremes have been murder, rape, pillage, and the extermination of small communities." Among cases "which have come to the knowledge of the Federal authorities," the following were cited in *Tiempo*.

November 25, 1944, the evangelical church house of La Gloria, Veracruz, was burned as well as nine houses of Protestants. Seven people, among them five children, died in the disaster. A little later the Catholics expelled from the village sixty families who were affiliated with the Church of God.

May 27, 1945, in Santiago, the Catholic priest led an assault on the homes of Protestant pastors Feliciano Juarez and Vicente Garita. The preachers were lynched and quartered and their homes dynamited.

June 1, 1945, the parish priest of Caulote, Michoacan, burned the Lutheran temple. (Lutheran was used to mean any evangelical church; this congregation was Pentecostal.) Urged on by him, the Catholics abused the women and beat up the men. The evangelicals who succeeded in escaping fled to the mountains. One hundred five arrived in Mexico City seeking protection.

January 15, 1946, in Neblinas, Hidalgo, various Sinarquistas (a fanatical religious-political organization), led by Candido Munoz and Julio Bautista, and spurred on by the local priest, attacked the evangelicals who were gathered there. Many were wounded and others expelled from the village. They beat the pastor, then hung him from a tree.

On July 31, 1946, agents of the federal police, Marcelo Fernandez Ocano and Leopoldo Arena Diaz, arrived at San Felipe de Santiago to investigate atrocities committed by the

Catholics. The priest, Pedro Juarez, had the mob take them to the mayor's office. Both were tortured. Fernandez Ocano was scalped alive with a machete and his eyes were plucked out with a nail. Afterwards they clipped off his ears, broke his teeth with blows, and clubbed him until his bones were broken. When he was dead, his body was cut in pieces and thrown to the dogs. Arena Diaz succeeded in escaping. Perhaps this is the only time that justice acted to punish the monstrous crime. Some of the fanatics who took part in the offense were detained in the Toluca jail. However, the priest, Pedro Juarez, was still at liberty to spur further violence.

March 8, 1947, in Ameca, Jalisco, the Catholic priest, after a scuffle that he himself provoked, kidnapped several Protestants, carried them to his church and, using inquisitional methods, obliged them, under threat of death, to be baptized according to the rite of the "Holy Mother."

April 13, 1949, in Rioverde, San Luis Potosi, the body of Samuel Juarez was found with eighty-five knife wounds in it. This heinous crime was attributed to the vengeance of the priest, Jose Maria Rosales, whose abuses against the people had been halted by the Protestant minister.

On December 7, 1950, for the second time in the same year, the Catholics attacked the church building of the Presbyterian Church in Tixtla, Guerrero. At the cry of "Long live Christ the King" they broke the furniture, raped the women, and wounded the men, according to the exhortation of the priest, Adalberto J. Miranda.

Sunday, January 27, 1950, in the town of Mayoro, twenty-one people gathered in the home of Francisco Garcia to dedicate themselves to their prayers. Soon afterward the bells of the Catholic church began to sound, and a few minutes afterward a mob of fanatics armed with clubs, machetes, axes, and hoes, fell upon the Protestants. All of them received wounds and blows. The pastor, Agustin Corrales, was dragged with a rope from the saddle horn and left for dead at Kilometer No. 115 on the highway to Queretaro.

January 1952, in Zacamitla, Veracruz, two individuals shot and killed the Protestant catechist, Miguel Martinez. This occurred three days after the priest, Jose Perez, had said in the pulpit: "I promise you, my children, that I will go to the front with you to finish off these evangelicals with clubs."

*Tiempo* quoted the archbishop of Mexico as responding, "We lament the happenings, . . . but we do not have any control over the people in this respect. It is to be regretted that the Protestant ministers go to Catholic people to diffuse their faith. We have always tried to avoid these embarrassing acts; but the people have their beliefs and, good or bad, we cannot take them away from them."

*Tiempo* called his response "insincere, false, and contradictory," noting that Article Twenty-Four of the Mexican constitution established complete religious freedom in one's church building or in his private home.

The *Tiempo* report and subsequent articles in leading Mexico City newspapers exerted strong pressure upon the Mexican Catholic hierarchy. The attacks and atrocities tapered off. News reports of similar Catholic persecutions in Colombia provoked disgust among United States Catholics. Word went out from the leadership that the violence was counterproductive and had to cease. Except for infrequent attacks in remote areas, the persecution in Mexico was halted.

## Martyrdom among the Chamulas

Christians were martyred in other Mexican tribes where elders opposed converts of Bible translation ministries. The most noteworthy martyrdoms occurred in the zone of Chiapas, near the Guatemala border.

The Chamula Indians were catechized and baptized by priests after the Spanish conquest. Like most other Mexican Indians, they simply absorbed Catholic symbols and rituals into their pagan belief system. Around 1850 the elders drove out the foreign priests and announced they were returning to the faith of their fathers. In a form of mockery, they impaled a young boy on a cross and declared that he was their savior.

The Chamulas were not again threatened with change until the late 1960s when Wycliffe translators Ken and Elaine Jacobs moved to the market town of Las Casas near Chamula territory. A young Chamula named Domingo showed up at their door seeking work. They agreed to hire him for garden work if he would teach them their language. In the process of language study and Bible translation, Domingo became a believer. He then told the Jacobs that he wanted to return home.

When he saw them again, he asked if they would come to dedicate his new house. "Chamulas have always dedicated their new houses to evil spirits," explained Domingo. "I want to dedicate my house to the true God and His Son, Jesus." The Jacobs made the trip into Chamula territory and participated in the dedication. They felt it wise not to spend the night and returned to Las Casas about midnight.

Domingo next reported nine families "trusting in Jesus and meeting for worship and Bible study" at his house. "Enemies have tried to kill us and burn my house down," he told the Jacobs. "But we will go on following Jesus."

A few weeks later Domingo brought forty Chamula refugees to the Jacobs. "The elders ran us out," he said sadly. "We have nowhere to go and nothing to eat."

The Jacobs took the crowd in. Then Ken and Domingo went to the local police. An official went into the tribe and demanded that the elders allow the evangelicals to come back. "If you resist," he warned, "we will send in soldiers."

Most of the Chamula Christians returned home. One evening a band of Chamula men surrounded the house of a Christian family. Inside were four young sisters and an eighteen-year-old babysitter. They tossed gasoline on the thick, thatched roof and set the house on fire. When the girls ran out, they opened fire. The babysitter was hit, but escaped to the house of her uncle and was saved. One of the young sisters was burned to death. The other three were wounded running from the house. One died on the way to the hospital in Las Casas.

The killers were not apprehended. The persecution continued. At one point the Chamula elders held 160 believers in their crude jails. When the Mexican army threatened to intervene, they let the prisoners go.

More threats and harassment followed. The Chamula Christians stood firm, never resorting to violence themselves. They grew to a thousand strong, worshiping in small chapels all over Chamula territory.

In the early 1990s, 584 Chamula Christians fled their villages and went into "exile," petitioning government officials for intervention. Their pleas went largely unanswered. In 1994, the 584 returned to their homes and were again attacked. The "president" of the group and his wife and daughter were killed.

## Missionary Martyrs

Two foreign missionaries, Ancel Allen and Nyles G. Huffman, are among those martyred in Mexico in this century. Both were affiliated with a small United States-based mission called "Air Mail from God" which later merged with Trans World Missions. Huffman was director of the mission; Ancel Allen was a new recruit.

Fresh from Moody Bible Institute, Ancel and his wife, Naomi, began work in August 1956. They would fly low over villages, dropping Gospels which contained invitations to write for a free Bible correspondence course. Ancel flew the plane and Naomi dropped the Gospels to excited people below. During the first five weeks they dropped fifty-five thousand Gospels.

Ancel was looking forward to seeing the first responses from the Gospels he had dropped. The first letters came on September 21, 1956, the date of his last flight.

This time he flew alone, never expecting to be hit. When he did not return at the expected time, 3:30 p.m., Naomi went to her room and prayed especially for him. "The answer the Lord gave me," she recalls, "was, 'everything is all right.'"

Later news came that his crashed plane had been found with his body inside. The attackers had tried to hammer over the bullet holes in the fuselage without success. They had also tried to dig the bullets from his body with a knife in an effort to disguise the cause of death.

No one was ever charged with the crime nor was any motive ever proven. Naomi was not bitter. "The people who shot at Ancel did so because they had never received the Word," she wrote.

They didn't know that Christ died for their sins. The Christian villagers who took such wonderful care of Ancel's body and were such a help to me, did so because they had received and believed the Word. They purchased the casket, the plot in the cemetery, and took care of the service. . . . After the service, the native Christians accompanied us to the cemetery, and just as the sun was going down, the women of the church sang songs and lovingly placed over the grave flowers gathered from the mountainside. It is for such a transformation as this in the lives of the Mexican people that Ancel gave his life, and it is for such a transformation as this that I am continuing in the work that Ancel and I began together.

Air Mail from God continued flying. About two years later Director Huffman's plane was shot down. His attackers were never caught either.

In 1977, an independent Mexican Protestant evangelist was hacked to death in the plaza of Ejutla, Oaxaca, a state with a large Indian population. The Catholic Mother Superior in Ejutla subsequently warned evangelicals never to come back. They continued to evangelize there.

Martyrdoms also occurred in another Oaxacan town, Santa Rosa Matagallinas, where four Baptists were reportedly murdered, others wounded, and still other evangelicals harassed by local people acting at the behest of their parish priest.

*Christianity Today* (March 2, 1979) quoted Presbyterian Nicolas Fuentes, head of the Mexico City-based National Committee for Defense of Evangelicals: "Our evangelical chapels are destroyed, we are forbidden to preach, and our pastors are persecuted. In this committee, we receive a minimum of twenty cases per year of flagrant violations against evangelicals by Catholic mobs."

## Martyrs of the 1980s and 1990s

Murders of evangelical workers continued with the killers rarely brought to justice. A pastor from Anchorage, Alaska, was killed outside of Mexico City on a main highway. He was traveling with another pastor from Alaska and their two wives. The newspapers associated the killings with highway robbery. A missionary said it "was nothing but a conspiracy by [radical elements] of the Catholic church."

In the previous month (December 1985), the missionary reported two missionary couples had been "killed near the same section," and "a year or so ago, three Mexican pastors were killed by Communists in a town in [the state of] Oaxaca. The other few Christians in the village had to escape for their life and went to live in the basement of the Presbyterian church in Oaxaca City."

On June 3, 1992, Melecioi Gomez Vazques, a thirty-two-year-old Presbyterian lay preacher in the state of Chiapas, was brutally shot and axed in an ambush in the town of Saltillo. The killing was believed to have been carried out by local leaders trying to drive Protestants from villages. Saltillo leaders had reportedly threatened to kill one male church member after another until all were dead.

# 32

# Central America

## *Panama, Guatemala, Honduras, El Salvador, Nicaragua, and Costa Rica*

C entral America, like Mexico, was conquered and Catholicized by Spain in the sixteenth century. For three hundred years no religious dissent was tolerated. In the old Guatemalan capital of Antigua, relics of the Inquisition can still be seen. One niche formed a straitjacket where heretics were chained while water dripped on their heads until they either recanted or went mad. More troublesome heretics were reportedly roasted alive in a huge oven. Other dissenters were hung from metal rings attached to the ceilings.

The breakup of Spain's Central American Federation in 1838 produced five independent nations—Guatemala, Honduras, El Salvador, Nicaragua, and Costa Rica—and weakened the power of the Catholic hierarchy. One by one the countries adopted constitutions guaranteeing religious freedom and separation of church and state. Panama, which broke off from Colombia in 1903, became the sixth nation in what is now Central America.

## The First Evangelicals

The first evangelical missionaries arrived in the latter half of the nineteenth century. German Moravians came first, then Presbyterians (at the personal request of the president of Guatemala), then the Central American Mission (CAM), which today has the largest number of field workers of any mission.

The pioneer missionaries were welcomed with volleys of curses and stones. Wrote Miss Eleanor M. Blackmore, an early CAM worker in Nicaragua: "I'm stoned and cursed and hooted in every street. I don't know one road in the whole city where I can walk in which there are not houses where they lie in wait to stone me. . . . We don't want pity. We count it an honor thus to be trusted to suffer, but we do covet your prayers." Their converts experienced more persecution. Many were beaten and some were threatened with death for identifying with the evangelicals.

## The First Missionary Martyrs

The deadliest peril for the pioneers was yellow fever. In 1894 Mr. and Mrs. H. C. Dillon and bachelor Clarence Wilbur were crossing Nicaragua enroute to El Salvador when all three became violently ill, suffering fever, chills, and congestion of the eyes, gums, and tongue, and vomiting dark blood—symptoms of yellow fever. Wilbur died in the town of Granada and was buried in an isolated grave since public cemeteries were reserved for Catholics and could not be profaned by Protestant remains.

The Dillons reached a ship and started for home. They were hardly out to sea when Mrs. Dillon died. Mr. Dillon recovered and eventually remarried. Three years after his first wife died, he was stricken again in the tiny village of El Paraiso in western Honduras. After several weeks at the brink of death, he passed away and was buried by the local believers in a board coffin—a great honor, since the impoverished nationals customarily buried their own dead in a simple grass mat.

Dillon's second wife, Margaret, remained at El Paraiso, living in a small shack and sleeping on a hard straw mattress. She trained Honduran evangelists who ministered in area villages. Fifteen years passed without a furlough. Visiting missionary colleagues noticed how pale she was and insisted she take a rest. The dread fever hit her while she was packing. Unable to walk, she was carried in a hammock thirty-six miles by Honduran men to a mission station. They arrived Friday, June 6, 1913. She died the following Sunday morning.

Yellow fever was conquered. Persecution cooled. Evangelicals became more accepted. There are now substantial evangelical communities in all the Central American countries.

## A Family Is Murdered

Many national evangelicals have paid a heavy price for their commitment to Christ in Central America.

The Juan Campos family lived in a village a few miles from Managua, Nicaragua. From a visit to the capital, their daughter brought home a little red book she had found in a garbage heap. Señora Campos was using a page to roll a cigarette when Juan grabbed up the book and began to read. A loud, swaggering man given to bouts of drinking, he had never before shown interest in religion. What he read in the New Testament so intrigued him that he went into Managua and hunted up the address of the publisher listed on the flyleaf. CAM missionaries led him to Christ.

Juan Campos became one of the most effective evangelical preachers in the country. Several years later, in 1957, a young man became infatuated with the Campos's granddaughter. Since Juan was her guardian, the youth asked his permission to marry her. "Are you a believer?" the preacher asked. The youth shook his head. "Then until you become one of us, I cannot give her to you. It is written in God's Word that a believer should not be unequally yoked together with an unbeliever."

The suitor stormed off in a rage and returned with his machete. Catching the family unaware, he hacked the preacher and his wife and granddaughter to death. Then he vandalized the house to give the appearance of robbery.

News of the brutal crime stunned the small country. The president of Nicaragua expressed his dismay and said, "We need more pastors like Juan Campos."

## A Recent Missionary Martyr

Only one evangelical missionary is known to have been murdered in Central America during the last century. The circumstances and motives surrounding his death are still murky.

In the summer of 1974 Canadian Gilbert Reimer, one of eighteen missionaries of the Gospel Missionary Union serving in Panama, returned to Panama City after leading a Christian youth camp in the country. He never reached home. His body was found floating in a canal.

He had been stabbed and beaten to death, but no valuables had been taken from his body. A police investigation led nowhere. Neither the identity of the murderers nor their motives is yet known.

One theory circulated that the killing was a case of mistaken identity. Another story spread that he was counseling a drug addict and the supplier became angry over losing a customer and took revenge. Whatever the reason, the fragrance of Gil Reimer's concern for Panamanian young people lingers in Panama today.

## Honduras

On June 25, 1975, Honduran army troops stormed a Catholic training center for peasant leaders in the town of Juticalpa. The peasants were demanding that the government speed up promised land redistribution. They had previously blocked bridges and invaded several large estates, and were now planning a hunger strike. In the June melee six Catholic lay workers were killed.

That same day two Franciscan foreign missionaries, Frs. Michael Cypher of Wisconsin and Ivan Betancourt of Colombia, disappeared. A special squad of government investigators, set up as a result of pressure from the Catholic hierarchy, found the bodies of the two priests and seven others at the bottom of a well in front of the hacienda of rancher Jose Manuel Zelaya.

Further investigation uncovered these facts: Fr. Cypher was walking into Juticalpa with a man who needed medical treatment when overtaken and arrested by soldiers. Fr. Betancourt was stopped while taking three women visitors to town. Both priests and the three women were taken to rancher Zelaya's home where they and four others were interrogated, beaten, shot, mutilated, and then thrown into the well. The murderers dropped dynamite into the well to destroy the evidence, but the powder failed to ignite.

The rancher, the provincial army commander, and two accomplices were indicted for murder. The government ordered all Catholic priests, monks, and nuns to leave the area. Bishop Nicholas D'Antonio, a U.S. citizen, left only after ranchers offered a five-thousand-dollar bounty for his head.

The Honduran Catholic hierarchy gave the slain priests a martyr's funeral. A spokesman noted that the peasants had been promised land in the spring by a previous president, Oswaldo Lopez Arellano. He had been deposed after disclosure by the U.S. Securities and Exchange Commission that the American-owned United Brands Company (formerly United Fruit) had paid Honduran officials $1.25 million in bribes for lowering of export taxes on bananas.

Evangelicals have found Honduras to be a fertile field during the past decade. Protestants numbered over 10 percent of the population by 1990. Poverty still prevails in this the poorest of the "banana" republics.

## El Salvador

On March 12, 1977, Father Rutilio Grande left his home in the town of Aguilares El Sol with an older man and a boy to celebrate mass in an outlying rural church. Their car was ambushed and all three were killed.

Fr. Grande was perhaps the best-known priest in tiny El Salvador. He was president of the Priests' Senate and headmaster of the Jesuit high school as well as being pastor of a rural parish. He had recently protested the beating of peasants by soldiers and had joined with other Jesuits in supporting land reform. Big landowners in the area claimed he had incited the peasants.

Following his murder, townspeople crowded a midnight mass held at the Aguilares church to express their sorrow. Salvadoran archbishop Oscar Romero called him "Salvador's first Christian martyr, a dedicated man of God who worked for the very poor."

The archbishop then pronounced excommunication on all who would commit violence against a priest.

After the funeral, a landowners' group called the White Warrior Union announced that it would begin assassinating other Jesuits in El Salvador on July 21. The government also denounced social activist priests as a tiny minority in league with Marxists.

Throughout 1977 and 1978 attacks on peasants continued, but no more priests were killed. A Catholic investigator claimed to have heard at least forty separate stories of murders, disappearances, or jailings of persons against whom no charge was made. Several Catholic religious communities reported terrorism to Archbishop Romero that included killings, kidnappings, and gang rapes of women and young girls by soldiers. They said the terrorism was aimed directly at Catholic leaders and teachers in rural areas.

## Archbishop Romero

Archbishop Romero was even-handed in his condemnation of evil government practices and violent guerrilla attacks. However, he became identified as the voice of the poor. On February 2, 1980, six weeks before his murder, Romero told a conference of Latin American bishops about the rampant injustice and inhumane treatment of poor people in his country. He told them that defending the poor now brought about something new in their church persecution. He went on to enumerate some of the atrocities of the past three years: six priests killed as martyrs; fifty priests attacked; many others tortured and expelled; hundreds and even thousands of peasants, delegates of the Word, catechists, assassinated or tortured. Romero emphasized how the ordinary poor Christian people bore the brunt of these persecutions.

On the night before he was assassinated, Romero pleaded with the army, in a radio broadcast, "Stop the oppression." He did not mince his words, he even ordered them in God's name to stop the killings.

On March 24, 1980, Archbishop Romero was celebrating mass in a hospital in San Salvador. The Gospel reading during the service had been, "Jesus replied: 'The hour has come for the Son of Man to be glorified. I tell you the truth, unless a grain of wheat falls to the ground and dies, it remains only a single seed. But if it dies, it produces many seeds. The man who loves his life will lose it, while the man who hates his life in this world will keep it for eternal life'" (John 12:23-25, NIV).

Romero took these words as the text of his sermon. He pointed out how his own work was bound to bring risks to his own personal safety, but that anyone who is killed in Christ's service is just like the grain of wheat. It dies. But the reality is that it only appears to die. He continued: "If they kill me I shall rise again in the Salvadorean people. As a pastor, I am obliged by divine decree to give my life for those I love—for all Salvadoreans, even for those who may be about to kill me. From this moment I offer my blood to God for the redemption and resurrection of El Salvador."

Soon after saying these words, Romero was gunned down on the steps of the altar. The bullets had hit him in the stomach. He was rushed into the emergency area of the hospital, but died within minutes.

## Disappearances

Three American nuns and a lay churchwoman were shot on a highway in 1981. Some speculated that they ran a roadblock and were fired on by Salvadoran security forces. The brother of one of the nuns reacted strongly to the implication that the women had been involved in violence themselves.

Eight years later six Jesuit priests were found murdered at a university. Their killers were presumed to be a right-wing death squad. The Jesuits were known to have been sympathetic with the effort by leftist rebels to overthrow the government and set up a socialist regime.

In 1981, Pastor Salvador Rodriguez of Chapeltique Baptist Church and an unidentified woman member of his congregation were presumed to have been murdered by a right-wing death squad. The two victims had received letters warning that they were placing their lives in danger by continuing in social ministries. Two Baptists who received letters fled.

This same year, Pastor Jose Alfredo Lainez y Cisneros was pulled from his pulpit and beaten to death by extremists. His murderers may have been incensed over his work as project manager of a World Vision relief project. Said World Vision's Paul Goddard: "I remember him as a little Pentecostal pastor with no teeth. He was a simple pastor trying to do good for his flock. He probably never understood the politics [of El Salvador] at all."

On September 21, 1988, ten peasants were massacred by government soldiers. Three months later the Lutheran Church office in the capital was bombed, and printed death threats were distributed by right-wing extremists.

The Salvadoran government became more moderate when Jose Napoleon Durate was elected president. Four years later, in 1988, Durate was diagnosed as having terminal cancer.

Attacks by leftist guerrillas slacked off in 1991 after the collapse of the Soviet Union, which many believed had trained leftist Salvadoran guerrillas in Cuba. By 1992 the situation appeared to be much less volatile than in the 1980s.

## Guatemala

In the summer of 1978 a priest was killed by vigilantes for defending peasant rights in Guatemala. About the same time, according to *Christianity Today*, the army massacred more than one hundred peasants protesting seizure of their land by well-to-do ranchers.

On July 29, 1981, unidentified gunmen shot to death Rev. Stanley Rother, an American missionary priest from Oklahoma. Rother had worked in Guatemala for thirteen years and had been warned six months before that he was a target for assassination. His father, Franz Rother, said his son had been friendly with peasant groups opposed to the Guatemalan government. "They have the rich and poor [in Guatemala]," said the father, "and the rich don't want the poor people to get any aid because they wanted to keep them downtrodden so they could make slaves out of them."

Two months later terrorists shouting anti-American slogans invaded the home of American Mennonite missionary John Dave Troyer of Mio, Michigan. The gunmen herded Troyer, his wife, their five children, and Gary Miller, a visiting Mennonite missionary from Virginia, into the yard and ransacked the house. Then after setting fire to the mission's truck, they opened fire on the two men. Troyer was killed. Miller incurred a wound to the chest, but survived.

During the turbulent 1980s death squads terrorized and murdered hundreds of Guatemalans believed to be sympathetic to groups opposed to government policies on land reform. During this same period evangelical Christianity grew rapidly. By the end of the decade over one-fourth of the people were believed to be evangelicals, with some missionaries predicting that Guatemala would become the first country in Latin America to attain an evangelical majority.

## Nicaragua

The Capuchin Catholic fathers reported in 1976 that Pastor Hernandez, minister of the Evangelical Chapel of Sofana, members of his family, and sixteen other persons disappeared or were shot in 1974 by the Nicaraguan National Guard.

The reputable Amnesty International published a long report August 15, 1977, documenting the arrest without warrants of 303 peasants in northeast Nicaragua, all of whom have not been heard from since. Amnesty International also cited the shooting of four men, eleven women, and twenty-nine children "in cold blood" by National Guardsmen in the village of Varilla in January 1977.

Nicaragua became the scene of a bloody war between leftist and rightist elements. General Anastasio Somoza Debayle occupied the little poverty-stricken nation until 1972 when he resigned. When a leftist rebellion threatened to overthrow the government, strong man Somoza was elected president again in 1974. Martial law was imposed in December, after officials were kidnapped by the Marxist Sandinista guerrillas. Nationwide strikes eventually led to full-scale civil war. Months of fighting ended, though only temporarily, when Somoza fled in 1979.

The Communist Sandinistas soon took power, proclaimed a rule by decree, and began aiding leftist guerrillas in El Salvador. In 1983 Salvadoran Contra guerrillas launched an offensive against the Sandinistas. A Contra request for military aid was refused by the U.S. Congress. However, funds were diverted secretly by certain White House officials.

In 1990 an election was held. Violet Barriso de Chamorro, the widow of a murdered newspaper editor, won a surprising upset victory over the Sandinista candidate. Her leadership became shaky when she permitted the Sandinistas to control part of the government.

During this turbulent era much blood was shed. Many evangelicals had supported the Sandinistas for the overthrow of Somoza and adoption of land reforms. In 1986, Baptist health worker Nestor Antonio Castilblanco and three other men were reportedly killed by Contra guerrillas. According to reports, an armed band invaded the health worker's home and took him, his two brothers, and a brother-in-law captive. The invaders burned the four men's homes to the ground, ransacked the Baptist mission clinic, and tortured the men before stabbing them to death.

The Sandinistas also killed many civilians. In one of the most shocking incidents, Cayetano Salgado Zamora, his son Ernesto, and fifteen other members of the Assembly of God church in the town of Pablito were handed a note after services, inviting them to meet with certain people about a bank loan. At the meeting they were detained by Sandinista soldiers and taken to a mountainside area known as Santo Domingo. There, the Sandinista soldiers forced them to dig their own graves before being executed. Their bodies were found several weeks later.

The bodies of many other victims of Sandinista torture and execution were subsequently discovered by the Puebla Institute and other human rights groups.

# 33

# Brazil

## The World's Leading Mission Field

Since the doors of China closed, Brazil has become the leading mission field for evangelical mission agencies. Over three thousand foreign missionaries serve in Brazil today. The Southern Baptist Convention alone has some three hundred workers scattered over this huge country that ranks seventh in the world in population and is larger than the United States in area, excluding Alaska.

Almost all evangelical groups are growing rapidly, especially Pentecostals. Twenty-five thousand Brazilians crowd into a single Pentecostal church in Sao Paulo each Sunday. Brazil, which had a Lutheran president from 1974 to 1979, is also the most populous Catholic country in the world. Seventy-three percent of the 157 million are claimed as Catholic, but only 12 percent are believed to practice their religion. Over 17 percent of Brazilians are Protestants.

## Martyrs to Indians

Only five evangelical missionaries have been martyred in Brazil in this century. They were killed in two groups by hostile Indians.

From the sixteenth century to present times, the treatment of Indians is one long saga of cruelty and horror. Portuguese settlers took Indian lands for farming, women for concubines and household servants, and men for field hands. Rubber and gold hunters used and abused Indians as desired and sometimes shot them for sport. Some immigrants to Brazil became millionaires through the exploitation of Indians.

It is no surprise that Brazil's Indian population has plummeted from several million to little more than two hundred thousand. Nor is it any wonder that Indians whose hearts have not been changed by the gospel have attacked missionaries venturing into the jungle with the noblest of motives.

## The Nhambiquara Massacre

Protestant efforts to reach and evangelize the mysterious tribes of Amazonia began shortly after World War I. In May 1924, three Americans set out from Cuiaba in south central Brazil to contact the untamed devil-worshiping Nhambiquara Indians. The group included Arthur F. Tylee and Alexander Hay, two young missionaries with the Inland South American Missionary Union, and Rev. L. L. Legters, a rough-and-ready U.S. evangelist who had longed for the evangelization of South American Indian tribes.

Tylee, a wiry young intellectual who had studied six languages, was from Worcester, Massachusetts. He had made a profession of faith in Christ at fifteen, but in college had drifted away. His experiences in France during World War I showed him that education was no substitute for Christian faith. After the war he enrolled at Harvard Law School, but soon became dissatisfied and transferred to the Moody Bible Institute. At Moody he learned about the pioneer work of the Inland South American Missionary Union. He and his fiancée, Ethel Canary, also a Moody student, were accepted by ISAMU shortly after graduation. They were to be married as soon as he located a permanent station.

There was no road into the interior from Cuiaba. The three Americans and their mule drivers followed an old telegraph line that had been built in 1909 to warn of a possible military invasion from Bolivia. Day after day the explorers pushed along in the sweltering heat and clouds of mosquitoes. After weeks of debilitating travel through soggy forests and swampy marshes, they reached Juruena. No mecca for tourists, it was only a relay station staffed by Brazilian employees who occupied a few pole houses in clearings.

They asked the telegraph operator about Nhambiquaras. "They come in to trade now and then," he said. "We keep our guard up. They're wild fellows and have a reputation for killing anybody who crosses their path." The first Nhambiquaras showed up a few days later, stark naked and slender with bronze skin and straight black hair. Arthur Tylee recorded his impressions:

> . . . Here was the raw article; the Indian; the wild Indian; the absolutely uncivilized Indian. Instead of repulsion or fear, such a feeling of love toward them rose within me that it seemed as though I must tell them how much I loved them and how God loved them even to the giving of His Son for them. . . .

The three moved on to the next telegraph station and then turned back, stopping at a Nhambiquara village. The chief received them cordially and in broken Portuguese invited them to return. "As soon as possible," Tylee assured.

A week after their marriage, Arthur and Ethel were on their way to Juruena where they planned to build a house. The Brazilians remembered Arthur. "You can live in the station until you build your house," the operator told them. It was only one room and the only piece of furniture was a canvas chair, but the Tylees welcomed his offer gladly.

At the time the Brazilians were fearful of an Indian attack. Four months before, the station's food supply had run short. Six Brazilians had gone to a Nhambiquara village to buy food even though they were warned not to go. The chief was said to be angry over the killing of his brother by a Brazilian. When the six did not return on schedule, a search party was sent out. The searchers found only the graves of their friends.

The Tylees noticed that no Brazilian ever stepped outside his house without carrying a gun and long knife. "You'd better be prepared," they warned the missionaries. "These Indians can look friendly one minute and the next minute kill you." The missionaries had brought guns only for protection against snakes and wild animals. "Better that we die," Arthur told Ethel, "than ever shoot a Nhambiquara in self-defense. Otherwise, all our preaching will come to an end."

They decided to build their house at a Nhambiquara campsite about a kilometer northeast of the station. They wanted to avoid any trouble between the Brazilians and the Indians.

Every day the Tylees looked for Indian visitors. Five months later they saw seven coming over a hill. They were armed with bows and arrows but appeared friendly and claimed they had not killed the six Brazilians. They stayed an hour, then left after promising to return and bring some wild honey. The next day fifteen came and stayed for several hours.

The Indians were hard to predict. Most days they were friendly. Other times they seemed to be testing the missionaries. Twice, Arthur felt the cold steel of a long knife at his throat. Each time he merely smiled and pretended that the Indian was joking.

The health of both Tylees deteriorated. Their temperature went up and down from fevers. Food supplies often ran short and they had to live off *mandioca*, a kind of jungle potato. Once Ethel almost died from beriberi.

After bachelor Albert McDowell came to help in the work, they took an extended furlough. They returned two years later in glowing health, bringing a registered nurse, Mildred Kratz, whom they had known at Moody, and a fair-haired, brown-eyed baby. Little Marian Tylee quickly charmed the Indian visitors. The Indians tried to teach her words, which she parroted back with a lisp that sent them into convulsions of laughter.

Nhambiquaras were now coming regularly. Some worked for wages in a model garden. During the furlough Arthur had had soil samples analyzed and was trying to introduce new crops to the Indians. Groups often stayed for supper and overnight, joining the missionaries in prayers and hymn singing.

The Nhambiquaras built huts near the Tylees where they stayed on extended visits. Everything continued to go well. Arthur's language notebook filled up with Nhambiquara words and phrases. Nurse Kratz did medical work and helped Ethel with teaching. Albert McDowell also treated the sick.

In 1929 a flu virus was brought in by Brazilian visitors and quickly spread among the Indians. The missionaries were kept busy treating patients. One Nhambiquara, Manoel, died at their house. His friends immediately tied his body to the back of an Indian for transport back to his village and burial.

Ten months passed. Late in the evening of October 27, 1930, three Indians came with news that some of their friends had died from the flu—a story later discovered to be untrue. Saturday, four days later, ten Indians came. Sunday, more Indians arrived. They acted morose and sullen. When Ethel asked one if he wanted to spend the night, he replied angrily, "No. It is too dangerous. Manoel died here."

Early Monday morning the crowd increased. Still the missionaries sensed no trouble. The Indians were only a little quieter than usual.

Suddenly Ethel heard a weird call. She looked and saw an Indian grasp Nurse Kratz in a tight grip. When she tried to go to Mildred's aid, another Indian, who had always been friendly before, pinned her arms back. "Let me go!" she shouted, and he did.

The Indians were murmuring in low tones and it was impossible to catch what they were saying. Instinctively, Ethel ran toward the bedroom where baby Marian was still asleep. A hoe handle crashed against her head. She fell, tried to get up, and was hit twice more. Afterwards she recalled seeing a revolver on a table and, remembering what Arthur had said, dismissing the idea of using it.

Dazed and with blood streaming from her nose and mouth and wounds on her head, Ethel crept to Marian's bed. The baby seemed to sigh. Ethel turned around and saw Mildred Kratz lying on the dirt floor. Instinctively, she pulled an arrow from the nurse's body. She crawled across the room and found Arthur. Three Brazilians were lying nearby. Ethel later recalled:

> It was perhaps the blackest hour of all. Up to this time it seemed only a question of bearing the pain patiently until I would be released from all suffering forever and be with my Lord and loved ones. But now—could I pick up the broken threads of my life and go on without the one who had been more than life to me? The brain was too numb to even think of what it would be like but I was conscious of a Presence and Strength with me far greater than my own and out of the blackness of human despair spoke the voice of One who had gone that way before: "The cup which my Father hath given me, shall I not drink it?" With the question came also the reply, "Even so, Father, for so it seemed good in thy sight." Then Romans 12:1 came to my mind: "I beseech you . . . by the mercies of God, that you present your bodies a living sacrifice, holy, acceptable unto God." I thought, "It will be harder to be a living sacrifice than a dying sacrifice, but I must be."

Somehow Ethel managed to get to the telegraph station. The operator telegraphed for Albert McDowell who was at another station down the line. Albert arrived at 9:00

p.m. and cleansed and bandaged Ethel's deep scalp wounds. The next morning, Albert and the Brazilians laid the bodies to rest under trees across from the mission house. Baby Marian was buried in her father's arms.

The Brazilians at Juruena wanted to punish the Indians. "My loved ones are already with the Lord," Ethel said. "I want no revenge." Years later, one of the Brazilian workers at the telegraph station told another missionary, "Her faith brought me to the Savior."

After a period of recuperation, the widow went back to the United States. For the next twenty-five years she was a "living sacrifice," speaking in churches, Bible conferences, Bible schools and colleges, presenting the challenge of the lost tribes. It is a reasonable guess that hundreds of young Christians heard the call of God through her impassioned pleas and volunteered for foreign missionary service. She never remarried and died September 7, 1955, in West Branch, Michigan, at the age of sixty-one.

And the Nhambiquaras?

In 1937 a missionary went back to Juruena and found only a few charred posts and a pile of ash-covered rocks to mark the site of the massacre. "But we found another building which will never perish," he wrote, "erected by the testimony of His servants—a living temple of living stone—hearts that are open to the gospel and lives that are bearing faithful witness to Christ." He referred to the Brazilians converted through the witness of the missionaries there.

The year before, missionary work had been reopened among the Nhambiquaras at an outpost called Campos Novos. The Indians were slow in responding, but after several years they came to trust the missionaries fully. In the years since, intertribal fighting and disease have wiped out large segments of the tribe on the Brazilian side. But a ministry at two stations continues to this day.

## The Kayapo "Big-Lips"

In the 1920s north central Brazil was just as trackless as the state of Mato Grosso in the south. The only highways were the yellow tributaries of the Amazon that drained a basin over three times larger than Texas. Life in scattered white settlements at the mouths of rivers consisted of long periods of boredom shattered by moments of terror. Brazilians attacked Indians. Indians took revenge, usually killing Brazilian males and taking the women and girls captive. Then the cycle of terror started all over again.

In the Xingu River area the Kayapo "Big-Lips" were most feared. The deformity resulted from a tribal custom of stretching out the lower lip an inch or more by a wood disc inserted into the flesh. Just the sight of a Big-Lip warrior, his body painted jet black, sent a white running for his gun.

The first missionary to attempt to reach the Big-Lips was Ernest Wotton, a member of the Heart of Amazonia Mission, then affiliated with the Worldwide Evangelization Crusade and later absorbed into The Unevangelized Fields Mission. Wotton had been challenged by Fenton Hall, a young English bachelor who had died from malaria while trying to Christianize the Guajajara Red Indians.

Wotton hired a young civilized Indian couple, Jacinto and Caroline, as guides and set out from the outpost town of Nova Olinda at the confluence of the Xingu and the Rio-Zinho rivers. With a crew of rowers, they started up the Rio-Zinho in a long canoe, looking for Kayapos.

Rounding a bend, they surprised an Indian fishing. The protruding lower lip told them he was from the tribe they were seeking. But upon sight of the visitors, he ran back into the jungle. The missionary ordered the rowers to swing into a sand bar. Leaping out, he and Jacinto waded ashore. The young Caroline followed.

"We want to be your friends. Come," Jacinto called. About a dozen Big-Lips crept cautiously out of the jungle and stopped near the men. While Wotton and Jacinto's attention was diverted, others grabbed Caroline and carried her screaming into the jungle. Jacinto yelled for a rifle. The frightened rowers announced they were leaving. The missionary and guide could come if they wished. There was no choice. The sobbing husband waded to the canoe, leaving his wife at the mercy of the wild Kayapos.

Ernest Wotton made several more tries. Eventually his health broke and he had to give up.

In 1928 a young Australian couple, Fred and Mabel Roberts, came to Brazil. Before the year was out, Mabel contracted malaria. "I have done all I can," she whispered to Fred. The young husband conducted her funeral service and buried her beside the grave of Fenton Hall.

After Mabel's death, Fred felt God wanted him to pick up the mantle of Ernest Wotton. Two other young missionaries volunteered to go with him. Fred Dawson, a fellow Australian, said, "If the Lord calls me to lay down my life for Christ and the Indians, I am willing." Fred Wright, an Irish athlete, was also ready to die if necessary.

The Three Freds, as they came to be called, went to Nova Olinda in 1935. There they stored most of their belongings and bought a boat and motor, eliminating the need for a crew. Fred Wright's last letter to his home prayer-partners indicated the depth of their commitment:

> I do not know when you will receive this, or even if you receive it at all. . . . Once we leave civilization, it may be months or even years before we can come down with mail. It may be that we shall never get down again; God only knows.
>
> As far as we can ascertain, the Kayapos are very numerous. We are quite aware that, humanly speaking, we are as good as dead men, but brethren, stand by us as one man. Do not criticize. We are beyond criticism as we go forward in the Name of the Lord and under His command, after having fully counted the cost.
>
> Finally, it is well to remember that Calvary was and is the greatest victory of all times. Death to the Christian is not defeat. Should the Lord will that we be taken, our prayer is that more men and more money be rushed out to follow up this advance. Let our generalship be

greater than that of our archenemy, the devil, and set aside all sentiment for the sake of the spread of the Gospel of our Lord Jesus Christ in that day.

They were never seen alive again.

Months later, missionaries Horace Banner and Jock Johnstone reached Nova Olinda. They hired two Brazilian youths and started up the Rio-Zinho. They came to some long impassable rapids and found where the Three Freds had made wheels from a large tree trunk to apparently make a cart for portaging the canoe past the rapids. In the woods nearby they came upon a straw-thatched shack and beyond that a large abandoned village. When they found a charred piece of wood with a round two-inch hole, the Brazilians refused to go further. The wood was evidently from the cart built to carry the canoe.

The two missionaries stuffed a brief record of their trip into a bottle and tied the bottle to a tree hoping that the missing men might find it. They returned to Nova Olinda, hired other boatmen, and came back to the village. The bottle was gone and there were tracks of Indians all around.

This time they had brought three canoes. Leaving one canoe and a crew at the rapids, they pushed further upriver. On the eighth day they reached a giant cataract, which they called Smoke Falls. At the foot of the falls they recovered the Three Freds' boat and motor. The prow of the boat was smashed and the motor had been stripped of some parts. They searched the riverbank nearby and found a heap of bloodstained, ant-eaten clothing.

Banner and Johnstone reported to their home office in London that the Three Freds could be considered dead. The story was picked up by newspapers throughout the British Commonwealth. It was discussed and prayed over in hundreds of missionary groups and churches. A book about the Three Freds aroused more interest. The Heart of Amazonia Mission received hundreds of letters pledging prayer. Many writers, including Christians in Africa, sent money. Some volunteered for service in Amazonia.

Two years later hundreds of wild Kayapos swarmed into Nova Olinda. These Big-Lips were not attacking but seeking refuge from tribal enemies. Horace Banner got the news and hurried back. Stepping ashore, he was surrounded by the naked Indians from the very tribe for which the Three Freds had given their lives. Among the group was the woman, Caroline, who had been kidnapped years before. She now had a new husband and conducted herself as one of the wild ones.

The missionary found another kidnapped woman, Magdalena, willing to talk. She recalled a party of warriors returning to the camp with revolvers, felt hats, and sport shirts. They bragged of killing three strange white men, she said.

The Indians at Nova Olinda were anxious to revenge their defeat. Night after night the men held war dances. Then they began leaving in relays. The women, children, and old men stayed behind.

About a week later the warriors began trickling back. Many burned with fever. Some had died. None had found the enemy. Banner and Frank Houston, a new missionary, felt God had intervened and brought them back.

The government Indian Protection Service put the Indians in the hands of the missionaries. Then, in 1938, all of the Indians left.

Banner and Houston went upriver and built a mission house, praying that the Indians would settle there. Within a month the first contingent came out of the jungle and built a communal house next to the missionaries. Other groups came and built more houses. The missionaries began language studies and taught the Indians new ways to grow crops.

The missionaries were hesitant to ask about the fate of the three Freds, believing that the Indians might fear reprisals. One day an Indian asked if they had heard "about three white men like yourselves" who were killed. "Yes," Banner replied, "but tell us what you know." The informant said he had only heard about the killings from others.

Horace Banner passed around a photo of the Three Freds. Various Indians volunteered details until the sad story was pieced together. The missionaries used the opportunity to explain their purpose in coming to the Indians and God's love for them.

The killers were named, but the Indians said none were in the camp. A few weeks later a party of strange warriors arrived. Among them were two of the alleged murderers. The missionaries befriended them and invited them to attend Sunday services. One evening as Horace Banner played a hymn on his concertina, one of the men came and handed over his war club. Then he sat down and listened attentively to the music.

## No More Martyrs

The sacrifice of Arthur Tylee and his baby, nurse Mildred Kratz, and the Three Freds spurred other missionaries to push deeper into the Amazonian jungles of Brazil. The frontier was pushed further and further back. Yet there are still many tribes that have not been reached, even today.

There have been no more missionary martyrs in Brazil's Amazonia.

## Brazil's Catholic Martyrs

Recent clashes between Roman Catholic priests and Brazilian authorities are concentrated in economically depressed northeast Brazil where priests are participating in land reform movements and protests by impoverished peasants.

The situation here is similar to that in Nicaragua, El Salvador, Honduras, and Guatemala. Powerful landowners are allied with the government, the military, and conservative bishops of the Catholic hierarchy. A new breed of Catholic clergy, supported by a few Protestants, preach social change through revolution if necessary. Skillful Marxist agitators eagerly capitalize on discontent.

The Catholic activists looked to Archbishop Helder Camara of Recife (formerly Pernambuco), Brazil, for leadership. He had powerful links to many world Catholic figures, yet this did not prevent alleged murders, imprisonments under false pretenses, and torture of priests and nuns.

Archbishop Camara's "Justice and Peace" movement claimed three priests were martyred before 1985. Father Rudolf Lunkenbein was killed July 15, 1976, while defending the rights of Indians against encroaching land grabbers. Father Joao Bosco Penido Burnier was gun whipped and shot in the state of Mato Grasso after he came upon four military policemen torturing two women and protested. Bishop Adriano Hipolito da Costa was mutilated by "hoodlums" representing a group of wealthy Brazilians.

The movement also cites the arrest of Sister Maurina Borges da Silveira, a forty-three-year-old Franciscan nun, for allowing a group of young people to meet at her orphanage and discuss politics. After being forced to strip, she was beaten and given electric shocks, then told to stop praying and renounce Christ for He could not help her. Her archbishop, who had been silent on politics, excommunicated her torturers.

Altogether, the Catholic social activists claim that seventy-nine persons fighting for social justice died under torture during a nine-year period.

The small minority of Protestants who participated included Paul Wright, the son of U.S. missionaries, and United Methodist missionary Fred Morris. Young Wright was arrested in 1973 and has not been heard from since. Morris was seized and tortured, allegedly for sending reports to *Time* magazine on problems in northeastern Brazil and for associating with supposed Communists.

# 34

# Uruguay, Argentina, and Chile

## *The Southern Stretch*

Argentina and Chile occupy the long southern tail of South America. Uruguay is tucked between Argentina and Brazil on the north. These countries were settled and Catholicized by Spanish soldiers and priests in the sixteenth century. They threw off the shackles of Spain in the early nineteenth century. They permitted limited Protestant missionary work years before other nations to the north. The first Protestant church on the west coast of the Western Hemisphere, south of California, was opened in Chile in 1856. At that time missionaries were allowed to evangelize only non-Spanish speaking foreign immigrants. Spanish work was prohibited for many years in both Chili and Argentina by intolerant Catholic hierarchies allied with civil and military authorities. Early evangelicals suffered the same stonings, beatings, imprisonments, and family and social pressures that Protestants experienced elsewhere in Latin America before the 1950s.

## The First Martyrs

No evangelical missionaries died in connection with their service in Uruguay, Argentina, and Chile during the twentieth century. However, fifteen were martyred in the preceding century. Their story, which has inspired national believers ever since, deserves telling.

In 1842 Captain Allen Gardner, who had resigned from the British Royal Navy to serve God full time, sailed into the Strait of Magellan. Unfriendly Indians kept him moving along until he finally found a group who said he might build a church for them.

The pioneer went home and tried to interest mission boards in the work. When all turned him down, he organized the Patagonian Missionary Society.

Seven years and two more trans-Atlantic voyages later, the mission had seven members, including the founder. Before leaving England the last time, he arranged for a vessel to bring supplies periodically from the Falkland Islands. Then he and six associates put to sea in a tiny ship with six months of stores.

On December 5, 1850, they went ashore on the coast of the remote island of Tierra del Fuego. The Indians they had hoped to evangelize drove them back to their ship, and they took refuge in Spanish Harbor. The first supply ship did not arrive until January 1852. By then it was three months too late. The crew found all seven dead of starvation. Captain Gardner's last diary entry read: "Great and marvelous are the loving-kindnesses of my gracious God unto me. I neither hunger nor thirst, though five days without food."

The tragedy awakened English Christians to the need for evangelizing the Indians in southern South America. A party of eight sailed six years later. Seven of the eight were massacred by aborigines while conducting a worship service on shore. Others took their places. The mission's name was changed to the South American Missionary Society. There are churches in southern Chile and Argentina today which have connections to the pioneer work.

## Church Growth in Dark Times

Evangelicals have made great gains in Uruguay, Argentina, and Chile in recent years. The most rapid growth has been among indigenous Pentecostals in Chile. One of every twelve Chileans is a Pentecostal or Methodist Pentecostal. In 1974 the president of Chile participated in the dedication of a Methodist Pentecostal cathedral in Santiago that seated fifteen thousand. Nothing like this had ever happened before.

Church growth has spiraled alongside inflation, political terrorism, and turmoil. Argentina has been in almost daily crisis since the fall of strongman Juan Peron. One military government has succeeded another, each failing to stop rightist and leftist killings and to curb the world's worst inflation.

The Catholic church is split. Many priests and laymen with leftist ties have been arrested and reportedly tortured. Some have been killed in alleged revenge of leftist terrorism against political leaders and security forces.

The worst violence against priests apparently was in retaliation for a leftist bomb explosion that killed twenty policemen. A wave of killings followed the murders, climaxed by the assassination of three priests and two seminarians in a parish residence in Buenos Aires. The priests belonged to the Irish Pallottine order and were shot in the back of the head. None had engaged in political activities.

The killing of the five clerics in July 1976 brought the wrath of the Catholic hierarchy down on Argentine officials, but did not stop the bloodshed.

Democratic rule returned to Argentina in 1983. Six years later the nation was plagued by severe inflation. The hyperinflation sparked rioting which led to harsh economic measures.

Protestant missionaries and national pastors have thus far not been targets of terrorists in Argentina. In recent years Protestant leaders have enjoyed more public favor than Catholics because of their charitable works and avoidance of politics.

## Terrorism in Uruguay

Little Uruguay (population 3.1 million), long a haven of political liberalism, was hit by terrorism in the late 1960s. In succeeding years many foreign diplomats and businessmen were abducted by the leftist, urban Tupamaros guerrillas. However, no missionaries were attacked or kidnapped. In 1973 the violence provoked a military takeover which brutally suppressed the terrorism. The military allowed the return of civilian rule in 1985. With a Protestant population of 3.1 percent, evangelical missionaries continue to be welcomed with some 115 missionaries in the country.

## Marxism in Chile

Chile, according to leading evangelicals there, came to the brink of disaster in 1973. Only an "act of God in answer to our prayers," they say, brought the downfall of the Marxist government and prevented a massacre of middle- and upper-class leaders.

The basic facts of what happened in Chile are well known. Marxist Salvador Allende, head of Chile's Socialist Party, won the presidency in 1970 by a narrow plurality, receiving 36.3 percent of the vote in a three-man race. Allende became the first Marxist president of a nation ever freely elected.

Chile became a mecca for leftists all over Latin America. Allende quickly established diplomatic relations with Communist states, including Cuba. He expropriated many banks, industries, and large farms, and nationalized the properties of four large U.S. corporations. Chile's economy fell into a tailspin. Inflation skyrocketed. Production declined. Food became scarce.

In the 1973 election Allende's opposition, the Democratic Confederation, retained control of both the senate and the chamber of deputies. Subsequently, the Chilean Congress and Supreme Court declared Allende's expropriation of property illegal under the nation's constitution. Allende refused to retreat. His Communist allies, according to evangelical sources, stockpiled quantities of Russian and Chinese arms.

The Marxist government virtually ignored church organizations except for welcoming support from leftist priests. Evangelicals, however, saw a storm of persecution ahead. Many pastors began secret prayer meetings asking for divine intervention.

## A "Miracle" or a Tragedy?

September 11, 1973, the "miracle," as it was called later by many evangelical leaders, happened. Chilean military commanders surrounded and bombarded the presidential palace. Allende died in the successful coup. Afterwards it was announced that the military had acted after learning of Plan Zeta, which the Marxists planned to initiate on September 17. The military leaders said the plan called for liquidation of thousands of Chileans in the initial purge (a thousand influential people were to be killed in one city alone), with expectations that as many as 10 percent of Chile's population might have to be killed before a classless Marxist society was formed.

The new government under Army General Augusto Pinochet began rounding up leading leftists. Thousands of foreign leftist refugees fled the country with assistance from the United Nations and the World Council of Churches. Reports were leaked to newspapers claiming brutal torture and killing of political prisoners inside Chile. Supporters of the new government countered that the stories were vastly exaggerated by Communist propaganda mills. Nevertheless, the new government was criticized and condemned, both in the United States and elsewhere. The censure became heavier after it was learned that the U.S. Central Intelligence Agency had worked for Allende's downfall.

Some Protestant churchmen abroad came down hard against the new government. A number of American evangelical leaders abhorred the coup, but most waited to hear from their brothers and sisters in Chile. The answer came in a formal declaration by representatives of practically all the evangelical bodies in Chile:

> Chile fell without fear into the clutches of international Marxism whose national leaders, in spite of not representing the majority, knew how to deceive with false promises many Chileans who desired needed changes. . . . Once in power, they brought about chaos and the breakdown of the institutional structures, leading the country to a slow death, poisoned by hatred and divested of our most cherished spiritual values.
>
> The pronouncement of our Armed Forces in the historical process of our country was God's answer to the prayers of all the believers who recognized that Marxism was the expression of satanic power of darkness in its highest degree. . . . We, the Evangelicals, . . . recognize as the maximum authority of our country the Military Junta, who in answer to our prayers freed us from Marxism.

Rev. Rogelio Aracena, a Chilean Methodist pastor and district leader of Campus Crusade for Christ in Chile, came to the United States to present the evangelical viewpoint. He said inflation had exceeded 1,000 percent under three years of Allende. University students, he noted, had been ordered to spread Marxism in public surveys. Christian students who refused to participate had been forced to leave their schools.

Missionaries wrote their home constituencies to explain what had happened. One pointed out that "some Chilean priests" along with "quite a few French and other European priests . . . were frankly favorable" to Allende. "To these must be added a goodly number of ex-priests who were openly Marxists." He conceded that the new government had jailed "a few evangelical pastors," but "not for preaching the gospel. They were directly involved in Marxist politics though they may not have been aware of where this philosophy would lead them eventually."

Right-wing rule continued until 1989, when General Pinochet was rejected by a plebiscite. Pinochet accepted the rejection and announced presidential elections. Voters removed Pinochet from office and elected Patricio Aylwin as president.

Rapid evangelical growth has continued with over five hundred evangelical organizations in the country. Over 22 percent of the population is Protestant. The largest church body is the Pentecostal Methodist Church with over three hundred thousand members.

# 35

## Paraguay and Bolivia

### *Inland Countries*

Landlocked Paraguay has never fully recovered from a nineteenth-century war against Brazil, Argentina, and Uruguay that took the lives of almost every able-bodied male in the country. Still abysmally poor, Paraguay existed as a police state in the iron grip of dictator Alfredo Stroessner from 1954 to 1988.

Most of the 5.6 million people are *mestizo,* of mixed Indian and Spanish ancestry. Fifty thousand or more pure Indians still survive in the jungled, swampy Chaco (hunting ground). The British Anti-Slavery Society accuses the Paraguayan government of practicing a policy of extermination towards many of these Indians, charging that most men have been killed and the women and children sold into slavery.

### A Mennonite Martyr

Missionaries with the New Tribes Mission (the largest mission in Paraguay) and Mennonite workers have hazarded their lives in trying to evangelize the wild Indians of Paraguay. The only martyr has been Mennonite Cornelius Isaak. The Mennonite knew that Ayore Indians in Bolivia had killed five New Tribes missionaries in 1943 (see next section). Nevertheless, he set out in the summer of 1958 to contact Ayores in Paraguay. He died of a spear wound received in his first contact with the wild Indians.

The missionaries in Paraguay's Chaco have continued trying to tame the wild forest dwellers with love and the gospel. They, too, are grieved at cruelty shown toward the Indians by "civilized" Paraguayans. But they make their protests known in quiet, personal diplomacy, scrupulously avoiding political involvements to which the government might object.

Most other evangelical missionaries in Paraguay also avoid political entanglements. The dictator regarded their work favorably and years ago permitted Billy Graham to hold an eight-day crusade in Asuncion, the capital. It was the first evangelical meeting ever held on public grounds in this country.

## "Martyrs" for Land

One and one-half percent of the wealthy elite own 89 percent of all land. To promote a fairer distribution of farmlands, a group of priests set up the Christian Land League. A story soon surfaced that the Paraguayan government intended to liquidate leaders of the League.

Seven foreign Jesuit priests and two Disciples of Christ missionaries were arrested and deported. Three Paraguayan priests were seized, then released. Seven Paraguayan workers for the Friendship Mission of the Disciples of Christ were also taken into custody and of these three remained in prison.

The Committee of Churches for Emergency Aid, headed by a Catholic bishop and two prominent Protestants, claimed the government was holding around six hundred political prisoners. Three "Christians" fighting for social justice, they said, had been martyred in prison and many others tortured. The government denied this and blamed the trouble on Marxist subversives. M. Frisco Gilchrist, a twenty-five-year Disciples of Christ missionary veteran and one of those expelled, replied that in Paraguay it had become a crime to help the poor. The Disciples' Friendship Mission which the government closed, calling it an "arsenal . . . and resistance center," was only developing self-help projects and encouraging poor people to organize cooperatives, the ex-missionary claimed. Charges of communism, he added, were often an excuse to arrest and mistreat rivals to the Stroessner regime.

Relations between the government and the Roman Catholic hierarchy deteriorated. The archbishop of Asuncion refused to attend meetings of the Council of State, explaining that his conscience forbade him to participate in the "institutional violence" that plagued Paraguay.

In 1989, General Alfredo Stroessner, who had ruled since 1945, was ousted in a military coup led by General Andrew Rodriguez. Rodriguez was elected president.

A new relationship has dawned between Roman Catholics and evangelicals. Leaders of both groups have petitioned the government to end historic recognition of Roman Catholicism as the state's official religion. A proposed new constitution would grant unprecedented freedoms to the 165,000 evangelicals among Paraguay's four million people. Osvaldo Velasquez, president of the Evangelical Baptist Convention, calls the proposed constitution a "pleasant surprise . . . They are recognizing that we, as Christians, have a contribution to make to the country."

## Bolivia—Target of Communists

Bolivia has long been a special target for Marxists. Che Guevera was killed there in 1967 while leading a guerrilla band. Slightly smaller than Texas and Colorado combined, Bolivia is strategically bordered by five other nations coveted by Marxists. It has a history of clerical domination, genocidal wars, military rule, an imbalance between extreme wealth and grinding poverty, and ethnic and economic conflicts between the Indian underclass (65 percent of the population) and the ruling Spanish oligarchy.

## Mountain Indians Die for Christ

Ten million Quechua Indians, speaking a variety of related dialects, populate cold, barren plateaus and hidden mountain valleys in western South America. One and a half million of these live in Bolivia. Only one in twenty is literate. Quechuas have been among the most difficult people in the world to reach with the gospel. Only a small percentage are believers today. The majority are in bondage to the angry gods of their ancestors.

In Bolivia hundreds of Quechua evangelicals have been ostracized from their communities, blamed for crop failures, and severely persecuted. Many believers have had their homes burned. Some have been killed or stoned.

Missionaries and national church leaders believe the key to Quechua evangelization is Scripture translation. Wycliffe personnel in Bolivia have finished translating New Testaments in all the major Quechua dialects.

## Martyrs in the Jungle

Wild Bolivian Indians roam the eastern jungle bordering Brazil and Paraguay. They have long been the concern of Wycliffe, the South American Mission, and the New Tribes Mission.

Six New Tribes missionaries have been martyred in heroic attempts to take the gospel to tribesmen who have long suffered inhumane abuse from traders, rubber hunters, and white adventurers.

The first five martyrs were among the first members of the mission founded by Paul Fleming in 1942. A missionary to Malaysia, Fleming had returned to Michigan weak from malaria. He shared with a young pastor, Cecil Dye, his dream of taking the gospel to remote tribes that other missions had not yet reached. From their talks evolved an interdenominational mission to *new tribes*, hence the name.

Two years later Cecil and Dorothy Dye and their three children, Cecil's younger brother, Bob, and his wife, Jean, newlyweds Dave and Audrey Bacon, George Hosbach, and Eldon Hunter arrived in Bolivia. Their goal was to establish a mission with the Ayores, a tribe that a Bolivian official called "impossible to tame. They attack any civilized person who comes near them," he warned. "Slip up and club their victims in their hammocks. You'll never come back alive." Other Bolivians made the same predictions.

The married men moved their families to remote Santo Corazon in the heart of a jungled area where several nomadic tribes roamed at will. From here the five men planned to launch their first missionary journey looking for Ayores and pushing their base camps further and further into the wilds.

The men went without guns. An American reporter had planned to accompany them, but backed out upon learning they were going in unarmed. "I don't know God that well," he said.

They left November 10, 1944, after telling two colleagues, Clyde Collins and Wally Wright, "If you don't hear anything inside a month, come and make a search for us." The married men did not mention that to their wives.

The month passed. Clyde and Wally and four Bolivian men followed their trail over a hill and along a rocky river. They came upon a group of Ayores. The frightened Indians ran away. A little farther on they found a cracked camera lens, one of Cecil's socks, George's machete, and some other personal items, but no bodies. While they were camped, Wally was wounded by an arrow. They gave up and went back.

A second and larger search party of Bolivians moved into the jungle. They picked up the missionaries' trail and followed it to an abandoned Ayore plantation. There they found more personal belongings.

An army commander wanted to send in troops on a revenge raid. The wives pleaded, "Don't go. We want to reach them for Christ." The soldiers did not go.

More months passed, then a year. Jean Dye and other missionaries moved to a railway camp deeper into Ayore country. Dorothy and Audrey went home on furlough. One day in 1948 a band of naked Ayores suddenly appeared at the camp. The missionaries gave them gifts and tried to make friends. The Indians took the gifts and melted back into the jungle. Six weeks later the Indians returned and spent the night. Some remained. They told of another clan who had killed five whites years before and had thrown their bodies into the river.

The following year, Degui, a friendly Ayore, brought an Indian boy to Jean. The boy told of five tall white men coming to his village. "Your countrymen are dead," he told Jean. "Our warriors killed them and buried their bodies."

Jean came down with malaria and went home to see a doctor. She now believed the five were dead. Among the survivors, only Audrey held out hope. Six months later Jean returned to Bolivia. Dorothy and her three children, and Audrey and daughter Avis also went back.

Degui brought another Ayore who added more to the previous story. In time still others would add more details until the wives had a fairly accurate account of what had happened to the men.

## How the Five Were Killed

A man named Ejeene was hoeing his crops when he saw the five men coming. They were extending knives and clothing as gifts. Ejeene ran to the village shouting, "*Conjnone! Conjnone!* (Civilized! Civilized!)"

The women and children darted into the jungle. The men came running from their gardens and hid behind their huts. They armed themselves with spears, clubs, and bows and arrows. From their hiding place they watched the five walk into the center of the circle of huts and place gifts on the ground. An impatient Ayore, Ajarmane, suddenly released an arrow. It hit one man in the shoulder. A companion pulled it out, then all five began walking rapidly away.

After the five left, the Ayore men rushed for the gifts. One, Upoide, was angry because he did not get a machete. "I'm going after the Conjnone and get me a machete," he shouted.

He found them sitting on a log. They motioned him near, holding out more knives, machetes, and pointing to heaven. Upoide walked up to the smallest man (Dave Bacon) and extended his hands. Dave gave him a machete and hugged him.

Upoide was still angry. He pulled back, whirled and pierced Dave with a spear. As Dave struggled to pull the weapon out, other Ayores ran up. One named Aburasede struck him on the head with a club and killed him.

The other Ayores now felt they must follow suit, or the dead man's companions would take vengeance. They closed in on the missionaries, hurling spears and wielding clubs. In the confusion of the melee, one missionary managed to run through the crowd. Datide, another warrior, overtook him and struck him down.

The shouts brought other Indians running. Ejeene, the man who had spotted the missionaries first, yelled, "They are descendants of our ancestor, *Corabe* [White Butterfly]. You shouldn't have killed them. They were not bad." The war chief, Amajane, who had been away, arrived. He agreed that the missionaries must have been descendants of a legendary white woman who at one time had lived with the Ayores. He lectured the killers sternly but did not punish them.

## The Fate of the Killers

Relatives of the killers who became Christians told the missionary widows, "We're sorry our men killed your husbands. They didn't know better."

"We understand," the wives assured them. Audrey added, "It was worth my husband's death to see you come to know Christ."

What happened to the killers? Four died in the jungle before having a chance to hear the gospel. Two of these were killed by tribal enemies. Upoide, the one whose anger triggered the massacre, was the first to come to the mission station. When assured that the three widows had forgiven him, he became the first of the killers to accept Christ. Ajarmane, the one who had shot the arrow, was next. The remaining killers also heard the gospel but made no profession of faith.

And the widows? Jean Dye married Larry Johnson, an instructor at New Tribes' language school, thirteen years after her husband's death. She serves with him at the school in Camdenton, Missouri. Dorothy Dye also serves here. One of her children, Paul, is a missionary to the Guica Indians of Venezuela. Audrey Bacon married Rollie Hoogfhsagen. They serve at New Tribes headquarters in Sanford, Florida.

As for the rest of the Ayores—a permanent Christian Ayore settlement was established. The community became a base for other missionaries launching advances into jungle areas never before penetrated. No further missionary killings have been charged to Ayores in Bolivia.

## Another "New Tribes" Martyr

One dark January evening in 1944 Bruce Porterfield sat down in his home in Lansing, Michigan, to read the paper after a hard day's work. The story of how five missionaries had presumably been killed by Stone-Age Indians in Bolivia caught his attention. That evening he committed himself to follow in their footsteps.

Six years later he and his wife, Edith, arrived in Bolivia in the midst of a revolution. They survived the shooting that blazed around them and joined other missionaries at a backwoods river town named Cafetal. Here they heard of the wild Nhambiquaras who had attacked the Tylee family and Mildred Kratz in Brazil.

In January 1951, they were joined by a big, ambling bear of a bachelor named Dave Yarwood. A farm boy from Washington State, Dave loved the outdoors and was anxious to join the expedition to reach the Nhambiquaras.

The next month, Bruce, Dave, and colleague Jim Ostewig began their hunt. Meeting no success, they returned to Cafetal. August came and they were still no closer to making contact. Then on a turtle egg hunt they ran smack into four naked Indians. Nhambiquaras! The Indians took some gifts and vanished into the jungle.

In September they met up with eight Nhambiquaras. These Indians came right up and gave them bear hugs. Then they began touching the missionaries all over.

Other encounters followed. The Indians indulged in painful horseplay, suddenly seizing one of the missionaries around the neck and almost choking the breath from him.

The dangerous game of hide and seek continued. Sometimes the missionaries were able to eat meals with the Indians. Sometimes they learned a few Nhambiquara words.

After one stay of several days at an outlying camp, Dave suggested that the others go back to Cafetal and stock up on supplies. "I'll hang around here and keep up the contact," he said. Bruce did not want to leave him alone. But Dave insisted.

Bruce was glad to spend a few days with his wife. But he could not get his mind off Dave. He visualized him lying in his bunk reading his Bible. He recalled the time Dave had put his arm around a Nhambiquara and told him in English of God's love. The Indian put his lips to Dave's ear after each sentence and whispered back, in precise English, every word Dave told him. The Nhambiquaras were remarkable mimics. The Indian thought it was a joke.

Before Bruce could go back, a riverboat captain stopped to tell him that Dave was dead. Three Brazilian tax collectors looking for rubber hunters had come across Dave's body. By the description Bruce knew that it really was his friend.

Bruce and Jim went back and found Dave's remains. The shafts of two arrows trimmed in turkey feathers were sticking out of his back. Two more were in his chest. They buried the body, gathered up the few personal effects which the Indians had not taken, and went back to Cafetal. Dave's diary told part of the story. December 4, the day before he was killed, nine Nhambiquaras came to see him. He learned some more words. "On the whole . . . the atmosphere was friendly," he wrote. "We'll see what happens tomorrow." That was the last entry.

The shock of Dave's murder drove Bruce into a deep depression. It was two months before he emerged from his "Dunkirk of the soul" and accepted an invitation from another missionary to help reach the wild Macurapis. They made a contact, then he joined another New Tribes' man in search for wild Yuquis. These efforts led to some hair-raising incidents, but his faith was renewed and he continued the quest for more lost tribes.

In his book *Commandos for Christ* (Harper and Row) Bruce Porterfield expressed the New Tribes Mission's purpose.

> It is for us to furrow the ground. It is for others to plant the seed and reap the harvest. And as surely as day follows night, the harvest will come. And it will be rich, the result of all the hard plowing, sowing, and watering that has been done, in tears, heartaches, suffering, and blood. . . .

Bolivia remains one of the poorest countries in the world. The growing of coca for use in making cocaine has led to clashes between police and coca growers and to increased anti-U.S. feeling among the farmers. Missionaries must be careful about what they say.

Evangelical Christianity continues to grow, although in 1992 Protestants represented only 5 percent of the population.

# 36

## Peru and Ecuador

### *Land of the Incas*

The same sacrificial purpose has motivated missionaries to risk their lives in reaching tribes in Peru and Ecuador. Besides the mountain Quechuas, about fifty jungle groups have challenged the evangels of the gospel on the eastern side of the snow-capped Andes in these two countries.

The gold-seeking Spaniards baptized the mountain Indians, then robbed their Inca rulers of precious treasures at sword point. But the conquistadors stopped short of the forbidding jungle east of the Andes. Only a few intrepid traders and priests dared to cross the rugged mountains and search for the mysterious brown denizens of the forest. Many never returned.

### Dawn over Amazonia

The first evangelical missionaries ventured into the vast Amazonian forests early in the twentieth century. First in Peru were the Church of the Nazarene and the Christian and Missionary Alliance. The Nazarenes began work among the head-hunting Aguarunas, a tribe that had massacred an entire settlement of white farmers around 1900. First in Ecuador was the Gospel Missionary Union (GMU) which established a station among the feared Jivaro headhunters on an upper Amazon tributary.

The pioneer missionaries faced unimaginable hardship in the rain forests of Peru and Ecuador. Some walked overland for two to three weeks, then canoed down swift, often flooded rivers to reach their stations in uncharted tribal territories ruled by powerful chiefs. It seems a miracle that none were killed by Indians who knew whites only as enemies. However, tropical diseases left many missionaries with broken health and shortened life expectancies.

## Jungle Base Saves Lives

By 1946 only a half dozen tribes in Peru and Ecuador had been entered. Reaching the remainder appeared impossible until the Wycliffe Bible Translators developed a central jungle base in Peru. It was the idea of Wycliffe's founder, Cameron Townsend, to have a dispensary, commissary, radio communication center, and an airline at the hub of operations in an area larger than Texas. Missionaries in trouble could get help fast. Under Townsend's direction, Wycliffe also established ties with the Peruvian government, bringing the umbrella of national protection over Bible translators at their far-flung posts.

Wycliffe began work in Peru in 1946 and ultimately placed workers in around fifty tribes. Not one translator has been killed by Indians, although there have been some close calls.

Two single women, Lorrie Anderson and Doris Cox, entered Shapra territory when it was ruled by Chief Tariri, the most feared headhunter in Peru. Tariri later told Cam Townsend, "Had you sent two men we would have killed them. Had you sent a man and wife we would have killed the man and kept the woman for a wife. You sent two young women, calling me 'brother.' I had to protect them." After his dramatic conversion, Tariri became a sensation in Peru and a celebrity to Christians in Europe and the United States.

The Mayorunas were feared more than the Shapras. By 1969 they had killed hundreds of Peruvians and kidnapped many white women for wives in raids on government outposts. A peaceful entry was made that year by seventeen-year-old Ronald Snell, who had grown up in another tribe, and translator Harriet Fields. Miss Fields and her partner, Harriet Kneeland, lived among the Mayorunas for many years while they worked on a translation of the New Testament.

## Martyrs to Maoism

Natural disasters, a lagging economy, and Marxist terrorism prepared the way for a military coup in 1968. After twelve years of military rule, Peru returned to democratic leadership in 1980 under former President Fernando Belaunde. However, with civil government, unrest increased. Murderous terrorist activities of the Marxist Maoist "Shining Path" group caused some twenty-three thousand deaths and $20 billion worth of damage from 1980 to 1992.

Among these casualties were two World Vision leaders in Peru whom Shining Path terrorists targeted in 1991, in the capital of Lima. Norman Tattersall of Canada died immediately in the machine-gun attack. Jose Chuquin of Colombia, hit by twenty-two bullets, died a short while later.

The leader of the Maoist group, Abimael Guzman Reynosa, was captured by police. Guzman's capture dealt a severe blow to the terrorist group, but did not stop the terrorism. The murderous Shining Path continues to receive funds from cocaine producers in the mountains.

The Maoist terrorists sprang up among the poor Quechua Indian population who live in poverty-stricken villages in high valleys and plateaus of the Peruvian Andes. Christians and other Quechuas who dared oppose the terrorists were killed. Not without cost, the gospel continued to go forward amidst the guerrilla war.

On September 6, 1992, Romulo Saune, the leader of the Christian Quechuas in Peru, was killed in a confrontation which also took the lives of three other Christians in his family. Saune and his relatives were returning from a visit with believers in a remote village when their vehicle was stopped at a guerrilla roadblock. Suddenly the guerrillas began "spraying the people with machine-gun fire," said Tom Claus, a Mohawk Indian and close friend of Saune for sixteen years. "Romulo was killed immediately." At only thirty-nine, "he was very young to die, but in his short life he had achieved so much for God and his Indian people and his work must have been finished when God called him home."

Only three months before, Romulo Saune had received the World Evangelical Fellowship's first Religious Liberty Award.

Claus called Saune "a martyr for Christ, just like Stephen in the Bible. He died with his boots on . . . after preaching the Word at his home church where his dad is the pastor. His eighty-five-year-old grandfather was also a pastor there, but was tortured and murdered by the Shining Path" in 1990, Claus reported.

Claus came to know Saune when he went to Peru to help conduct a seminar for Quechua Indians at the Wycliffe Bible Translators Center in Ayacucho, the Peruvian highland city where the Shining Path movement began. Saune, Claus said, had been working on the Bible translation for the Quechuas since he was seventeen. More recently, he had purchased a "lovely training center compound just fifty miles east of Lima, the capital city, to disciple and teach Quechua Indian pastors and church leaders." Romula Saune, Claus added, "also held short-term Bible institutes in Indian villages all over. God used him in a powerful way."

The martyrdom of Romulo Saune has spurred Peruvian Quechua Christians to new heights of faithfulness. Church growth is expected to continue in the wake of his death. Neither the gates of hell nor the crazed Maoist terrorists will prevail against the will of God.

# ECUADOR—MISSIONARY STORY OF THE CENTURY

In Ecuador occurred the most publicized missionary massacre of the twentieth century, when five young stalwarts representing three mission societies were killed by Auca Indians in January 1956.

Jim Elliot was from Portland, Oregon. At Wheaton College he was president of the Student Foreign Missions Fellowship. A perceptive thinker and writer, he wrote in college: "He is no fool who gives what he cannot keep to gain what he cannot lose." He was married to Elisabeth Howard, from a prominent Christian publishing family in Philadelphia. The Elliots had an infant daughter.

Pete Fleming was from Seattle, and at twenty-seven was a year younger than his friend Jim Elliot. Pete had recently received his M.A. in literature. He was married to his childhood sweetheart, Olive, and they had three young children.

Ed McCully, the oldest son of a Milwaukee bakery executive, attended Wheaton and starred on the football team. He had won the National Hearst Oratorical Contest in San Francisco in 1949 and studied at Marquette University Law School. He and his wife, Marilou, had an eight-month-old son.

Roger Youderian was raised on a Montana ranch. He attended Northwestern Schools in Minneapolis where he met his wife, Barbara. They joined the Gospel Missionary Union and were working with Mr. and Mrs. Frank Drown among the head-hunting Jivaros when the Elliots, Flemings, and McCullys arrived.

Nate Saint, the most animated of the lot, had been flying missionaries in and out of stations in the Ecuadorean jungle since 1948 for Missionary Aviation Fellowship. Builder, inventor, and skilled pilot, Nate had devised an alternate fuel system for single-engine planes and an ingenious method of lowering a bucket by using a spiraling line to the ground. "During the last war, we had to be willing to be expendable," he wrote. "A missionary constantly faces expendability." Nate was married to a nurse, Marj, whom he had met in the service. They had three children.

## The Challenge of the Aucas

None of the five came to Ecuador anticipating the Auca project. Once in Ecuador they kept hearing about these feared Indians who had never been tamed by soldiers or missionaries. The first Jesuit priest to enter Aucaland, Pedro Suarez, had been murdered in 1667. After the Jesuits gave up, the Aucas were left alone for over two hundred years. Then the rubber hunters came, burning Indian homes, raping, torturing, killing, enslaving, and later the oil companies, searching for black gold.

Missionaries often talked about how the Aucas might be reached. Nate Saint had flown all around their territory and longed and prayed for the day when they might know of his Savior.

Nate's older sister, Rachel, a Wycliffe member, learned of a young Auca girl named Dayuma, who had fled to the outside after her father had been killed by the tribe. In 1955 Rachel began studying the language with her at a hacienda.

## "We Decided It Was the Lord's Time"

While Rachel was learning the Auca language, Jim Elliot, Ed McCully, and Nate Saint studied maps and talked about how entry might be made. One evening they pored over the maps for several hours before adjourning for midnight cocoa. "We decided it was the Lord's time," Nate wrote on October 2.

Pete Fleming joined up. Nate then thought of Roger Youderian, not knowing that Roger was discouraged over his work among the Jivaros. When Nate asked if he would help with the Auca project, he volunteered. Roger made five.

All knew the danger. Jim Elliot had told his wife, Betty: "If that's the way God wants it to be, I'm ready to die for the salvation of the Aucas."

They made careful plans. Their main base would be at Shell Mera where the World Radio Missionary Fellowship, sponsors of the missionary radio station HCJB in Quito, had a hospital. For an advance base, they cleared off an old air strip at Arajuno, a camp abandoned by Shell on the very edge of Auca territory. From here they would fly out and look for an Auca clearing to make gift drops. If the Indians responded favorably, a ground contact would be attempted.

## The Operation Gets Underway

After flying over the area for several days, Nate located a large thatch house in a clearing. Using Nate's invention, they let down a gift machete, wrapped in canvas and decorated with colored streamers. When they flew back over, the gift was gone. The next time Nate passed over "Terminal City" Ed McCully spotted three Aucas through binoculars. They dropped more gifts. On succeeding passes, Nate flew lower, calling through a loudspeaker Auca phrases learned from Dayuma: "We like you! We like you! We have come to visit you." Each time they dropped a bucket of gifts, with Nate circling to keep the drop spiraling down towards the drop zone. The people on the ground smiled and waved, and one day they put a live parrot in the bucket as a reciprocal gift. Another day, December 23, they put in squirrels, another parrot, and a smoked monkey tail.

The next step was to find a landing place as close to the clearing as possible. The Curaray River was nearby and the missionaries went looking for a sandbar. They christened the site selected "Palm Beach."

## D-Day

Tuesday, January 3. They huddled at Arajuno for a final prayer meeting, then sang a favorite hymn:

> We rest on Thee, our Shield and our Defender;
> Thine is the battle, Thine shall be the praise;
> When passing through the gates of pearly splendor
> Victors, we rest with Thee through endless days.

Johnny Keenan, another MAF pilot, flew in. He would stand by to see if the first landing turned out okay.

About 8:00 a.m. Nate began ferrying in the men and supplies to Palm Beach. After the last landing he buzzed Terminal City, calling to the Aucas, "Come tomorrow to the river!" The Indians looked puzzled.

He flew back to Arajuno, leaving the others to sleep on the beach, and returned the next morning. He and Pete checked out Terminal City again. Some of the Indians seen the day before were missing. They must be on their way to the river, the two decided.

When Nate and Pete got back, the others had a tree house up and were walking along the beach holding up gifts and shouting welcomes across the river. Nate got on the radio to Shell Mera and brought Marj up to date.

The "neighbors" did not show on Wednesday. The five spent a second night in the tree house. The next morning Nate and Pete went up for reconnaissance. They saw only women, children, and an old man at Terminal City. While they were gone Jim and Roger hiked downstream and found Auca footprints. They judged them to be at least a week old. Nate and Pete took another look at Terminal City. This time they saw an Auca kneel and point in the direction of Palm Beach. They flew back to the sandbar rejoicing.

## Aucas!

Nothing else happened until 11:15 a.m. Friday when three naked Aucas suddenly appeared on the far bank of the river—a young man, a woman about thirty, and a girl around sixteen. Jim waded across, seized the hands of the man and woman, and led them back to the spot where the plane was parked. The girl splashed across on her own.

The missionaries used all the phrases they could remember. The Aucas jabbered and smiled. The men took pictures and displayed a copy of *Time*.

The Auca man, "George," kept touching the plane. Nate opened the passenger door and with little urging George jumped in. Nate took off and flew over Terminal City with George shouting gleefully all the way. When they landed back on the beach, the Auca leaped out, clapping his hands in delight.

At 4:15 p.m. Nate radioed Marj reporting their favorable progress.

The girl, "Delilah," and George left. The woman stayed by the beach fire. When the missionaries came down from the tree house the next morning, she was gone. But the fire was still warm.

Saturday, no neighbors came to visit. Nate and Pete flew low over Terminal City. The people they saw looked afraid. The women and children ran to hide. "Come, come, come to the river," Nate invited. Pete tossed some gifts. A man looked up and smiled. It was George.

## "Pray for Us. This Is the Day!"

Sunday morning, Nate went up alone and spotted a group of Auca men walking towards the camp. He flew back to the beach with the good news and radioed Marj. "A commission of ten is coming. Pray for us. This is the day!" He set the next scheduled transmission at 4:30 p.m. and signed off.

At 4:30 p.m. Marj switched on the radio at Shell Mera. Nothing. She kept trying. The radio must be out, she thought. The wives prayed and tossed and turned that night.

Monday, January 9, Johnny Keenan took off for Palm Beach. A few minutes later he radioed that the plane had been stripped of fabric. There was no sign of the men. Obviously, something was wrong.

## Bodies Are Sighted

Wycliffe pilot Larry Montgomery, an American reserve officer, was at Shell Mera. He contacted Lt. General William K. Harrison, commander in chief of the U.S. Caribbean Command in Panama, to report the five missing. Radio station HCJB broadcast the news and asked for prayers. Newspapers headlined around the world: FIVE MISSIONARIES MISSING IN ECUADOR.

A search party led by missionary Frank Drown started overland. Johnny Keenan made his fourth flight over Palm Beach and saw a body he could not identify. Johnny made another pass and sighted a second body in the river.

The big U.S. Air Force planes roared in. They could not land at Palm Beach. Wednesday night, rain fell in torrents. Thursday, two Navy fliers went in with a chopper. They found four bodies in the river. All had been speared to death.

Major Nurnberg, one of the chopper pilots, flew to Shell Mera and described the clothing to the wives. Pete, Roger, Jim, and Nate were identified. The major speculated that the first body seen by Johnny was Ed and it had been washed away by the rain.

The overland search party arrived Friday and buried the four. *Life* magazine photographer Cornell Capa landed in a chopper in a heavy downpour just as the last body was being dropped into the grave. His photos and the accompanying story in *Life* made the Auca massacre the missionary story of the century.

The next day the U.S. Air Force flew the five widows over to see the common grave. Peering down at the scar of white sand, Olive Fleming thought of 2 Corinthians 5:1: "For we know that if our earthly house of this tabernacle were dissolved, we have a building of God, an house not made with hands, eternal in the heavens."

Why had the Indians attacked after the initial friendly encounter? Frank Drown noted that Indians are naturally curious about something new and will accept it. But after thinking about it, they may feel threatened and attack in fear.

Life had to go on for the wives. Barbara Youderian returned to work among the Jivaros. Betty Elliot helped with Quechua ministries, then wrote the first book about the martyred five, *Through Gates of Splendor* (Harper and Row). Marj Saint took a new missionary job in Quito. Marilou McCully went home to have her second child, then returned to work with Marj. Olive Fleming's plans were undecided.

## Why Did God Let It Happen?

Response from the civilized world came swiftly. Some church leaders thought the men had died needlessly. Others felt God had allowed the men to die for a great purpose.

Part of that purpose seemed evident immediately. An American naval officer was shipwrecked shortly after reading the story. As he floated alone on a raft he recalled a sentence from Jim Elliot which a reporter had quoted: "When it comes time to die, make sure that all you have to do is die." He prayed for salvation, spiritual and physical. Both prayers were answered. From Iowa, an eighteen-year-old boy wrote that he had turned his life "over completely to the Lord." He wanted to take the place of one of the five. Indeed, in succeeding months, missions were deluged with offers to "take the place" of the Auca martyrs.

The work with the Aucas was only beginning. The Auca girl, Dayuma, now a Christian, went back to her people. Her family greeted her with joyful amazement. They thought she had been eaten by a foreign cannibal. She said the missionaries had come in friendship to tell them about a Savior. "Just as you killed the foreigners on the beach, Jesus was killed for you," she told them.

## Matchless Love

One month later Rachel Saint (Nate's sister) and Betty and little Valerie Elliot hung their hammocks among the Aucas. Valerie played with the children of her father's killers.

Rachel and Betty gradually learned the reason for the murders and the identity of the six killers. "We thought foreigners would kill and eat us," one Auca said. Another confessed that he had cried after the killings.

An older man, "Uncle Gikita," admitted that he had advanced on Nate Saint as the pilot held his hands high, pleading for mercy. "I speared him," he said. When the other missionaries shot in the air, the other Auca men had run. The old man called them back and they killed Ed, Pete, Roger, and Jim.

Gikita accepted Christ; so did Kimo, another of the killers. "Jesus' blood has washed my heart clean," Kimo told Rachel. "My heart is healed." The other four killers—Nimonga, Dyuwi, Minkayi, and Tona—soon believed also.

Betty Elliot returned to the States. Wycliffe's Dr. Catherine Peeke came to help Rachel with the tedious language analysis and translation of the New Testament into Auca. Nine years after the killings, the first published copies of the Gospel of Mark in Auca were dedicated at "God's Speaking House." Kimo, now the Auca pastor, prayed, "Father God, You are alive. This is Your day and all of us have come to worship You. They brought us copies of Your Carving, enough for everybody. We accept it, saying, 'This is the truth.' We want all of your carving."

Special guests for the dedication were Wycliffe's Ecuador Director, Don Johnson, his wife, Helen, and Steve and Phil Saint. Steve, fourteen, had visited his Aunt Rachel several times and was a beloved friend to the Aucas. He read a verse in Auca during the service.

## Auca Killer Baptizes Nate Saint's Son and Daughter

Steve stayed on after the other visitors left. Later he received a letter from his sister Kathy, fifteen, saying that she would like to show her faith by being baptized by the Aucas. Steve decided that he would be baptized at the same time.

Marj and Phil, the younger brother, came for the occasion. The baptisms were held on Palm Beach at dawn. Kimo talked to Steve and Kathy and two Auca teenagers who were to be immersed about the meaning of baptism as a witness of resurrected life in Christ. Then he baptized them.

Afterwards, Kimo and Dyuwi led the group to the site of the missionaries' graves. The two forgiven killers, Marj and Rachel, and the four teenagers sang the hymn which the five men had sung just before leaving to meet the Aucas: "We rest on Thee, our Shield and our Defender. . . ."

## The First Auca Martyr

Still there is more. The Christian Aucas felt compelled to reach a longtime enemy clan downriver. The missionaries helped them locate the group and flew over and dropped gifts, using Nate's invention. Tona, one of the six killers, volunteered to take the gospel to his downriver brothers. Axed from behind, he cried, "I'm not afraid. I'll die and go to heaven." "We'll help you go," his attackers shouted. In his dying breath, Tona whispered, "I forgive you. I'm dying for your benefit."

These downriver Aucas later came to the Christian community where Rachel and Catherine were staying. Many became Christians.

## Auca Update

The rippling effect of the Auca incident continues. More Aucas are coming to Christ. More people are being won by missionaries who initially felt God's call at the news of the massacre of the five. The Auca killers have traveled abroad to tell what God has done. Kimo and his friend Komi were a sensation at the World Evangelism Congress in Berlin. Uncle Gikita and others joined Rachel for a series of missionary rallies in major cities in the United States.

At least eight books, including *Through Gates of Splendor*, and hundreds of newspaper and magazine follow-up articles have been written about the Aucas and the five missionaries they killed. One book is *The Diary of Jim Elliot*, compiled and edited by Elisabeth Elliot (Fleming H. Revell).

The "Auca incident" is enshrined in the missionary history of the church and in the past of Ecuador as well. The president of the predominantly Roman Catholic country flew to Wycliffe's jungle base at Limoncocha to meet the forgiven Auca killers personally. On the tenth anniversary of the five martyrs' death, Ecuador issued commemorative postage stamps honoring each man.

And the widows? Four remarried. Olive Fleming wed a professor at Trinity Evangelical Divinity School in Chicago. Betty Elliot, after losing her second husband, Addison Leitch, to illness, married an institutional chaplain in Georgia. She has become one of the most respected and best-known Christian writers on the evangelical scene. The former Marilou McCully is living in quiet privacy with her Christian husband. Marj Saint became the wife of Dr. Abe Van Der Puy, president of World Radio Missionary Fellowship. Barbara Youderian, who chose not to remarry, moved to Quito to serve as hostess at the guest house of the Gospel Missionary Union.

## Revival Follows the Storm

The Auca experience has eclipsed persecution of evangelical Christians in Peru and Ecuador. Many missionaries and nationals among Indians and Spanish-speaking people have been beaten, stoned, and spat upon. Some have lost their jobs and been alienated from families and old friends for the sake of the gospel, though none are known to have been killed. As recent as the late 1960s, a Gospel Missionary Union medic, Dr. Donald

Dilworth, was beaten so severely by a mob of crazed Quichuas that nearly one hundred stitches were required to close his wounds.

Overreaching all of the persecution is news from GMU missionaries of an unprecedented turning to Christ by Quichuas in Ecuador. In one province alone the Christian community has grown to around sixteen thousand. Ecuadorean Christian Quichuas are now going as missionaries to mountain Indians in Colombia, Peru, and Bolivia. Nevertheless, isolated persecutions have continued. Two Quichua believers in a mountain province were killed in 1985. In 1987, Antonio Zuma, a twenty-eight-year-old Quichua pastor, was killed in a mob attack during a Sunday morning worship service. Zuma and other believers were assaulted with boards and stones during a service at a church member's house. The mob was reportedly incited by local bar owners whose business had been hurt by the growth of the church.

The people of Ecuador continue to be responsive to the gospel. Evangelicals have increased six-fold since 1960. A severe earthquake in 1987 and economic problems have left the nation vulnerable to civil unrest. The missionaries and national Christians, mindful of martyrs of the past, bravely carry on.

# 37

# Colombia

## *Banquet of Hope*

With Colombia we have traveled almost full circle around South America, omitting only Venezuela, which borders Colombia on the northeast, Guyana, French Guiana, and Suriname (formerly Dutch Guiana). No missionaries or national Christian workers are known to have been martyred in these countries, although evangelicals in Venezuela experienced Catholic persecution before the 1950s.

Colombia, however, is uniquely a land of martyrs to fanaticism and intolerance. No other Latin American nation approached the persecution heaped upon evangelicals there in the 1940s and 1950s. Not even Mexico experienced widespread violence of such intensity upon godly pastors and Christian believers.

## Conservatives versus Liberals

Of all the Spanish American countries, Colombia was closest to Spain until the rise of the Liberal Party. In contrast to the Conservative Party which stood for a centrally governed church-state, the Liberals believed in decentralized federal government, separation of church and state, and religious freedom. The Liberals excommunicated the Jesuit order three times and once banished the powerful archbishop of Bogota for declaring that the church was over the state. Rivalry between the two parties caused nearly a hundred civil wars before 1899 when the War of a Thousand Days took over one hundred thousand lives.

Conservatives held control until 1930 when Liberals were swept back into office. The Liberals trimmed clerical power and removed from the constitution a concordat with the

355

Vatican giving the Catholic Church power over education, marriage, morality, family life, and religious activities. The Catholic hierarchy was incensed and worked feverishly to get back the presidency.

## "False Prophets" and "Devouring Wolves"

In 1944, when evangelicals were coming under attack all over the continent, sixteen Colombian bishops ordered a letter read in every Catholic church in the country to incite attacks on Protestants. The epistle called Protestant ministers "false prophets" and "devouring wolves." "Protestants," the bishops said, "come to our country to carry out a work of destruction; they come not only to steal our faith . . . but to ruin our national and social structure." Opposition to Protestant "propaganda" was both a religious duty and "an act of true patriotism," and Catholics should avoid Protestants and give complete devotion to "Our Lady . . . who has always killed off all heresies."

The following year Pope Pius XII urged Colombian Catholics not to permit "the sacred deposit of your faith . . . to be contaminated by that propaganda, as audacious as it is cunning, which wishes to convert into a mission land, a people who count in their glorious history four centuries of irreproachable Christianity."

## Passions Are Inflamed

The storm kept building. A Colombian priest published a book, *Protestantism in Colombia*, in which he called Protestants "undesirable foreigners," a "virus," and an "infection." He asked Colombians to strive for "the final extirpation of Protestantism from our midst." The required religious text in most public high schools justified persecution of Protestants and defended the infamous Spanish Inquisition and the Massacre of St. Bartholomew's Day.

Attacks on Liberals escalated. As a result of a Liberal split, a Conservative was elected president in 1946 with only 41 percent of the popular vote. In 1948 the most popular Liberal leader, who would undoubtedly have been elected the next president, was assassinated. Riots flared in Bogota and spread across the country. The Conservative president dissolved Congress and claimed dictatorial powers. Before the undeclared civil war was over, two hundred thousand Colombians were dead.

## The Great Persecution Begins

The Conservative politicians and their allies in the church hierarchy set out to destroy the Protestant "scourge." Mobs and vigilantes, sometimes led by priests, attacked practically at will while town officials looked the other way. Local police often joined in the attacks.

Every accusation imaginable was thrown against Colombian Protestants and missionaries. They were destroying national unity by damaging religious uniformity. They were agents of international Communism. They were trying to legalize divorce. Missionaries were paying poor Catholics to apostatize. Protestant schools were infecting the nation with moral disease. Protestant pastors were helping revolutionaries trying to overthrow the government.

From 1944 to 1958 at least 120 evangelicals or members of evangelical families were killed. Five martyrs were under age four. Eighty-eight Protestant churches and chapels were destroyed by fire or dynamite. An additional 183 houses of worship and 206 Protestant primary schools were closed by official orders. Over fifteen thousand evangelicals were driven from their homes. Protestant children were shut out of public schools.

In the Department (state) of Huila, Pastor Perez and his twelve-year-old son Bernardo were arrested in November 1953, when the violence was at its peak. Soldiers hung the boy by a thumb and demanded a confession that his family were bandits. When he denied this, the tormentors asked if they were evangelicals. "Yes," he gasped, "but we don't hurt anyone."

They turned to the agonized father. "How many people have you killed?"

"I have killed no one," he answered. "I follow God's Word which does not permit us to kill or do evil against anyone."

Having no witnesses, the soldiers had to let the two go. "If we arrest you again," they warned, "you and your entire family will be killed. Not a seed of this wickedness will remain."

Around midnight the following May 19 an armed mob burst into the Perez home without warning. They shot both parents and attacked the seven children with machetes. One boy, David, was slashed on the arm and neck but managed to drag a younger sister across the yard and over a fence. An enraged man caught up with them and literally severed the little girl's hand from her brother's grasp. David was the only one who escaped alive.

Christian and Missionary Alliance missionaries Lee and Ruth Tennies became David's second parents. Five years later he graduated from the Alliance Bible Institute in Armenia, Colombia, and became a pastor.

## More Colombian Martyrs

Pedro Moreno, a young preacher, was arrested for evangelizing around Saboya, Colombia. The police promised to release him if he would sign a statement pledging to stop spreading the evangelical message. He refused and was thrust into a cell.

Only one evangelical family lived in Saboya. The father, Juan Coy, brought food and encouragement to Pedro and tried to obtain his release. One night a trusted friend warned Juan, "Be careful. The police have a plot to leave Pedro's cell door open. If he walks out, he'll be shot on the spot for escaping." Sure enough, the prisoner did find his door open. He stayed inside.

Then they learned of a second plot. Pedro would be released and shot as he left the jail. The release came through. Juan went to the jail and talked to Pedro. They decided to trust God for protection. Pedro cautiously stepped from his cell, dashed out the jail door, and leaped into a passing truck. The driver took him out of the city and today Pedro Moreno is an evangelical pastor in Colombia.

After failing to kill the preacher, the fanatics decided to take revenge on Juan Coy. They went to his farm and waited until he had finished his evening milking. When he appeared on the path, they opened fire and killed him. But the evangelical witness survived. Today there is an evangelical church in Saboya attended by three hundred people.

One of the worst atrocities occurred in July 1951, in the state of Meta. A priest issued orders for all Protestants in a town to be exterminated. Ten policemen and four civilians, armed with rifles and submachine guns, burst into the home of Carlo Arturo Gahona, an evangelical connected with the Worldwide Evangelization Crusade. "Long live the Holy Catholic Church!" they shouted. "Down with the Protestants!" Turning their guns on the helpless family, they martyred three sons, a daughter-in-law, and three grandchildren. One of the three grandchildren, four-month-old Carlos Arturo, was pitched across the patio onto a pile of broken bottles and died vomiting blood.

## Colombia's First Evangelical Missionary Martyr

The veteran evangelical missionaries were greatly loved and respected by Colombian evangelicals. One of the most honored was Ernest Fowler, who had served thirty-two years in Colombia with the Gospel Missionary Union and the Latin American Mission. The product of a devout Methodist couple, Ernie had grown up on a Montana ranch. He had made many trips through the rugged Colombian Andes, training national evangelists and encouraging churches. Once threatened with death during the persecution, he had the courage of a Daniel and the compassion of a Barnabas.

In 1966 Ernie was looking forward to reducing the language of the Yupka Indians to writing and translating the Bible. But first he felt his family deserved a summer vacation high up in the mountains near the Venezuelan border. Another missionary couple loaned them their home, and Ernie, his wife Eva, three children—Valerie, John, and Alison—and a Colombian girlfriend of Valerie's, Elvira, moved in. A few days later two other missionary kids, Peter Clark and David Howard Jr., arrived to enjoy the summer with them.

On Wednesday, August 3, Ernie took Valerie and Elvira for a hike and met seven strangers on the trail. "We're policemen looking for Communists," they said. At their request, Ernie handed over his shotgun and machete. But when he asked for a receipt, two of the "policemen" drew their guns and shot him dead. Surprisingly, the bandits did not harm the horrified girls. They made a few obscene remarks then headed down the trail. The stunned girls rushed to Ernie's body and turned him over. His mouth was full of blood and his eyes were rolled back.

The girls ran back to the house with Valerie shouting, "They shot Daddy!" The house was in a shambles. "Oh, they've killed Mother and the boys, too," Valerie moaned. A frightened whisper came from behind a wall. "Quiet. Are there any bandits around?" When assured that the men had left, the others came out of hiding.

The seven men had come by the house first and told Eva the same story. Suddenly they drew guns and demanded money and jewels. When she handed over the few pesos she had, one tried to tear her wedding band off her finger, while the others vandalized the house. After forcing the family into a side room, they left.

Eva and the children spent the night in some bushes near Ernie's body. It took them all day Thursday to dig a grave in the rocky, mountain soil. A Christian neighbor came by and took the news to other missionaries who came and helped with the burial. Soldiers pursued the bandits without success.

Scores of tributes came to the Fowler family. A Catholic priest sent "brotherly greetings" and spoke of Ernie's death "not as a bereavement but rather as a departure to the Lord."

## Banquet of Hope

Two years after Ernie Fowler's martyrdom an Evangelism-in-Depth campaign trained thirty thousand evangelicals in personal witness and follow-up. These believers visited 143,000 Colombian homes and distributed half a million gospel tracts. That same year the Roman Catholic hierarchy invited evangelicals to participate in the Church's thirty-ninth International Eucharistic Congress held in Bogota. The congress included hundreds of neighborhood Bible studies in which evangelicals participated with joy.

Miracles kept recurring in the seventies as evangelicals grew in number and respect. The most significant event came on October 19, 1977, when evangelicals sponsored a Banquet of Hope, similar to the National Prayer Breakfast of Washington, D.C. The top leaders of both political parties were invited as guests of honor to hear a message by Evangelist Luis Palau.

The celebration began about noon in the courtyard of the national government building. Hundreds of evangelicals participated in the prayer and praise service. Some knelt while others fell prostrate on the concrete shouting, "Glory to God!" There were short testimonies. "Many were killed for this day," declared a pastor. "Now we are the church victorious." "If they put a bullet through my chest, that will not stop the power of the gospel," vowed another.

The formal banquet was scheduled that evening in the Red Room of posh Hotel Tequendama in downtown Bogota. Would the president and other high leaders come? At precisely 8:30 p.m. President Alfonso Lopez Michelsen, the four major candidates for the next year's presidential election, the heads of the four major labor unions, judges, ambassadors, and many other high officials walked in. They heard Evangelist Palau declare, "Christ is Colombia's only hope. Only He can solve the moral crisis in this nation." The entire program was broadcast to the nation.

Sitting near the president were pastors who had been in jail twenty years before. Some had lost loved ones in the great persecution. Tears flowed freely. One pastor summed up his feelings: "The road to evangelization of our nation is paved with the blood of our martyrs."

## The Murder of Wycliffe's Chet Bitterman

Even as Colombian evangelicals celebrated the end of Catholic persecution, Marxist terrorist groups were forming in the jungles. They were especially upset with Christian organizations, such as the Wycliffe Bible Translators, who were helping the poor rise from their poverty through education and better farming methods. In January 1981, the M-19 group, the most notorious of the Marxist guerrilla organizations, decided to kidnap and use as a negotiating tool Al Wheeler, director of the Wycliffe office in the Colombian capital of Bogota.

Early in the morning of January 19, an M-19 member disguised as a policeman knocked on the office door. When the door was opened, six hooded and armed terrorists burst inside and ordered the Bible translators not to leave. They took the twelve adults and five children to the living room, tied their hands and feet, and gagged them. When they couldn't find Wheeler, the invaders took the man who seemed to be most in charge, linguist Chet Bitterman, and sped away.

Four days later the terrorists made their demand: Bitterman would be executed unless Wycliffe and all its members left Colombia by 6:00 p.m., February 19.

Wycliffe refused to leave. Wycliffe leader Bernie May summed up Wycliffe's commitment by asking: "If something is worth living for, isn't it worth dying for, too?"

President J. Robert McQuilkin of Columbia Bible Institute, which Chet had attended in North Carolina, said: "Once you start giving in to terrorists, you jeopardize every missionary the world over."

Wycliffe's aging founder, William Cameron Townsend, advised: "Never think of people as enemies. Look on them as your friends. They may be fighting you because they don't understand you."

The terrorists called for President Reagan to intervene. The *New York Times* and the *Washington Post*, they said, would have to publish their manifesto, if Bitterman's life was to be spared.

The Colombian government quickly declared that the United States had nothing to do with Wycliffe and its companion organization, the Summer Institute of Linguistics. Wycliffe and SIL had a contract with the national government with which any negotiations must be handled, the government spokesman said.

Prayer chains were formed across the hemisphere as the February 19 deadline approached. The kidnappers sent letters written by Chet to the local newspapers saying, "I'm being treated well." A photo showed him playing chess with his captors. A tape delivered to a radio station confirmed that he was witnessing to them.

"We've talked. We've argued. We've even become friends," Bitterman said on the tape. "We respect each other though we view the world from opposite poles."

The guerrillas sent a letter from Chet to his wife, Brenda, in which he requested a Spanish Bible. In the letter, he quoted from the Psalms and other books in the Scripture.

Garcia Herraros, a Catholic priest, expressed his solidarity with the captive Bible translator in an open letter published on the front page of the Bogota newspaper, *El Tiempo*: "When one is taken prisoner as a result of dedicating himself to the task of making the Word of God available, the suffering that results can only be converted into a crown of heroism, sainthood, and martyrdom."

One of Chet's two little daughters asked her mother: "When's Daddy coming back to play with us?"

Chet's wife, Brenda, prayed with friends: "Lord, thank you for choosing Chet. We know you don't make mistakes."

The deadline for Chet's threatened execution was only hours away when the terrorists sent word they were extending the time for two weeks. Rumors and threats circulated all over Bogota. One caller said Chet would be killed in twenty-four hours unless all members of the Bible translation group agreed to leave Colombia. When this short deadline passed, there was hope that Chet might be released.

The climax to the painful episode came on March 7. Three men in their late twenties hijacked a minibus in Bogota. After binding, gagging, and blindfolding the driver, they drove to a hideaway, picked up Chet, and drove around for several hours. The bus driver later told police: "I heard one shot. Then the guerrillas fled to a getaway car."

The bus driver freed himself and called police. Following instructions from an anonymous caller, they found Chet's body in the abandoned bus. Brenda's father and several Wycliffe members identified the victim as Chet. Later that day the body was flown over the Andes to Wycliffe's operational base at Loma Linda for burial in the presence of family, co-workers, and Colombian friends.

The drama of Chet's kidnapping and murder was played out in newspapers and over broadcast stations around the world. Hundreds wrote to the Bitterman family and to Wycliffe's office, stating that they had made faith commitments. Some asked for applications to serve with Wycliffe. Declared Chet's mother, Mary: "Lives have already been changed through the kidnapping, so who knows what might happen now because of Chet's death."

## Continuing Murders

On May 8, 1999, evangelical pastor Rincon Galindo, his wife, her sister, and a neighbor were murdered in Cali by a group of people who have never been caught.

According to Pastor Hector Pardo, at least twenty-five evangelical pastors were killed and three hundred churches were closed in 1999. The majority of the murdered pastors belonged to Assembly of God churches.

## Miracles and the Drug Menace

Government crackdowns and the discrediting of Soviet Communism hit Marxism hard in Colombia. A new evil—drug-trafficking—rose up to overshadow the danger from leftist guerillas.

Government arrests of drug lords sparked a series of retaliation killings. August 18, 1989, Luis Carlos Galan, the ruling party's presidential candidate for the 1990 election, was assassinated. This was followed by the slaying of two other presidential hopefuls, several judges, and a number of other Colombian leaders who dared oppose the drug lords.

The center of the drug trade was in and around the city of Medellin. Following the 1989 murder of Luis Carlos Galan, more than eight Medellin churches held simultaneous all-night prayer vigils. Christ for the City missionary Oscar Vera sent a plea to the Latin American Mission: "Please, I need prayer for the protection of my life and for the lives of leaders at my church. We have been threatened."

Vera was spared, but others were not. An estimated three hundred bands of hired killers, working for drug traffickers, with an average of ten per group, patrolled Medellin. Many of the three thousand or so killers were boys in their early or mid-teens.

During the long Mother's Day weekend in 1991, 112 persons were murdered in Medellin, another illustration, according to the local newspaper *El Mundo*, of "the horrifying dance of death that has taken control" of the city. "There isn't a family in Medellin that does not have an open wound caused by this cursed violence," said *El Mundo*. "How far must the barbarity go before this problem is resolved?"

Believers in Medellin kept praying. Miracles began happening, beginning at Bellavista Prison in Medellin where an average of three inmates were being killed each week. More than three hundred prisoners were converted to Christ. Newspapers and TV news told of prisoners studying Scripture, getting baptized, worshiping, and even turning in home-made weapons to the authorities. The media reported that during a nine-month spiritual awakening, not a single prisoner had been killed or wounded in violence at Bellavista Prison. TV reporter German Castro told viewers on national television that more than the new constitution then being drafted, "Colombians need God in their hearts."

At one church, a seventeen-year-old paid killer became a Christian. Young Bayron could not continue living in his community because of threats from his former gang associates. He moved in with two church leaders and buried his submachine gun in the yard because he didn't want to kill anymore. Yet his mother became angry: "Son, have you become an idiot with all those evangelicals? Dig up your gun and bring me money for food."

One Friday Bayron got a telephone call, asking that he come and pray for someone. It was a trap. When he did not return by nightfall, friends went to a local morgue. They found Bayron's body and the corpses of twelve other young people slain a few hours before.

As the drug wars continued in Colombia, more and more believers put themselves in danger of becoming martyrs like Bayron.

## Looking to the Future

Isolated persecution of evangelicals by Catholic extremists continues in parts of Latin America. But such religious persecution is seldom incited by Catholic clergy. To the contrary, Catholic clergy in many areas now welcome evangelical missionaries and some endorse evangelistic crusades. A rural bishop in Colombia even proposed to a Baptist missionary, "Let's buy a plane and share its use and expenses." Some members of the Catholic hierarchy in Latin America now candidly admit that much of the population is Catholic in name only.

Except in Peru and possibly Nicaragua, Marxism is hardly the threat it once was. In Colombia and Bolivia the greatest danger for Christian workers comes from drug traffickers.

Meanwhile, opportunities for evangelical growth continue bright. Officials in Latin nations are taking notice of the moral and economic changes in tribal groups that have become believers. One of the most noted miracles is the change in the Motilone Indians, who once were known as the last head-hunting tribe in Colombia. To reach the Motilones, independent missionary Bruce Olsson entered Motilone territory and was held captive for several months during which he was put before a firing squad. The command was given and eighteen submachine guns fired. When the smoke cleared, Olsson was still shackled to the tree. The executioners had fired blanks.

In the big cities, the crusades of evangelist Luis Palau are producing results comparable to the Billy Graham meetings in the United States a decade and more ago. In these areas and elsewhere, God's people remain faithful. They are spurred on by the heritage and sacrifice of the thousands of Christian martyrs of the twentieth century who gave their lives for the sake of Christ and the gospel.

# Index